GLOBAL/LOCA.

ASIA-PACIFIC: CULTURE, POLITICS, AND SOCIETY

Editors: Rey Chow, H. D. Harootunian, and Masao Miyoshi

GLOBAL

LOCAL

CULTURAL PRODUCTION

AND THE TRANSNATIONAL IMAGINARY

Rob Wilson and Wimal Dissanayake, Editors

DUKE UNIVERSITY PRESS   *Durham and London 1996*

© 1996 Duke University Press
All rights reserved
Printed in the United States of America on acid-free paper ∞
Typeset in Minion by Keystone Typesetting, Inc.
Library of Congress Cataloging-in-Publication Data
appear on the last printed page of this book.

CONTENTS

●

III   GLOBAL/LOCAL DISRUPTIONS

GLOBAL/LOCAL

INTRODUCTION:

TRACKING THE GLOBAL/LOCAL

Rob Wilson and Wimal Dissanayake

●

[C]apitalism is at the crossroads of all kinds of formations. Always by nature neo-capitalism, it invents, for the worst, its eastern face and its western face, and reshapes both.—Gilles Deleuze and Félix Guattari, *On the Line*

There are tendencies [in global capitalism] going in opposite directions. On the one hand, there's a tendency toward this international centralization of power. There's also an opposite tendency. All around the world, there's much more involvement in grass-roots organizations, there's regionalism [and moves toward developing] more local autonomy.—Noam Chomsky, *Spin* interview (1993) with Jerry Brown

No space disappears in the course of growth and development: the *worldwide does not abolish the local.*—Henri Lefebvre, *La production de l'espace*

Postmodern culture-workers, on the verge of becoming the "symbolic engineers" and critical self-consciousness of global capital,[1] stand at the crossroads of an altered and more fractal terrain everywhere we gaze at century's end: a new world-space of cultural production and national representation which is simultaneously becoming more *globalized* (unified around dynamics of capitalogic moving across borders) and more *localized* (fragmented into contestatory enclaves of difference, coalition, and resistance) in everyday texture and composition. The contributions to this volume, gathered from various sites and across cultural disciplines, track this contemporary interface of global forces, images, codes, sites, genres, and technologies of transnationalization with those more local communities, tactics, and symbolic strategies of cultural location that confront and challenge them in the production of locality, local subjects, national situations, and the making of everyday space and public spheres of existence.

The global/local assemblage would, as sublated agent of the "world system," refigure one-way models of domination to the social formations of the modern nation-state and, in its more optimistic formulations, activate multiple lines of social invention, contestation, mobility, reimagining, coalition, and flight. Regions and region-states increasingly override national borders and older territorial forms and create special economic zones of uneven development and transcultural hybridity. This global/local synergy within what we will track as the *transnational imaginary* enlivens and molests the textures of everyday life and spaces of subjectivity and reshapes those contemporary structures of feeling some culture critics all too commonly banalize as "postmodern" or hypertextually consecrate as "postcolonial" resistance. Too much of cultural studies, in this era of uneven globalization and the two-tier information highway, can sound like a way of making the world safe and user-friendly for global capital and the culture of the commodity form.

The ongoing process of disruption and manipulation by global discourses and technologies is all too uncritically being rearticulated as a process of *translating the transnational* structurations of nation, self, and community into "translational," *in-between* spaces of negotiated language, borderland being, and bicultural ambivalence.[2] It is no longer adequate to map the globe into binary zones of center and periphery as an eternally Manichean space of colonial victimization nor even as Edward Said's rich culturescape of "contrapuntal" imperialism. Still, whatever our attitude toward the creative-destructive dynamic driving the contemporary phases of global capitalism, the local goes on being micromapped and micromined into so many consumer zones. If Coca-Cola Incorporated can claim in the 1990s, "We are not a multinational, we are a multilocal," cultural studies must enter a brave new world of simulated and multimarketed locales/locals with the politics of resistance all but drained from the bottle.

The geopolitics of global cultural formations and local sites are shifting under the pressures of this new "spatial dialectic" obtaining between mobile processes of *transnationalization* and strategies of *localization* or regional coalition. All along the Pacific Rim and inside the multiplex Asia/Pacific, outsourcing and immigration have created mingled processing zones and "global cities" of crosshatched and circular flow like Los Angeles, Vancouver, Taipei, Honolulu, or Seoul in which "all that was local becomes increasingly globalized, all that is global becomes increasingly localized."[3] Such regions, variously located, can virtually override national borders via the flextime flow of commodities, peoples, labor diasporas, images, and informations. "*Globloc,*" Mitsuhiro

Yoshimoto informs us, has become the latest Japanese media coinage to describe this process of interface between global technologies and local adaptations within the discourse of Japanese postmodernity/fashion. Within these spaces of uneven modernity, we are witnessing not so much the death and burial of "local cultural originality," as Fanon once feared within residually colonial structures of national modernity, as their rehabilitation, affirmation, and renewal in disjunctive phases and local reassertions: if at times euphoric in its quirkiness, globalization discourse is marked as well by what have been called "Lilliput strategies" of tying down and impeding transnational flows and globally dispersed work chains by linking "local struggles with global support" and connecting "local problems to global solutions."[4]

The nation-state, in effect, having been shaped into an "imagined community" of coherent modern identity through warfare, religion, blood, patriotic symbology, and language, is being undone by this fast imploding heteroglossic interface of the global with the local: what we would here diversely theorize as the *global/local* nexus. The dissolution and disinvention of *e pluribus unum* narratives can be seen happening in the United States from various angles and within multiple genres of discourse.[5] In discrepant situations of postmodern decolonization nonetheless, cultural workers (like Paik Nakchung urging the progressively national dimensions of the "people's literature" movement in South Korea in his wide-ranging interview with Fredric Jameson or Ping-hui Liao showing how the public sphere in Taiwan becomes a space of bargaining and negotiation for national memory and indigenous reemergence) do seek, by means of a heightened articulation of geopolitical location to Asian/ Pacific cultural heritage, "to recover the concreteness of space that capitalism makes disappear."

Henri Lefebvre predicted, in the aftermath of "1968" experienced as a global/local crisis in social modernity, that the process of mass urbanization would be superseded (in David Harvey's overview of Lefebvre's space-oriented poetics) by "the production of [everyday] space, that was binding together the global and the local, the city and the country, the centre and the periphery, in new and quite unfamiliar ways."[6] According to Lefebvre's prescient analysis of situated possibility in *La production de l'espace,* the "abstract space" of global capital would go on being fractured from within by enduring ties to religion, place, city, country, and, above all, by amplified segregations of class: "Today more than ever, the class struggle is inscribed in space," he suggested.[7] Lefebvre called this global-local dialectic "the principal contradiction" suturing the new world-space of late capital and sought to aggravate the very discrepancy "between the capacity to conceive and treat space on a global (or worldwide) scale on the one hand, and its fragmentation of procedures and processes, all fragmentary themselves, on the other."[8] These spaces of the local, within the practice of everyday life under global capital, can provide the spawning ground for those various "surreptitious creativities" of reuse, recoding, and deterritorialized invention that, in a related analysis of space viewed as everyday practice, Michel de Certeau saw emerging in the interstices and against the grain of capital's disciplinary structures.[9]

Lefebvre prefigured the rise of post-Fordist geographers in the 1980s like David Harvey, Mike Davis, Edward Soja, Neil Smith, and Katharyne Mitchell (see her analysis of the Pacific Northwest as a conjunction of global capitalist flows and local resistances, in this collection) for whom the local (both as spatial materiality and as symbolic metaphor) is already thoroughly global in its uneven and contradictory makeup, as well as in the work of transpacific filmmakers like Ridley Scott or Stephen Okazaki for whom Tokyo and Southern California comprise an interlocked Asian/Pacific space. Cultural workers confront a sprawling, unevenly modernized world, all too clamorously here, in which "socio-political contradictions are realized spatially" in the cities, places, and cultures where capital would globalize and install its everyday operations.[10] Because this postmodern space remains alive with class contradiction and sedimented with dynamics of modernization that suppressed "local knowledges" and subjects, cultural workers can seek to articulate if not aggravate "conflicts between local powers and central powers, wherever they may occur in the world" without systematic planning, without the assumption of vanguard theory, without the delusion of any total space-time alternative.[11] Local spaces of contested identification and belonging, if scrappy and minor in this micropolitical sense, can still generate what Raymond Williams called "resources of hope" within contexts of transnationalization, that master-narrative of globalized production in which "the products you are responsible for and the company you serve have become denationalized" from bounded national locations/identities such as "U.S.A.," "Mexico," or "Japan."[12]

Simultaneous with the rise of "global localization" as a marketing strategy implemented by transnational corporations like Sony and Coca-Cola in the late 1970s and throughout the 1980s to bypass national borders and infiltrate transnational corporations (TNCs) as regionally adept and flexibly situated "insiders," the rise of "critical regionalism" as an aesthetic of rearguard resistance rearticulated borders as spaces, genres, and enclaves of cultural preservation and community identity to be set against global technologies of modernization or image-cultures of the postmodern.[13] Akio Morita, after the transnational purchase of Columbia Pictures in 1989 by Sony, told *Newsweek* readers the flexible strategy to sustain profits in the Third Wave: "We are still expanding our facilities in this country [United States]. I don't like the word 'multinational.' I don't know what it means. I created a new term: 'global localization.' That's our new slogan."[14] Transnationalization of corporate identity, thus, implies a process of *global localization:* crossing borders and segmenting markets via flexible production.

The dialectical countermovement to pressurize the local into a community of resistance took place in Hawaii as in Great Britain, organized around different allegiances to place, race, and class, as the essays by Wilson and Featherstone would here particularize. So situated, the local need not embody a regressive politics of global delinkage, bounded particularity, and claims of ontological pastness, where locality becomes some backward-gazing fetish of purity to disguise how global, hybrid, compromised, and unprotected everyday identity already is. Globalization, paradoxically, has led to a strengthening of local ties, allegiances, and identity politics within different nation-state formations, even though what may emerge is what Stuart Hall calls that more "tricky version of 'the local' which operates within, and has been thoroughly reshaped by 'the global' and operates largely within its logic."[15]

Our hypothesis of the "global/local" linkage would suggest and maximize linkage, disjuncture, and fracture at the neo-capitalist border: the counterlogic of the *both/and.* Attempts to rise to the quasi-totalizing task of making a model or sustaining a vision of a "world system" via the cultural politics of "cognitive mapping" will involve representing an intensified vision of the local situation. At the very least, we feel the need to read the articulations and relocations of theory as the contradiction-ridden activity of cultural production (producing uneven cultural capital) in what Rey Chow calls the tricky thicket of "cosmopolitan diasporic space."[16] In Colin MacCabe's unpacking of "cognitive mapping" as a necessary postmodern strategy for locating and actualizing geopolitical orientation, deftly expanded across the Pacific Rim in the "geopolitical aesthetic" of Fredric Jameson, this tactic of representative location implies "[one] model for how we might begin to articulate the global and the local. It provides a way of linking the most intimately local—our particular path through the world—and the most global—the crucial features of our political planet."[17] Mapping, tapping into, and tracking this "local motion," to use a Hawaiian expression for place-bound tactics, can be figured as implying, at some primary level of collective agency, geopolitical location on the trajectory of transcultural/transnational informations and commodity flows: it is a way of keeping alive the hidden totality of social relations that does not sublate the local into the global. We need not posit the global/local in some endlessly binary master/slave opposition in which the "merely" local is undone, insignificant, or displaced by a "binary machine" logic sustaining the dominant discourses of social science or political economy.[18]

Pluralization and relativization are processes, stressed within the newer globalization theories of postmodern social theory, that would give more power to local heterogeneity and locally situated political struggles within the world-system model.[19] Attention to local conjunctures needs to be linked, at all points, to global processes without falling into the by-now-tired modernist binary of the universal (global) sublating the particular (local), explained through a colonizing master-narrative of undifferentiated homogenizing forces meeting endlessly specific and hyper-detailed adaptations doomed to defeat. Such an abstractly oppositional formulation of the global/local, as James Clifford has observed, "*either* favors some version of 'globalism' self-defined as progressive, modern, and historically dynamic *or* favors a localism 'rooted' (not routed) in place, tradition, culture, or ethnicity conceived in an absolutist mode."[20] Wary of any prefabricated metanarrative of teleological development, we can approach global/local space as one that disturbs prior analytical categories—with a spatial dialectic acknowledging the agency of social imagination and cultural labors.

What we would variously track as the "transnational imaginary" comprises the *as-yet-unfigured* horizon of contemporary cultural production by which national spaces/identities of political allegiance and economic regulation are being undone and imagined communities of modernity are being reshaped at the macropolitical (global) and micropolitical (cultural) levels of everyday existence. Given these macroeconomic transformations underway, can there emerge strategies of "transnational solidarity" within such a space? Can we even imagine a transnational community that is not wholly given over to the dominant rationality of capital? Must the cross-border linkages and synergies at the global/local interface be tied to the dynamics of mastery and logics of profit even as they render the modular nation-state into a "dysfunctional" organization.[21] The global/local tracks the space of a disorientation, the rendering and deforming local of Western universality as standard, center, and dominant knowledge.

Local struggles, such as the national situation of South/North Korea, can be registered as a relational, multidimensionally conflicted social space of global contradiction. If local struggles figure as allegories of larger, more systemic alteration, then part and whole will have to be rethought and reimagined as figuring the contemporary world-system of global capital in all its concreteness. *Praxis*, if one can still posit such a slogan of transnational solidarity, has to be multilayered, addressing both the most immediate local concerns and the larger global horizon in which, to invoke another example, contemporary capitalism as a tourist apparatus can cannibalize and decontextualize the local Pacific into some "ex-primitive" simulacrum.[22]

Even as the political space of contemporary Hawaii, like Maori New Zealand, undergoes a renewed struggle for indigenous sovereignty and the recovery of lands alienated to the American nation-state, the influx of some six million tourists per year creates a porous space on Oahu, which "suffers the greatest number of tourists per square mile of any place on earth."[23] This indigenous Pacific is deformed and troped, on a daily basis of mass-tourist banalization, into "lovely hula hands" beckoning the transnational tourist with exotic/erotic redemption from the cyborg labor of late capitalist everyday life. "Let's start thinking in terms of local development rather than multinational expansion," urged Mililani Trask for *Ka Lahui Hawai'i* in a recent forum on Hawaiian sovereignty one hundred years after American annexation, positing the development of local Costco warehouses on tax-free native land as a micropolitical tactic to alter the tourist-based economy. The local posits interstitial spaces of alternative imagining: modes of living and memory undoing the dominant space-time of the nation-state and the transnational superstate.

If the world-system of capitalism has thrived since the days of Captain Cook and Adam Smith maximizing "the wealth of nations" upon circulating spectacles and discourses of social difference and cultural heterogeneity, it now also thrives on a "time-space compression" in which "some localized aesthetic image" of place or native sovereignty runs the risk of being marketed and defined by postmodern regimes and codes of neo-capital accumulation.[24] Given transculturalization and the relentless to-and-froing of informations and commodities across national borders, we could multiply examples of such displacement: fears of rootlessness at the shopping mall give way to global nightmares of electronic propinquity, cultural vanishment, and semiotic overload.[25]

From the Atlantic to the New Pacific, a moral tactic for cultural studies becomes urgent: the rise of the global economy entails articulating a "global cultural economy" at the micropolitical level of everyday struggle and affirming a "local motion" asserting the force of a "disjunctive synthesis."[26] If panic, apolitical emptiness, and schizophrenia do reign, deterritorialized spaces and individuals can be actualized in between the dominant arrangements of social space "as a local-global correlation of becomings-other" disorganized around the counterlogic of the *both/and*.[27] Against all odds, the local posits the terrain of disjunctive global/local cultural flows, unpredictable outcomes, temporary autonomous zones, nonsynchronized spaces where indigenous imagination might achieve renewed social agency or a multicultural community, say, can articulate place-bound identity or construct ethnic survival. Risking the articulation, as well, of some "hidden totality" of capital in its latest phase of globalization, the dominant note in this collection, *Global/Local*, aims to unsettle the hybridity discourse normative to postcolonial analysis with trenchantly situated readings that stress enduring asymmetries of domination, injustice, racism, class dynamics, and uneven spatial development.

The first six essays in this collection attempt to come to terms with ongoing processes and forces of globalization that are disrupting local communities, nations, and regions into something else, whether nightmarish, hybrid, or neo-sublime. In "The Global in the Local," Arif Dirlik reaches back into formations of Chinese Marxism and Third World socialism and forward into agendas of guerrilla marketeering to theorize the social dynamics of local spaces as still figuring quasi-socialist, or at the very least heteroglossic, alternatives of space-time within the capitalist world system that has achieved hegemony across the twentieth century. Dirlik presents a richly conjunctural notion of the local read as a "site both of promise and predicament" that has, in contemporary contexts, already "been worked over by modernity" and the disorganizing dynamics of global capital. This is a "critical localism" wary of romantic nostalgia for communities past, hegemonic nationalism, or a museumifying historicism that would imprison the present in the past and disguise oppression in a neo-ethnic sheen.

Engaged in providing a refigured sociology of "global culture" as a multiple formation of homogeneous technologies meeting heterogeneous adaptations, Mike Featherstone would ground his disciplinary assessment of transnational sociology within the culture-laden dynamics of working-class communities of localized identity in Thatcher's Great Britain. Given the rise of globalized technologies and the standardized spaces and products of modernity, localism can become a way to hold on to "a particular bounded space" posited around close-knit social ties of kinship, community, and residency. Assuming an oversimplified image of unified community, Featherstone argues, even a nation can embody such localism, as "a geographically bounded space which is sedimented with symbolic sentiments." The notion of the boundary Featherstone presents does show how fully *relational* any localism as social formation is and how embedded in struggle, tension, and contradiction. Even nostalgia can be a critical tool if one is cognizant of the newer forces of domination and wary of sentimental idealizations. Intensified globalization provokes a further range of reactions "which seek to rediscover particularity, localism and difference" in the unevenness of race, class, and gender. This new localism of postmodernity seems creolized, evermore cagily constructed. Tourism, as in the case of the Ainu in Northern Japan who stage their crafts and customs for the Tokyo gaze, can be manipulated to serve the recovery of cultural identity. Featherstone's essay suggests, finally, the conjunction of social science with cultural studies now emerging to theorize global/local conjunctions whether located in England, Japan, or Brazil.

With trenchant geopolitical insight into the ruses of "postcoloniality" discourse or a "multiculturalism" tied to social formations of the nation-state, Masao Miyoshi presents a critical assessment of transnationalization as a domineering process in which "the administrative and occupational mode of colonialism is irreversibly being replaced by an economic version—especially after the end of the Cold War." This is the period which megatrend thinkers along the Asian-Pacific Rim, for example, would celebrate as the rise of a decommunized co-prosperity sphere. Miyoshi's analysis in "A Borderless World?" of indigenous peoples assumes the dynamics of "colonized space" as a starting point for political struggle, already molested by social formations of capital: "Once absorbed into the chronopolitics of the secular West," Miyoshi warns, "colonized space cannot reclaim autonomy and seclusion; once dragged out of their precoloniality, the indigenes of peripheries have to deal with the knowledge of the outside world, irrespective of their own wishes and inclinations."

The odds deepen against the emergence and survival of such local formations rooted in culture and place: transnationals, no longer tied to national allegiances and GNPs like multinationals, are even more adrift and mobile, deterritorialized, ready to consume any local or indigenous site of resistance/difference within the ideology of a "borderless" co-prosperity sphere that has all the makings of a transnational oversoul. Identity politics must engage with these forces of transnationalization before the grounds of identity are already undone. Perhaps this vision of global capital is oversystematized and stable and insufficiently cognizant of the local, but Miyoshi's call to critical wariness de-

mands attention to the forces of global inequality and the games that transnational cultural critics play to think of something else or nominate themselves as
professional subalterns.

With a grim logic that seemingly suspends the politics of resistance or
place, Mitsuhiro Yoshimoto's "Real Virtuality" shows the circulatory power of
contemporary capitalism not only to commodify but to simulate life-world and
body, to turn history into image and "commodity-image" into the resources of
expanding profit for transnational corporations we belatedly metonymize
as "Hollywood." This off-ground process Yoshimoto tracks as *virtualization,*
"which constitutes the basic dynamic of capitalism" in its pure form. Moving
from real to virtual, national image-cultures and narrative structures are thus
threatened with subsumption "under the general uniformity of the global image culture." This simultaneously creates the disjunctive space, within imagined
communities, "of global integration and national/ethnic separatism." Having
become ideal commodities, images and spectacles are produced and consumed
instantly, of which the Gulf War was just one global instance simulating a
"strong America" on a slagging economic base. What Brian Massumi has
tracked as a cycle of "image accumulation/image shedding" becomes crucial to
this post-Fordist phase of globalizing capital,[28] given over to a dynamic of
hyper-circulation of imagery that lends itself to the survival not of Detroit but
to a transnationalized Hollywood (financed by Japan) turning Japan into con-
sumable image. Yoshimoto's global/local assumes a world-space of decontex-
tualized representations, no longer constrained by location: "images without
end."

Focusing upon the emergence of what he calls the "independent transnational film" genre and the territory of "transnational liminality," Hamid Naficy
highlights the "claustrophobic configuration of space" as represented by Turkish and Iranian filmmakers working in exile. Oddly, the compression of space-
time does not expand but shrinks the locus of action—the iconography of
possibility for these global migrants—into suitcases, buses, cages, cramped
rooms, prisons, TV sets. Transnationality suggests the transformation of place
into interstitial spaces of "agonistic liminality": "to be in transnationality," for
Naficy, does not mean to belong to operations of capital with its masculinist
sense of space as adventure, movement, action; but to be in between, uprooted,
homeless, "to belong to neither of the two modes of dystopia or utopia."

"In transnational genre, it is the enclosed claustrophobic spaces, often in
the form of prisons, which both express and encode the (melo)drama of transnational subjectivity" in Naficy's reading of the genre—so unlike the trans-

pacific if not transworld sense of heteroglossic space given in a Pacific Rim action film like *Blade Runner*. Even cyberspace can be confining, a machinic prisonhouse for capital and the state to play out their logics and enlist happy cyborgs. Perhaps this clash of claustrophobia and some variously inflected nostalgia for immensity and the sacred comprises the mingled space of exilic transnationality. Agoraphobia may be a sensible reaction to public spaces given over to the ideology of consumerism and colonizing the dreams and consciousness of the transnational subject, as Naficy's reading of *Agora* (1992) suggests. Given such phobias, *transnational* should not become just another name for "international" or, worse yet, "cosmopolitan" mobility. With uncanny insight into international media spectacles, Ella Shohat and Robert Stam's essay questions the power/knowledge dynamics of any vision of globality, as such spectacles and narratives remain linked to uneven centers and structures of domination it would be misleading to sublimate as "postcolonial."

In the second section of this book, "Local Conjunctions," global processes, interactions, genres, and codes are focused through local settings and cultural images—from Japan to Hollywood, from Canada to India—that would contest any comforting reading of postcolonial hybridity. Karen Kelsky's "Flirting with the Foreign" offers a deft, speculative, situated ethnography of the gender and racial dynamics in contemporary Japan, specifically as these internal dynamics are disturbed by the material and libidinal mobility of the "office lady" culture in transnational settings. These women are constructed by Japanese patriarchal discourse as "yellows cabs" embodying the global tourist economy and its new forms and flows of cosmopolitan cultural traffic. Given the export-oriented outreach of Japan, these Japanese tourists in resort and border spaces "have appropriated the gaijin males as reflexive symbols" that reflect back upon the gender and racial hierarchies of Japan, signifying the male as native/authentic and the woman as contaminated by the foreign/global. Such encounters can refract the local ingredients of the Japanese national imaginary and its insular struggles to reinscribe differences between male and female, rich and poor, Japanese and black and white at the transnational border.

Film, still the crucial genre of transnational production and global circulation for refigured narratives, offers speculative ground for the transnational imaginary and its contention within national and local communities. Most of the essays in *Global/Local* engage with this contemporary mode of cultural reproduction and would demystify the politics of the transnational spectacle. In "Desiring the Involuntary: Machinic Assemblage and Transnationalism in De-

leuze and *Robocop 2*," Jonathan L. Beller exposes the filmic construction of
cyborgian subjectivity in a world of transnational endocolonization wherein
"the distinction between the inside and the outside of a world-system becomes
obsolete." As "machinic assemblage" of the transnational state, as agent of a
quasi-Deleuzian unconscious, Robocop embodies a technologized image of
our worst fears—subjective evacuation—and everyday hopes—of flight, becoming other, political refragmentation into local autonomous zones. Moving from
police work to the reproductive pleasures of sports entertainment, Beller offers
a complex foray into the transnational image-machine of Hollywood, reading
Robocop as a transnational intertext figuring the shifting powers of America in
the residually interstate world-system. Finally, Katharyne Mitchell offers a fully
situated critique of the global flows and local accommodations and resistances
aggravating racial, ethnic, and national tensions in the Asia/Pacific dimensions
of Canada.

The third section, "Global/Local Disruptions," examines discrepant locations and genres in which local resistance movements and cultures are threatened with absorption into the mediations of capital. Dana Polan's essay, "Globalism's Localisms" establishes an intertextual film archive which represents
these uneven yet at times hopeful dynamics, for example, industrial Pittsburgh
being turned into a site of postmodern film production. Christopher L. Connery's "The Oceanic Feeling and the Regional Imaginary" examines the various
ways Pacific Rim cultures, emerging from the cold war order into the new
Asia/Pacific of APEC, have figured the Pacific Ocean into a new frontier of
economic co-prosperity and cultural reinvention. From literature to political
economic discourse, this "borderless" regionality signifies the promises and
delusions of "oceanic consciousness" and is disfigured by the uneven politics of
transnationalization.

Burrowing archivally into this Pacific location, Rob Wilson's essay on
"*Goodbye Paradise:* Global/Localism in the American Pacific" looks into "local"
literary and film production in Hawaii to articulate contradictions between
multicultural American imaginings, transnational tourism in a microstate, and
the decolonizing politics of location associated with the Hawaiian sovereignty
movement. These discrepant localisms and neo- and subnational communities
of the Pacific local are framed within the larger dynamics of transnational
capital, which disfigures the daily life around Bamboo Ridge through the mediations of tourism. Ping-hui Liao, who has already mapped the Taiwanese cultural politics of the February 28, 1947, incident as renarrated in contemporary
scholarship and the film *City of Sadness* (1989),[29] again holds out for "counter-

public spheres (or alternative minor public spheres)" within media whereby local memories, heterogeneous forces, and resistances in Taiwan cannot be globally effaced. In a fully dialectic reading of global impacts upon and local transformations of a Taiwanese genre, the literary supplement as transformed into a medium of cultural critique and oppositional social theory, Ping-hui Liao shows how "global cultural flows can be appropriated, [as Taiwanese] writers tend to work through indigenous and imported genres and discourses, mingling local knowledge with information from abroad, to establish a sphere of criticism in which a mobile vision of the global and the marcopolitical may open up possibilities for contestation and resistance." The complexity of the Asia/Pacific local as a ground of national identity is given at once more global audibility and more local impact. On a related level, Paik Nak-chung's interview with Fredric Jameson offers a powerful case study of South Korea as a critical space where these various social formations of modernity—the local, the national, the transnational—contend for domination on a dynamic peninsula divided by the capitalist/communist binary that drove the cold war imaginary and its paranoid subjects. While attentive to local contradictions at all points, both critics adhere to a mobile vision of the "macropolitical" that would allow for resistances within an uneven system of power to alter that system and disturb its self-understanding via liberal master-narratives of co-prosperity and freedom.[30]

Paul Bové's "Afterword," with the trenchant and relentlessly critical insight that characterizes his scholarship, frames the overall problematics of the local/global conjunction as these discourses of memory and speculation effect residual formations of the nation-state and the emerging transnational superstates and zones: forces, as Bové summarizes, refiguring the disciplines and tactics of cultural studies, social research, historical memory, and intellectual obligation. Even if we can get beyond an older dialectical reading of the worldwide abolishing the local, the global/local need not be the rallying cry for an ecstatic postmodernity celebrating a simultaneously homogeneous and fragmented "schizo-space" or the pleasures of nomadic theory-travel.[31] Even as everyday space is colorfully internationalized at century's end and the growth of speculative capital grows more mobile and unevenly concentrated in "global cities" of transnational service-production like Tokyo, New York, and London, the end result may be no less than the postnational installation of "an ideology of globalism, whereby localities are seen as powerless in an era of global economic forces."[32]

These new times are global/local times. The forging of politics and ethical obligations in the face of such injustices and uneven benefits, retooled to fit the changing cultural and political-economic circumstances, still matter. This collection of essays—situated in different geopolitical locations, working through discrepant genres and discourses of contemporary purport, mingling criticism with cultural invention, refusing political despair—should contribute to the unfolding analysis of the "transnational imaginary" that effects local projects, regional emergences, and national subjects in their situated struggles to achieve a just, decent, and compassionate community.

Notes

1   See Robert B. Reich, *The Work of Nations: Preparing Ourselves for Twenty-First-Century Capitalism* (New York: Alfred A. Knopf, 1991), who buttresses his portrayal of corporate transnationalization with the contradictory claim that, despite "competition from foreign symbolic analysts," "America's symbolic-analytic zones remain, for the most part, wondrously resilient," p. 240.

2   On "this hybrid location of cultural value—the transnational as the translational," see Homi Bhabha, "The Postcolonial and the Postmodern," *The Location of Culture* (London and New York: Verso, 1994), p. 173 ff. For a geopolitically situated critique of *postcolonial* discourse as a version of flexible production, see Arif Dirlik, "The Postcolonial Aura: Third World Criticism in the Age of Global Capitalism," *Critical Inquiry* 20 (1993): 328–56. Also see the critiques of postcolonial discourse by Ella Shohat and Robert Stam and by Masao Miyoshi in this collection, as applied to the genres of world history and film/novel analysis.

3   Edward W. Soja, *Postmodern Geographies: The Reassertion of Space in Critical Social Theory* (London: Verso, 1989), p. 217; and Mike Davis, *City of Quartz: Excavating the Future in Los Angeles* (New York: Vintage, 1992) on the globalization of the regional economy, p. 101. Different disciplinary articulations of these global/local interactions are simultaneously reforming anthropology, cultural geography, and sociology, especially in the United States and Great Britain: see Clifford Geertz, *Local Knowledge* (New York: Basic Books, 1983); J. Friedman, "Being in the World: Globalization and Localization," in *Global Culture: Nationalism, Globalization and Modernity,* ed. Mike Featherstone (London: Sage, 1990); *Culture, Globalization and the World-System,* ed. Anthony King (Binghamton, N.Y.: Department of Art and Art History, 1991); and Etienne Balibar and Immanuel Wallerstein, *Race, Nation, Class: Ambiguous Identities* (London and New York: Verso, 1991).

4   Frantz Fanon, *Black Skin, White Masks,* trans. Charles Lamm Markmann (New York: Grove Weidenfield, 1967), pp. 14–18; Jeremy Brechner and Tim Costello, "The Lilliput Strategy: Taking on the Multinationals," *Nation* 259 (Dec. 19, 1994): 757–760. On the older "Manichean" space of colonized local peripheries as "two zones [which] are opposed but not in the service of a higher unity," see Frantz Fanon, *The Wretched of the*

Earth, trans. Constance Farrington (New York: Grove Press, 1968), p. 38 ff., as well as the more hybrid, "contrapuntal" reading of global space as an imperial legacy in Edward W. Said, *Culture and Imperialism* (New York: Alfred A. Knopf, 1993); and Ackbar Abbas on Hong Kong as a porously global city of colonial/transnational "hyphenization," "Building on Disappearance: Hong Kong Architecture and the City," *Public Culture* 6 (1994): 441–459.

5   On the "trojan nationalisms" of modernity readying to expand and implode into global/local contestation, from Canada and the United States to Japan and India, see the astute analysis of Arjun Appadurai, "Patriotism and Its Futures," *Public Culture* 5 (1993): 411–429. On the multiply situated, racially and ethnically coded refiguring of the American national imaginary and canons of imagined community, see the two special issues of *boundary 2* edited by Donald Pease: "New Americanists: Revisionist Interventions into the Canon," vol. 17 (Spring 1990); and "New Americanists 2: National Identities and Postnational Narratives," vol. 19 (Spring 1992); as well as Amy Kaplan and Donald Pease, eds., *Cultures of United States Imperialism* (Durham, N.C.: Duke University Press, 1994); and Lauren Berlant, "The Theory of Infantile Citizenship," *Public Culture* 5 (1993): 395–410, on America/United States as divergent forms of the national symbolic-imaginary within processes of transnationalization.

6   David Harvey, "Afterword" to Henri Lefebvre, *The Production of Space,* trans. Donald Nicholson-Smith (Oxford: Blackwell, 1991), p. 431. As Bruce Robbins warns of the global/local interface as a problem of political agency, "The move in geography to study the smaller, sub-regional units known as localities came at a time [in the 1980s] when the worldwide restructuring of the capitalist economy seemed at once to be increasing the scale of global interconnectedness and, in direct proportion, to be decreasing the power of the human agents concerned *to grasp or resist its operations*" (emphasis mine): "Comparative Cosmopolitanism," *Social Text* 31/32 (1992): 176.

7   Lefebvre, *The Production of Space,* p. 55. On Vancouver, Canada as an Asian/Pacific site of localist production and community of resistance to the contemporary influx of Hong Kong hypercapital, see Katharyne Mitchell's essay in this collection, "In Whose Interest? Transnational Capital and the Production of Multiculturalism in Canada."

8   Lefebvre, ibid., p. 355. On the complicated post-Lefebvrean politics of "spatial metaphors" as tactics locating and mobilizing postmodern struggles toward decentralization and marginalization, see the essays in material geography gathered in *Place and the Politics of Identity,* ed. Michael Keith and Steve Pile (London and New York: Routledge, 1993), especially Neil Smith and Cindi Katz, "Grounding Metaphor: Towards a Spatialized Politics," pp. 67–83.

9   Michel de Certeau, "Walking in the City," *The Practice of Everyday Life,* trans. Steven Rendall (Berkeley: University of California Press, 1984), p. 96.

10 Ibid., p. 365.

11 Ibid., p. 379.

12 Kenichi Ohmae, *The Borderless World: Power and Strategy in the Interlinked Economy* (New York: Harper, 1991), p. 94. Christopher L. Connery's essay in this collection

exposes the neo-capitalist sublimations of space, ocean, and region in Ohmae's narrative of expanding co-prosperity across the Asia/Pacific region of APEC and NAFTA.

13   For articulations of "critical regionalism" as a place-bound aesthetic emerging during the 1980s, see Kenneth Frampton, "Towards a Critical Regionalism: Six Points for an Architecture of Resistance," *The Anti-Aesthetic: Essays on Postmodern Culture*, ed. Hal Foster (Port Townsend, Wash.: Bay Press, 1983); and Rob Wilson, "Blue Hawaii: Bamboo Ridge as 'Critical Regionalism,'" in *What Is in a Rim?: Critical Perspectives on the Pacific Region Idea*, ed. Arif Dirlik (Boulder, Colo.: Westview Press, 1993).

14   Interview with Morita, *Newsweek*, October 9, 1989, p. 66. Ohmae credits Morita for the invention of this global/local incorporation: "What is called for [in the borderless interlinked spaces of transnational production] is what Akio Morita of Sony has termed global localization, a new orientation that looks both ways" and can bypass national protectionism and state regulation (*Borderless World*, 93). Japanese social scientists, policy planners, and economists began to think of the Asia-Pacific region as a distinctive "community" around 1963.

15   Stuart Hall, "Culture, Community, Nation," *Cultural Studies* 7 (1993): 354. Also see Stuart Hall, "The Local and the Global: Globalization and Ethnicity," in Anthony King, ed., *Culture, Globalization and the World-System*, pp. 19–39.

16   Rey Chow, *Writing Diaspora: Tactics of Intervention in Contemporary Cultural Studies* (Bloomington: Indiana University Press, 1993), pp. 118–119. Chow is quite vigilant against the tendency of transnational cultural critics, benefiting from metropolitan cultural capital, to declare "subaltern" status.

17   Preface to Fredric Jameson, *The Geopolitical Aesthetic: Cinema and Space in the World System* (Bloomington: Indiana University Press, 1992), p. xiv. Jameson's reading of urban spaces and "global cities" of cultural production in Taiwanese and Chinese film as figuring the dynamics of economic globalization remains exemplary in this regard: "Urban PRC film, however, seems to take a very different stylistic turn [from Taiwanese film], as though its relations were not those that led into the Chinese land mass, but rather the discontinuous vertical openings onto the media and the Pacific Rim, that is to say, onto whatever is fantasized as the West" (118). On the "internal heterogeneity" of contemporary Taiwan film versus the more "transnational hybridity" of Hong Kong film, see Chris Berry, "These Nations Which Are Not One: Identity and Postcoloniality in Recent Hong Kong and Taiwan Film," *SPAN* 34/35 (1992): 48–58.

18   See Gilles Deleuze and Félix Guattari, *On the Line*, trans. John Johnston (New York: Semiotext(e), 1983), pp. 77–80, on the binary logic of "abstract overcoding machines" narrating the self-knowledge of the Western nation-state: "a huge abstract machine that overcodes the monetary, industrial, and technological flux" of the global economy and its zigzag deterritorializations (111–112).

19   For one version of this dominant theme in globalization theory's refiguring of Wallerstein's world-system model, see Johann P. Arnason, "Nationalism, Globalization, Modernity," in *Global Culture*, pp. 222–225.

20   James Clifford, "Borders and Diasporas," talk given at the Center for Cultural Studies,

University of California at Santa Cruz, April 3–4, 1992. For a related problematic articulating local appropriations of global media, see Ien Ang, "Global Media/Local Meaning," *Media Information Australia* 63 (1991): 4–8, who maximizes local semiotics as a potential site of resistance via recoding: "If, in other words, the global is the site of the homogeneous (or the common) and the local the site of the diverse, then the latter can—in today's [technologically] integrated world-system—only constitute and reconstitute itself in and through concrete reworkings and appropriations of the former."

21   Kenichi Ohmae, "Rise of the Region State," *Foreign Affairs* 72 (1993): 93: "Nation states by definition require a domestic political focus, while region states [like Singapore's 'growth triangle' with Indonesia, Malaysia and Thailand, or Hong Kong linked to Shenzhen] are ensconced in the global economy" (83).

22   On "global tourism" becoming a cultural dominant cannibalizing the local Pacific and indigenous forms of identity/place, see Dean MacCannell, *Empty Meeting Grounds: The Tourist Papers* (London and New York: Routledge, 1992): "ex-primitives" performing ethnic authenticity are devoured by the image-culture and commodity logic of "cannibal-capitalism" (59).

23   Haunani-Kay Trask, "Lovely Hula Hands: Corporate Tourism and the Prostitution of Hawaiian Culture," in *From a Native Daughter: Colonialism and Sovereignty in Hawai'i* (Monroe, Maine: Common Courage Press, 1993), p. 184. If the Ainu in contemporary Japan can use tourism as an apparatus by which to win recognition as an ethnic minority within the Japanese nation-state, "Hawaiians," as Jonathan Friedman remarks, "are acutely aware of the potential de-authenticating power of commodification [via tourism]": see Friedman, "Being in the World: Globalization and Localization," in *Global Culture*, pp. 323–324.

24   David Harvey, "Capitalism: The Factory of Fragmentation," *New Perspectives Quarterly* 9 (1992): 42–45. Explaining the rise of place-bound poetics and "some localized aesthetic image" during the 1980s, Harvey argues that, within postmodern regimes of flexible reproduction, "Capitalist hegemony over space [through technologies of 'space-time compression'] puts the aesthetics of place very much back on the agenda," *The Condition of Postmodernity: An Enquiry Into the Origins of Cultural Change* (Oxford: Blackwell, 1990), p. 303.

25   Arjun Appadurai, "Disjuncture and Difference in the Global Cultural Economy," *Public Culture* 2 (1990): 3.

26   Interview with Arata Isozaki, *New Perspectives Quarterly* 9 (1992): 19–20. Isozaki is describing his own architectural style—mingling Japanese motifs and local forms with those globalized technologies and image-spaces (like Disneyland) signifying Euro-American modernity—as "schizophrenic eclectic."

27   Brian Massumi, *A User's Guide to Capitalism and Schizophrenia: Deviations from Deleuze and Guattari* (Cambridge: MIT Press, 1992), pp. 141 and 112.

28   Ibid., p. 200. According to the global logic of this "commodity-image" infiltrating the postmodern psyche as well as colonizing exterior space, " 'Postmodernity' is the presence of the consumer/commodity axis of the capitalist relation in every point of social

space-time: endocolonization accomplished" (133). For a much differently inflected analysis of the "global-local duality," in which globalization becomes a process by which different local communities can "fashion a global opposition politics" and begin to network "new forms of grassroots political agency" in border spaces of multilocality, see Michael Peter Smith, "Can You Imagine?: Transnational Migration and the Globalization of Grassroots Politics," *Social Text* 39 (1994): 15–33.

29   Ping-hui Liao, "Rewriting Taiwanese National History: The February 28 Incident as Spectacle," *Public Culture* 5 (1993): 281–296.

30   For a trenchant discussion of *micropolitical* (local) and *macropolitical* (global) levels of cultural production and self-understanding, as these qualify nation-state formations and official narratives of identity, see Jonathan Arac and Harriet Ritvo, eds., "Introduction," *Macropolitics of Nineteenth-Century Literature: Nationalism, Exoticism, Imperialism* (Philadelphia: University of Pennsylvania Press, 1991).

31   Michael Smith and Steve Pile, intro., *Place and the Politics of Identity*, p. 2.

32   Saskia Sassen, *The Global City: New York, London, Tokyo* (Princeton, N.J.: Princeton University Press, 1991), p. 334. As a related work of global/local cultural studies, see Andrew Ross's discussion of the World Trade Center as an icon and structure of transnationalization all too unevenly reconfiguring and disrupting the local into "two-tier" space, "Bombing the Big Apple," in *The Chicago Gangster Theory of Life: Nature's Debt to Society* (London and New York: Verso, 1994): "The large-scale development of the WTC was an especially arrogant example of the giantism of urban renewal and its record of evictions and displacements [resulting in] the new 'global city' of finance capital and its two-tier post-Fordist service sector/professional economy" (112–113).

I GLOBALIZATIONS

●

THE GLOBAL IN THE LOCAL

Arif Dirlik

●

About ten years ago, a movie called *Local Hero* (directed by Bill Forsyth) appeared on the screens of artsier movie theaters in the United States. The movie narrates the study of a friendly confrontation between a global oil company located in Houston, Texas, and a small town on the Scottish coast, which the corporation plans to buy out and to raze so that it may build a complex for its North Sea oil operations. The corporation seeks to bargain the townspeople out of their property—since, we are told, they are not mere Third World people who may simply be pushed out of the way. The locals, though excited by the promise of unimagined wealth, not only prove to be crafty negotiators, but in the end manage to humanize the initially very urban young company executive sent there to do the negotiating, as well as the tough but spacy owner of the company (played beautifully by Burt Lancaster), both of whom end up falling in love with the place and its inhabitants. The film ends with the CEO scrapping the planned oil complex in favor of building a research laboratory where refineries and docks were to have been. The locals win, the town wins, the environment wins, and the corporation is happy—except for the young executive who is shipped back mercilessly to Houston, and the jungle of urban life and global corporate operations, with only memories of what might have been.

The film in its execution conveyed all the warmth of its message, but what seemed most remarkable about it at the time was its romantic nostalgia for the concretely (and, therefore, humanely) local against the abstractly (and, therefore, dehumanizingly) global. In hindsight it seems romantic still, but somewhat less nostalgic. We know that the humanization of one corporate CEO does not add up to the humanization of capital, and we are even more aware than before that the salvaging of one local community from the ravages of capital does not stop the onslaught of capital on community. We have learned, if anything, that to save one community it may be necessary to destroy another.

What makes *Local Hero* seem less nostalgic is the emergence in the intervening decade of a concern with the local as the site of resistance to capital, and the location for imagining alternative possibilities for the future. Romantic the movie may have been, but within the context of what was to follow, its nostalgia for the local community appears as something more than a mere fabulation of a past irrevocably lost; it appears as a nostalgia that becomes an active ingredient in the formation of a contemporary discourse on the local which has rescued "fabulation" itself from the opprobrium of a more "realistic" time to render it into a principle for the reconstruction of the local.[1] It would seem by the early nineties that local movements, or movements to save and reconstruct local societies, have emerged as the primary (if not the only) expressions of resistance to domination: from the tree-hugging women of the Chipko movement in Northern India to the women workers of the maquiladora industries of the United States-Mexican border, from indigenous people's movements seeking secession from colonialist states to the western Kansas counties that wish to secede from Kansas and the United States because they feel abused by their governments, local movements have emerged as a pervasive phenomenon of the contemporary world.[2] These movements find resonance in radical social theory in the increasing frequency with which the term "local" appears in considerations of the present and the future of society globally. In this theorizing the "local" retains the concrete associations of the local community—as in *Local Hero*—but more as reference than as specific description (or prescription); the meaning (the very scope) of the local is subject otherwise to negotiation in accordance with those considerations.

I reflect on the "local" as a site both of promise and predicament. My primary concern is with the local as a site of promise and the social and ideological changes globally that have dynamized a radical rethinking of the local over the last decade. I am interested especially in the relationship between the emergence of a global capitalism and the emergence of concern with the local as a site of resistance and liberation. Consideration of this relationship is crucial, it seems to me, in distinguishing a "critical localism" from localism as an ideological articulation of capitalism in its current phase. Throughout, however, I try also to remain cognizant of the local as a site of predicament. In its promise of liberation, localism may also serve to disguise oppression and parochialism. It is indeed ironic that the local should emerge as a site of promise at a historical moment when localism of the most conventional kind has reemerged as the source of genocidal conflict around the world. The latter, too, must surely enter any consideration of the local as a site of resistance to and liberation from oppression. In either case, the local that is at issue here is not the "local" in any conventional or traditional sense, but a very contemporary "local" that serves as a site for the working out of the most fundamental contradictions of the age.

Rethinking the Local

It is too early, presently, to sort out the factors that have contributed to the ascendancy of a concern with the local over the last decade, and any such undertaking must of necessity be highly speculative. What the "local" implies in different contexts is highly uncertain. Suffice it to say here that a concern for the local seems to appear in the foreground in connection with certain social movements (chief among them ecological, women's, ethnic, and indigenous people's movements) and the intellectual repudiation of past ideologies (chief among them, for the sake of brevity here, the intellectual developments associated with postmodernism).

Why there should be a connection between the repudiation of past ideologies and the reemergence of the local as a concern is not very mysterious. Localism as an orientation in either a "traditional" or a modern sense has never disappeared, but rather has been suppressed or, at best, marginalized in various ideologies of modernity. Localism does not speak of an incurable social disease that must sooner or later bring about its natural demise; and there is nothing about it that is inherently undesirable. What makes it seem so is a historical consciousness that identifies civilization and progress with political, social, and cultural homogenization and justifies the suppression of the local in the name of the general and the universal. Modernist teleology has gone the farthest of all in stamping upon the local its derogatory image: as enclaves of backwardness left out of progress, as the realm of rural stagnation against the dynamism of the urban, industrial civilization of capitalism, as the realm of particularistic culture against universal scientific rationality, and, perhaps most importantly, as the obstacle to full realization of that political form of modernity, the nation-state.[3]

This teleology has been resisted not only in the name of "traditional" localism, that sought to preserve received forms of local society, but by radical critics of modernity as well. Antimodernism rendered the local into a refuge from the ravages of modernity. Socialists, while not resisting modernity per se, have sought to localize modernity so as to render it more manageable—

beginning with the social experiments of the utopian socialists and culminating in Peter Kropotkin's plans for "industrial villages" as the foundation for anarchist society.[4] Karl Marx and Friedrich Engels, who rejected "utopian" in favor of "scientific" socialism nevertheless saw in "abolishing the contrast between town and country" one of the keys to resolving the problems of capitalist society, which had brought this contrast "to its extreme point."[5] Third World revolutions in the twentieth century would perpetuate these concerns for local society; especially those revolutions which, compelled by force of circumstances to pursue agrarian strategies of revolution, had to face local societies and their participation in revolution as a condition of revolutionary success. In these cases, ironically, local society would also emerge as a source of national identity, against the cosmopolitanism of urban centers drawn increasingly into the global culture of capitalism.[6]

The teleology of modernity, nevertheless, was to emerge victorious in the twentieth century over earlier socialist doubts about its consequences. The concern for the local persisted in the thinking of agrarian utopians and anarchists, but they, too, were to be marginalized for their insistence on the continued relevance of the local.[7] In the immediate decades after World War II, the modernizationist repudiation of the local prevailed in both bourgeois and Marxist social science.

It is not surprising, therefore, that the local should appear in contemporary discourse hand in hand with the repudiation of modernist teleology, the rejection as ideology of the "metanarratives" which have framed the history of modernization, whether capitalist or socialist. "Postmodernism," which has been described as "incredulity toward metanarratives," provides a convenient if loose term for characterizing the various challenges to modernist teleology, not because those who do so think of themselves as "postmodernists," but because every such challenge in its own way contributes to the making of a postmodern consciousness. Be that as it may, the repudiation of modernist teleology implies that there is nothing natural or inherently desirable about modernization (in capitalist or socialist form) and that the narrative of modernization is a narrative of compelling into modernity those who did not necessarily wish to be modern. This critique, too, is not necessarily novel, but long has been fundamental to the radical criticism of capitalism; from Marx and Engels to Kropotkin, radicals in the nineteenth century rejected the "naturalness" of capitalist development and pointed to coercion as key to the global success of capitalism. Marx, however, viewed it as a progressive development whereas Kropotkin viewed complicity in development (with specific reference to the nation-state) as the consequence of "brainwashing thanks to . . . education deformed and vitiated by the state, and our state prejudices"—which may be one reason among others that anarchism has made something of a comeback among radicals in recent years as Marxism has suffered for its association with modernization.[8]

The repudiation of the metanarrative of modernization, and its redirection of attention to coercion over teleology in development, have had two immediate consequences. First, it rescues from invisibility those who were earlier viewed as castaways from history, whose social and cultural forms of existence appear in the narrative of modernization at best as irrelevancies, at worst as minor obstacles to be extinguished on the way to development. Having refused to die a natural death, but instead come into self-awareness as victims of coercion, they demand now not just restoration of *their* history, further splintering the already cracked facade of modernity. The demand is almost inevitably accompanied by a reassertion of the local against the universalistic claims of modernism.[9]

The repudiation of the metanarrative of modernization, secondly, has allowed greater visibility to "local narratives." Rather than an inexorable march of global conquest from its origins in Europe, the history of modernization appears now as a temporal succession of spatially dispersed local encounters, to which the local objects of progress made their own contributions through resistance or complicity, contributing in significant ways to the formation of modernity, as well as to its contradictions. Also questioned in this view are the claims of nationalism which, a product itself of modernization, has sought to homogenize the societies it has claimed for itself, suppressing further such local encounters, and the "heterogeneity" they imply.[10]

Were it simply an ideological phenomenon, the postmodern repudiation of the metanarrative of modernity could be dismissed as a momentary loss of faith in modernity, another instance of those chronic failures of nerve that seem to attend moments of crisis in development, especially on occasions of transition, that will go away as soon as the transition has been completed and the crisis resolved. If so, this new round of antimodernism might be at best a passive enabling condition that allows us to hear previously inaudible voices, that will be muted again as soon as the business of development is once again under way, with capitalism having disposed of the competition that for nearly a century shaped and "distorted" its development.

It is possible that the disillusionment with capitalism, accompanied by a loss of faith in socialism that gathered force in the 1980s to reach its culmination in the fall of socialist states in 1989, has played a fundamental part in the resurgence of an antimodernism that has redirected the attention of radicals to local solutions to problems of development. It is more than possible, as I will argue below, that rather than signal the death of developmentalism, this new round of antimodernism has something to do with a new phase in the development of capitalism. What is not so certain is that the concerns expressed by this antimodernism will go away once the crisis of transition has been overcome, because these concerns are not merely ideological but the very products of the ecological, social, and political consequences of development. They are responses to a real crisis created by developments within capitalism and the whole project of modernity, and solutions to the crisis (as in the past) will have to be factored into considerations of further development. Above all, however, what is likely to give these concerns lasting power is that they express the demands not just of the powerless victims of development, although that is significant enough, but of formerly powerless groups who have acquired new power by virtue of the process of development itself, who now seek to redefine it in accordance with their own interests and perceptions.

It is neither necessary nor possible to recapitulate here what these groups are, except in the broadest terms to indicate the ways in which their emergence from invisibility and silence contributed to the questioning of metanarratives of development. Primary within the United States are the emergence into politics of Afro-Americans and women in the 1960s, followed (and due to the stimulus they provided) by other ethnic and indigenous people's movements. Globally, Third World revolutions (especially in China, followed by Vietnam) played a major part in questioning earlier (capitalist *and* socialist) models of development, but even more important in the long run have been the emergence from the 1970s of successful instances of capitalist development in the Third World which, having achieved success, proceeded to question the assumptions of Eurocentric models of development, countering the latter with models of development that claimed inspiration in native cultural and ideological norms; I have in mind here the cultural claims of East Asian societies.

I will say more about the latter in the next section in connection with the emergence of a global capitalism. A few words are necessary here concerning the various "people's movements" in the United States (and elsewhere in the First World), which called into question not just the claims of capitalist society, but received notions of socialism as well. Most obvious is the questioning by women, ethnic, racial, and indigenous peoples of the socialist claims to the centrality of class as the fundamental problem of capitalist society. The result was not only a more thorough examination of social categories in political organization, but also a greater awareness of the political manipulation of social categories; that is, the imposition on social complexity of reductionist interpretations of categories to rationalize ideological rule in the name of the groups so represented. The response to categorical reductionism was to assert the historicity and contextuality of social categories, which was to find expression in the works of E. P. Thompson, Eugene Genovese, and the so-called "new social history" which their works inspired.[11] What is important here is that new consciousness of the historicity of social categories drew attention to the local culture of the people in social movements against earlier emphases on a one-to-one relationship between social existence and ideology.

Even before the crisis of socialism became evident in the 1980s, and postmodernism became a household word, developments in social movements and in the relationships between the "Three Worlds" called into question the spatial and temporal teleology of development, as well as the conceptual teleology that had characterized earlier radical thinking. However, it is necessary to note that whatever the material circumstances that rendered "postmodernism" intelligible and plausible, it was the generation that came of age with these developments that was to play the crucial part in its articulation. The concern for the local (whether literally local or in reference to the "local" needs of social groups) gathered force simultaneously with the repudiation of teleology. I can do no more than suggest here that an ecological consciousness, which has done much to reassert the primacy of the local (as the most viable location for living in harmony with nature), was a product of the same circumstances and obviously bore some relationship to the shift in social and political consciousness.

Development as maldevelopment; adjustment to nature against the urge to conquer it; the porosity of borderlands against the rigidity of political forms, in particular the nation-state; heterogeneity over homogeneity; overdetermination against categorically defined subjectivities; ideology as culture and culture as daily negotiation; enlightenment as hegemony; "local knowledge" against universal scientific rationality; native sensibilities and spiritualities as a supplement to, if not a substitute for, reason; oral against written culture; political movements as "politics of difference" and "politics of location"—the list could go on. It enumerates elements of a postmodern consciousness that serve as enabling conditions for a contemporary localism, but also produce it. The consciousness itself is an articulation not of powerlessness, but of newfound power among social groups who demand recognition of their social existence and consciousness against a modernity that had denied them historical and, therefore, a political presence. Governor John D. Waihee III of Hawaii, refer-ring to the Hawaiian sovereignty movement, acknowledged recently that what seems possible today would have been unimaginable only two decades ago.[12]

The suspicion of Enlightenment metanarratives for their denial of differ-ence makes for a suspicion of all metanarratives which suppress or overlook differences, allows for localized consciousness, and points to the local as the site for working out "alternative public spheres" and alternative social formations.[13] This is the promise held out by the local. The local, however, also indicates fragmentation and, given the issues of power involved, political and cultural manipulation as well. This is the predicament. That traces of earlier forms of exploitation and oppression persist in the local, albeit in forms worked over by modernity, aggravates the predicament.

This predicament becomes more apparent when we view the problem of the local from the perspective of the global: the local as object of the operations of capital, which provides the broadest context for inquiry into the sources and consequences of contemporary localism. The emergence of the concern for the local over the last two decades has accompanied a significant transformation within capitalism with far-reaching economic, political, social, and cultural consequences. This transformation, and its implications for the local, need to be considered in any evaluation of the local as source of promise and predicament.

"Global Localism"

David Harvey and Fredric Jameson, among others, have perceived a relation-ship between postmodernism and a new phase in the development of capi-talism that has been described as late capitalism, flexible production or accu-mulation, disorganized capitalism, or global capitalism.[14] Global capitalism represents a further deterritorialization, abstraction, and concentration of cap-ital. In a fundamental sense, global capitalism represents an unprecedented penetration of local society globally by the economy and culture of capital; so that the local understood in a "traditional" sense may be less relevant than ever. It is ironic then that capital itself should justify its operations increasingly in the language of the local. The irony allows us to see the local in all its contradictoriness.

Fundamental to the structure of the new global capitalism (the term I prefer) is what Frobel and others have described as "a new international divi-sion of labor": in other words, the transnationalization of production where, through subcontracting, the process of production (of the same commodity even) is globalized.[15] The international division of labor in production may not be entirely novel, but new technologies have expanded the spatial extension of production, as well as its speed, to an unprecedented level. These same technologies have endowed capital and production with unprecedented mobility, so that the location of production seems to be in a constant state of change, seeking for maximum advantages of capital over labor, as well as to avoid social and political interference (hence, flexible production). For these reasons, analysts of capitalism perceive in global capitalism a qualitative difference from similar practices earlier—and a new phase of capitalism.

Second is the "decentering" of capitalism nationally. In other words, it is increasingly difficult to point to any nation or region as the center of global capitalism. More than one analyst (in a position of power) has found an analogue to the emerging organization of production in the northern European "Hanseatic League" of the early modern period, that is the period before the emergence of nation-states (one of them describing it as a "high-tech Hanseatic League"); in other words, a network of urban formations, without a clearly definable center, whose links to one another are far stronger than their relationships to their immediate hinterlands.[16]

The medium linking this network together, thirdly, is the transnational corporation, which has taken over from national markets as the locus of economic activity; not just as a passive medium for the transmission of capital, commodities, and production, but as a determinant of the transmission and its direction. While the analogy with the Hanseatic League suggests decentralization, in other words, production is heavily concentrated behind this facade in the corporation. One articulate spokesman for the new economic order suggests that the share of decision-making for production between the corporation and the market is roughly 70 to 30 percent.[17] With power lodged in transnational corporations, which by definition transcend nations in organization and/or loyalty, the power of the nation-state to regulate the economy internally is constricted, while global regulation (and defense) of the economic order emerges as a major task. This is manifested not only in the proliferation of global organizations, but also in efforts to organize extranational regional organizations to give coherence to the functioning of the economy.

Fourthly, the transnationalization of production is the source at once of unprecedented unity globally and of unprecedented fragmentation (in the history of capitalism). The homogenization of the globe economically, socially, and culturally is such that Marx's predictions of the nineteenth century, premature for his time, finally seem to be on the point of vindication. At the same time, however, there is a parallel process of fragmentation at work: globally in the disappearing of a center to capitalism and locally in the fragmentation of the production process into subnational regions and localities. As supranational regional organizations, such as the European Economic Community, Pacific Basic Economic Community, the North American Free Trade Zone (to mention some that have been realized or are the objects of intense organizational activity) manifest this fragmentation at the global level, localities within the same nation competing with one another to place themselves in the pathways of transnational capital represent it at the most basic local level. Nations, themselves, it is arguable, represented attempts historically to contain fragmentation, but under attack from the outside (transnational organization) and the inside (subnational economic regions and localities), it is not quite clear how this new fragmentation is to be contained.[18]

A fifth important (perhaps the most important) consequence of the transnationalization of capital may be that for the first time in the history of capitalism, the capitalist mode of production appears as an authentically global abstraction, divorced from its historically specific origins in Europe. In other words, the narrative of capitalism is no longer a narrative of the history of Europe; so that, for the first time, non-European capitalist societies make their own claims on the history of capitalism. Corresponding to economic fragmentation, in other words, is cultural fragmentation or, to put it in its positive guise, "multiculturalism." The most dramatic instance of this new cultural situation may be the effort over the last decade to appropriate capitalism for the so-called Confucian values of East Asian societies, which is a reversal of a long-standing conviction (in Europe and East Asia) that Confucianism was historically an obstacle to capitalism. I think it is arguable that the apparent end of Eurocentrism is an illusion, because capitalist culture as it has taken shape has Eurocentrism built into the very structure of its narrative, which may explain why even as Europe and the United States lose their domination of the capitalist world economy, culturally European and American values retain their domination. It is noteworthy that what makes something like the East Asian Confucian revival plausible is not its offer of alternative values to those of Euro-American origin, but its articulation of native culture into a capitalist narrative. Having said this, it is important to reiterate that the question of world culture has become much more complex than in earlier phases of capitalism.

The fragmentation of space, and its consequences for Eurocentrism, also imply a fragmentation of the temporality of capitalism: the challenge to Eurocentrism, in other words, means that it is possible to conceive of the future in ways other than those of Euro-American political and social models. Here, once again, it is difficult to distinguish historical reality from ideological illusion, but the complexity is undeniable.

Finally, the transnationalization of production calls into question earlier divisions of the world into first, second, and third worlds. The Second World, the world of socialism, is for all practical purposes, of the past. But the new global configuration also calls into question the distinctions between the First and Third Worlds. Parts of the earlier Third World are today on the pathways of transnational capital and belong in the "developed" sector of the world economy. Likewise, parts of the First World marginalized in the new global economy are hardly distinguishable in way of life from what used to be viewed as the Third World. It may not be fortuitous that the North-South distinction has gradually taken over from the earlier division of the globe into the three worlds—so long as we remember that the references of North and South are not merely to concrete geographic locations, but metaphorical references: North denoting the pathways of transnational capital, and, South, the marginalized populations of the world, regardless of their actual location.

Ideologues of global capital have described this condition as "global regionalism" or "global localism," adding quickly, however, that "global localism" is 70 percent global and only 30 percent local.[19] They have also appropriated for capital the radical ecological slogan, "Think globally, act locally."[20] The terms capture cogently the simultaneous homogenization and fragmentation that is at work in the world economy. Production and economic activity (hence, "economic development") becomes localized in regions below the nation, while its management requires supranational supervision and coordination. In other words, the new pathways for the development of capital cut across national boundaries and intrude on national economic sovereignty, which renders irrelevant the notion of a national market or a national economic unit and undermines national sovereignty from within by fragmenting the national economy.[21] Similarly, the necessity of supranational coordination transforms the functions of the nation-state from without, incorporating it within larger regional or global economic units.

The situation created by global capitalism helps explain certain phenomena that have become apparent over the last two to three decades, but especially since the eighties: global motions of peoples (and, therefore, cultures), the weakening of boundaries (among societies, as well as among social categories), the replication in societies internally of inequalities and discrepancies once

associated with colonial differences, simultaneous homogenization and fragmentation within and across societies, the interpenetration of the global and
the local (which shows culturally in a simultaneous cosmopolitanism and localism of which the most cogent expression may be "multiculturalism"), and the
disorganization of a world conceived in terms of "three worlds" or nation-
states. Some of these phenomena have also contributed to an appearance of
equalization of differences within and across societies, as well as of democratization within and between societies. What is ironic is that the managers of this
world situation themselves concede the concentration of power in their (or
their organizations') hands; as well as their manipulation of peoples, boundaries, and cultures to appropriate the local for the global, to admit different
cultures into the realm of capital only to break them down and to remake them
in accordance with the requirements of production and consumption, and
even to reconstitute subjectivities across national boundaries to create producers and consumers more responsive to the operations of capital. Those who do
not respond, or the "basket cases" which are not essential to those operations—
four-fifths of the global population by their count—need not be colonized; they
are simply marginalized. What the new "flexible production" has made possible
is that it is no longer necessary to utilize explicit coercion against labor, at home
or abroad (in colonies); those peoples or places that are not responsive to the
needs (or demands) of capital, or are too far gone to respond "efficiently,"
simply find themselves out of its pathways.

Much of what I have described above as the conditions for the production
of contemporary localism (a postmodern consciousness, embedded in new
forms of empowerment) appears in this perspective as a product of the operations of global capitalism. It should also be apparent from the above that the
local is of concern presently not only to those who view it as a site of liberation
struggles, but, with an even greater sense of immediacy, to managers of global
capital as well as to those responsible for the economic welfare of their communities. I will take up the latter in the next section. The concern for the local on
the part of capital, and what the operations of capital may imply for the local, is
apparent in the following analysis by an advocate of "guerrilla marketing."

> 1984 is here, the problem is how to manage it. The answer we propose,
> gentlemen, is guerrilla marketing. Just as the guerrilla fighter must know
> the terrain of the struggle in order to control it, so it is with the multina-
> tional corporation of today. Our terrain is the world. Our ends can be
> accomplished with the extension of techniques already in the process of

development. The world market is now being computer micromapped into consumer zones according to residual cultural factors (i.e., idioms, local traditions, religious affiliations, political ideologies, folk mores, traditional sexual roles, etc.), dominant cultural factors (i.e., typologies of life-styles based on consumption patterns: television ratings, musical tastes, fashions, motion picture and concert attendance, home video rentals, magazine subscriptions, home computer software selection, shopping mall participation, etc.), and emergent cultural factors (i.e., interactive and participatory video, mobile micromalls equipped with holography and super conductivity, computer interfacing with consumers, robotic services, etc.). The emergent marketing terrain which must be our primary concern can only be covered totally if the 304 geographical consumption zones already computer mapped (the horizontal) can be cross-referenced not only with the relatively homogeneous "conscious" needs of the macroconsumer units, but also with the heterogeneous multiplicity of "unconscious" needs of the microconsumer (the vertical). This latter mapping process has so far readily yielded to computer solution through the identification and classification of a maximum of 507 microconsumption types per macroconsumption unit. Through an extension of this mapping, even the most autonomous and unconventional desires may be reconstructed for the benefit of market extension and control. Emergent marketing strategies must move further beyond the commodity itself and toward the commodity as image, following marketing contingencies all the way down. And here, precisely, is the task of guerrilla marketing: to go all the way with the images we create and strike where there is indecision (flowing from constructed situations without determinant outcomes just like the guerrilla fighter). For the multinational of today profits are necessary but not sufficient conditions for growth which our whole history shows to be equivalent to survival. We remain dependent on market control and extension. But now this requires more than the control of production and consumption—to grow we must sell a total image. Like guerrilla fighters, we must win hearts and minds. This task can be accomplished by constructing and reconstructing them all the way down in what can only be viewed as an endless process.[22]

Cleansed of its computer vocabulary, this text would read very much like one of those local analyses upon which guerrilla revolutionaries have based strategy.[23] But the resemblance does not stop there. As with guerrilla struggle, where the requirements of a fluid strategy called forth a need for organizational flexibility in order to deal with diverse circumstances without abandoning long-term organizational goals, the imperatives of guerrilla marketing, too, have resulted in a reconceptualization of the transnational corporation as an organization. "Global localism" implies, organizationally, that the corporation domesticate itself in various localities without forgetting its global aims and organization. This has created for companies organizational problems that resemble closely those of a centralized Communist party engaged in guerrilla warfare. The CEO of one such company, who chooses to describe his company as "multi-domestic" rather than multi- or transnational, describes the organizational problems his company faces much as Mao Zedong used to describe problems facing the Communist party in China. "ABB (Asea Brown Boveri) is an organization with three internal contradictions. We want to be global and local, big and small, radically decentralized with centralized reports and control. If we resolve those contradictions, we create real organizational advantage."[24]

The radical slogan of an earlier day, "Think globally, act locally," has been assimilated by transnational corporations with far greater success than in any radical strategy. The recognition of the local in marketing strategy, however, does not mean any serious recognition of the autonomy of the local, but is intended to recognize the features of the local so as to incorporate localities into the imperatives of the global. The "domestication" of the corporation into local society serves only to further mystify the location of power, which rests not in the locality but in the global headquarters of the company which coordinates the activities of its local branches. To recall what I cited above from Kenichi Ohmae, "global localism" is "70 percent global and 30 percent local." The guiding vision of the contemporary transnational corporation is to homogenize the world under its guidance. The same CEO writes: "Are we above governments? No. We answer to governments. We obey the laws in every country in which we operate, and we don't make the laws. However, we do change relations *between* countries. We function as a lubricant for worldwide economic integration"[25] (emphasis in the original).

Some lubricant, that "changes" the relations it facilitates! It points to a crucial point, nevertheless. The transnational corporations of the day, much like radical guerrillas, do not just respond to circumstances, but create the conditions for their success. To achieve this end, however, they must first grasp social, political, and cultural relations in their full complexity. The goal of analysis itself is not social need but the teleology of the organization, although that teleology must be articulated to local languages in order to acquire legitimacy transnationally.

From the perspective of global capitalism, the local is a site not of liberation but manipulation; stated differently, it is a site the inhabitants of which must be liberated from themselves (stripped of their identity) to be homogenized into the global culture of capital (their identities reconstructed accordingly). Ironically, even as it seeks to homogenize populations globally, consuming their cultures, global capitalism enhances awareness of the local, pointing to it also as the site of resistance to capital.

This is nevertheless the predicament of the local. A preoccupation with the local that leaves the global outside its line of vision is vulnerable to manipulation at the hands of global capital which of necessity commands a more comprehensive vision of a global totality. Differences of interest and power on the site of the local, which are essential to its reconstruction along nontraditional, democratic lines, render the local all the more vulnerable to such manipulation as capital plays on these differences and the advocates of different visions and interests seek to play capital against one another.[26] The local in the process becomes the site upon which the multifaceted contradictions of contemporary society play out, where critique turns into ideology and ideology into critique, depending upon its location at any fleeting moment.

Considerations on the Local as Site of Resistance

In the first section above, I suggested that the postmodern repudiation of Enlightenment metanarratives and the teleology of modernity has allowed the reemergence of the local as a site of resistance and the struggle for liberation.[27] It is the struggle for historical and political presence of groups suppressed or marginalized by modernization, I argued further, that has dynamized this postmodern consciousness and has produced the contemporary notion of the local, which must be distinguished from "traditional" localism if only because such struggles are themselves informed by the modernity that they reject. This is the local as it has been worked over by modernity. It finds expression presently in the so-called "politics of difference," that presupposes local differences (literally, or metaphorically, with reference to social groups) both as a point of departure and as a goal of liberation.

My discussion of global capitalism is intended to support this thesis, while introducing into the consideration of the local as a contemporary phenomenon what I take to be a crucial dimension that is missing from most postmodernist discussions of the subject. Postmodernist repudiation of metanarratives and teleology has made also for a suspicion of universalizing "foundational" explanatory themes, in particular Marxist ideas of totality and class. Totalities do not go away because they have been repudiated. Global capitalism, both in its disorganizing of earlier structures and the reconfiguration of global relations (including class relations, now more global than ever), points to just such a totality that produces, and provides the context for, the contemporary phenomenon of the local. To the extent that it refuses to recognize this context, the idea of the local is prey to the manipulations of capital, and the ideology of "global localism." I have argued elsewhere that to the extent that postmodern criticism fails to account for the totality that is its context, its ideological criticism becomes indistinguishable from an ideological legitimation of the social forms that are the creation of global capitalism.[28] It is crucial, therefore, that postmodern cultural criticism reconnect with actual movements of resistance to capital that continue to be informed by practices of resistance that are coeval with the history of capitalism. Postmodernism needs the connection to restore a sense of the structures of oppression and inequality, to check its slide into political irrelevance upon the slippery slopes of a fluid narcissism. The latter needs postmodernism for its articulation of the pitfalls to liberation that are implicit in teleological notions of change, and conceptual teleologies that bind in reductionist categories a social existence and consciousness that is shifting, complex, and contradictory. Such rigid visions of history, rather than look at the process of the struggle for liberation as the source of alternative futures, seek to contain with predetermined visions of the future a process that needs to be an open-ended process of multiple social negotiations.

The intrusion of global capitalism into local societies has been accompanied by a proliferation of local movements of resistance in recent years in which women's and ecological movements are particularly prominent. These movements already show a keen appreciation of the relationship of local to global struggles, as well as a sharp sensitivity to the complexities of movement building that is indicative of a contemporary consciousness. An example is provided in the following statement by Rachel Kamel, a union activist connected with the American Friends Service Committee. After describing the plight of workers (mostly women) in the United States, the Mexican maquiladoras, and the Philippines, as they are played off against one another by transnationals, and suggesting several ways of coordinating resistance, Kamel writes:

Each of the projects we have described may seem tiny, especially when contrasted to the size and power of transnational corporations. Yet each is also a small step toward building a movement that could bring together hundreds of local grassroots campaigns, within the United States and internationally.

At this writing, the idea of a broad-based, multinational movement to tackle the problems of the global factory is still a vision. What we have tried to document in this guide is that the global factory is composed of thousands of concrete local situations—and that each of us, whatever setting we live and work in, can take small, accessible actions to confront our specific situations.

By understanding that every local story is part of a global "big picture," we can open up space for dialog and sharing of experiences—especially across barriers of language, nationality, gender, race and class. And as that process of communication moves toward networking and coalition-building, the vision of a multi-national movement can become a reality. (emphasis mine)[29]

Note that Kamel describes corporations as "transnational," while using the older term "multinational" to describe resistance movements. Also noteworthy is the complexity of the situations she describes. Kamel deems essential to the success of local organizing four constituencies: labor unions, community groups, religious institutions, and local government.[30] These constituencies must be brought together, and still leave open spaces for dialogue among the groups she enumerates in the statement above. Hardly a proponent of post-modern consciousness could wish for greater complexity and contradiction!

The affirmation of the local, and of diversity thus defined, is not without its own problems, as activists such as Kamel and Vandana Shiva are well aware. One such problem is the celebration of premodern pasts which, in the name of resistance to the modern and the rationalist homogenization of the world, results in a localism or a "Third-Worldism" that is willing to overlook past oppressions out of a preoccupation with capitalist or Eurocentric oppression and that in the name of the recovery of spirituality affirms past religiosities that were themselves excuses for class and patriarchal inequalities. One consequence of global capitalism is that there are no longer any local societies that have not been worked over already by capital and modernity; insistence on local "purity" may well serve as excuses for a reactionary revival of older forms of oppression, as women in particular have been quick to point out in India and among the indigenous people's movements in North America.[31] The local is valuable as a site for resistance to the global, but only to the extent that it also serves as the site of negotiation to abolish inequality and oppression inherited from the past, which is a condition of any promise it may have for the future. It is neither possible nor desirable to dismiss the awareness that is the product of modernity as just another trick of Eurocentrism.

What this points to is a "critical localism" which, even as it subjects the present to the critical evaluation from past perspectives, retains in the evaluation of the past the critical perspectives afforded by modernity. Excluded from this localism are romantic nostalgia for communities past, hegemonic nationalist yearnings of a new kind (as with the so-called Confucian revival in East Asia), or historicism that would imprison the present in the past. An example of the latter are well-intentioned but misguided efforts in China scholarship recently to assert a "China-centered" view of history; well-intentioned because these efforts seek to rescue Chinese history from its subjection to the hegemony of Euro-American teleologies and concepts; misguided because the effort is accompanied by assertions that Chinese themselves are incapable of doing this because they have been tainted by Western concepts and, therefore, have lost touch with their own past. Such efforts, which deny to the Chinese contemporaneity while giving born-again EuroAmericans the privilege of interpreting China's past for the Chinese, are reminiscent of nineteenth-century Europeans who, claiming historicalness for themselves while denying it to others, appropriated the meaning of history for the whole world, especially the Third World.[32] At the other extreme is that ethnocentrism in the critique of hegemony, which falls into affirmations of pre-Western ethnicities and spiritualities, without accounting for the problem of oppression in general, which has not been the monopoly of the West or of capitalism, even though it may have been carried to unprecedented levels in the modern world in the denial of alternative modes of existence. The dilemmas faced by struggles against Euro-American and capitalist oppression, I believe, should not be evaded by sweeping under the rug premodern forms of oppression. As a first cut, it is necessary to distinguish stateless communities (or those communities where state organization and local community coincided, such as tribal organizations around the world)[33] from communities that provided excuses for far-flung state organizations, such as the premodern empires of China, India, and the Ottoman Empire. The former are easier to sympathize with, the latter much less so, as the affirmation of premodern pasts in their case, however antihegemonic in terms of their relationship to the West, barely disguises national chauvinisms of a new kind—as in the case of the Confucian revival, for instance, which is not unrelated to assertions of a "Greater Chinese" economic region. These two positions are quite different in their sources and implications; and it is important to distinguish Euro-Americans speaking for Third World pasts from those of Third World peoples speaking for their pasts in efforts to rescue their identities from "death by assimilation" (in the words of the writer, Frank Chin). Nevertheless, both positions are problematic; it is not only silly to deny the undeniable—that economic and cultural conjunctures for the past century have defined the conditions of existence for non-European or American peoples—but also socially (distinct from politically) reactionary to ignore past forms of oppression of various dimensions that have been brought to the forefront of historical consciousness by these conjunctures. It is the continued existence of such forms of oppression, compounded and overdetermined now by new forms of oppression, that makes Marxist and gender analyses in particular as relevant as ever to critical understanding.

The local as I use it here has meaning only inasmuch as it is a product of the conjuncture of structures located in the same temporality but with different spatialities, which is what gives rise to the problem of spatiality and, therefore, of the local, in the first place. The conjunctural situation also defines the culture of the local, which is stripped of its reification by daily confrontation between different cultures and appears instead in the nakedness of its everyday practice. Unlike under conditions of isolation and stability, where culture appears timeless in its daily reproduction (if such is ever entirely the case), the conjunctural situation reveals cultural activity as an activity in production and ceaseless reconstruction. That culture is thus constructed does not imply that the present is, therefore, immune to the burden of the past; only that the burden itself is restructured in the course of present activity. Neither does it mean that the past is unimportant; it only underlines the claims of the present, of the living, on the past, rather than the other way around. Culture is no less cultural for being subject to change through the "practice of everyday life" (the term is Michel de Certeau's), of which it is as much source as product. It is the prevalence of cultural conjuncture as a condition of life globally that has brought forth the sharp consciousness of culture as an ongoing construction of everyday practice. This prevalence has been illuminated in the works of Pierre Bourdieu and Marshall Sahlins, who have argued out the implications for culture and history of conjunctures between past and present, between different social and cultural structures (which problematize the relationship between different presents, as well as between the present and the past), and even between structure and event, especially where the event is of an unprecedented nature such as the contacts of non-European peoples with Europeans.[34]

The immediate question here is what this ongoing construction of culture implies in terms of the resistance of the local to the global. Ashis Nandy has written that:

> When two cultures of unequal secular power enter into a dialogue, a new hierarchy inevitably emerges, unless the dialogue creates a shared space for each participant's distinctive, unstated theory of the other cultures or, in its absence, each participant's general theory of culture. The concept of cultural relativism, expressed in the popular anthropological view that each culture must be studied in terms of its own categories, is limited because it stops short of insisting that every culture must recognize the way it is construed by other cultures. It is easy to leave other cultures to their own devices in the name of cultural relativism, particularly if the visions of the future of these other cultures have already been cannibalized by the worldview of one's own. It is less easy to live with an alien culture's estimate of oneself, to integrate it within one's selfhood and to live with that self-induced inner tension. It is even more difficult to live with the inner dialogue within one's own culture which is triggered off by the dialogue with other cultures because, then, the carefully built cultural defences against disturbing dialogues—and against the threatening insights emerging from the dialogues—begin to crumble.[35]

Nandy's view of cultural dialogue has been inspired by the approach to culture of Mohandas Gandhi, who, Richard Fox tells us in his recent illuminating study of Gandhi, believed that "cultures change through collective experiments,"[36] experiments that had the present for their point of departure but opened up to diverse pasts in their pursuit of "truth." The local, I would like to suggest here, is the site for such experimentation. The "experimentation," however, has to be global in compass. Resistance that seeks to reaffirm some "authentic" local culture, in ignoring the conjunctures that produced it, is condemned to failure; if only because the so-called authentic local culture is daily disorganized by the global forces (e.g., guerrilla marketeers) that seek to reconstitute it, to assimilate it to the global homogenization that it seeks.

This is the second problem with the local as a strategic concept of resistance, which is even more serious: the assimilation of the local into the global, so that different localities become pawns in the hands of global capital in its guerrilla warfare against societies globally. This may, indeed, be the most serious challenge facing resistance/liberation movements in our day: how to deal with global companies that, at the least sign of interference with their activities (be those labor demands or efforts to restrict the harm they inflict on local societies and ecologies), threaten to pick up and move to new localities, which new technologies enable them to do or, more accurately, which is a major goal of the development of new technologies? How does resistance deal with a General Motors, which holds entire communities and cities in suspense in shutting down production plants, waiting to see the outcome of communities competing with one another in offering better and sweeter deals to the corporation to keep it in their respective communities to save jobs—and the livelihood of the entire community? Local resistance under the circumstances must be translocal both in consciousness and action if it is to be meaningful at all (a big "if," and possibly cause for a widespread sense of futility globally). The dilemma is heightened by the fact that local consciousness, which is necessary as the basis for resistance, contradicts the translocal activity and consciousness that is a necessity of successful resistance. If this contradiction is overcome, the very fragmentation of the globe by capital may be turned to an advantage by resistance movements: the demand for the authentically local against its exploitation as a means to assimilation may "overload" global capitalism, driving it to fragmentation.[37]

Apart from the part it plays in resistance to global capitalism, how the local may serve as a building block for the future is a question to which Henry Giroux has provided a suggestive answer. Giroux's "border pedagogy" is derivative of postmodern/postcolonial "politics of difference," but dissatisfied with the affirmation of difference as an end in itself, which he rightly perceives to be subversive of meaningful politics, he seeks ways to formulate new kinds of "unity in diversity" that may serve as grounds for "nontotalizing politics."[38] "Nontotalizing politics" must attend "to the partial, specific, contexts of differentiated communities and forms of power," not "to ignore larger theoretical and relational narratives" but to "embrace the local and the global."[39] Especially important is his idea of "formative narratives" which cogently expresses the considerations I have suggested above:

> The postmodern attack on totality and foundationalism is not without its drawbacks. While it rightly focuses on the importance of local narratives and rejects the notion that truth precedes the notion of representation, it also runs the risk of blurring the distinction between master narratives that are monocausal and formative narratives, that provide the basis for

historically and relationally placing different groups or local narratives within some common project. To draw out this point further, it is difficult to imagine any politics of difference as a form of radical social theory if it doesn't offer a formative narrative capable of analyzing difference within rather than against unity.[40]

I stated above that the meaning of the local in contemporary discussions is uncertain and have refrained throughout from burdening it with a definition that might have constricted analysis. The boundaries of the local need to be kept open (or porous) if the local is to serve as a critical concept. The contemporary local is itself a site of invention; the present is ultimately the site for the global.

Notes

1 Subramani, *South Pacific Literature: From Myth to Fabulation* (Suva, Fiji: University of the South Pacific Press, 1985), for a case for postmodernist fabulation.

2 For the movements referred to, see Vandana Shiva, *Staying Alive* (London: ZED Books, 1988); Rachel Kamel, *The Global Factory: Analysis and Action for a New Economic Era* (Philadelphia: American Friends Service Committee, 1990); Maivan Lam, *The Age of Association: The Indigenous Assertion of Self-Determination at the United Nations,* unpublished manuscript cited with the author's permission.

3 For extended discussions of this problem, see Peter A. Kropotkin, "The State: Its Historical Role," in *Selected Writings on Anarchism and Revolution,* ed. P. A. Kropotkin (Cambridge, Mass.: MIT Press, 1975), pp. 211–264; and Raymond Williams, *The Country and the City* (New York: Oxford University Press, 1973).

4 Leo Loubere, *Utopian Socialism: Its History since 1800* (Cambridge, Mass.: Schenkman Publishing, 1974), and Peter Kropotkin, *Fields, Factories, and Workshops of Tomorrow,* intro. and ed. Colin Ward (New York: Harper & Row, 1974).

5 As Raymond Williams notes, it was to be forgotten in the twentieth century that Marx and Engels placed a great deal of emphasis on abolishing the division of labor between town and country. Item 9 of the program for socialism in the *Communist Manifesto* reads: "Combination of agriculture with manufacturing industries; gradual abolition of the distinction between town and country, by a more equable distribution of the population over the country." Karl Marx and Friedrich Engels, "Manifesto of the Communist Party," in *The Marx-Engels Reader,* ed. Robert C. Tucker (New York: W. W. Norton, 1972), pp. 331–362, 352.

6 Arif Dirlik, *Anarchism in the Chinese Revolution* (Berkeley: University of California Press, 1991), and Arif Dirlik, "Mao Zedong and 'Chinese Marxism,'" in *The Encyclopedia of Asian Philosophy* (London: Routledge, in press), for further discussion.

7 I have in mind here thinker-activists such as Ivan Illich and Murray Bookchin who have

consistently upheld the significance of the local and the "vernacular." Among their many works, see, for examples, Ivan Illich, *Shadow Work* (Salem, N.H.: Marion Boyars, 1981), and Murray Bookchin, *Post Scarcity Anarchism* (Palo Alto, Calif.: Ramparts Press, 1971).

8   Kropotkin, "The State," p. 252.

9   For a cogent statement, see Russell Means, "The Same Old Song," in *Marxism and Native Americans,* ed. Ward Churchill (Boston: South End Press, n.d.), pp. 19–33. The implications for our understanding of the state of the restoration of local, stateless societies into history (left out of history by virtue of their statelessness) is the theme of Pierre Clastres' *Society against the State,* translated by Robert Hurley in collaboration with Abe Stein (New York: Zone Books, 1987). Writes Clastres: "It is said that the history of peoples who have a history is the history of class struggle. It might be said, with at least as much truthfulness, that the history of peoples without history is the history of their struggle against the state" (p. 218).

10   Partha Chatterjee, *Nationalist Thought and the Colonial World—A Derivative Discourse* (London: ZED Books, 1986), discusses this problem at length.

11   For a further discussion of this problem, with reference to the work of E. P. Thompson and Eugene Genovese, see Arif Dirlik, "Culturalism as Hegemonic Ideology and Liberating Practice," *Cultural Critique* (Spring 1987): 13–50. For the ways in which such problems appeared in contemporary movements, which simulated this new awareness, see Frances Fox Piven and Richard A. Cloward, *Poor People's Movements: Why They Succeed, How They Fail* (New York: Random House, 1977). For a work that brings together postmodernity and the legacy of such social movements, and relates them explicitly to the problem of the local, see Henry Giroux, *Border Crossings: Cultural Works and the Politics of Education* (New York and London: Routledge, 1992). A distinguished pedagogue, Giroux describes himself as "a critical populist," who is heir to the legacies "of the IWW, Bill Haywood, C. Wright Mills, Martin Luther King, and Michael Harrington. In other words, people who speak to people in a language that dignifies their history and experience" (p. 13).

12   "A Century After Queen's Overthrow, Talk of Sovereignty Shakes Hawaii," *New York Times,* November 8, 1992, "National Report."

13   Giroux, *Border Crossings,* pp. 21–22.

14   David Harvey, *The Condition of Postmodernity* (Cambridge, Mass.: Basil Blackwell, 1989), and Fredric Jameson, "Postmodernism, or, The Cultural Logic of Late Capitalism," *New Left Review* 146 (July–August 1984): 59–92.

15   F. Frobel, J. Heinrichs, and O. Kreye, *The New International Division of Labor* (Cambridge, Mass.: Cambridge University Press, 1980). "Disorganized Capitalism" comes from Claus Offe, *Disorganized Capitalism* (Cambridge, Mass.: MIT Press, 1985), and Kent C. Trachte, *Global Capitalism: The New Leviathan* (Albany, N.Y.: State University of New York Press, 1990). Other noteworthy books on the subject are Leslie Sklair, *Sociology of the Global System* (Baltimore: Johns Hopkins University Press, 1991), which spells out the implications for the Third World of global capitalism, and Robert Reich,

The Work of Nations (New York: Alfred A. Knopf, 1991). Reich's book incorporates his contributions to the *Harvard Business Review,* with such suggestive titles (in the present context) as "Who is Us?" and "Who is Them?" For "subcontracting," see Garry Gereffi, "Global Sourcing and Regional Divisions of Labor in the Pacific Rim," in *What Is in a Rim? Critical Perspectives on the Pacific Region Idea,* ed. Arif Dirlik (Boulder, Colo.: Westview Press, 1993), pp. 51–68.

16   Riccardo Petrella, "World City-States of the Future," *New Perspectives Quarterly* (Fall 1991): 59–64. See also, "A New Hanseatic League?" *New York Times,* February 23, 1992, E3.

17   Kenichi Ohmae, "Beyond Friction to Fact: The Borderless Economy," *NPQ* (Spring 1990): 20–21.

18   This phenomenon is addressed in most of the works cited in note 15.

19   Ohmae, "Beyond Friction to Fact," p. 21. Also see James Gardner, "Global Regionalism," *NPQ* (Winter 1992): 58–59.

20   "The Logic of Global Business: An Interview with ABB's Percy Barnevik," *Harvard Business Review* (March–April 1991): 90–105.

21   This is the basic argument of Reich, *The Work of Nations.*

22   From a conference on marketing held at the Research Triangle Park, North Carolina, February 27, 1987. Quoted in Rick Roderick, "The Antinomy of Post-Modern Bourgeois Thought," paper presented at the Marxism and Society seminar, Duke University, March 1987, pp. 1–2. Quoted with the author's permission.

23   See, for example, Mao Zedong's meticulous "mapping" of local Chinese social relations and structure in his *Report from Xunwu,* trans. with an intro. and notes Roger R. Thompson (Stanford, Calif.: Stanford University Press, 1990). The implications of the report are drawn out by Roxann Prazniak in her review essay, "The Art of Folk Revolution," *Peasant Studies* 17, no. 3 (Spring 1990): 295–306.

24   "The Logic of Global Business," p. 95.

25   Ibid., p. 105.

26   For a fascinating discussion involving Hawaii, see Jeff Tobin, "Cultural Construction and Native Nationalism: Report from the Hawaiian Front," in *Asia/Pacific as Space of Cultural Production,* ed. Arif Dirlik and Rob Wilson (Durham, N.C.: Duke University Press, 1995).

27   This is what Michel Foucault has referred to as the "insurrection of subjugated knowledges," in his "Two Lectures," in Michel Foucault, *Power/Knowledge: Selected Interviews and Other Writings, 1972–1977,* ed. Colin Gordon (New York: Pantheon Books, 1980), pp. 78–108, 81.

28   Arif Dirlik, "The Postcolonial Aura: Third World Criticism in the Age of Global Capitalism," *Critical Inquiry* 20 (1994): 328–356.

29   Kamel, *Global Factory,* p. 75.

30   Ibid., p. 26.

31   Meera Nanda, "Is Modern Science a Western, Patriarchal Myth? A Critique of the Populist Orthodoxy," *South Asia Bulletin* 11, nos. 1 & 2 (1991): 32–61.

32 For a seminal and influential work to argue this position, see Paul Cohen, *Discovering History in China* (New York: Columbia University Press, 1984).

33 For an excellent account of indigenous people's movement and their relationship to existing states, see Maivan Lam, *The Age of Association: The Indigenous Assertion of Self-Determination at the United Nations.* Also see note 2 above.

34 See Pierre Bourdieu, *The Logic of Practice* (Stanford, Calif.: Stanford University Press, 1990) and Marshall Sahlins, *Islands of History* (Chicago: University of Chicago Press, 1985).

35 Ashis Nandy, *Traditions, Tyranny, and Utopias: Essays in the Politics of Awareness* (Delhi: Oxford University Press, 1987), pp. 16–19.

36 Richard G. Fox, *Gandhian Utopia: Experiments with Culture* (Boston: Beacon Press, 1989), p. 26.

37 I owe to Wallerstein this notion of "overloading the system" as a means of resistance. See Immanuel Wallerstein, "Development: Lodestar or Illusion?" in *Unthinking Social Science: The Limits of Nineteenth Century Paradigms* (London: Polity Press, 1991), p. 124. What I have in mind here may be illustrated by an episode from South Pacific culture. In his analysis of oral traditions in the South Pacific, Subramani observes that South Pacific writers have, "in some instances, rediscovered their oral literatures by reading translations of them by European researchers." The goal of European researchers in undertaking this kind of activity around the globe, at least initially, was to understand the natives to better control, convert, or assimilate them. With a new cultural consciousness that aims at liberation, these same "researches" now serve the cause of liberation and the assertion of local identity against assimilation. Subramani, *South Pacific Literature*, p. 32.

38 Giroux, *Border Crossings*, p. 79. For "unity in diversity," see Yuji Ichioka, " 'Unity Within Diversity': Louis Adamic and Japanese Americans," *Asian/Pacific Studies*, no. 1 (1987), Duke University, Asian/Pacific Studies Institute.

39 Giroux, *Border Crossings*, p. 79.

40 Ibid., p. 54.

LOCALISM, GLOBALISM, AND

CULTURAL IDENTITY

Mike Featherstone

●

Introduction

It is one of today's clichés to say that the world is becoming smaller and interconnected; that, in effect, it has become one place. One of the terms which points to the heightened consciousness of this process, globalization, has gradually become rooted in popular discourses over the last decade to the extent that we not only see references to the globalization of money markets, fashion, and advertising industries, but also the globalization of diseases such as AIDS and the illicit drug and pornography industries as well. Of course, not everyone is affected by, or conscious of, these globalization processes to the same extent. It could be argued that this is one of the problems in attempting to formulate a theory of globalization, that the theories often adopt a totalizing logic and assume some master process of global integration which it is assumed is making the world more unified and homogeneous. From this perspective the intensification of global time-space compression through the universalizing processes of the new communications technology that aggravate the power of the flows of finance and commodities means that local cultures inevitably give way. Our experiences and means of orientation are seen as divorced from the physical locations in which we live and work. The fate of our residence and work seems to be in the hands of agencies in parts of the world foreign to us. Localism and a sense of place give way to the anonymity of "no place spaces" or simulated environments in which we are unable to feel totally at home.

At the same time there is also the sense that such monological accounts which equate the success of the globalization process with the extension of modernity, that "globalization is basically modernity writ large," miss the cultural variability of non-Western nation-states and civilizations. It is insufficient to assume that their cultures will simply give way to modernity or to regard their formulations of national particularity as merely reactions to Western modernity. Rather the globalization process should be regarded as opening up the sense that now the world is a single place with increased, even unavoidable, contact. We necessarily have greater dialogue between various nation-states, blocs, and civilizations, as well as a dialogical space in which we can expect not only cooperation and consensus but a good deal of disagreement, conflict, and clashing of perspectives. Not that participating nation-states and other agents should be regarded as equal partners to the dialogue. Rather, they are bound together in increasing webs of interdependencies and power balances. Because of this increased complexity and sensitivity to change, and the capacity to transmit information about shifts in fortune, it is more difficult to retain lasting and oversimplified images of others. It can be argued that the difficulty of handling increasing levels of cultural complexity, and the doubts and anxieties they often engender, are reasons why "localism," or the desire to return home, becomes an important theme—regardless of whether the home is real or imaginary, temporary, syncretized, or simulated, or whether it is manifest in a fascination with the sense of belonging, affiliation, and community attributed to the homes of others. What does seem clear is that it is not helpful to regard the global and local as dichotomies separated in space or time; rather, it would seem that the processes of globalization and localization are inextricably bound together in the current phase.

Localism and Symbolic Communities

Within the sociological tradition, the term local and its derivatives, locality and localism, have generally been associated with the notion of a particular bounded space with its set of close-knit social relationships based upon strong kinship ties and length of residence.[1] There is usually the assumption of a stable homogeneous and integrated cultural identity that is both enduring and unique. In this sense it was often assumed that members of a locality formed a distinctive community with its own unique local culture—something which turns the location of their day-to-day interactions from a physical space into a "place." Much of the research on localities which developed within urban sociology and community studies was influenced by two main assumptions. The first assumption was derived from nineteenth-century models of social change in which the past was regarded as entailing simpler, more direct, strongly bonded social relationships, as we find in the paired oppositions: status and contract (Maine), mechanical and organic solidarity (Durkheim), and community and association (Toennies). The latter terms, drawn from the ideal types delineated in Toennies's influential *Gemeinschaft und Gesellschaft,* have been used to emphasize the historical and spatial continuum between small relatively isolated integrated communities based upon primary relationships and strong associations of the modern metropolis. The work of Toennies and other German theorists have helped sanction over-romantic and nostalgic depictions of "the world we have lost" to the relentless march of modernization. The second assumption, taken from anthropology, emphasized the need to provide ethnographically rich descriptions of the particularity of relatively isolated small towns or village. We have, for example, studies of small rural communities in the west of Ireland[2] or North Wales.[3] Yet here and in other community studies researchers soon became preoccupied with the problems of delineating the boundaries of the locality. It soon became clear that the most isolated community in Britain or the United States was firmly plugged into national societies. The illusion of spatial isolation which drew researchers in to focusing upon the rich particularity of local traditions soon gave way to an acceptance that the "small town was in mass society" to paraphrase the title of one of the American studies of the 1950s.[4] The intention here, and in earlier influential studies such as Middletown[5] and Yankee City,[6] was to examine the ways in which local communities were being transformed by the processes of industrialization, urbanization, and bureaucratization. These modernizing processes were perceived to be all pervasive and heralded "the eclipse of community" to use the title of a book by Maurice Stein which discussed this literature.[7]

In Britain there were also a number of studies of localities, some of which provided rich descriptions of the particularities of working-class life. In studies such as *Coal Is Our Life, Working Class Community,* and *Class, Culture and Community,*[8] we get a strong sense of a distinctive working-class way of life with its occupations' homogeneity, strictly segregated gender roles with male group ties and the "mateship" code of loyalty dominant both in work and leisure (drinking, gambling, sport)—women were largely confined to the separate home sphere. The classic account of this culture which captures the fullness of everyday working-class life was provided by Richard Hoggart's account of his Leeds childhood in *The Uses of Literacy.*[9] Hoggart documented the sayings, songs, sentimentality, and generous indulgences of working-class life (the Sunday afternoon big meat tea, the Saturday night "knees-up" and singing in the pub, the charabanc seaside outings at which all the saved-up money had to be squandered, the belly-laugh survival humor and vulgarity, the larger-than-life characters and general emotional warmth and group support, the gossip and knowledge of family histories and local institutions).[10] As has been pointed out there is a danger of taking this picture of working-class life as the definitive one, the real working-class community, and missing its particular location in time and space—the northern working-class towns of the 1930s.[11] The same era that produced working-class film star heroes, Gracie Fields and George Formby. Both epitomized the working-class sense of fun and capacity to mock and deflate pretentiousness. They had a strong sense of community and loyalty to place; the retention of a local accent showed their unwillingness to lose their roots and reinforced their apparent "naturalness," which made them forever seem a Lancashire lad and lass at heart. Here we think of Gracie Fields in films such as *Looking on the Bright Side, Sing as We Go, Keep Smiling,* and *The Show Goes On.*[12] George Formby likewise maintained an irrepressible cheerfulness, the "cheeky chappie," the little man forever playing the fool, yet possessing local knowledge with which to outsmart the upper-class "toffs" in films such as *Off the Dole, Keep Fit,* and *No Limit.*[13] The films of both Fields and Formby showed Britain very much as a class-divided society, and both achieved fame through their ability to poke fun at middle- and upper-class decorum and the respectability, formality, and reserve which the BBC typified.

The films were important in their attempt to present society from the bottom up, and their capacity to install a sense of pride in working-class localism. They presented a contrast to the accounts of working-class life provided by the middle and upper classes. For some in the upper echelons of society the working class were akin to an exotic tribe. Frances Donaldson, for example, remarks that the upper and middle classes regarded the working class as quasi-foreign, and when they moved amongst them with a view to improving their lot "they did so as anthropologists . . . or missionaries visiting a tribe more primitive than themselves."[14] George Orwell's famous *The Road to Wigan Pier* was written in this style as he had received an upper-class, public school education at Eton which provided him with a keen sense of social distinctions.[15] One memorable passage that sticks in the mind and epitomized Orwell's frequent discomfort with aspects of working-class life was the uneasiness with which he received his daily breakfast slice of bread and dripping. Each time it was put on his plate it always contained a black thumbprint, left by the coal miner he was lodging with who always cut the bread after slopping out the chamber pots. Here we have an example of what Elias refers to as the "disgust function," the feeling of revulsion which those who have developed more refined taste and bodily controls can experience when they encounter the habits of common people.[16] In this type of writing, in which all is revealed about "darkest England," we frequently get swings from emotional identification, the desire for the immersion in the directness, warmth, and spontaneity of the local community, to revulsion and disgust.

In this context, it is worth recalling that the audience for accounts of working-class life has a long history going back to Engels and Charles Booth in the nineteenth century. It is still evident in the dramatic exposé style of many of the accounts written by "one of us" about "the people of the abyss," to mention the title of one of Jack London's books. This sense of an anthropologist parachuted into the alien depths of deepest working-class England was still to be found in the 1950s in the publicity for Richard Hoggart's *The Uses of Literacy* (1958), where the inside cover of the first Penguin edition suggested that the book sought "to remedy our ignorance" about "how the other half lives."[17]

Hoggart's book is noticeable for its sympathetic descriptions of traditional working-class life in the face of modernization. The culture which was made and reproduced by working-class people was seen as under threat from the mass media and commercialization. Many of these negative influences originate in the United States, and he has little time for television, milk bars, jukebox boys, and other elements of the "candy-floss world" of mass culture. The tensions within working-class culture as it encountered the forces of the affluent society, consumerism, and mass culture are captured in a series of novels from the late 1950s and 1960s, many of which were made into films. Here we think of Alan Sillitoe's *Saturday Night and Sunday Morning* (1958), Stan Bairstow's *A Kind of Loving* (1960), David Storey's *This Sporting Life* (1960), and the films from Ken Loach: *Up the Junction* (1965), *Poor Cow* (1967), and *Kes* (1967), which explored the earthiness and richness of life within the closed working-class community with occasional glimpses of the modernizing processes.[18] Here one thinks of the central character in the much acclaimed film version of *Saturday Night and Sunday Morning*, Arthur Seaton, a working-class hero if there ever was one, played by Albert Finney, who although he finally succumbs to marriage, in the last moments of the film defiantly casts a stone at the newly built modern suburban housing estate which is to be his future.

As Bernice Martin reminds us, many of the accounts of working-class life focus upon its directness and simplicity of emotional expression.[19] To the middle-class observer it is too often the "immediate gratification," the ritual swearing, the aggression, sexuality, drinking, and violence which attract attention. Yet these features are actually liminal movements of working-class life, a part which is too often mistaken for a whole. The moments of brotherhood and "communitas" are necessarily limited moments of "framed liminality," moments of "anti-structure" in which celebration and taboo-breaking are planned for, in stark contrast to the careful budgeting and time management and careful concern for reputation and respectability in routine everyday life.[20] It is the representations of these liminal moments which provide a rich repertoire of images. Here one thinks of, for example, Ridley Scott's *Hovis Bread* commercial which is packed with nostalgic images of a nineteenth-century northern English working-class town set to a mournful refrain from Dvořák's *New World Symphony* played by a brass band. Or the former British Prime Minister Harold Macmillan reminiscing about the people in his northern working-class constituency of Stockton-on-Tees: "Wonderful people, the finest people in the world," he remarked in a television interview, in a voice heavy with emotion and a tear in the corner of his eye, which almost had us believing he believed the Stockton working class to be the true organic community.

Many of these images of working-class community, therefore, help to foster myths of belonging, warmth, and togetherness which suggest the mythical security of a childhood long relinquished. There is nothing so powerful as the image of an integrated organic community in the childhood one has left behind.[21] Geoffrey Pearson has provided an important account of the ways in which successive generations always recourse to the myth of "the good old days," the existence of a less violent, more law-abiding and harmonious community in the past of their childhood or parent's times.[22] As one goes further and further back into history one finds successive displacements of this golden age back to the 1950s, 1930s, 1900s, 1870s, and so on. Successive generations invest in a form of nostalgia in which the past seems to be more simple, emotionally fulfilling, with relations more direct and integrated, an image of coherence and order. Here the assumption is that one's identity and those of one's significant others are anchored in a specific locale, a physical space which becomes emotionally invested and sedimented with symbolic associations so that it becomes a place. As Bryan Turner remarks, nostalgia, or the loss of a sense of home, is a potent sentiment in the modern world.[23] Particularly so for those groups who are ambivalent about modernity and retain the strong image of the alleged greater integration and simplicity of a more integrated culture in the past.

When we speak of a locality, then, we should be careful not to presume an integrated community. There are problems with establishing the extent to which localities were integrated in the past. We have to be aware of the location in time-space and social space of those who make such pronouncements and that they might be painting a nostalgic and overunified picture. It is also important that we do not operate with the view that localities are only able to change through the working out of a one-way modernization process entailing the eclipse of community and the local culture.

Usually when we think of a locality we have in mind a relatively small place in which everyone can know everyone else, that is social life based upon face-to-face relations. It is assumed that the intensity of the day-to-day contacts will generate a common stock of knowledge at hand which makes misunderstandings less frequent. It is the regularity and frequency of contacts with a group of significant others which are held to sustain a common culture. While the existence of such an integrated set of "core values" or common assumptions rooted in everyday practices may be overstated at both local and national levels, there is a further dimension of cultural integration which must be referred to.[24] This is the generation of powerful, emotionally sustaining rituals, ceremonies, and collective memories. Durkheim, in his *Elementary Forms of the Religious Life,* placed particular emphasis upon the way in which a sense of the sacred was generated in emotionally bonding periods of "collective effervescence." Over time the intense sense of involvement and excitement which bound people together tends to diminish, yet the use of commemorative rituals and ceremonies can be understood as acting like batteries which store and recharge the sense of communality. Outside the regular calendar of ceremonies which reinforce our family, local, and national sense of collective identity, it is also possible to draw on collective memories. As Halbwachs reminds us, collective memories refer to group contexts in the past which are periodically reinforced through contact with others who shared the initial experience.[25]

Nations as Communities

Yet are there limits to the size of the group and place to be considered a local community? Could a nation be considered a local community? If we examine the origins of the term, it refers not only to the modern nation-state, but also draws on the meaning of "*natio,*" a local community, a domicile family condition of belonging.[26] There is often a clear reluctance to accept that the nation could ever embody the type of bonding typically attributed to the local community, especially by Marxists with international sympathies. Hence Raymond Williams remarks:

"Nation" as a term is radically connected with "native." We are *born* into relationships which are typically settled in place. This form of primary and "placeable" bonding is of quite fundamental human and natural importance. Yet the jump from that to anything like the modern nation-state is entirely artificial.[27]

This contrasts with the position of Benedict Anderson, who argues that "all communities larger than the primordial village of face-to-face contact (and perhaps even these) are imagined. Communities are to be distinguished not by their falseness/genuineness, but by the style in which they are imagined."[28] In this sense a nation may be considered as an imagined community because it provides a quasi-religious sense of belonging and fellowship which is attached to those who are taken to share a particular symbolic place. The place is symbolic in that it can be a geographically bounded space which is sedimented with symbolic sentiments; the configuration of the landscape, buildings, and people have been invested with collective memories which have sufficient emotional power to generate a sense of communality. Certain places may be enshrined with a particular emblematic status as national monuments and used to represent a form of symbolic bonding which overrides and embodies the various local affiliations people business. Indeed, it can be argued that this is an essential part of the nation-building process in which the nation-state actively encourages the cultivation and elaboration of the "*ethnie*," or ethnic core.[29] In this sense the creation of a national community is invented, but it is not invented out of nothing. Anthony Smith emphasizes the need for a common repository of myths, heroes, events, landscapes, and memories that are organized and assume a primordial quality. In the eighteenth century with the birth of nationalism in Europe, there was a deliberate attempt by cultural specialists (or proto-intellectuals) to discover and record the vernacular customs and practices, legends and myths, the culture of the people, which it was assumed was fast disappearing.[30] In effect, the expanding strata of the indigenous intelligentsia sought to pull together and weave into a coherent form this body of popular cultural sources which could be used to give the past a sense of direction and construct a national identity. This can be linked to what Gellner, Anderson, and others regard as a crucial factor in the construction of nationalism: the availability of a print culture which can interconnect people over time and space.[31] The possibility of the nation therefore depends upon the development of the book, the novel, and the newspaper alongside a literate reading public capable of using these sources throughout the territorial area and thus able to imagine themselves as a community. It can be argued that the development of the film industry facilitates this process even better, as film provides an instantiation and immediacy which are relatively independent of the long learning process and institutional and other supports necessary to be able to assimilate knowledge through books.[32]

The nation, therefore, becomes represented through a set of more or less coherent images and memories which deal with the crucial questions of the origins, difference, and distinctiveness of a people. In this sense it has a quasi-religious basis as it is able to answer some of the questions of theodicy in a world which is subject to processes of secularization. The sacrifice and suffering people are willing to undergo for the nation must in part be understood with respect to the capacity of the discourses, images, and practices that sustain the nation and provide a sense of overarching meaning and significance which transcends death or renders death meaningful through subsuming the individual under a sacred totality. Yet the fact that a national culture is constituted as a unique particularity, points to the rise of the European nation-states, and their power struggles and elimination contests, in which the mobilization of the population through the idea of the distinctiveness of the nation and its difference from its neighbors attained significance. In this sense the external pressures of the figuration of significant others to which the nation-state belongs and the escalating power struggles can make the identity of the nation more important. It has been argued that conflicts heighten the sense of the boundary between the "in-group" and the "out-group." Hence Georg Simmel, who had written at length about the capacity of external conflicts to unify the internal structure of a group, remarked on the way in which the German reaction to the Great War resulted in a strong wave of social ecstasy and intensification of social bonds which unified the nation.[33] Clearly both Simmel and Durkheim were surprised at the intensity of the enthusiasm and sentiments aroused by the Great War, and as Marcel Mauss points out later, had he lived, would no doubt have been horrified to see the heightened realization and intensification of the sacred which occurred in the Nuremberg rallies of the 1930s.[34]

Simmel's writings are important because he gives us a sense of the multidimensional and relational nature of social life. A local culture may be a common set of work and kinship relationships which reinforce the practical, everyday lived culture which is sedimented into taken-for-granted knowledge and beliefs. Yet the articulation of these beliefs and sense of the particularity of the local place will tend to become sharpened and more well-defined when the locality becomes locked into power struggles and elimination contests with its neighbors. In such situations we can see the formation of a local culture in which the particularity of its own identity is emphasized. In this case the locality presents an oversimplified, unified image of itself to outsiders. This image, to use a metaphor of Cohen, can be likened to the local community's face, or mask.[35] This does not mean that inside the locality social differentiation has been eliminated and relationships are necessarily more egalitarian, simple, and homogeneous, rather its internal differences and discourses may very well be complex. What is at issue here is the direction of focus. Internally we may be able to consider the community as incorporating all sorts of independencies, rivalries, power struggles, and conflicts. Many community studies document these conflicts: here one thinks of Elias and Scotson's account of the struggles between the established and the outsiders.[36] Yet under certain circumstances such struggles may be forgotten, as, for example, when the locality is brought into conflict with another locality, or the region is involved in interregional disputes. In such situations one's own particularity is subsumed into some larger collectivity and appropriate cultural work undertaken to develop an acceptable public face for it. This process entails the mobilization of the repertoire of communal symbols, sentiments, and collective memories. It is the shifts in the interdependencies and power balances which increase the local people's consciousness of the symbolic boundary between themselves and others which is aided by the mobilization and reconstitution of symbolic repertoires with which the community can think and formulate a unified image of its difference from the opposite party.[37] As we shall go on to see, it is the capacity to shift the frame and move between varying range of foci, the capacity to handle a range of symbolic material out of which various identities can be formed and reformed in different situations, which is relevant in the contemporary global situation. Here we have the sense that the contemporary world has not seen a cultural impoverishment, an attenuation of cultural resources. Rather, there has been an extension of cultural repertoires and an enhancement of the resourcefulness of various groups to create new symbolic modes of affiliation and belonging, to rework and reshape the meaning of existing signs, and to undermine existing symbolic hierarchies, for their own particular purposes in ways which become difficult for those in the dominant cultural centers to ignore. This shift has been aided and abetted by various sets of cultural specialists and intermediaries with sympathies for the local.

The strength of the sentiments which become embodied in the nation and their resilience over time, it has been argued, has been underestimated by some theorists who miss the role of the nation in the nation-state and assume that the national sentiments are a by-product of the modernization process devised to facilitate the integration of the nation-state and are subsequently proved redundant and undermined by the modernizing process.[38] In addition, there are often tendencies to underestimate the ways in which the formation of the nation and nationalism draw upon cultural resources which have yet to be modernized, such as the cultural memories, symbols, myths, and sentiment surrounding the ethnic core.[39] This suggests that the stock sociological contrast between tradition and modernity may not be that useful. This is noticeable in the case of nation-states such as Japan, which, it is argued, cannot be fit into the assumed developmental logic of modernization.[40] In effect, Japan managed to impose a restrictive and particularistic project of modernity and was able to protect it against universalistic challenges.[41] This would point to the continuing importance of cultural factors in the development of nation-states and in their relations with other nation-states.

As has been already mentioned, the bilateral interactions that occur between nation-states, especially those which involve increasing competition and conflict, can have the effect of unifying the self-image of the nation, as well as the image or national face which is presented to the other. An increase in the regularity and intensity of contacts, as nation-states become bound up in regional figurations (their reference group of significant others), can intensify the pressures to form a distinctive and coherent identity. It is important to emphasize that this process, in addition to external presentation of the national face, also has an internal dimension and depends upon the power of resources particular groups possess to mobilize the ethnic core. They will endeavor to mobilize different aspects of the ethnic core to suit their own particular interests and aspirations; in effect, the process of cultural formation of a national identity is one which always entails the part being represented as a whole: a particular representation of the nation is presented as unanimous and consensual.

Here one thinks of Margaret Thatcher's Downing Street statement on news of victory in the Falklands War in 1982: "We are one nation tonight." Such statements also point to the fragility of particular formulations of national identity; while to be legitimate they have to draw upon a finite and recognizable repository of the ethnic core, they are also subjected to a continuous process of struggle to develop and impose alternative formulations. The fragility and volatility of the emotional sentiments embodied in the nation, and the struggle over the legitimacy of the representation, therefore suggest that we should consider the national cultures in processional terms. When we consider processes of the formation and deformation of national identity, we should also be clear that it is easier to identify a common ethnic core where there has been a long-term process of national formation in European nations as is the case in Britain and France. That we should be wary of taking their individual cases as the model for nation formation is evident when we consider the case of newer nations, especially those endeavoring to construct a multicultural sense of identity. The case of Australia is interesting in this context, and there are now a number of studies about the attempts to generate a unified national identity: to "invent Australia," through the cultivation of representations of particular places such as Ayers Rock or Bondi Beach and particular historical events such as Gallipoli.[42]

It can be argued that the images that are constructed through television and the cinema are a necessary part in the process of the formation of a nation, especially in their capacity to bridge the public and the private. It is evident that a nation is an abstract collectivity which is far too big to be directly experienced by people. Hence it is not only the existence of civic rituals, such as Remembrance Day, royal weddings, etc., which provide the sense of the sacred which binds the nation together; increasingly it is the representation of these events which is crucial.[43] For people whose knowledge of these events is restricted to viewing television in their living room, it is clear that the television does not merely represent such events, but also constructs them. Yet it is not a question of a passive audience taking in the event, as Dyan and Katz have argued, it is also possible for individuals and families to reconstitute the ceremonial space in the home by observing rituals, dressing up, and "participating" in the knowledge that countless others are doing the very same thing.[44] Hence an "atomized" audience can occasionally be united via television media events.

Yet it is insufficient to see the process of imagining the nation as purely the product of internal factors. It is clear that in the Second World War the British film industry played an important part in mobilizing a national identity through the production of representations of the common foe.[45] Hence we should not consider cultures in isolation, but endeavor to locate them in the relational matrix of their significant others.[46] It can be argued that it is not the isolation of the nation which is the crucial factor in developing an image of itself as a unique and integrated national culture; rather it is the need to mobilize a particular representation of national identity in response to the unavoidable contacts, interdependencies, and power struggles which nation-states become locked into with their significant others. This means we should not focus only on bilateral relations between nation-states because nation-states do not just interact they form a *world* as increasingly their interactions take place within a global context. This global context has seen the development of its own body of formal and taken-for-granted procedures based upon processes and modes of integration which cannot simply be reduced to the interests and control of individual nation-states.[47] The independent development of diplomatic conventions and procedures, international law which forms a nexus of underpinning ground rules for international conflicts, are one set of examples.[48] Another would be the independent power of multinational corporations to act independently to weaken the integrity of national culture through their capacity to direct the flow of cultural goods and information from the dominant economic centers to the peripheries—the cultural imperialism thesis would be a strong case of this type of argument. At the same time the perception and extent of these processes can increase nation-states' sensitivity to the need to preserve the integrity of their own national traditions and can be used to promote counter- or de-globalizing and fundamentalist reactions.

One effect, then, of the globalization process—the increasing contact and sense of the finitude of the world, the consciousness that the world is one place—is a clashing of different interpretations of the meaning of the world formulated from the perspective of different national and civilizational traditions. The density and multidirectionality of the talk which takes place on the global stage necessarily demands that nation-states take up a position as they find it increasingly impossible to silence the other voices or consider opting out. Hence we have a plurality of national responses to the process of globalization which cannot be conceived as reducible to the ideas generated from Western modernity. One of the problems entailed in mapping the contemporary global condition is this range of different national cultural responses which continue in various ways to deform and reform, blend, syncretize, and transform the alleged master processes of modernity.

With respect to theories of modernity there is often the assumption that modernization necessarily entails the eclipse of the national tradition and cultural identity. Yet it can be argued that theories of modernity which emphasize a relentless process of instrumental rationalization which effectively "empties out" a society's repository of cultural traditions and meanings are misconceived. Weber's notion of the imposition of an "iron cage," a new bureaucratized serfdom, or "Egyptification" of life and the related arguments about the progressive commodification, rationalization, and disenchantment of the world by critical theorists such as Habermas would seem to be difficult to substantiate.[49]

Knorr Cetina, for example, argues that if we examine everyday practices closely, they testify to the presence of "meaning" and "tradition," of "the body" or "intimacy," of "local knowledge," and everything else that is often thought to have been bred out of "abstract systems."[50] In effect the everyday practices of participants, even if they work within highly technicized organizations, operate with and by means of fictions. Hence, if we observe the practices in local environments, we find that the shared, deeply cherished classifications people use are a form of the sacred. Modernity has not meant a loss of magic and enchantment or a reduction of the fictional use of symbolic classifications in local institutions.

This notion of modernity points toward postmodernism and postmodernity, with the latter term not to be understood as a new epoch which is now replacing the modern age, but a growing awareness of the limits of the claims of the project of modernity. There are, of course, many problems involved in trying to produce definitions of postmodernism and postmodernity.[51] Put simply, postmodernism points to the problem of handling cultural complexity, of having to deal with what from the point of view of established, well-ordered categories appears to be a disorder which cannot be adequately incorporated into existing classifications or ignored. It is possible to identify a number of features here. Firstly, postmodernism entails a loss of confidence in the master-narratives of progress and enlightenment which have been central to Western modernity. The confidence in the universality of this project is replaced by an emphasis upon contingency, incoherence, and ambivalence. There is a greater awareness of multicoding, hybridization, and cultural syncretism. Secondly, there has been a democratization and popularization of forms of knowledge and cultural production and dissemination which were previously monopolized or tightly controlled by established groups. This, of course, is only a partial shift, but one sufficiently noticeable to create a sensitivity to those formerly excluded from, or allocated a residual role within, existing classifications. Hence we have an appreciation of the legitimate particularity of local knowledge and outsider perspectives as manifest in, for example, feminism and post-colonialism. Hence there is an emphasis on plurality, on contested and irreconcilable *histories*, as opposed to a unified unidirectional history. It is in this sense that Vattimo speaks of "the end of history," the end of the sense of a singular unified stream of history stemming from the West, which all other civilizations, cultural traditions, and nation-states will inevitably flow into.[52]

Globalization and Cultural Identity

If globalization refers to the process whereby the world becomes increasingly seen as "one place" and to the ways in which we are made conscious of this process, then the cultural changes which are thematized under the banner of the postmodern would seem to point in the opposite direction to a consideration of the local.[53] Yet, this is to misunderstand the nature of the process of globalization. It should not be taken to imply that there is, or will be, a unified world society or culture—something akin to the social structure of a nation-state and its national culture, only writ large. Such outcomes may have been the ambition of particular nation-states at various points of their history, and the possibility of a renewed world state formation process cannot be discounted in the future. In the present phase it is possible to refer to the development of a global culture in a less totalistic sense by referring to two aspects of the process of globalization. Firstly, we can point to the existence of a global culture in the restricted sense of "third cultures": sets of practices, bodies of knowledge, conventions, and lifestyles which have developed in ways which have become increasingly independent of nation-states. In effect there are a number of trans-societal institutions, cultures, and cultural producers who cannot be understood as merely agents and representatives of their nation-states. Secondly, we can talk about a global culture in the Simmelian sense of a cultural form: the sense that the globe is a finite knowable bounded space, a field into which all nation-states and collectivities will inevitably be drawn. Here the globe, the planet earth, acts both as a limit and the common bounded space on which our encounters and practices are inevitably grounded. In the second sense the result of the increasing intensity of contact and communication between nation-states and other agencies is to produce a clashing of cultures, which can lead to heightened attempts to draw boundaries between the self and others. From this perspective the changes that are taking place as a result of the current phase of intensified globalization can be understood as reactions which seek to rediscover particularity, localism, and difference, all of which generate a sense of the limits of the culturally unifying, ordering, and integrating projects associated with Western modernity. Hence in one sense it can be argued that globalization produces postmodernism.

If we examine the first aspect of the globalization process, it is evident that the problems of intercultural communication in fields such as law have led to the development of mediating "third cultures."[54] These were initially designed to deal with the practical problems of intercultural disputes, but as with the development of the European Court of Justice and other institutions and protocols in international law, they can achieve autonomy and function beyond the manipulation of individual nation-states. In addition we can point to the further integrating effects of the internationalization of the world financial markets following the move to twenty-four hour trading after the "Big Bang" of October 1986.[55] The process of deregulation encouraged the de-monopolization of national legal systems and a more meritocratic market ethos in which international lawyers become part of a group of new professionals, which includes: corporate tax accountants, financial advisers, and management consultants. To these groups we might add a further category of "design professional," those cultural specialists and intermediaries working in the film, television, music, advertising, fashion, and consumer culture industries.[56] The deregulation of markets and capital flows can therefore be seen to produce a degree of homogenization in procedures, working practices, and organizational cultures. In addition we can point to some convergences in the lifestyle, habitus, and demeanor of these various sets of professionals. There are also similarities in the quarters of the cities they live and work in. Yet it should be emphasized that such groups are not to be found in every city or even every national capital. They are concentrated in various world cities such as New York, Tokyo, London, Paris, Los Angeles, and São Paulo.[57] It is the integration of the particular services located in particular quarters of these world cities which produces transnational sets of social relations, practices, and cultures. The process of globalization is therefore uneven, and if one aspect of it is the consciousness of the world as a single place, then it is in these select quarters of world cities that we find people working in environments which rely upon advanced means of communications which overcome time-space separation. Here we find the most striking examples of the effects of time-space compression, as new means of communication effectively make possible simultaneous transactions which sustain "deterritorialized cultures."

It is when we take the next step and assume that such areas are the prototypes for the future and that the international economy and communications networks will produce similar homogenizing effects in other areas of national societies that we run into problems. It is here that some would make the mistake of assuming that the extension of various social and cultural forms to different parts of the world is necessarily producing a homogenization of content. That is, the globalization process is seen as producing a unified and integrated common culture. Hence we find theories of cultural imperialism and media imperialism that assume local cultures are necessarily battered out of existence through the proliferation of consumer goods, advertising, and media programs stemming from the West (largely the United States). Such theories share with theories of mass culture a strong view of the manipulability of mass audiences by a monolithic system and an assumption of the negative cultural effects of the media as self-evident, with little empirical evidence about how goods and information are adapted and used in everyday practices.[58] Of course it is possible to point to the availability of Western consumer goods—especially major brands of food, drink, cigarettes, and clothing—following the business and tourist trails to the remotest parts of the world. It is also clear that certain images, for example, the tough guy hero fighting against innumerable odds, have a strong appeal in many cultures. Hence we find Rambo movies played throughout southern and eastern Asia so that "remote villagers in rural Burma could now applaud Rambo's larger-than-life heroics only days after they hit the screens of Wisconsin."[59] Paul Theroux recalls that when he visited the Solomon Islands he found that Rambo was one of their folk heroes and that remote villagers would link up a video-recorder to a generator to play tapes of the movie.[60] Such accounts are by now legion—yet how are we to read them?

One possibility is to attempt to outline some of the absorption/assimilation/resistance strategies which peripheral cultures can adopt toward the mass and consumer culture images and goods originating from metropolitan centers.[61] In the first place it is apparent that once we investigate actual cases the situation is exceedingly complex. It is not just a question of the everyday practical culture of local inhabitants giving way to globally marketed products. Such market culture/local culture interactions are usually mediated by the nation-state, which in the process of creating a national identity will educate and employ its own range of cultural specialists and intermediaries. Some of these may well have been educated in world cities and have retained strong networks and lifestyle identifications with other transnational "design professionals," managers and intellectuals and para-intellectuals. Some of these may even be official "cultural animateurs" employed by the ministry of culture, in some cases perhaps with one eye on national cultural integration and one eye on the international tourist trade. Hence, depending on the priority it gives to the nation-forming project and the power resources that the nation-state possesses, it can reinvent memories, traditions, and practices with which to resist, channel, or control market penetration. Some nation-states, for example, will invest in locally produced film and television programs. Yet as we have previously mentioned, such experiments in cultural engineering are by no means certain to succeed unless they can find a base to ground themselves in local forms of life and practices. Hence the scenario of "cultural dumping" of obsolete American television programs on a powerless nation-state on the periphery is only one possibility from a range of responses. It also has to be set alongside the activities of cultural gatekeepers, brokers, and entrepreneurs within the major cities of the nation-state in conjunction with colleagues abroad in the world cities collaborating upon what aspects of the local popular culture—music, food, dress, crafts, etc.—can be packaged and marketed in the metropolitan centers and elsewhere. In many cases it may be that various forms of hybridization and creolization emerge in which the meanings of externally originating goods, information, and images are reworked, syncretized, and blended with existing cultural traditions and forms of life.

In the case of the effects of global television, it is important to move beyond oversimplified, oppositionally conceived formulations which stress either the manipulation or the resistance of audiences. In recent years the pendulum has swung toward the latter populist direction with its claim that a new cultural studies orthodoxy has emerged around the assumption of the creativity and skillfulness of active audiences and consumers.[62] Television and the new communications technology are frequently presented as producing both manipulation and resistance, on the one hand, and the homogenization and fragmentation of contemporary culture, on the other hand.[63] The new communications technology is presented as producing a global Gemeinschaft which transcends physical place through bringing together disparate groups who unite around the common experience of television to form new communities.[64] This means that the locality is no longer the prime referent of our experiences. Rather, we can be immediately united with distant others with whom we can form a "psychological neighborhood" or "personal community" through telephone or the shared experience of the news of the "generalized elsewhere" we get from watching television. Hence as Morley remarks, "Thus, it seems, locality is not simply subsumed in a national or global sphere: rather, it is increasingly bypassed in both directions; experience is both unified beyond localities and fragmented within them."[65] Yet this is not to suggest that the fragmentation of experience within localities is random or unstructured. Access to power resources creates important differentials. Just as there are "information rich" nations on a global level there are also "information poor" ones. Within localities there are clear differentials, with the wealthy and well-educated most likely to have access to the new forms of information and communications technology through possession of the necessary economic and cultural capital.[66] Here we can also point to Mary Douglas and Baron Isherwood's concept of "informational goods," goods which require a good deal of background knowledge to make their consumption meaningful and strategically useful, as is the case with personal computers.[67] On the other hand, it is the sense of instantiation and immediacy presented by television which appears to make its messages unproblematically accessible. American soap operas, Italian football, or the Olympic Games all have an apparent immediacy and intelligibility which could be misunderstood as producing a homogeneous response. Yet these global resources are often indigenized and syncretized to produce particular blends and identifications which sustain the sense of the local.[68]

A further problem with the homogenization thesis is that it misses the ways in which transnational corporations increasingly direct advertising toward various parts of the globe which is increasingly tailored to specific differentiated audiences and markets. Hence the global and the local cannot be neatly separated as we find in the statement by Coca-Cola, "We are not a multinational, we are a multi-local."[69] Here we can usefully refer to the term "globloc," the fusion of the terms global and local to make a blend. Apparently the term is modeled on the Japanese *dochaku,* which derives from the agricultural principle of adapting one's farming techniques to local conditions and was taken up by Japanese business interests in the 1980s.[70]

The various combinations, blends, and fusions of seemingly opposed and incompatible processes—such as homogenization and fragmentation, globalization and localization, universalism and particularism—points to the problems which are entailed in attempts to conceive the global in terms of a singular integrated and unified conceptual scheme. Appadurai has rejected such attempts at theoretical integration to argue that the global order must be understood as "a complex, overlapping, disjunctive order."[71] It can be best conceived as involving five sets of non-isomorphic flows of people, technology, finance, media images and information, and ideas. Individual nation-states may attempt to promote, channel, or block particular flows with varying degrees of success depending upon the power resources they possess and the constraints of the particular configuration of interdependencies they are locked into.

It is, of course, important that we examine the evidence from systematic studies which focus upon particular localities to examine the effects of these flows on particular groups of people. It can be argued that one particularly important site where the various flows of people, goods, technology, information, and images cross and intermingle is the world city. These are the sites in which we find the juxtaposition of the rich and the poor, the new middle-class professionals and the homeless, and a variety of other ethnic, class, and traditional identifications, as people from the center and the periphery are brought together to face each other within the same spatial location in cities such as London, Paris, New York, Los Angeles, as well as Bangkok, Rio de Janeiro, Mexico City, São Paulo, and Manila.[72] The sociospatial redevelopments of the inner areas and docklands of some large Western cities in the 1980s have been regarded by some as examples of "postmodernization."[73] Yet, it can also be argued that many of the cultural factors associated with this process—the post-modern emphasis upon the mixing of codes, pastiche, fragmentation, incoherence, disjunction, and syncretism—were characteristics of cities in colonial societies, decades or even centuries, before they appeared in the West.[74] From this perspective the first multicultural city was not London or Los Angeles but probably Rio de Janeiro, Calcutta, or Singapore. At the very least this points to some of the problems involved in defining the modern and the postmodern and their family of associated terms, a more nuanced and elaborated notion of cultural modernity which goes beyond Eurocentric notions of the homogenizing effects of industrialization, urbanization, and bureaucratization. It suggests a global conception of the modern, which rather than being preoccupied with the historical sequences of transitions from tradition to modernity and post-modernity, instead focuses upon the spatial dimension, the geographical relationship between the center and the periphery in which the first multiracial and multicultural societies were on the periphery not the core. Cultural diversity, syncretism, and dislocation occurred there first. The interdependencies and power balances which developed between Western nation-states such as England and France and colonial societies clearly form an important, yet neglected aspect of modernity; an aspect which is noticeably absent from those accounts which derive from those working in the classic tradition deriving from French and German theorists.[75]

It is the very process of intensified flows of people from the ex-colonial countries to the Western metropolitan centers in the postwar era that has made us increasingly conscious of this colonial aspect of the development of modernity and the question of cultural identity. The inward movement of people, as well as images and information, from places which for many in the West were constructed through oversimplified racist and exotic stereotypes of "the Other," means that new levels of complexity are introduced into the formulation of identity, cultural tradition, community, and nation. This challenges the notion of one-way flows from the center to the peripheries, as the dominant centers in the West become not only importers of raw materials and goods, but of people too.[76] The visibility and vociferousness of "the rest of the West," means that cultural differences once maintained between societies now exist within them.[77] The unwillingness of migrants to passively inculcate the dominant cultural mythology of the nation or locality raises issues of multiculturalism and the fragmentation of identity. In some cases this provoked intensified and extremist nationalist reactions, for example, the racist campaigns of Le Pen in France and Britain's 1980s Falklands War with its "little Englanderism." This can lead to a complex series of reactions on the part of immigrants. For some ethnic groups this entails a retreat into the culture of origin (in Britain a reidentification with the Caribbean, Pakistan, India, or Bangladesh) or into fundamentalist religions from the home country. For others this may entail the construction of complex counterethnicities as in the case with young second generation Afro-Caribbeans who have developed identities around the symbols and mythologies of Rastafarianism.[78] For yet others the prospect of a unified single identity may be impossible and illusory as they move between various identities. Some third generation young blacks in Britain constantly shift between British, Caribbean, black, subcultural, and various gender identifications. For example, the film *My Beautiful Laundrette,* by Stephen Freers and Hanif Kureishi, has central characters who are two gay men, one white, one brown, with the latter's Pakistani landlord uncle throwing black people out onto the street. Such characters do not present positive unified identity images and are consequently not easy to identify with.[79]

It can be argued that the problems involved in trying to live with multiple identities helps to generate endless discourses about the process of finding or constructing a coherent identity.[80] Yet in contrast to those arguments that assume that the logic of modernity is to produce an increasingly narrow individualism—a narcissistic preoccupation with individual identity which was common in the 1970s—today we find arguments which emphasize the search for a strong collective identity, some new form of community, within modern societies. Maffesoli for example, sees the process of development from modernity to postmodernity as entailing a movement from individualism to collectivism, from rationality to emotionality.[81] In this sense, postmodernity is seen as sharing with its premodern antecedents an emphasis on emotionality and the cultivation of intense feelings and sensory experiences, such as were found in the spectacles of the Baroque. Here Maffesoli speaks of postmodernity as fostering the emergence of ephemeral postmodern *tribes,* which are to be found especially amongst young people in large cities such as Paris. These groupings provide a strong sense of localism and emotional identification (*Einfuhlung*) through the tactile embodied sense of being together. Yet they are regarded as *neo*-tribes because they exist in an urban world where relationships are transitory, hence their identifications are temporary as people will necessarily move on and through the endless flow of sociality to make new attachments.[82] The subject of tribalism, both in its traditional sense of exclusive membership of a group based upon kinship ties and strong identification with a locality or region, and in the sense of the emergence of more transitory neo-tribes, is currently attracting a good deal of public interest.[83]

This interest has been subjected to the process of global marketing by various arms of the tourist industry, which it is predicted will become the world's leading industry by 1996.[84] Of course for many tourists the ease with which they can now travel to the more exotic and remote parts of the world amounts to a step into a tourist reservation in which they enjoy "home puts"— all the accustomed comforts of home in terms of food, drink, living space, television programs, and other facilities, plus sea, sand, and sun.[85] In effect, they are locals whose contact with another set of locals in the tourist location is highly regulated and ritualized. It has been argued that this particular set of tourists are being replaced by more sophisticated post-tourists who seek a whole range of experiences and direct encounters with locals, some of whom are not at all worried that what they are presented with is a simulation of a local culture, and are interested in the whole paraphernalia of the "behind the scenes" and the construction of the performance and set.[86] Such staged simulations of localities can vary from reassuring clear cartoon-style parodies (the Jungle Cruise in the Magic Kingdom) to small-scale "walk-in, see and touch" simulations of the key buildings and icons which in the popular imagination are taken to represent a national culture (the World Showcase at Epcot) to the whole heritage industry efforts to preserve and restore full-scale living and working examples of "the past."[87] Some would see this as part of a wider shift away from the imposition of abstraction and uniformity through modernist architecture to a postmodern struggle for place, to reinvent place and rehumanize urban space.[88]

In yet other situations it is the locals themselves who are asked to take part in staged authenticity for tourists. Here the tourists are granted the privilege of moving around the living, working locality in which the real inhabitants perform for them. Hence MacCannell discusses the case of Locke, California, the home of the last survivors of Chinese farm laborers, which was a company town and was sold to tourist developers in 1977 who marketed it as "the only intact rural Chinatown in the United States."[89] Here the inhabitants along with the town became museumified, presented as the last living examples of "a way of life which no longer exists."

MacCannell also discusses examples of "enacted or staged slavery," such as the deal struck between MCI Incorporated and the Masai of Kenya covering wage rates, admission fees, television and movie rights, etc., which could allow the Masai to earn a living by perpetually *acting Masai*.[90] Also interesting in this context is Dennis O'Rourke's film *Cannibal Tours* which follows a group of wealthy European and North American tourists up the Sepik River in Papua New Guinea aboard a luxury cruise ship.[91] Such situations vary a great deal in both the objectives of the tourists and the relative power of the parties involved. In the case of New Guinea, the tribesmen were well aware of the unequal exchange and hard bargains which the wealthy tourists invariably strike and that the middlemen and local representatives of the tourist agencies had creamed-off the money. The tribespeople here do not have sufficient power resources to manipulate the degree of openness and closure of the boundary of the locality in their own terms. In other cases this can lead to what MacCannell refers to as "the hostile Indian act," in which ex-primitives typically engage in hatred, sullen silence, and freezing out.[92] For their part, the cannibal tourists achieve a safe package version replete with vicarious thrills of the "heart of darkness," while fulfilling a theme in the popular imagination, a visit to the place of "the Other." At the end of each day, they return to the home comforts and familiar Western surroundings of the cruise ship.

In the case of some communities of Inuit in Alaska, it is possible for tourists to make visits to tribespeople and participate in their way of life on a much more complete basis. Here the tourist lives with the tribe and takes part in a wide range of activities—there is no tour ship to retreat to and only individuals or small groups are admitted to the tribe on a strictly regulated basis under the supervision of government agencies. The Inuit use the money they get to buy essential supplies and equipment (bullets for hunting rifles, etc.) in order to maintain a partly modernized, yet independent version of their traditional way of life. They are in a situation in which they possess sufficient power resources to be able to manipulate the boundary of their community to their own advantage and maintain their sense of cultural identity. A further example would be the Ainu who were a "hunter and gatherer" people inhabiting the northern Japanese island of Hokkaido, which only became officially integrated into Japan after the Meiji Restoration. During the 1970s an Ainu cultural movement developed which not only established schools for the teaching of their language and traditions, but also in certain areas established traditional village structures to produce handicraft goods, so that tourists could come to witness their traditional lifestyles.[93] Tourism, then, has been consciously manipulated for the purposes of the reconstitution of Ainu cultural identity.

For other cultural movements tourism may cease to be seen as a resource, but may be identified as a major element in the process which is destroying localism and ethnic identities. The Hawaiian cultural movement, developed since the 1970s, has reacted against the long-term process which has incorporated Hawaii into the U.S. economy and seen the development of a multiethnic Hawaii in which Hawaiians became a minority in their own land, with their numbers reduced from 600,000 to 40,000 during the first century of contact, along with the stigmatization and disintegration of the Hawaiian language and customs. The tourist industry, the dominant force since the decline of the plantation economy, became identified with the taking of land and the commodification and trivialization of Hawaiian culture as exotica. Instead of the old system with its homogeneous model of Western modernist identity at the top and backward and quaint Hawaiians at the bottom, with those at the bottom threatened with assimilation, it is argued that in its place a polycentric system has emerged.[94] The new model moves between two poles: the Hawaiian cultural movement's opposition to tourist development and its attempts to establish and defend its own authentic sense of the past and the newer more up-market tourism which seeks on the one hand to modernize and develop and to define those who stand in its way as lazy and backward and on the other hand to recreate a nostalgic vision of the former plantation Hawaii. This nostalgic vision has little acceptance from the Hawaiian movement, which wishes to develop a particular identity and way of life which resists the whole enterprise of being an object for someone else's gaze.[95]

Concluding Remarks

Anthony King has remarked that all "globalizing theories are self-representations of the dominant particular," acutely pointing to the problem of the location of the theorist who necessarily writes from a particular place and within a particular tradition of discourse, which not only endow him with differential power resources to be able to speak, but also to be listened to.[96] Many of our Western taken-for-granted assumptions about the world have immense power because their very self-evident quality does not encourage the possibility of dialogue. Hence we have a number of theories about the ways in which the West was able to impose its particular vision of the "exotic Other" on distant parts of the world. Yet this should not be taken to allow us to remain bound to the view that our representations must remain trapped within the particularism of our fantasy-laden projections, for the question of evidence cannot be completely dispensed with. It took an American anthropologist of Sri Lankan origins to raise doubts about one of the powerful Western myths about the Pacific: that Captain Cook was deified by the Hawaiians. Obeyeskere demonstrates through careful research that it wasn't the Hawaiians who deified Captain Cook, but the Europeans who projected the myth of native deification onto the Hawaiians to bolster their own civilizing myths.[97] The discovery of this reversal was made possible in part through Obeyeskere's knowledge of Asian societies, where he could find no local evidence to support assumptions of the deifications of Westerners by overcredulous natives, and in part through his attribution of commonsense practical rationality to the Hawaiians; the latter is in contrast to those who emphasize the enduring strength of their culture through the inflexibility of their cosmological categories. As members of "the rest" come increasingly to reside in the West and are able to make their voices heard, we can expect many more accounts which challenge the "self-representations of the dominant particular." At the same time, important as the drive for deconceptualization is, there remains the problem of reconceptualization, the possibility of the construction of higher level, more abstract general models of the globe. Here we can make a number of points.

The first is to do with how we conceptualize the globe. To identify it as a single place is perhaps to give it a sense of false concreteness and unity.[98] For many of the people in the world the consciousness of the process of globalization, that they inhabit the same place, may be absent, or limited, or occur only spasmodically. To some extent an appropriate model to represent this might be a heap, a congeries, or an aggregate.[99] Clearly, this is one way of understanding the notion of a global culture: the sense of heaps, congeries, and aggregates of cultural particularities juxtaposed together on the same field, the same bounded space, in which the fact that they are different and do not fit together, or want to fit together, becomes noticeable and a source of practical problems. It can be argued that the study of culture, our interest in doing justice to the description of particularities and differences, necessarily directs us toward an ideographic mode in which we are acutely aware of the danger of hypostatizations and overgeneralizations.

At the same time there are clearly systemic tendencies in social life which derive from the expansive and integrating power of economic processes and the hegemonizing efforts of particular nation-states or blocs. From this perspective there is a need for practical knowledge modeled in systematic form which yields technically useful information and rational planning. Models in which differences have to become domesticated, turned into variables to further integration. In this sense certain aspects of the world are becoming more amenable to systems analysis as the world becomes more integrated through systemic practices and takes on systemic properties. Yet when we consider the relationship between the system and culture, it is argued that a shift away from the powerful hegemonic control over the system could be accompanied by a concomitant shift in cultural categories. Friedman, for example, has argued that while all cultures are plural and creole in terms of their origins, whether or not they identify themselves as such depends upon further processes.[100] Hence our capacity to notice, look for, or advocate pluralism and the defense of particularity may not depend upon the actual extent of these characteristics, but be a function of relative changes in our situation which now gives us "permission" to see them. He remarks:

> In fact it might well be argued that the pluralist conception of the world is a distinctly western mode of apprehending the current fragmentation of the system, a confusion of our own identity in space. When hegemony is strong or increasing cultural space is similarly homogenized, spaghetti becomes Italian, a plural set of dialects become a national language in which cultural differences are translated into a continuum of correct to incorrect, or standard to non-standard.[101]

In some ways this conception is similar to that developed by Elias in which he argues that in situations in which established groups are firmly in control relationships with outsider groups are more hierarchical and the dominant group is able to colonize the weaker with its own pattern of conduct. The established are able to develop a collective "we-image" based upon a sense of superiority and "group charisma," an image which is inseparable from the imposition and internalization of a sense of "group disgrace," a stigmatized sense of unworthiness and inferiority by the outsider group. The outsiders are invariably characterized as "dirty, morally unreliable and lazy."[102] At the same time this colonization phase of the relationship between the established and the outsiders can give way with a shift in interdependencies and the relative power balance to a second phase, that of "functional democratization." In this second phase of differentiation and emancipation, people become enmeshed in longer and denser webs of interdependencies, which the established group finds difficulty in controlling. Outsider groups gain in social power and confidence and the contrasts and tensions in society increase. In this second phase, it is possible that many of the unified models, which are seen as doing an injustice to particularity and complexity, become subjected to critique and rejection. Interest develops in constructing models and theories which allow for notions of syncretism, complexity, and seemingly random and arbitrary patterns.[103] These concluding remarks are, of course, speculative, and there are many difficulties in trying to use established-outsider models in situations where there are increasing numbers of participants in the global "game." The boundaries between collectivities can be breached or ignored, yet at the very least my analysis of the global/local relationship perhaps does suggest that we should not be too hasty to dispense with theories of social relations altogether.

Notes

1   For discussions of localism and locality, see P. Cooke, "Locality, Structure and Agency: A Theoretical Analysis," *Cultural Anthropology* 5, no. 1 (1990); C. Bell and H. Newby, *Community Studies* (London: Allen and Unwin, 1971); and A. Cohen, *The Symbolic Construction of Community* (London: Tavistock, 1985).

2   See C. M. Arensberg, *The Irish Countrymen* (1937; rpt. Garden City, N.Y.: Natural History Press, 1968) and C. M. Arensberg and S. T. Kimball, *Family and Community in Ireland* (London: Peter Smith, 1940).

3   Ronald Frankenberg, *Communities in Britain* (Harmondsworth: Penguin, 1966).

4   Arthur Vidich and J. Bensman, *Small Town in Mass Society* (Princeton: Princeton University Press, 1958).

5   D. Lynd and H. Lynd, *Middletown in Transition* (New York: Harcourt Brace, 1937).

6   W. L. Warner and P. S. Lunt, *The Social Life of a Modern Community* (New Haven: Yale University Press, 1941).

7   Maurice Stein, *Eclipse of Community* (New York: Harper, 1960).

8   Norman Dennis, F. Henriques, and C. Slaughter, *Coal Is Our Life* (London: Tavistock, 1956); Brian Jackson, *Working Class Community* (London: Routledge, 1968); B. Williamson, *Class, Culture and Community* (London: Routledge, 1982).

9   Richard Hoggart, *The Uses of Literacy* (Harmondsworth: Penguin, 1958).

10   Ibid., see especially chap. 5, "The Full Rich Life."

11   C. Critcher, "Sociology, Cultural Studies and the Postwar Working Class," in *Working Class Culture*, ed. J. Clarke, C. Critcher, and R. Johnson (London: Hutchinson, 1979).

12   See J. Richards, *The Age of Dream Palace: Cinema and Society in Britain 1930–1939* (London: Routledge, 1984), especially chap. 10.

13   Ibid., especially chap. 11.

14   See F. Donaldson, *Edward VIII*, as quoted in Paul Fussell, *Abroad: British Literary Travelling between the Wars* (Oxford: Oxford University Press, 1980), p. 74.

15   It is interesting to note that the term "Wigan Pier" was coined by George Formby Sr. who ironically confounded the grime of a mining town with the delights of a seaside resort (see J. Richards, *The Age of the Dream Palace*, p. 191).

16   N. Elias, *The Civilizing Process, Volume I: The History of Manners* (Oxford: Blackwell, 1978). See also Pierre Bourdieu, *Distinction: A Social Critique of the Judgement of Taste*, trans. R. Nice (London: Routledge, 1984), and M. Featherstone, *Consumer Culture and Postmodernism* (London: Sage, 1991), especially chap. 9.

17   S. Laing, *Representations of Working Class Life 1957–1964* (London: Macmillan, 1986), p. 47.

18   See S. Laing and P. Stead, *Film and the Working Class* (London: Routledge, 1989).

19   B. Martin, *A Sociology of Contemporary Cultural Change* (Oxford: Blackwell, 1981), p. 71.

20   V. Turner, *The Ritual Process: Structure and Anti-Structure* (Harmondsworth: Allen Lane, 1969).

21   S. Hall, "Old and New Identities," in *Culture, Globalization and the World-System*, ed. A. King (London: Macmillan, 1991), p. 46.

22   Geoffrey Pearson, "Lawlessness, Modernity, and Social Change," *Theory, Culture, and Society* 2, no. 3 (1985).

23   Bryan Turner, "A Note on Nostalgia," *Theory, Culture, and Society* 4, no. 1 (1987).

24   See Featherstone, *Consumer Culture*, especially chap. 9.

25   M. Halbwachs, *On Collective Memory* (Chicago: University of Chicago Press, 1992). See also D. Middleton and D. Edwards, eds., *Collective Remembering* (London: Sage, 1990).

26   T. Brennan, "The National Longing for Form," in *Nation and Narration*, ed. Homi Bhabha (London: Routledge, 1990), p. 45.

27   Raymond Williams, *Towards 2000* (London: Chatto and Windus, 1983), p. 180; as quoted in Brennan, "The National Longing," *Nation and Narration*, p. 45.

28   Benedict Anderson, *Imagined Communities* (rev. ed., London: Verso, 1991), p. 6.

29   A. D. Smith, "Towards a Global Culture?" *Theory, Culture, and Society* 5, no. 2–3 (1990).

30   See P. Burke, *Popular Culture in Early Modern Europe* (London: Temple Smith, 1978).

31   See E. Gellner, *Nations and Nationalism* (Oxford: Blackwell, 1983); see also Benedict Anderson, *Imagined Communities*.

32   See S. F. Moore, "The Production of Cultural Pluralism as a Process," *Public Culture* 1, no. 2 (1989); see also, A. Higson, "The Concept of National Cinema," *Screen* 30, no. 4 (1989).

33   P. Watier, "The War Writings of Georg Simmel," *Theory, Culture & Society* 8, no. 3 (1991).

34   S. Moscovici, "Questions for the Twenty-First Century," *Theory, Culture & Society* 7, no. 4 (1990).

35   See Cohen, *The Symbolic Construction of Community*.

36   N. Elias and J. Scotson, *The Established and the Outsiders* (London: Cass, 1965; rev. ed., London: Sage, 1995).

37 See Cohen, *The Symbolic Construction of Community*.

38 See Arnason, "Nationalism, Globalization and Modernity," in *Global Culture*, ed. M. Featherstone (London: Sage, 1990).

39 See Smith, "Towards a Global Culture?"

40 See N. Sakai, "Modernity and Its Critique: The Problem of Universalism and Particularism," in *Postmodernism and Japan*, ed. H. Harootunian and M. Myoshi (Durham, N.C.: Duke University Press, 1989); see also Mitsuhiro Yoshimoto, "Postmodernism and Mass Images in Japan," *Public Culture* 1 (1989): 8–25.

41 See M. Maruyama, *Thought and Behavior in Japanese Politics* (London: Oxford University Press, 1969); see also Johann Arnason, "The Modern Constellation and the Japanese Enigma," Parts I and II, Theses Eleven 17 and Eleven 18 (n.p., 1987).

42 See R. White, *Inventing Australia* (Sydney: Allen and Unwin, 1981); J. Fiske, B. Hodge, and G. Turner, eds., *Myths of Oz* (Sydney: Allen and Unwin, 1987); A. Game, "Nation and Identity: Bondi," *New Formations* 11 (1990).

43 David Chaney, "The Symbolic Form of Ritual in Mass Communications," in *Communicating Politics*, ed. P. Golding (Leicester: Leicester University Press, 1986).

44 D. Dayan and E. Katz, "Articulating Consensus: The Ritual and Rhetoric of Media Events," in *Durkheimian Sociology: Cultural Studies*, ed. J. Alexander (Cambridge: Cambridge University Press, 1988).

45 See Higson, "The Concept of National Cinema."

46 See A. Gupta and J. Ferguson, "Beyond 'Culture': Space Identity and the Politics of Difference," *Cultural Anthropology* 7, no. 1 (1992).

47 See Arnason, "Nationalism, Globalization and Modernity."

48 See A. Bergesen, "Turning World-System Theory on Its Head," in *Global Culture*, ed. M. Featherstone (London: Sage, 1990).

49 See H. Haferkampf, "Beyond the Iron Cage of Modernity," *Theory, Culture & Society* 4, no. 1 (1987). Some of these criticisms apply to the recent work of Anthony Giddens on modernity (*The Consequences of Modernity* [Oxford: Polity Press, 1990] and *Modernity and Self-Identity* [Oxford: Polity Press, 1991]). For a critique of his neglect of the cultural dimension and assumption that globalization is merely modernity writ large, see Roland Robertson "Social Theory, Cultural Relativity and the Problem of Globality," in *Culture, Globalization, and the World-System*, ed. A. D. King (New York: Macmillan, 1991).

50 K. Knorr Cetina, "Primitive Classification and Postmodernity: Towards a Sociological Notion of Fiction," *Theory, Culture & Society* 11, no. 3 (1994).

51 See Featherstone, *Consumer Culture*.

52 G. Vattimo, *The End of History* (Oxford: Polity Press, 1988).

53 See R. Robertson, "Globality and Modernity," *Theory, Culture & Society* 9, no. 2 (1992); *Globalization* (London: Sage, 1992); R. Robertson, "On the Concept of Globalization: The Limitations of the Local-Global Distinction," mimeo, University of Pittsburgh.

54 V. Gessner and A. Schade, "Conflicts of Culture in Cross-border Legal Relations," *Theory, Culture & Society* 7, nos. 2–3 (1990).

55 Y. Dezalay, "The *Big Bang* and the Law," in *Global Culture,* ed. M. Featherstone (London: Sage, 1990).

56 A. King, "Architecture, Capital and the Globalization of Culture," in *Global Culture,* ed. M. Featherstone.

57 See A. King, *Global Cities* (London: Routledge, 1990); S. Sassen, *Global Cities: New York, London, Tokyo* (Princeton, N.J.: Princeton University Press, 1991); S. Zukin, *Landscapes of Power: From Detroit to Disney* (Berkeley: University of California Press).

58 J. Tomlinson, *Cultural Imperialism* (London: Pinter, 1991).

59 P. Iyer, *Video Nights in Kathmandu* (London: Black Swan, 1989), p. 12.

60 Paul Theroux, *The Happy Isles of Oceania: Paddling the Pacific* (New York: Putnam, 1992), p. 178.

61 U. Hannerz, "Scenarios for Peripheral Cultures," in *Culture, Globalization and the World-System,* ed. A. King (London: Macmillan, 1991).

62 Meaghan Morris "Banality in Cultural Studies," in *Logics of Television,* ed. P. Mellencamp (Bloomington: Indiana University Press, 1990).

63 D. Morley, "Where the Global Meets the Local: Notes from the Sitting Room," *Screen* 32, no. 1 (1991).

64 J. Meyrowitz, *No Sense of Place* (Oxford: Oxford University Press, 1985).

65 Morley, "Where the Global Meets the Local," p. 9.

66 Ibid., p. 10.

67 Mary Douglas and Baron Isherwood, *The World of Goods* (Harmondsworth: Penguin, 1980).

68 See M. Canevacci, "Image Accumulation and Cultural Syncretism," *Theory, Culture & Society* 9, no. 3 (1992). Canevacci, for example, mentions how the Brasillian Indios at Iguacu Falls not only were fans of Italian football and identified with Rud Guillot of Milan, but also used video cameras both to communicate amongst themselves and to produce images for the outside world.

69 Quoted in Morley, "Where the Global Meets the Local," p. 15.

70 Robertson, "On the Concept of Globalization"; see also, T. Luke, "New World Order or New World Orders? Power, Politics and Ideology in the Informationalizing Global Order," in *Global Modernities,* ed. M. Featherstone, S. Lash, and R. Robertson (London: Sage, 1995).

71 A. Appadurai, "Disjunction and Difference in the Global Cultural Economy," *Theory, Culture & Society* 7, nos. 2–3 (1990).

72 E. Berner and R. Korff, "Strategies and Counter-Strategies: Globalization and Localization from the Perspective of the Sociology of Group Conflict," mimeo, University of Bielefeld, 1992.

73 See P. Cooke, "Modernity, Postmodernity and the City"; see also, S. Zukin, "The Postmodern Debate over Urban Form," *Theory, Culture & Society* 5, nos. 2–3 (1988).

74 See A. King, "The Times and Spaces of Modernity," in *Global Modernities.*

75 H. K. Bhabha, "'Race,' Time and the Revision of Modernity," *Oxford Literary Review* 13 (1991).

76   This is not just a question of the flow between the West as the center and "the rest" as the periphery. As J. Abu-Lughod has indicated, we have to consider the proliferation of multiple cores and especially how the cultures of the rising cores in Asia are diffusing within their own circuits ("Going Beyond the Global Babble," in *Culture, Globalization and the World-System,* ed. A. D. King [London: Macmillan, 1991]). This also means raising the question of the relations between the hosts and migrants into these new cores—for example Japan.

77   S. Hall, "The Question of Cultural Identity," in *Modernity and Its Futures,* ed. S. Hall, D. Held, and T. McGrew (Oxford: Polity Press, 1992).

78   Ibid., p. 308.

79   S. Hall, "Old Identities and New," p. 60.

80   On multiple and dispersed identities, see G. Marcus, "Past, Present and Emergent Identities: Requirements for Ethnography in Late Twentieth Century Modernity," in *Modernity and Identity,* ed. S. Lash and J. Friedman (Oxford: Blackwell, 1992); on cultural dislocation, see Gupta and Ferguson, " 'Beyond' Culture."

81   M. Maffesoli, *Le Temps des tribus* (Paris: Klinckcieck, 1988; English translation forthcoming, London: Sage, 1995).

82   See also discussions in Z. Bauman, *Modernity and Ambivalence* (Oxford: Polity Press, 1991).

83   See D. Maybury-Lewis, "On the Importance of Being Tribal," *Utne Reader* 52 (July–August 1992); *Millennium: Tribal Wisdom and the Modern World* (New York: Viking Penguin, 1992).

84   J. Urry, "The Tourist Gaze and the 'Environment,' " *Theory, Culture & Society* 9, no. 3 (1992).

85   U. Hannerz, "Cosmopolitans and Locals in World Culture," *Theory, Culture & Society* 7, nos. 2–3 (1990); see also, Bauman, *Modernity and Ambivalence.*

86   J. Urry, *The Tourist Gaze* (London: Sage, 1990).

87   For discussion of Walt Disney World, see S. J. Fjellman, *Vinyl Leaves: Walt Disney World and America* (Boulder, Colo.: Westview Press, 1992).

88   D. Ley, "Modern, Post-Modernism and the Struggle for Place," in *The Power of Place,* ed. J. A. Agnew and J. A. Duncan (Boston: Unwin Hyman, 1989).

89   D. MacCannell, *Empty Meeting Grounds: The Tourist Papers* (London: Routledge, 1992), chap. 8.

90   Ibid., p. 18.

91   See N. C. Lutkehaus, " 'Excuse Me, Everything is Not All Right: An Interview with Filmmaker Dennis O'Rourke," *Cultural Anthropology* 4, no. 4 (1989); E. M. Brunner, "Of Cannibals, Tourists, and Ethnographers," *Cultural Anthropology* 4, no. 4 (1989); see also MacCannell, *Empty Meeting Grounds.*

92   MacCannell, *Empty Meeting Grounds,* p. 31.

93   J. Friedman, "Being in the World: Globalization and Localization," p. 320.

94   J. Friedman, "Narcissism, Roots and Postmodernity: The Constitution of Selfhood in the Global Crisis."

95   For a further account of the complexity of localized identities, see John Kirkpatrick, "Trials of Identity in America," *Cultural Anthropology* 4, no. 3 (1989): 301–311.

96   Anthony D. King, "The Times and Spaces of Modernity (or, Who Needs Postmodernism?)" in *Global Modernities*, ed. M. Featherstone, et al. (London: Sage, 1995).

97   G. Obeyeskere, *The Apotheosis of Captain Cook* (Princeton, N.J.: Princeton University Press, 1992).

98   John Tagg, "Globalization, Totalization, and the Discursive Field," in *Culture, Globalization, and the World-System* (London: Macmillan, 1991).

99   See N. Elias, *Involvement and Detachment* (Oxford: Blackwell, 1987); see also, Moore, "The Production of Cultural Pluralism."

100   Jonathan Friedman, "Cultural Logics of the Global System," *Theory, Culture, and Society* 5, nos. 2–3 (1988).

101   Ibid.

102   Stephen Mennell, *Norbert Elias* (Oxford: Blackwell, 1989).

103   See Michel Serres, *Rome: The Book of Foundations* (Stanford: Stanford University Press, 1991).

A BORDERLESS WORLD?

FROM COLONIALISM TO TRANSNATIONALISM AND THE DECLINE OF THE NATION-STATE

Masao Miyoshi

●

Discourse and practice are interdependent. Practice follows discourse, while discourse is generated by practice. As for the discourse on colonialism, there is a long lineage of engagements with the history of colonialism. One recalls papers by practitioners such as John Locke, Edmund Burke, James Mill, and Thomas Macaulay early on, and critiques of the practice by Hobson, Lenin, Luxemburg, and Schumpeter among many others since the height of imperialism. Numerous metropolitan fiction writers are obsessed by the presence of remote colonies from Melville and Flaubert to Conrad and Gide. Actually, hardly any Western writer from Jane Austen to Thomas Mann, from Balzac to D. H. Lawrence could manage to escape from the spell of modern expansionism. The modern West depends on its colonies for self-definition, as Edward Said's newest book, *Culture and Imperialism,* argues.[1]

In the area of literary theory and criticism, however, the discourse on colonialism has a surprisingly brief history. One needs to remember that writers of the Negritude Movement and other Third World writers such as Aimé Césaire, C. L. R. James, Frantz Fanon, and George Lamming[2] began to voice their views from the oppositionist perspective soon after the end of World War II.[3] And, yet, it was only fifteen years ago—well after the disappearance of administrative colonization from most regions of the world—that the discourse on colonialism entered the mainstream of Western theory and criticism.[4] Examining history from the perspective of personal commitment to resistance, Said's *Orientalism* in 1978 dramatically heightened the consciousness of power and culture relations, vitally affecting segments of disciplines in the humanities.[5] In other words, it was not until years after the end of formal colonialism between 1945 and 1970 that theory was enabled to negotiate issues of colonialism as an admissible factor in criticism. The time gap of a good many decades in literary history is interesting enough if only because it demonstrates the discipline's habitual unease and disinclination in recent times to engage with extratextual matters, especially those concerning the imminent transfer of powers and resources. The history of decolonization and the memory of administrative and occupational colonialism, dangerously verging on nostalgia at times, form the base on which colonial and minority discourses have been built in recent years.[6]

The circumstances surrounding this process of "liberation" and "independence," however, have no widely accepted narrative as yet. Does colonialism only survive today in a few places such as Israel, South Africa, Macao, Ireland, and Hong Kong? Does the rest of the world enjoy the freedom of postcolonialism? The problem we face now is how to understand today's global configuration of power and culture that is both similar and different vis-à-vis the historical metropolitan-colonial paradigm. This paper is concerned with such transformation and persistence in the neocolonial practice of displacement and ascendancy and with its specular engagements in discourse. The current academic preoccupation with "postcoloniality" and multiculturalism looks suspiciously like another alibi to conceal the actuality of global politics. This paper argues that colonialism is even more active now in the form of transnational corporatism.

We might begin with the beginning of the decolonization process.[7] The end of the cold war in 1989 has enabled us to look back at the history of the past half-century—or even longer—from a perspective informed by truly radical change. We are, for instance, once again reassessing the end of World War II, which fundamentally altered the world system. The destruction of German and Japanese aggressions did not result in the full resuscitation of the hegemony of the European industrial states. The Western European nations, especially Britain and France, were too fatally injured to be able simultaneously to rebuild their domestic industrial bases and to sustain their military forces to dominate their colonies. In retrospect, we see that the Soviet Union kept up the front of a military superpower while disastrously wrecking its production and distributive systems. The avowed war objective of Germany and Japan—liberation and decolonization through a new world order (*die neue Ordnung* and *sekai shin chitsujo* in Axis slogans)—was a total sham; the colonized of the world that had sided with their master states in World War II seized the day and would not settle for less than independence and autonomy. Liberation was demanded and allowed to take place over several subsequent decades, albeit under varying circumstances.

After World War II, independence appeared to have ended the humiliating and exploitive colonial domination that had lasted anywhere from decades to centuries in countries covering at least 85 percent of the earth's land surface. And yet freedom and self-rule—for which the colonized had bitterly struggled often at the cost of immense sacrifice—were unexpectedly elusive. Decolonization neither effected emancipation and equality nor provided new wealth or peace. Instead, suffering and misery continued nearly everywhere in an altered form, at the hands of different agencies. Old *compradors* took over, and it was far from rare that they went on to protect their old masters' interest in exchange for compensation. Thus the welfare of the general population saw little improvement; in fact, in recent years it has worsened in many old-colonies with the possible exceptions of the East Asian Newly Industrialized Economies (NIES) and the Association of Southeast Asian Nations (ASEAN).[8] The "postcolonial" deterioration that Basil Davidson recently called "the black man's burden" was a result of double processes of colonization and decolonization, which were inextricably intermeshed.[9] We are all familiar with the earlier stage. As the colonizers drew borders at will, inscribing their appropriation on a map, tribes were joined or fragmented. Those who were encircled by a more or less arbitrary cartographic form were inducted into servitude on behalf of the distant and unseen metropolis. Western culture was to be the normative civilization, and the indigenous cultures were banished as premodern and marginal. And although subaltern resistance proved far more resilient than anticipated, and colonial programs were never really fulfilled anywhere, the victor's presence was powerful enough in most places to maintain a semblance of control and order despite unceasing resistance and opposition.

With the removal of formal colonialism after World War II, the cartographic unit that constituted a colony was now perceived both by the departing colonizers and the newly freed to be a historically autonomous territory, that is to say, a modern nation-state, with a national history, national language, national culture, national coherence, and finally a state apparatus of its own as symbolized by a national anthem, flag, museum, and map. The entity was, however, no more than a counterfeit reproduction of, and by, its former conqueror in many places, having neither a discrete history nor logic that would convince the newly independent citizens of its legitimacy or authenticity. Earlier, while struggling against the oppressors, self-definition was not difficult to obtain: opposition articulated their identity. Once the Europeans were gone, however, the residents of a colonial territory were thrown back on their old disrupted site that had in the precolonial days operated on a logic and history altogether different. The liberated citizens of a colony now had to renegotiate the conditions of a nation-state in which they were to reside thereafter. Retroversion to nativism might have been an option, but the Third World was fraught with inequalities and contradictions among various religions, tribes, regions, classes, gender, and ethnicities that had been thrown together in any given colonial territory. And production and distribution were often horrendously inefficient. The golden age of a nation-state's memory proved to be neither pure nor just, nor even available, but a utopian dream often turned into a bloody nightmare. The hatred of the oppressors was enough to mobilize toward liberation but was inadequate for the management of an independent state. As Fanon had predicted early in the game, attempts at nativism indeed ended in disastrous corruption and self-destruction, and they are still ongoing events in many parts of the world. Once absorbed into the "chronopolitics" of the secular West, colonized space cannot reclaim autonomy and seclusion; once dragged out of their precolonial state, the indigenes of peripheries have to deal with the knowledge of the outside world, irrespective of their own wishes and inclinations. And yet the conditions of the modern nation-state are not available to most former colonies.[10]

One recalls that Western industrialized nations had the luxury of several centuries—however bloody—to resolve civil strifes, religious wars, and rural/urban or agricultural/industrial contradictions. Former colonies had far less time to work them out, and they had been under the domination of alien powers. Thus most former colonies have yet to agree on the logic and objective of a geographic and demographic unit. The will to fragmentation battles with the will to totalization. One cannot forget that there were countless cases of overt and covert interventions by the United States and other colonial powers through economic, political, and military means. Peaceful progress has been structurally denied to them. Alliances among Third World states against First World domination, such as the Bandung Conference (1955), the Organization of Petroleum Exporting Countries (OPEC, 1960), UN Conference on Trade and Development (UNCTAD, 1964), and the New International Economic Order (NIEO, 1974), have all performed poorly, ultimately surrendering to the Bretton Woods system, which the victorious West established in 1944 for the postwar management of the ruined world with the World Bank, International Monetary Fund (IMF), and General Agreement on Tariffs and Trade (GATT) as the three central economic instruments.

It is widely agreed that the nation-state is a modern Western construction. It can be further argued that the gradual ascendancy of the nation-state around 1800 in the West was a function of colonialism. Earlier at the beginning of the modern period, the European monarchs sponsored adventurist projects, which were further propelled thereafter by the bourgeoisie's greater need for markets and resources to form a policy of colonial expansion. About the same time, as the industrial revolution increased production efficiency, urban areas received the influx of a large percentage of agricultural labor, creating a pool of surplus population.[11] These potentially rebellious unemployed and displaced workers needed to be depressurized in the marginal areas of the labor market. Toward that end, the organizers of colonialism had to persuade their recruits and foot soldiers about the profitability as well as the nobility of their mission. Voyaging into distant and savage regions of the world was frightening enough, and the prospects of sharing the loot were far from assured. Above all, bourgeois leaders had to conceal their class interests, which sharply conflicted with the interests of the population at large. They needed crusaders and supporters who trusted their good faith, believed in the morality of their mission, and hoped for the eventual wealth promised for them. Thus they made the myth of the nation-state (that is, the belief in the shared community ruled by a representative government) and the myth of *mission civilisatrice* (that is, the voyagers' racial superiority over the heathen barbarians) seem complementary and indispensable. In such an "imagined [or manufactured] community," the citizens were bound by kinship and communality; they were in it together.[12] In the very idea of the nation-state, the colonialists found a politicoeconomical as well as moral-mythical foundation on which to build their policy and apology.

Thus the development of Western colonialism from the sixteenth to the middle of the twentieth century coincides with the rise and fall of the nation-state. The fate of the nation-state in recent years, however, is not synonymous with the "rise and fall of the great powers," as Paul Kennedy argues.[13] The bourgeois capitals in the industrialized world are now as powerful, or even far more powerful, than before. But the logic they employ, the clients they serve, the tools available to them, the sites they occupy, in short, their very identities, have all changed. They no longer wholly depend on the nation-state of their origin for protection and facilitation. They still make use of the nation-state structure, of course, but their power and energy reside in a different locus, as I will argue later on.

Even before 1945, Winston Churchill sensed that Britain had to yield its imperial scepter to the United States. If not at the Yalta Conference, by the time he was voted out of 10 Downing Street he knew the management of the world was now in the hands of the United States. He was of course right. Colonial history since 1945 converges with U.S. history. At the end of World War II, the United States economy was finally free from all scars of the Depression. In peacetime, however, prospects were far from rosy. To downscale wartime economy would mean a drastic rise in unemployment (a minuscule 1.2 percent in 1942) as well as an absolute plunge in production and consumption, resurrecting the nightmare of 1930. There were a series of labor strikes (steel, coal, rail, and port) in 1946; President Truman's veto of the Taft-Hartley Labor Act, which sought to curb strikes, was overturned by the Congress in 1947. It was under such circumstances of economic tension and unease that the president decided to contain "Communist terrorism" in Greece and Turkey in 1947, and the Marshall Plan was inaugurated to aid European reconstruction. The GNP had sunk ominously by 19 percent in 1946 but only by 2.8 percent in 1947; and if it remained at a stagnant 0.02 percent in 1949, the Korean War (whose origins are not as yet unambiguous)[14] saved the day: the GNP rose by 8.5 percent in 1950 and 10.3 percent in 1951.[15] Similarly, just about the time the peace treaty with North Korea was signed in 1953 (and resulted in a minor recession), the United States began to aid the French government in its anti-insurgency war in Southeast Asia, shouldering 75 percent of the cost; and the training of South Vietnamese troops commenced in 1955 after the catastrophic defeat of the French army at Dien Bien Phu in 1954. When President Eisenhower warned Americans against "the potential for the disastrous rise of misplaced power" in the hands of the "military-industrial complex" and the "scientific-technological elite," the security state system had already been firmly—perhaps irretrievably—established in the United States.[16] (One notes that this was the decade in which the universities expanded to absorb the returned GIs, lowering the female-male college attendance ratio well below the level in the 1920s.[17] And in literary theory and practice, conservative ideology and formalist aestheticism of course dominated.)

The cold war, regularly reinforced by hot "anti-Communist" skirmishes, then, was a dependable instrument for the U.S. economy to organize its revenues and expenditures and to maintain a certain level of production and distribution. One notes in this connection that "in every year from 1951 to 1990, the Defense Department budget has exceeded the combined net profits of all American corporations." The U.S. Constitution does not accord the president the top economic power; "nevertheless, he has acquired that capacity from his role as chief executive officer of the military economy's management. Subordinate to the president/CEO are the managers of 35,000 prime contracting firms and about 100,000 subcontractors. The Pentagon uses 500,000 people in its own Central Administrative Office acquisition network."[18] The Pentagon, in short, is the U.S. equivalent of Japan's Ministry of International Trade and Industry (MITI); it plans and executes a centrally organized economic policy. Thus it is more accurate to say that national security questions were essentially economic in nature. The U.S. economy, rather than merely reacting to uncontrollable foreign threats, actually guided world relations.

Soon after the recession in 1957 and 1958, the Kennedy administration sought to expand international trade by lowering the European Community tariffs through the GATT Kennedy Round. The so-called liberalization of trade in the early 1960s restored the integrated world market and encouraged direct foreign investment. The result was a marked rise in European investment by American enterprises. Such an expansion in international trade led to a rapid development of "multinational enterprises" and "transnational corporations," that is, giant companies that not only import and export raw and manufactured goods but also transfer capital, factories, and sales outlets across national borders, as will be explained more fully later on. And this history of economic organizations needs to be recalled here in the context of global decolonization.

The fracture of the British empire was accelerating throughout the 1960s with the loss of innumerable colonies one after another—from Cyprus, Nigeria, and Kenya to Jamaica, Malaysia, and Singapore.[19] Having lost Indochina and other colonies in the 1950s, France finally yielded Algeria in 1962. At the same time, the U.S. GNP increased at a brisk pace of 7 to 9 percent with fairly low inflation and unemployment rates. Economically and militarily invincible, the United States was ready to protect capitalist interests everywhere, but especially in Vietnam. If President Johnson tried to win support for his Great Society programs and the war on poverty by offering a Southeast Asian expedition to the conservative oppositions, his gamble was calamitous. As no one can easily forget, protests raged across the country, splitting the nation into doves and hawks, Clintons and Gores. On the antiwar demonstrators' enemy list, the names of defense-related corporations were conspicuous: General Motors, General Electric, Du Pont, and Dow Chemical, to name a few. And it is many of these corporations that began during the 1960s to set the pattern of systematic transfer of capital and factories overseas. There were other factors, too; technological innovations in automation, synthetic chemistry, and electronic engineering produced an enormous accumulation of capital and a remarkable improvement in communication and transportation as well. The U.S. policy of liberal trade was both a response to and an instigation of such a development.

In the late 1960s, the global domination of U.S. multinational corporations was unchallengeable. Mainly centered in the Western hemisphere, and less in Africa and Asia, U.S. foreign direct investment (FDI) amounted to a half of all the cross-border investments worldwide, far surpassing the British FDI that stood at 20 percent and the French FDI at less than 10 percent.[20] Transnational corporations meant U.S. transnationals then, and this pattern remained unchanged until the mid-1970s. The concentration of U.S. investments in Western Europe can be explained by four factors: high interest rates in Europe; the emergence of the European Economic Community (EEC); the U.S. tax laws favorable to overseas profits; and comparatively low costs of skilled labor in Europe. The serious task of controlling the world order for the West was still assigned to the U.S. government with its military and political programs of aid and intervention.[21]

Around 1970, European and Japanese transnational corporations (TNCs) emerged rapidly to compete with their U.S. counterparts, and their main target was none other than the advanced manufacturing industries in the United States itself. This bold move is explainable by several economic developments. First, the U.S. dollar was devalued after the Nixon administration froze wages and prices and suspended conversion of dollars into gold in 1971, making the U.S. attractive for foreign investment. Second, the U.S. market also became attractive again after the political instability and unpredictability in the rest of the world as a result of the fourth Middle East war of 1973 and its consequent oil embargo. Third, the European and Japanese industrial recovery was strong enough to wage a vigorous investment campaign in the United States. Finally, trade friction intensified in time, and European and Japanese manufacturers saw an advantage in building plants inside the U.S. market. The U.S. share of TNCs was still overwhelming, but in the 1980s it fell to 33 percent as against Britain at 18 percent, West Germany at 10 percent, and Japan at 8 percent.

In 1985 the United States negotiated a depreciation of the dollar at the G5 (or Group of 5) meeting in New York. The Plaza Agreement forced the dollar down by one half against the yen, raising Japan's currency value by 100 percent. Though aimed at an increase of U.S. export to Japan and a decrease of Japan's export to the United States, the measure was not really effective. Before long, moreover, Japanese TNCs realized the power of the strengthened yen, with which they proceeded to stage an aggressive campaign of investment, while cutting prices as much as they could to maintain their market share. What characterizes this stage of multinational development is, in addition to continued investment in the United States, a general concentration on four regional targets: tax havens (for example, Curacao in the Dutch Caribbean); OPEC nations; Asian NIES (South Korea, Taiwan, Hong Kong, and Singapore); and ASEAN countries (Thailand, Malaysia, Indonesia, the Philippines, Singapore, and Brunei). Many of these nations were ruled by authoritarian governments, which banned labor unions and opposition parties, thus achieving political "stability"—a minimal requirement for a large-scale TNC commitment. There has also been a gradual development of TNCs among OPEC, NIES, Mexico, and India, investing in each other as well as the United States. Also, small corporations (that is, those with capital outlays of between 100 and 500 million dollars) in both industrialized and less industrialized nations were active in transnationalizing their operations. And this coexistence of TNCs of various origins (including joint ventures) is what makes the analysis of economic hegemony so complicated and difficult.

What emerges from this is an increasingly tightly woven network of multinational investments among EC, North American, and East Asian countries, gradually transforming the multi*national* corporations into *trans*national corporations. The distinction between the two corporate categories is certainly problematic: the terms are frequently used interchangeably. If there are differences, they are more or less in the degrees of alienation from the countries of origin. The range of international trading might be explained developmentally as follows. First, domestic companies simply undertake export/import activities, linking up with local dealers. Then, the companies take over overseas distribution and carry out their manufacturing, marketing, and sale overseas. Finally, the transnational corporations denationalize their operations by moving the whole business system, including capital, personnel, and research and development. This final stage is reached when a corporation promotes loyalty to itself among shareholders, employees, and clients rather than to its country of origin or host countries. Thus, a multinational corporation (MNC) is one that is headquartered in a nation, operating in a number of countries. Its high-echelon personnel largely consists of the nationals of the country of origin, and the corporate loyalty is, though increasingly autonomous, finally tied to the home nation. A truly transnational corporation, on the other hand, might no longer be tied to its nation of origin but is adrift and mobile, ready to settle anywhere and exploit any state including its own, as long as the affiliation serves its own interest.[22]

Let me repeat here that a sharp distinction between a TNC and a MNC is impossible because the precise extent of the denationalization of a corporation is not readily determinable. There is, for instance, no systematic study of the TNC tax obligations as against their MNC counterparts or of their comparative patterns of foreign direct investment. MNCs are as self-regarding as TNCs; however, a recent tendency toward lesser national identification and greater corporate self-interest is discernible. In other words, despite the ongoing dependence on the state apparatus (for example, the military), multinational corporations are in the process of *de*nationalization and *trans*nationalization.

There are still relatively few corporations that completely fit the TNC specification, but there are examples such as Asea Brown Bovari among large-scale companies and Yaohan among smaller ones. Starting in Sweden, ABB, with annual revenues of over 25 billion dollars, has no geographic center.[23] Yaohan began as a Japanese grocery store chain, severed its Japanese ties, and moved first to Brazil and then—for now—to Hong Kong. It should be noted here that the corporate tax in Japan was 49.9 percent whereas in Hong Kong it stood at 16.5 percent in 1989.[24] Yaohan's chairman declares that his real target is the one billion Chinese in the twenty-first century.[25] Many MNCs on the other hand are alertly comparing opportunities in their home countries and host countries as they map out their strategies for maximizing profits.

TNCs of this type became more visible in the 1980s, although the loss of national sovereignty to the multinational companies had been discussed since the 1960s and even earlier.[26] That this development should take place in the 1980s was no accident. After President Carter's stagflation in the late 1970s, President Reagan had a clearly defined program to promote private interests, supposedly with the conviction that strong private sectors would necessarily benefit the populace as a whole (but, in all likelihood, by simply following the cue cards handed over by the corporate designers of the policy). During this decade the transfer of wealth from the poor to the rich was carried out with remarkable efficiency. Corporate taxes were cut. Public services such as education, welfare, and medicine were reduced in the name of efficiency, resulting in a marked reliance on private enterprises such as Federal Express and private security services instead of "inefficient" public institutions such as the U.S. Postal Service or municipal police departments. There even have been talks of privatizing penal systems and public universities.[27] This decade also witnessed the reduction of the income tax rates for the higher brackets. The top tax on wages in 1945 was 94 percent, and in the 1950s through the 1970s it was in the 87 to 70 percent range; with the advent of President Reagan's administration the top tax on wages fell to 50 percent, and in 1991 under Bush it stood at 28 percent.[28] Thus the top one percent of Americans received 60 percent of the after-tax income gains between 1977 and 1989, while the bottom 40 percent of families had actual declines in income. According to the May 6, 1991, issue of *Business Week,* the typical CEO's pay was more than eighty-five times that of a typical manufacturing worker's pay in the United States, while the comparable ratio in Japan was only seventeen times.[29] Kevin Phillips reports, however, that "the pay of top corporate executives . . . soared to 130 to 140 times that of average workers, even while real or inflation-adjusted wages continued their 1980's decline."[30] Examples of illicit and semi-illicit business practices are too many to be enumerated here—from dubious mergers and appropriations and junk-bond scams to the savings and loan industry scandal. The number of poor people in 1991 increased to 35.7 million, that is, 14.2 percent of the total population, which is the highest figure since 1964.[31] In such an atmosphere of intensified self-regard and self-interest, corporate managers took it for granted that their business was to maximize profits nearly regardless of consequences. They would go wherever there were lower taxes and greater profits.

It should be emphasized here that this move toward transnationalization was not just American but global. Leslie Sklair, in one of the most comprehensive studies of TNCs (from a Gramscian and feminist perspective), points out that "while there is no convincing evidence that the TNCs can bring salvation to the Third World, in many poor countries the TNCs are seen as responsible for the only bright spots in the economy and society. . . . [TNCs] are very widely sought after and they carry high prestige."[32] As mentioned earlier, not only industrialized nations but NIES and other economies also produce corporations that maximize profits by freely crossing national borders. However one may view the TNC practice, TNCs are not beholden to any nation-states but seek their own interests and profits globally. They represent neither their home countries nor their host nations but simply their own corporate selves.

There are of course many other contributing factors. TNCs are immensely powerful. Sklair points out that "in 1986, according to the World Bank, 64 out of 120 countries had a GDP (gross domestic product) of less than $10 billion. United Nations data for 1985–86 shows that 68 TNCs in mining and manufacturing had annual sales in excess of ten billion dollars, while all the top 50 banks, the top 20 securities firms, and all but one of the top 30 insurance companies had net assets in excess of ten billion" (S, pp. 48–49). That is, of the largest one hundred economic units, more than fifty are TNCs.[33] Because of the rapid development in sophisticated computer technology—often justifiably called the third industrial revolution—in communication, transportation, and manufacturing, the transfer of capital, products, facilities, and personnel has been unprecedentedly efficient. Private funds—to the amount of billions of dollars at one transaction—flow from one industrial center to another, totaling every business day nearly 1 trillion dollars at the Clearing House Interbank Payment System (CHIPS) in New York City alone.[34] It goes without saying that this development weakens the interventionary power of central national banks, such as the Bundes Bank of Germany, Nihon Ginko of Japan, and the Federal Reserve of the United States.

Post-Fordist production methods enable TNCs to move their factories to any sites that can offer trained and trainable cheap labor forces as long as there are tax inducements, political stability, adequate infrastructure, and relaxed environmental protection rules. Low civil rights consciousness, too, including underdeveloped unionism and feminism, is crucial; although female labor is abused everywhere, the wage difference between the sexes is still greater in the Third World—the target area for TNCs.[35] Global transportation is so efficient that the division of labor across national borders is now a given. Parts are produced in many places to be assembled—depending on particular tariffs, labor conditions, and other factors—at a locale strategically close to the targeted market.[36] There are innumerable joint ventures, such as GM and Toyota, or GE, RCA, and Thomson SA. Banks and other financial institutions also move across borders with increasingly fewer impediments.

In this MNC/TNC operation, at any rate, manufactured products are advertised and distributed globally, being identified only with the brand names, not the countries of origin. In fact, the country of origin is itself becoming more and more meaningless. The "Buy American" drive is increasingly a hollow battle plan: the Honda Accord is manufactured in Ohio from 75 percent U.S.-made parts, while the Dodge Stealth is made in Japan by Mitsubishi.[37] "In the new Boeing 777 program, the Boeing Company is manufacturing only the wings, nose structure, and engine nacelles. The rest of the wide-body airplane will come from hundreds of subcontractors in North America, Japan, and Europe."[38] Almost no TV sets are wholly domestic products. It was announced in 1992 that "Zenith Electronics Corp., the last U.S.-owned television company, is moving final assembly of all of its large-screen sets to Mexico."[39] A TNC selects the place of operation, in short, solely by a fine calculus of costs and profits, involving the entire process of research, development, production, distribution, advertising, marketing, financing, and tax obligations.

TNCs are faced with the task of recruiting workers thoroughly familiar with local rules and customs as well as the specific corporate policies for worldwide operation. For that purpose, their workers usually are of various nationalities and ethnicities. This aspect is significant in several ways. First, TNCs will increasingly require from all workers loyalty to the corporate identity rather than to their own national identities. Second, employees of various nationalities and ethnicities must be able to communicate with each other. In that sense, TNCs are at least officially and superficially trained to be color-blind and multicultural.[40] Despite the persistent recurrence of violent racist events in the United States, its immigration regulations were radically changed in 1965 to reject the ethnically defined quota system set out by the 1952 McCarran-Walter Act. In the revised Immigration Reform and Control Act of 1986 and the November 1990 reform bill, priorities are given to skills rather than ethnicities. TNCs, especially, are allowed to claim a quota from the category of 40,000 aliens with special abilities in addition to the general category of skilled experts and professionals.[41] Third, the need of a huge pool of such skilled workers creates a transnational class of professionals who can live and travel globally, while freely conversing with their colleagues in English, the lingua franca of the TNC era. The formation of the transnational class, or what Robert Reich calls "symbolic analysts" in his *The Work of Nations,* is itself a development that calls for further study, especially as this exclusive and privileged class relates—or does not relate—to those kept outside: the unemployed, the underemployed, the displaced, and the homeless.[42] The third industrial revolution, very much like the earlier two, creates an immense semiskilled and unskilled surplus labor, causing a huge demographic movement across the world and feeding into the mass underclass in every industrialized region.

Reich has little to say about the fate that awaits those who won't be able to move up to the class of privilege. The question remains, then, as to how the new elite managers compare to the professional class of modern industrial society and how they relate to those left marginalized and abandoned in the TNC structure.

Earlier, as traditional society transformed itself into bourgeois capitalist society in the West, intellectuals and professionals who served in the planning and execution of the capitalist agenda were led to think of themselves as free and conscientious critics and interpreters. In the age of TNCs, they are even more shielded and mediated by the complexity and sophistication of the situation itself because transnational corporatism is by definition unprovincial and global, that is, supposedly free from insular and idiosyncratic constrictions. If clear of national and ethnic blinders, the TNC class is not free of a new version of "ideologyless" ideology that is bent on the efficient management of global production and consumption, hence of world culture itself. Are the intellectuals of the world willing to participate in transnational corporatism and be its apologists? How to situate oneself in this neo–Daniel Bell configuration of transnational power and culture without being trapped by a dead-end nativism seems to be the most important question that faces every critic and theorist the world over at this moment, a question to which I will return later.

The decline of the nation-state has been accelerated by the end of the cold war. War activates nationalism and patriotism inasmuch as hostility deepens the chasm that cuts "them" off from "us." The binary alignment that was present in all foreign relations during the cold war was abruptly removed in 1989. With the demise of authoritarian socialist states, bourgeois capitalism looked as if it had triumphed over all rivals. Whether such a reading is right or wrong, the disappearance of "the other side," together with the end of administrative colonialism, has placed the nation-state in a vacant space that is ideologically uncontested and militarily constabularized. The choreographed display of high-tech destruction by the United States during the Gulf War could not conceal the lack of objective and meaning in that astounding military exercise. The Gulf War was the war of ultimate snobbery, all style, demonstrating power for the sake of power in a world after the cold war. The war expressed the contempt of the rich for the poor, just as military and political force were being replaced in importance by economic and industrial power. The single superpower, the United States, executed the war, of course, but as the "sharing" of the military expenses among the "allied nations" demonstrates, the war was fought on behalf of the dominant corporate structure rather than the United States, which seemed after all as no more than a mercenary. Does this mean that from now on the armed forces of the United States are in service of a corporate alliance with little regard for its own people's interests? Is the state apparatus being even more sharply cut off from the welfare of the people than before? Wealth that generates right and might seems to have overwhelmed power that creates wealth.[43]

Against the effective operation of TNCs, the nation-states more and more look undefined and inoperable. Although the end of the cold war also loosened the ties that bound nation-states such as the Soviet Union and Yugoslavia while encouraging separatist movements in Scotland, Spain, India, Canada, and many other places, these are expressions of ethnicism, not nationalism.[44] To quote from *The New International Economy,* these independence movements are "a kind of mirrored reflection of the decline of the viability of nationalism as a politically unifying force, a decline occasioned moreover, by the economic and political internationalization."[45]

Admittedly, it is more customary nowadays to regard as "nationalistic" the "ethnic cleansing" by the Serbs, the Muslim and Hindu antagonism in India, or Islamic fundamentalism, but it seems at least as sensible to think of such neorevivalism, neoracism, and neoethnicism in conjunction with the decline of the nation-state. The fragmenting and fragmented units in these sites of contestation in the world are newly awakened agents not for the construction of autonomous nations but for the abandonment of the expectations and responsibilities of the politicoeconomic national projects. Ethnicity and raciality are being brandished as the refuge from the predicaments of an integrated political and economic body. As globalization intensifies, neoethnicism is appealing because of its brute simplicity and reductivism in this rapidly altering and bewilderingly complex age. But over all the separatist aspirations—from Czechoslovakia, Yugoslavia, India, and Myanmar—hover the dark shadows of economic anxieties that none of these "nationalist" units have sufficiently recognized as they rush toward independence and purification. It is as if the inadequacy of the nation-state is now fully realized, and the provincial strongmen are all trying to grab a piece of real estate for keeps before all is incorporated and appropriated by transnational corporations.

Those who have thought of the nation-state as a historical bourgeois invention for the sake of protecting a national economy from the threats of free democracy might hail transnationalism's negative effect on the nation-state. To the extent that war was an unavoidable product of national economy, as argued by Marx in his 1848 *Communist Manifesto,* there is something exhilarating about the demise of the nation-state. At the same time, the state did, and still does, perform certain functions, for which there is as of now no substitute agency. It defines citizenship, controls currency, imposes law, protects public health, provides general education, maintains security, and, more important, guides the national economy (though little acknowledged in the United States, as I pointed out earlier), all with revenues raised through taxation. In enumerating these functions, however, it becomes indisputably clear that the list is not a list of achievements but of failures. In all these items, the state as a political authority seems biased and compromised. It is not the nation as an integrated whole but certain classes, the privileged in it, that receive a major portion of benefits from the state performing these tasks. The state fails to satisfy most of its sectors and leaves most of its citizenry resentful. Thus, there is a palpable aversion to taxation among all segments of population, rich or poor, although everyone knows that tax is the glue that keeps the nation-state coherent. The nation-state, in this sense, no longer works; it is thoroughly appropriated by transnational corporations. Thus for some, it is a sheer annoyance, but for a vast majority it serves as a nostalgic and sentimental myth that offers an illusion of a classless organic community of which everyone is an equal member. Such an illusion of national community stubbornly persists.

Let me give one more example of the use of the concept of nation-states. The formation of a highly complex web across national borders of industrial production and distribution—in a word, transnationalization—largely invalidates disputes over surpluses and deficits in trade. Reich rightly argues that wealth is accumulated at the site where managers and technicians carry out research and development, not where the corporations or manufactured goods originate.[46] As I mentioned above, the identification of the countries of origin of manufactured goods is becoming increasingly impossible, and parts of a product come from all over. The "local content" regulations are nearly impossible to enforce. The United States, for instance, imports as much as 30 percent from U.S. transplants overseas that have been established over the last several decades.[47] Further, MNCs and TNCs are indifferent as they create regions of poverty in the middle of their own countries of origin such as the United States and Britain. It is quite possible to argue that the trade protectionists, such as the so-called revisionists in the U.S.-Japan trade discourse, are conscious or unconscious participants in a patriotic scam to conceal the class interests involved in the bilateral trade friction. Protectionism benefits certain sectors of industry and hurts others, just as free trade does. In other words, protectionism and free trade grant favors to different portions of industry in the short run, although protectionism invariably hurts the consumers. Only when the coherence of a total nation-state is unswervingly desired and maintained can the practice of protectionism persuade the population at large. In the present world, however, there is no example of such unquestioned national coherence—not even the notorious Japan, Inc. The "revisionists" merely stir the residual patriotic sentiment so that they can keep the illusion of national unity a while longer.[48]

TNCs are obviously not agents of progress for humanity. First, since the raison d'être of TNCs is maximum profits, the welfare of the people they leave behind, or even the people in the area where they operate, is of little or no concern to them. The host governments that are eager to invite TNCs cannot be expected to be particular about the workers' employment conditions or the general citizens' public welfare. The framework of the nation-state is deteriorating also in the host nations that are often controlled by dictators and oligarchs. All TNCs are finally in alliance, though competitive in several basic aspects.[49] The transnational class is self-concerned, though aggressively extroverted in cross-border movement. Labor unions, which might be expected to offer assistance to workers, on the other hand, still operate within the framework of a national economy. It is at present simply unthinkable that transnational labor unions will take joint actions across national borders, equalizing their wages and working conditions with their cross-border brothers and sisters. Imagine UAW officials meeting with Mexican union representatives to negotiate together a contract with the GM management in a *maquila* plant.[50] TNCs might raise GNP or even per capita income, but such a raise does not guarantee a better living for all citizens. So who finally protects the workers inside the United States or outside? The TNCs are far more transnational than the labor unions, generating the unemployed and underemployed everywhere, from Detroit to Manila, from Taipei to San Diego. There is little to be expected as of now from the residual nation-state or its alternatives in the way of protecting these people. What we have heard so far in relation to the North American Free Trade Agreement from the Bush administration, the Clinton administration, or U.S. university experts promises very little indeed.[51] As Sklair summarizes, "The choice is more likely to be between more or less efficient foreign exploitative transnational corporations and highly protected and perhaps corrupt local, state, parastatal or private firms" (*S*, p. 117).

Second, the rapid formation of the transnational class is likely to develop a certain homogeneity among its members. Even without the formation of TNCs, the world has been turning toward all-powerful consumerism in which brand names command recognition and attraction. Everywhere commodities are invented, transported, promoted, daydreamed over, sold, purchased, consumed, and discarded. And they are the cultural products of the transnational class. The members of such a class are the leaders, the role models, of the 1990s and beyond; their one gift is, needs to be, an ability to converse and communicate with each other. Cultural eccentricities are to be avoided, if not banned altogether. National history and culture are not to intrude or not to be asserted oppositionally or even dialectically. They are merely variants of one "universal"—as in a giant theme park or shopping mall. Culture will be kept to museums, and the museums, exhibitions, and theatrical performances will be swiftly appropriated by tourism and other forms of commercialism. No matter how subversive at the beginning, variants will be appropriated aggressively by branches of consumerism, such as entertainment and tourism, as were rap music, graffiti art, or even classical music and high arts. Cable TV and MTV dominate the world absolutely. Entertainment and tourism are huge transnational industries by themselves. The return to "authenticity," as mentioned earlier, is a closed route. There is nothing of the sort extant any longer in much of the world. How then to balance the transnationalization of economy and politics with the survival of local culture and history—without mummifying them with tourism and in museums—is the crucial question, for which, however, no answer has yet been found.[52]

Third, workers in search of jobs all over the world are changing global demography in this third industrial revolution. They come, legally or illegally, from everywhere to every industrial center either in industrialized or developing nations. TNCs are in need of them, though they are unwilling to provide them with adequate pay or care. Cut off from their homes, migrant workers disappear into huge urban slums without the protection of a traditional rural mutual dependence system. The struggle for survival does not allow any leisure in which to enjoy their pastoral memory. For those exploited alien workers in inner cities, consumerism alone seems to offer solace, if they are fortunate enough to have money for paltry pleasures. In Mexico City or Seoul, in Berlin or Chicago, migrants mix and compromise alongside other aliens from other regions. Neither nativism nor pluralism are in their thoughts, only survival. "Multiculturalism" is a luxury largely irrelevant to those who live under the most wretched conditions. It is merely an "import strategy" of the TNC managers, as Mike Davis calls it.[53] In fact, it may very well turn out to be the other side of the coin of neoethnicism and neoracism.

Fourth, environmental destruction is a major consequence of the development of TNCs. Because TNCs often move across borders to escape from stringent environmental regulations, the host government is not likely to enforce the pollution control rules. The effects of the damage caused in industrialized areas as well as NIES and Third World regions, however, is not confined to these specific localities. The proposal made by Lawrence Summers of Harvard and the World Bank to shift polluting industries from developed countries to the " 'underpolluted' " Third World is as foolish as it is invidious.[54] The effects of environmental violence inescapably visit everyone, everywhere. Air pollution, ozone layer depletion, acid rain, the greenhouse effect, ocean contamination, and a disrupted ecosystem are finally unavoidable no matter where the damage originates. The TNCs might escape from the regulators, but we are all—with no exception—victims. Who is there to control the environmental performance of TNCs globally? Are we to rely on the good sense of corporate planners to fight off catastrophe? Can we trust the fugitives from law to protect the law?[55]

Finally, academia, the institution that might play the principal role in investigating transnational corporatism and its implications for humanity, seems all too ready to cooperate rather than deliberate. The technical complexity of the TNC mechanism requires academic expertise in sophisticated research, explanation, and management of immense information data. Those in economics, political science, sociology, and anthropology, as well as business administration and international relations, are not expected to be harsh critics of the TNC practice, being compliant enough to be its explicators and apologists. Critics and theorists in the humanities, too, are not unsusceptible to the attraction of global exchange, as I will argue once more before I close.

TNCs continue colonialism. Like pre-1945 colonialism, they operate over distance. While they homogenize regions, they remain aliens and outsiders in each place, faithful only to the exclusive clubs of which they are members. True, old colonialism operated in the name of nations, ethnicities, and races, and transnational corporatism tends toward nationlessness. But as I have already mentioned, even the historical nation-state was actually an enabling institution for international enterprises. British colonialism made possible the East India Company, just as the U.S. government made possible the domination of the United Fruit Company in Central America. Colonialism never benefited the whole population of an adventurist nation. As J. A. Hobson argued nearly a century ago and scholars since have confirmed, colonialism enriched the rich and powerful of the home country and the *compradors* at the expense of the populace at large.[56] The trickle-down theory of the 1980s was, as always, a wishful fantasy or, more likely, an unadulterated con game. It is indeed sobering to remember that the war in Vietnam was conducted at a huge cost to the United States as a whole, which of course gained nothing from the old exhausted South Asian colony of France. And yet there were a good number of stockholders, executives, entrepreneurs, and employees of the U.S. defense industry who amassed fortunes over the millions of dead and wounded bodies and impoverished souls, both Vietnamese and American. Japanese industrial recovery, too, owes a great deal to the Korean and Vietnam wars.

TNCs are unencumbered with nationalist baggage. Their profit motives are unconcealed. They travel, communicate, and transfer people and plants, information and technology, money and resources globally. TNCs rationalize and execute the objectives of colonialism with greater efficiency and rationalism.

And they are, unlike imperial invaders, welcomed by the leaders of developing nations. In order to exploit the different economic and political conditions among the current nation-states, they ignore the borders to their own advantages. When the need arises, however, they can still ask for the aid of the armed forces of their home/host states. And in the process patriotic rhetoric can be resurrected to conceal the true state of affairs, as the Gulf War clearly demonstrated. The military, in the meantime, is increasingly assuming the form of a TNC itself, being nearly nation-free. TNC employees, too, are satisfied with their locally higher wages. And yet there is no evidence that the whole population of a host country enjoys an improvement in welfare: let me repeat, a higher GNP or per capita income does not mean an equally enjoyed increase in wealth. As the host government represses labor organization and urban industrial centers generate surplus labor, wages can be lowered and inequality can intensify at least temporarily.[57] Authoritarianism is unlikely to diminish. Oppression and exploitation continue. Ours, I submit, is not an age of *post*colonialism but of intensified colonialism, even though it is under an unfamiliar guise.[58]

I am raising these issues as a participant in the discourse on colonialism. I have myself participated in a number of workshops and conferences on the subject. It is curious, however, how quickly "colonial" discourse has been replaced by "*post*colonial" discourse. There was a conference in Berkeley called "After 'Orientalism'" in the spring of 1992. Soon thereafter, there was another at Santa Cruz, this time entitled "Beyond Orientalism." During the subsequent fall, there were at least two more, one at Scripps College, called "Writing the Postcolonial," and another, though slightly different in orientation, at Santa Barbara, entitled "Translating Cultures: The Future of Multiculturalism?" And above all there is a three-year project on minority discourse at the Humanities Research Institute, at University of California, Irvine. These are all recent California events, but there are many meetings and conferences on the subject everywhere, converting academics—us—into frequent fliers and globe-trotters. And there is, of course, an outpouring of articles in scholarly publications.[59]

Such activities are presumably politically engaged intellectual exercises. But if practice follows discourse, discourse must follow practice. Very much like studies in New Historicism, these are efforts once again to distance political actuality from direct examination. Once again, we are sanitizing our academic discourse on the ongoing political conditions—this time around TNCs and their eager host governments. We might even be masking a secret nostalgia as we devote our scholarly attention to "postcoloniality," a condition in history that is safely distant and inert, instead of seeking alternatives in this age after the supposed end of history. Similarly, multiculturalism looks suspiciously like a disguise of transnational corporatism that causes, of necessity, havoc with a huge mass of displaced workers helplessly seeking jobs and sustenance. Los Angeles and New York, Tokyo and Hong Kong, Berlin and London are all teeming with "strange-looking" people. And U.S. academics quite properly study them as a plurality of presences. But before we look distantly at them and give them over to their specialists, we need to know why they are where they are. What are the forces driving them? How do they relate to our everyday life? Who is behind all this drifting? The plurality of cultures is a given of human life: "our own tradition" is a fabrication as it has always been, everywhere. It is impossible not to study cultures of others; the American curricula must include "alien" histories. But that is merely a beginning. In the recent rise in cultural studies and multiculturalism among cultural traders and academic administrators, inquiry stops as soon as it begins. What we need is a rigorous political and economic scrutiny rather than a gesture of pedagogic expediency. We should not be satisfied with recognizing the different subject-positions from different regions and diverse backgrounds. We need to find reasons for such differences—at least in the political and economic aspects—and to propose ways to erase such "differences," by which I mean political and economic inequalities. To the extent that cultural studies and multiculturalism provide students and scholars with an alibi for their complicity in the TNC version of neocolonialism, they are serving, once again, just as one more device to conceal liberal self-deception. By allowing ourselves to get absorbed into the discourse on "postcoloniality" or even post-Marxism, we are fully collaborating with the hegemonic ideology, which looks, as usual, as if it were no ideology at all.

Notes

Many of my friends have read this paper in various stages. I am thankful for the following for detailed and insightful comments and suggestions, although errors and misinterpretations are, of course, entirely my own: Martha L. Archibald, Carlos Blanco-Aguinaga, Paul Bové, Noam Chomsky, Arif Dirlik, Joseba Gabilondo, H. D. Harootunian, Takeo Hoshi, Stephanie McCurry, and Anders Stephanson. This essay originally was published in *Critical Inquiry* 19 (Summer 1993). © 1993 by The University of Chicago.

1   See Edward W. Said, *Culture and Imperialism* (New York: Alfred A. Knopf, Inc., 1993).

2   Some examples are Aimé Césaire, *Discours sur le colonialisme* (1955); C. L. R. James, *The Black Jacobins: Toussaint Louverture and the San Domingo Revolution* (1938), *A History*

of Negro Revolt (1938), *Beyond a Boundary* (1963), and many others; Frantz Fanon, *The Wretched of the Earth,* trans. Constance Farrington (1961), and *Studies in a Dying Colonialism,* trans. Haakon Chevalier (1961); and George Lamming, *In the Castle of My Skin* (1953), and *The Pleasures of Exile* (1960).

3 During the 1960s, black writers began to express to the white audience their anti-colonialist views as activists were promoting civil rights. Politically acceptable to many liberal academics, they were at the same time dismissed by "respectable" critics and scholars in academic disciplines.

4 Perhaps this is more conspicuously an Anglo-American phenomenon. In South America, for instance, the discourse on colonialism started everywhere—from Mexico to Argentina—much earlier, at the latest in the 1960s.

5 See Edward W. Said, *Orientalism* (New York: Pantheon Books, 1978). Of course, there had been numerous studies in history and political science in relation to imperialism, racism, slavery, colonies, and so on, and the political activism of the 1960s and 1970s had also made contributions to the change in the political consciousness of Western intellectuals. But before the appearance of Said's book, no text had made a serious inroad into the mainline Anglo-American disciplines of the humanities.

6 The state of colonization is obviously much harder to define than this abbreviated argument might suggest. Any example—say, of Palestine or Hong Kong—will at once display the particular complexities of individual circumstances. It does seem undeniable, however, that while oppression and suffering continue unabated, the administrative and occupational mode of colonialism is irreversibly being replaced by an economic version—especially after the end of the cold war. To complicate the situation further, the status of the aborigines in settlement societies such as Australia, Taiwan, the United States, Canada, and the Pacific islands, to take random examples, is far from clarified. Serious legal disputes are distinct possibilities in the near future in some of these areas, for example, in Hawaii and Australia.

7 There are six interrelated developments in post–World War II history, none of which should or could be considered in isolation. It is indeed possible to argue that any one of these developments needs to be studied in close conjunction *with every other.* They are: (1) the cold war (and its end); (2) decolonization; (3) transnational corporatism; (4) high-tech revolution; (5) feminism; (6) the environmental crisis. There are adjacent cultural coordinates such as postmodernism, popularization of culture, cultural studies, de-disciplinization, ethnicism, economic regionalism (tripolarism), and so on. The relationship between the two groups is neither homologic nor causal, but its exact nature requires further examination in a different context.

8 In many regions of the world, there were some improvements in general welfare. As to starvation, for instance, the ratio of the chronically undernourished to the total population in the Middle East, South America, and Asia has been reduced to nearly one-half between 1970 and 1990. In Africa, however, there is hardly any change in the same period. See Katsumata Makoto, "Kiga," *Sekai o yomu kii waado,* III (Tokyo: Iwanami Shoten, 1992), pp. 82–83.

9   See Basil Davidson, *The Black Man's Burden: Africa and the Curse of the Nation-State* (New York: Times Books, 1992). An Africanist journalist, Davidson may be overly influenced by his observations of Africa when he writes about the rest of the world. He is, for instance, much too pessimistic—and Orientalist!—as he predicts that aside from Japan no Third World nation will become industrialized.

10 This narrative of colonization/decolonization is obviously oversimplified and, worse, totalized. Again, the case of South America, for instance, does not apply in many important aspects. However, for an inclusive discussion of the decolonization/recolonization process, one would have to consult an entirely different essay with a different focus and emphasis.

11 A typically preindustrial society has about 80 percent of its population engaged in agriculture. A fully industrialized society has a very small agricultural worker population, about 5 percent. This transformation from agriculture to manufacturing and other industries has taken most industrialized nations around 200 years. Japan went through the process in less than a century, while the East Asian NIES are changing at the speed of less than a generation. The high cost paid for such a social change is to be expected. Industrialization and colonization converge in this development. And thus all industrialized nations are former colonizers. There is a later development of this process in industrialized societies now. As manufacturing technology improves productivity, manufacturing jobs are rapidly disappearing everywhere, and they are being replaced by service jobs. The manufacturing worker surplus urgently needs to find outlets that are nowhere visibly available. There is not even an equivalent of old colonies for these surplus workers. See Sylvia Nasar, "Clinton Job Plan in Manufacturing Meets Skepticism," *New York Times,* Dec. 27, 1992, p. A1. See also Motoyama Yoshihiko, *Minami to kita* (Tokyo: Chikuma Library, 1991), pp. 223–225.

12 See Benedict Anderson, *Imagined Communities: Reflections on the Origin and Spread of Nationalism,* 2d ed. (London: Verso, 1991). The book does not explain *who* imagined the community, however.

13 See Paul Kennedy, *Rise and Fall of the Great Powers: Economic Change and Military Conflict from 1500 to 2000* (New York: Random House, 1987).

14 See Bruce Cumings, *The Origins of the Korean War,* 2 vols. (Princeton, N.J.: Princeton University Press, 1981, 1990).

15 The figures are based on Table B-2—Gross National Product in 1982 Dollars, 1929–87, *The Annual Report of the Council of Economic Advisers,* in *Economic Report of the President* (Washington, D.C.: U.S. Government Printing Office, 1988), p. 251.

16 Dwight D. Eisenhower, "Liberty Is at Stake" (1961), in *Super-State: Readings in the Military-Industrial Complex,* ed. Herbert I. Schiller and Joseph D. Phillips (Urbana: University of Illinois Press, 1970), p. 32.

17 U.S. Office of Education, "Institutions of Higher Education—Degrees Conferred, by Sex, 1870–1970," U.S. Office of Education, *Biennial Survey of Education in the United States* (Washington, D.C.: U.S. Government Printing Office, 1971).

18 Seymour Melman, "Military State Capitalism," *Nation,* May 20, 1991, pp. 666, 667.

Melman, *The Demilitarized Society: Disarmament and Conversion* (Montreal: Harvest House, 1988), *Profits without Production* (New York: Alfred A. Knopf, 1983), and *The Permanent War Economy: American Capitalism in Decline* (New York: Simon and Schuster, 1974) are important studies on this subject.

19 Others include Tanzania (1964), Zanzibar (1963), Somaliland (1960), Aden (1967), Kuwait (1961), Malta (1964), Borneo (1963), Trinidad and Tobago (1962).

20 See Okumura Shigeji, "Takokuseki kigyo to hatten tojo koku," *Takokuseki kigyo to hatten tojo koku* (Tokyo: Tokyo Daigaku Shuppan Kai, 1977), pp. 11–12.

21 The history of U.S. interventions since the Vietnam War is long and wide-ranging. To pick only the most conspicuous (overt) operations: the Dominican Republic, Lebanon, Grenada, Panama, the Persian Gulf. In addition, there were of course numerous covert operations in Iran, Nicaragua, El Salvador, and other places.

22 These terms are used differently depending on the region and the times. In South America, for instance, the term *multinational* was not used in the 1960s and 1970s because it was felt that those giant corporations were all U.S.-based and not *multi*national. The term *transnational,* on the other hand, was felt to be more accurate because it suggested the *trans*gressiveness of these U.S. corporate managements. Now that there are Mexico-originated "multinational" giant corporations (such as Televisa, the biggest TV network in the world outside the United States), the term is becoming more commonly accepted. See John Sinclair, "Televisa: Mexico's Multinational," *Centro: Puerto Rican Studies Bulletin* 2, no. 8, unpaginated.

There are numerous publications treating the development of transnational corporatism. For instance, see Peter F. Drucker, *The New Realities: In Government and Politics, in Economics and Business, in Sociology and World View* (New York: Harper and Row, 1989) and Kenichi Ohmae, *The Borderless World: Power and Strategy in the Interlinked Economy* (New York: Harper Business, 1990), pp. 91–99. Perhaps the most important source of information, though little known, is the United Nations Center on Transnational Corporations, which publishes the biannual *CTC Reporter* as well as numerous specific reports on transnational corporate activities. The center published the *Bibliography on Transnational Corporations* in 1979.

23 Percy Barnevik, CEO of ABB, concluded a recent interview by remarking, "Are we above governments? No. We answer to governments. We obey the laws in every country in which we operate, and we don't make the laws. However, we do change relations *between* countries. We function as a lubricant for worldwide economic integration. . . . We don't create the process, but we push it. We make visible the invisible hand of global competition" (William Taylor, "The Logic of Global Business: An Interview with ABB's Percy Barnevik," *Harvard Business Review* 69 [Mar.–Apr. 1991]: 105).

24 See Terajima Jitsuro, *Chikyugi o te ni kangaeru Amerika: 21 seiki Nichi-Bei kankei e no koso* (Tokyo: Tokyo Keizai Shinposha, 1991), pp. 78–79.

25 There are several books on this supposedly family-owned but un-Japanese enterprise, all by admiring—and commissioned?—Japanese authors. See, for instance, Itagaki Hidenori, *Yaohan: Nihon dasshutsu o hakaru tairiku-gata shoho no hasso* (Tokyo: Paru

Shuppan, 1990) and Tsuchiya Takanori, *Yaohan Wada Kazuo: Inoru keiei to hito zukuri* (Tokyo: Nihon Kyobunsha, 1991). Reflecting the owner's faith, Yaohan is aggressive in evangelizing the doctrine of the Seicho-no-ie Temple among its local employees. Despite predictable conflicts with employees of other religions (for example, Muslims in Singapore), Yaohan insists that the doctrine is the key to its success.

26   For specific comments on this aspect of TNCs, see, for instance, Raymond Vernon, *Sovereignty at Bay: The Multinational Spread of U.S. Enterprises* (Harlow: Longman, 1971), and Stephen Hymer, *The International Operations of National Firms: A Study of Direct Foreign Investment* (Cambridge, Mass.: MIT Press, 1976). In this connection J. A. Hobson's foresight in his *Imperialism* (London: Allen and Unwin, 1902), especially in part 1, "The Economics of Imperialism," cannot be forgotten.

27   Amidst the fiscal crisis in the state of California, there have been rumors that the University of California, Berkeley, and UCLA are being considered for privatization. Though there has been no confirmation of the rumor, there has been no official denial either.

28   See Tom Petruno, "A Return to Rational Rates," *Los Angeles Times,* Jan. 29, 1992, p. D1.

29   See "Are CEOs Paid Too Much?" *Business Week,* May 6, 1991. The Japanese are very proud of this "democratic" distribution of wealth. Though it is to a large extent true and justifiable, wealth equity is not quite so real. For one thing, there is a huge sum being spent every year on executive perks such as free housing, free chauffeured car, free parking (no pittance in space-scarce Japan), plus the notorious entertainment expenses annually estimated, by one study, at $35.5 billion. See Robert Neff and Joyce Barnathan, "How Much Japanese CEOs Really Make," *Business Week,* Jan. 27, 1992, p. 31. The manifestation of wealth, power, and privilege obviously takes different forms from society to society.

30   Kevin Phillips, "Down and Out," *New York Times Magazine,* Jan. 10, 1993, p. 20.

31   See Robert Pear, "Ranks of U.S. Poor Reach 35.7 Million, the Most Since '64," *New York Times,* Sept. 4, 1992, pp. A1, A14; After President Bush's visit to Japan in late 1991, the comparative figures of the rich and the poor in the United States attracted a good deal of media attention. See also Nasar, "The 1980s: A Very Good Time for the Very Rich," *New York Times,* Mar. 5, 1992, pp. A1, A22; Petruno, "Investors Seeking Voice on Execs' Pay May Get It," *Los Angeles Times,* Feb. 7, 1992, pp. D1, D3; Linda Grant, "Corporations Search for Answers on Executive Pay," *Los Angeles Times,* Feb. 23, 1992, pp. D1, D9; James E. Ellis, "Layoffs on the Line, Bonuses in the Executive Suite," *Business Week,* Oct. 21, 1991, p. 34; Anne B. Fisher, "The New Debate over the Very Rich," *Fortune,* June 29, 1992, pp. 42–55; and Louis S. Richman, "The Truth about the Rich and the Poor," *Fortune,* Sept. 21, 1992, pp. 134–146; Lee Smith, "Are You Better Off?" *Fortune,* Feb. 24, 1992, pp. 38–48; Geoffrey Colvin, "How to Pay the CEO Right," Apr. 6, 1992, pp. 60–69. See also the feature on executive pay in *Business Week,* Mar. 30, 1992, pp. 52–58.

32   Leslie Sklair, *Sociology of the Global System* (Baltimore: Johns Hopkins University Press, 1991), pp. 101–102; hereafter abbreviated S. Among numerous books on the subject, Sklair's is singular for a sociopolitical vision that informs its economic analysis.

33 Also, it was said in 1973 that "of the 100 largest economic units in the world, only half are nation-states, the others multinational companies of various sorts" (Harry M. Makler, Alberto Martinelli, and Neil J. Smelser, introduction, in *The New International Economy,* ed. Makler, Martinelli, and Smelser [Beverly Hills, Calif.: Sage, 1992], p. 25).

34 See June Kinoshita, "Mapping the Mind," *New York Times Magazine,* Oct. 18, 1992, pp. 43–47, 50, 52, 54.

35 Female labor is cheaper than male labor everywhere, especially in the Third World. Thus the sexual division of labor is attracting some attention among economists. An extremely important topic, it urgently requires further study. See *S,* pp. 96–101, 108–9, 233–35. See also Maria Mies, *Patriarchy and Accumulation on a World Scale: Women in the International Division of Labour* (London: Zed, 1986), esp. chaps. 3 and 4.

36 There is a good deal of literature available on this subject. See, for instance, Folker Fröbel, Jürgen Heinrichs, and Otto Kreye, *The New International Division of Labour: Structural Unemployment in Industrialised Countries and Industrialisation in Developing Countries,* trans. Pete Burgess (Cambridge: Cambridge University Press, 1980), and Michael J. Piore and Charles F. Sabel, *The Second Industrial Divide: Possibilities for Prosperity* (New York: Basic Books, 1984).

37 Lee Iacocca, the former Chrysler chairman, said little about the Nagoya Mitsubishi factory when he accompanied President Bush to Japan in 1991 to complain about the Japanese automobile imports. The Stealth is made entirely in Japan except for the word *Dodge* etched in the front bumper. See David E. Sanger, "Detroit Leaning on Japan, in Both Senses," *New York Times,* Feb. 27, 1992, p. A1.

38 John Holusha, "International Flights, Indeed," *New York Times,* Jan. 1, 1992, p. 49.

39 "'Made in America' Gets Tougher to Determine," *San Diego Union-Tribune,* Feb. 2, 1992, p. A33.

40 This does not mean that TNCs are all capable of rationally and skillfully dealing with complex race issues in all regions. The Japanese MNC/TNC managers in the United States, for instance, have had many serious difficulties in understanding the racial and ethnic problems, often provoking their employees of both majority and minority ethnicities to take legal actions against them. The problem as I see it, however, arises not from their informed policies but their inexperience and ignorance in execution. The corporate managers are becoming alert enough to what is expected and demanded of them for the maintenance of their operation in alien lands.

41 See Kuwahara Yasuo, *Kokkyo o koeru rodosha* (Tokyo: Iwanami Shoten, 1991), pp. 127–43. The movements of both skilled and unskilled labor in the European community, too, offers an economic integration model par excellence.

42 See Robert B. Reich, *The Work of Nations: Preparing Ourselves for Twenty-First-Century Capitalism* (New York: Alfred A. Knopf, 1991). In his contribution to *The New International Economy,* Volker Bornschier concludes, "we know that personal income distribution is more unequal if the level of [multinational corporation] penetration is high. No empirical evidence is reported that MNCs reduce inequality in less developed countries in the course of their operation, whereas there are several hypotheses with preliminary

empirical support for the contrary" (Volker Bornschier, "World Economic Integration and Policy Responses: Some Developmental Impacts," in *The New International Economy*, pp. 68–69).

43 The first large-scale war after the end of the cold war, the war in the Persian Gulf, requires further analysis. First World intellectuals hardly protested, although the U.S. Congress was nearly evenly divided about the land-force invasion of Iraq before the actual event. Among several collections of essays about the war in the gulf, see *The Gulf War Reader: History, Documents, Opinions*, ed. Micah L. Sifry and Christopher Cerf (New York: Times Books, 1991). See also Christopher Norris, *Uncritical Theory: Postmodernism, Intellectuals, and the Gulf War* (London: Lawrence and Wishart, 1992).

44 David Binder and Barbara Crossette count forty-eight ethnic wars in the world in their "As Ethnic Wars Multiply, U.S. Strives for a Policy," *New York Times*, Feb. 7, 1993, pp. A1, A12.

45 Makler, Martinelli, and Smelser, introduction, in *The New International Economy*, pp. 26–27.

46 See Reich, *The Work of Nations*, esp. chap. 12.

47 "The ratio of the overseas production totals of TNCs to the TNC sales totals is 79 percent for Switzerland, 48 percent for Britain, 33 percent for the U.S., and 12 percent for Japan. And among the top three countries, the overseas production totals were greater than the export totals. The 1981 U.S. export totals were 233.6 billion dollars, while the overseas production totals were nearly twice as much, 482.9 billion dollars. The Japanese export totals were 152 billion dollars, while its overseas production totals were merely 30 billion dollars." Motoyama Yoshihiko, *Minami to kita*, pp. 196–97; my trans. See also Terajima Jitsuro, *Chikyugi o te ni kangaeru Amerika* (Tokyo: Tokyo Keizdi Shimposha, 1991), pp. 68–69, 160–62.

48 Reich's comments occasioned by the publication of Crichton's *Rising Sun* are eloquent on this. "The purpose of having a Japanese challenge is to give us a reason to join together. That is, we seem to need Japan as we once needed the Soviet Union—as a means of defining ourselves, our interests, our obligations to one another. We should not be surprised that this wave of Japan-as-enemy books coincides exactly with the easing of cold-war tensions" (Reich, "Is Japan Really out to Get Us?" *New York Times Book Review*, Feb. 9, 1992). To quote from Sklair, protectionism "acts as a bargaining counter for the rich, and a bluff for the poor, and mainly comes to life in its use as a rhetorical device to satisfy domestic constituencies. For example, desperate politicians tend to fall back on it to appease working class votes in the United States and the United Kingdom" (*S*, p. 71). Among the "revisionists" are Clyde V. Prestowitz Jr., James Fallows, Karel van Wolferen, and Chalmers Johnson.

49 Chiu Yen Liang, "The Moral Politics of Industrial Conflict in Multinational Corporations Located in Hong Kong: An Anthropological Case Study," 2 vols. (Ph.D. diss., University of Chicago, 1991) discusses a strike at a Japanese TNC in Hong Kong. Although overly detailed in description and confusing in analysis, there are many interesting observations of the TNC practice.

50 "In some, though not all, export oriented zones (EOZS) the rights of workers to organize is curtailed, either formally or in practice, and . . . trade unions are either suppressed or manipulated through government-TNC collaboration" (S, p. 95).

51 Some labor unions and some Democrats, including Bill Clinton, support NAFTA with reservations concerning worker retraining and enforcement of adequate environmental regulations in Mexico. But the specifics are not available. As to the overall gains and losses, obviously some industrial sectors will gain while others will lose. The questions are who will gain how much, who will lose how much, and when will the disparity be balanced out? As to the prospects of worker displacement, a group of researchers at the University of Michigan predicted that "as few as 15,000 to 75,000 American workers—out of a work force of 120 million—could lose their jobs over 10 years as a result of the pact" (Nasar, "Job Loss in Pact Is Called Small," New York Times, Aug. 17, 1992, p. D3). The details are not offered, but the prediction as reported is totally unconvincing. Nearly all in the management side agree that NAFTA will benefit everyone in the long run. No one spells out, however, how long that means. It remains to be proven that NAFTA will not be a disaster to the U.S. workers for a foreseeable future. See also Bob Davis, "Fighting 'Nafta': Free-Trade Pact Spurs a Diverse Coalition of Grass-Roots Foes," Wall Street Journal, Dec. 23, 1992, p. 1. Also see Arif Dirlik, After the Revolution: Waking to Global Capitalism (Middletown, Conn.: Wesleyan and New England University Press, 1994).

52 There are numerous works by the members of the Frankfurt school on this, especially Adorno and Benjamin. Also, see S, p. 42, and Dean MacCannell, Empty Meeting Grounds: The Tourist Papers (London: Routledge, 1991). Arif Dirlik, in his essay in this collection, "The Global in the Local," advocates a neo-Marxist localism to deal with this problem.

53 Mike Davis, City of Quartz: Excavating the Future in Los Angeles (London, 1990), pp. 80–81. See also Edward W. Soja, Postmodern Geographies: The Reassertion of Space in Critical Social Theory (London: Verso, 1989).

54 James Risen, "Economists Watch in Quiet Fury," Los Angeles Times, Jan. 8, 1993, p. A20.

55 See, for example, United Nations Centre on Transnational Corporations, Environmental Aspects of the Activities of Transnational Corporations: A Survey (New York: United Nations, 1985).

56 For recent studies, see, for instance, Lance E. Davis and Robert A. Huttenback, Mammon and the Pursuit of Empire: The Economics of British Imperialism (Cambridge: Cambridge University Press, 1986). They argue that the elite members of British society gained economically and the middle-class British taxpayers lost during the nation's imperial expansion.

57 See Kuwahara, Kokkyo o Koeru rodosha.

58 See Noam Chomsky's Year 501: The Conquest Continues (Boston: South End Press, 1993), esp. chaps. 3 and 4.

59 To name a few, Kwame Anthony Appiah, "Is the Post- in Postmodernism the Post- in Postcolonial?" Critical Inquiry 17 (Winter 1991): 336–57; Homi Bhabha, "Of Mimicry

and Man: The Ambivalence of Colonial Discourse," *October* 28 (Spring 1984): 125–33; Sara Suleri, "Women Skin Deep: Feminism and the Postcolonial Condition," *Critical Inquiry* 18 (Summer 1991): 756–69; Dipesh Chakrabarty, "Postcoloniality and the Artifice of History: Who Speaks for 'Indian' Pasts?" *Representations* 37 (Winter 1992): 1–26; and, most important, issue no. 31–32 of *Social Text*, which addresses the question of postcolonialism and the Third World. None of the articles, however, directly discusses the development of the TNC.

REAL VIRTUALITY

Mitsuhiro Yoshimoto

●

Image/Nation/Globalization

One of the highly contested issues among those who study the formation of
global image culture concerns the connection between global circulation of
images and national and regional boundaries. While national boundaries are
increasingly blurred in the new global formation, transnational capitalism has
paradoxically given rise to an increasing obsession with place or specific site. To
the extent that the formation of global systems signifies a legitimation crisis of
the nation-state, there is nothing particularly strange about the importance of
the local in the face of globalization. The relevant question is where the image is
to be situated in this new global dynamic. Are globally circulated images simply
subsumed under the bifurcating tendency of simultaneous globalization and
localization, or do they reinforce instead the identities of nation-states as a
counterforce against globalism and localism? It still remains to be seen what
kind of effect is being created on the drawing and redrawing of national and
other types of geopolitical boundaries by global dissemination of seemingly
identical images. The entanglement of these issues and questions can be observed, for instance, in the recent history of the cinema, which, in the words of
the late film theorist Christian Metz, is "peculiar to a historical epoch (that of
capitalism) and a state of society, so-called industrial civilization."[1] As the
market of image-commodity is globalized, however, the cinema's national specificity has become a highly contested issue. Production, distribution, and consumption of films are no longer possible outside of influences of global capital
which transgress national boundaries.[2] In other words, the idea of nationality

does not seem to provide the most useful way of thinking about the junction of the cinema and global capitalism.

Yet, despite the undeniable fact of globalization, we can hardly dispense with questions concerning nationhood. No matter how increasingly the autonomy of nation-states is being eroded, a cinema's national specificity cannot be subsumed under the general uniformity of global image culture or, put more bluntly, the global hegemony of contemporary American mass images. To say that Hollywood's hegemony on the global scale is an indisputable proof of global Americanization or American cultural imperialism does not account for the newness and significance of the state of image culture with which we are confronted. In spite of its continuing central position in the capitalist formation, the United States can no longer dictate the terms of exchange on the global market of industrial, financial, and even cultural capital. Too ambiguous to have an adequate critical valence, the notion of Americanization and various discourses of Americanism cannot account for a dynamic of transnational capitalism. It is important to recognize Americanization essentially as a discourse, which is distinct from any real process of molding other nations into hollow replicas of the United States. Once Americanization is understood as a discursive construct, there is no fundamental contradiction in the simultaneous occurrence of global integration and national/ethnic separatism in the contemporary world. Global integration and fragmentation are inseparable from mass and instantaneous dissemination of images on the global scale, which is not some contingent effect of global capitalism but the essential part of a globalizing dynamic. Thus, our task is not to analyze how the entire globe is engulfed into the massive process of Americanization but how "America" as a set of conflicting images is articulated to other sets of images, as the effect of which the identities of many other nations partially emerge. In the globalized space of image circulation, things American cannot have any intrinsic meanings or functions inescapably tied up with some variant of American nationalism;[3] moreover, the notion and/or critique of Americanization can even be a manifestation of other kinds of imperialist enterprises in disguise.[4] Finally, in the specific context of film studies, we need to take the extra precaution of not becoming an accomplice of neocolonialism. For the study of national cinemas has too often been a mirror of the geopolitical mapping of contemporary neocolonialism. Before we jump on the bandwagon of either globalist discourse on contemporary cinemas or a critique of American cinema, we need to better understand the ingrained bias of film studies with regard to national cinemas.[5]

Technology/Vision/Image

The analysis of globalization calls for a number of different methodologies and theoretical perspectives, any one of which cannot perhaps fully account for the complexity of its dynamic. Any totalizing thesis on globalization would be vulnerable to criticism, easily invalidated by counterexamples which contradict the logic of the thesis. However, precisely because of its complexity, globalization needs to be theorized and made comprehensible. The vast scale and intricacy of globalization can easily numb our senses, incapacitating us from comprehending the present and acting on the future. If we do not wish to be trapped in the state of complete powerlessness, we sometimes need to take a risk of being reductive. The urgency of understanding globalization far outweighs the danger of constructing a totalizing theory with gaps and holes.

The entanglement of the global and the local, and the problematic position of nation-states in globalization must not be examined only as political questions. They are first and foremost questions of image and technologies of representation. Globalization and image culture do not exist separately first and then interact with each other. Image culture has not merely been globalized, nor is globalization merely characterized by the ubiquitous dissemination of transnationally produced images. To some extent, "globalization of image culture" or "global image culture" is a misleading phrase or an oxymoron since on a fundamental level globalization and image are inseparable from each other. Here, at the risk of being too speculative, I would like to introduce the notion of virtualization, which underlies both the logic of globalization and the history of representational technologies.

To understand virtualization, we must go back to questions concerning image-sign and referentiality. Virtualization or virtuality is an outcome of a historical process in which a semiotic disposition of reality has gone through a series of transformations. The first significant moment of these transformations was marked by the invention of the vanishing point in perspective art during the Renaissance. Perspective painting is a semiotic system, which gives rise to what Brian Rotman calls "referentialist misreading."[6] In perspective painting, image as a sign effaces itself so that what is represented appears as unmediated reality. The vanishing point as a formal device creates an illusion of anteriority, by which a thing depicted appears to exist independent of its pictorial representation. Perspective art creates an illusion of pure, physical reality which, unmediated by human presence, can be faithfully represented with proper skill and artistry. We cannot escape a referentialist-illusion simply by pointing out that a painting is only a sign system signifying reality. What is fictitious is not only the idea of image as a faithful mirror of reality but also the dichotomy of image and reality, or representation and referent, in which the latter term is regarded as anterior to the former. What is concealed by perspective painting is therefore the fact that reality itself is an effect of signification or that reality is invented by a particular semiotic disposition, that is, the vanishing point as a formal system.

The second epochal moment in the history of representational technologies coincided with the invention of photography and film. While Renaissance perspective painting invented pure reality existing in an abstract space of Cartesian coordinates, photography and film perfected the fidelity of image as representation. However, if we see photographic image merely as a more developed form of perspective art, we end up overlooking its true significance. What was so new about photography was its introduction of time into a differential relation of reality and image. Instead of perfecting the perspective art's reality effect, photography gave rise to the illusion of the object's unmediated physical presence in real time. A photograph as a hyperreal image not only represents the object but also signifies the latter's absence in the present. The photographic image is a mnemonic trace of the object which once existed in the past. As Paul Virilio argues, a photographic device captures the "delayed-time presence, the presence of the past, that lastingly impressed plate and film."[7] In other words, what was at stake in the age of photographic image was no longer the reality of pictorial representation but what Virilio calls actuality of photographic and cinematic representation, which set in motion a dialectic of the real-time presence of the object in the past and the image as the trace of the past presence.

The latest phase of the development of representational technologies has been brought about by a digital image, which, unlike the photographic image, does not require any preexisting object. As analogue media, photography and film optically transfer the physical configuration of an object and chemically imprint light patterns onto the surface of film. The analogue image is produced through a process of transcription, which establishes continuous homologies between the original source and its analogous images. The process of analogue transcription moves irreversibly from the original to its copies, the quality of which progressively deteriorates as they are further removed from the original source. In contrast, a digital medium is a medium of discontinuity. The digital image does not have any analogous connection to the configuration of the original material because it is produced by conversion of formal features which can be recognized by human perception into abstract numbers calculated by computers. Unlike an analogue transcription, a digital conversion is a reversible process, in which there is no fundamental difference between the original and its copies. Since images produced by digital media are synthetic, consisting of numbers or mathematical abstractions, a digital image can be produced directly by manipulating numbers instead of digitizing an analogue image first. For digital media, the idea of the original is in the end irrelevant.[8]

The synthetic image of the computer does not represent the object's real-time presence in the past but presents the object which does not exist anywhere except as an effect of its own image. As digitally processed images are instantaneously transmitted without a loss of fidelity, a spatial distance is replaced by speed of circulation. Actuality of the photographic image therefore yields to virtuality of the "paradoxical presence, the long-distance telepresence of the object,"[9] which may or may not really exist. The collapse of a hierarchical relation of the object and the image dissolves the past as a temporal category while the future is transformed into the possible present. Computers' capacity to finish a complex calculation in an infinitesimal instant virtually realizes the future in the present. Dialectic of the past and the present, which made photography and film mnemonic repositories of the past, is replaced by algorithm of real time and delayed time. The digital image has also transformed the image's relation to reality irreversibly. High definition of the digital image can easily deceive human perception, so that it is possible to synthesize retroactively a "documentary" footage depicting an event which never happened in the past. The thing's presence in real space is eclipsed by the real-time presence of the image, which can no longer be true or false but plausible or implausible.

Despite the apparent primacy of spatiality in our globalized world, we cannot understand the mechanism of globalization if we exclusively focus on a spatial dichotomy of global/local, which is often discussed as the relation of the general and the particular. As many critics assert, the importance of space in the contemporary world of transnational capitalism is undeniable; however, we cannot fully understand the newly discovered importance of spatiality if we misrecognize it as the mere primacy of space over time. What has changed is not necessarily the relative importance of either space or time, but the relationship of the two. The world has been fundamentally altered by digital technologies. Time is no longer a linear extension consisting of the past, the present and the future; instead, the temporal linearity is now supplanted by intensive time,[10] for which the only meaningful distinction is that of real time and delayed time. Consequently, in the new global space, the dichotomy of the real and the imaginary plays a far less important role than that of the plausible and the implausible or the actual and the virtual. The concept of virtuality, then, refers to a new spatio-temporal continuum which continues to radically alter our sense of reality.

Globalization is inseparable from the sense of a closure. With no more "open" territorial land to conquer and colonize, imperialist expansion reached a dead end after the Second World War. The age of neoimperialism was inaugurated by the development of digital technologies and computers, which invented time as a new frontier. Although managed by a differential use of space on the global scale, even the neocolonial international division of labor exploits time through virtual realization of the future in the past.

Money/Image/Capital

Technologies of information and vision have played a fundamental role in the phenomenal development of virtual systems. Yet, it is misleading to see the ubiquity of virtuality only as a result of the "inexorable march of progress of representational technologies, of their military, scientific and investigative instrumentalization over the centuries."[11] Equally if not more important in the emergence of virtuality on the global scale is the force of capitalism whose basic dynamic is also dependent on the incessant process of virtualization.

Any examination of capitalism cannot escape from some key questions concerning the relationship between value, money, and capital. Money has two different functions, or there is what Deleuze and Guattari call the dualism of money: money as a means of payment and money as a means of financing.[12] But as Marx argues, they only refer to two different moments in the circulation processes: the circulation of commodities, C-M-C [Commodity-Money-Commodity], and the circulation of money, M-C-M [Money-Commodity-Money]. To the extent that its goal is to satisfy particular needs through acquisition of use-value, the cycle C-M-C is a finite process with a definite conclusion (i.e., consumption). In contrast, the movement of capital or the cycle of M-C-M is an infinite process because the outcome of the cycle, money, can be realized as value only if it is used, that is, only if it starts another cycle of M-C-M.

In the hypothetical transaction used by Marx as an illustration, 2,000 lb. of cotton is first purchased for £100 (M-C) and then resold for £110 (C-M); that is, £100 is exchanged for £110 (M-M). In order for this circular movement to become a process of capital accumulation, £110 cannot be used as a means of payment, that is, as a means of satisfying definite needs.[13] The only difference between the initial capital £100 and the outcome of this cycle £110 (M+ΔM) is not their quality but quantity, so that the only way for £110 to remain capital is a repetition of the same cycle in which £110 is reinvested as the original capital. In other words, capital can exist as capital only in circulation, outside of which there is simply no capital. Another way of stating this is that the emergence of capital and that of surplus value, so that capital that does not produce surplus value is a mere oxymoron. Similarly, to the extent that the beginning and end of the M-C-M cycle are both money, surplus value as such does not exist either. As Marx argues, "instead of simply representing the relations of commodities, it [value] now enters into a private relationship with itself, as it were. It differentiates itself as original value from itself as surplus-value, just as God the Father differentiates himself from himself as God the Son, although both are of the same age and form, in fact one single person; for only by the surplus-value of £10 does the £100 originally advanced become capital, and as soon as this has happened, as soon as the son has been created and, through the son, the father, their difference vanishes again, and both become one, £110."[14]

Capital, value, and money together constitute the Holy Trinity of capitalism: "Value therefore now becomes value in process, money in process, and, as such, capital. It comes out of circulation, enters into it again, preserves and multiplies itself within circulation, emerges from it with an increased size, and starts the same cycle again and again."[15] And to the extent that "the circulation of money as capital is an end in itself,"[16] capitalism becomes an automaton or an autotelic apparatus of difference producing new differences while deferring settling accounts ad infinitum. Moreover, this fundamental axiomatic of capitalism shows that there is no intrinsic relation between industrial production and capital accumulation or production of surplus value. In other words, even if it seems "in the information age, . . . *circulation* of objects replaces their *production* as the motor of the economy,"[17] in terms of the basic dynamic of capitalism, nothing has fundamentally changed in a transition from industrial to postindustrial or late capitalism.[18] As Marx argues, "industrial capital too is money which has been changed into commodities, and reconverted into more money by the sale of these commodities. Events which take place outside the sphere of circulation, in the interval between buying and selling, do not affect the form of this movement."[19] Even the high visibility and importance of financial capital in late capitalism is not necessarily a radical new development but a mere affirmation of the basic axiomatic of capitalism, according to which the accumulation of capital cannot happen outside of the M-C-M cycle.

Although it is not radically new, late capitalism is still sufficiently different from industrial capitalism and, therefore, deserves our critical attention. One of the ways to characterize industrial capitalism is the introduction of a particular regime of manipulating time, which can be represented by what has come to be known as Taylorism. Aiming at the maximization of labor productivity, Taylorism broke down the bodily movement of workers into discrete fragments, which are rationally reorganized in such a way that no waste would be created with regard to both time and space.[20] In order to analyze the least wasteful way of controlling the workers' bodies, their movement in labor process was recorded and analyzed according to a scientific method of measurement.

Important as it was, a Taylorist rationalization of labor power by itself was not a sufficient cause for a massive expansion of industrial capitalism. One of the most decisive turning points in the development of capitalism in the twentieth century was the advent and spread of Fordism, which consisted of two major innovations in the area of production and labor management: "the semi-automatic assembly-line, adopted between 1910 and 1914; and the $5.00, 8-hour day, inaugurated on 5 January 1914."[21] In order to cut the production cost as much as possible, Henry Ford broke down the production process into numerous components and arranged them into the assembly line, and the workers had to do only one kind of mechanically repetitive job, which did not require any skilled craftsmanship. Under Fordism, workers were uniformly homogenized and neutralized, and for the first time, they became mere labor commodities, comparable to raw materials and machine tools which could be used and manipulated for whatever purpose capitalists desired. At the same time, Fordism was not a mere revolution in mass production. Ford was well aware that mass production did not mean anything unless it was accompanied by mass consumption: the homogenized workers—the large inroad of a new wave of immigrants and laborers leaving small towns—were labor commodities to be used, and perhaps more importantly, they were also the potential consumers who would purchase the mass-produced commodities (e.g., Ford's own model T.). In other words, the lasting effect of Fordism in our twentieth-century world can be understood only if we see it as the first socioeconomic system dependent on the existence of the masses and the combination of mass production and consumption.

Fordism became the rule of the game in capitalist countries only after the Second World War, when the United States, whose hegemony was unquestioned, imposed various sociopolitical reforms and trade agreements upon Western Europe and Japan. Into this new world economy based on the combination of Fordism and variations of Keynesianism, an increasing number of former colonies, which became independent after 1945, were also incorporated.

The spread of Fordism was coterminous with the internationalization of the world economy, facilitated by the international flow of goods, people, and ultimately, information.

A crisis of Fordism came in the early 1970s in the collapse of the post–World War II economic system known as the GATT (General Agreement on Tariffs and Trade)–Bretton Woods system.[22] The end of the dollar's convertibility into gold and that of a fixed exchange system made financial capital more dominant than ever. In the new economic climate, the rigidity of Fordism is obsolete and has been replaced by the invention of what David Harvey calls flexible accumulation. The dissociation of space from place is further accelerated; the notion of time is replaced by that of speed. For the purpose of shortening turnover time, image and spectacle have emerged as ideal commodities, which can be consumed and disappear instantaneously. The economy or the material base is increasingly ephemeral: profit is believed to be just a matter of manipulating numbers on a video display terminal.

This transformation of industrial capitalism based on Fordist mass production into a new information-based capitalism of post-Fordism cannot but affect the film industry. In the United States, it is not Detroit but Hollywood that not only survived the crisis of capitalism in the early 1970s but also used that crisis successfully as an opportunity to restructure itself to cope with a new economic reality. While Detroit was still unaware of the obsoleteness of Fordist mass production in the post–oil crisis world, Hollywood was steadily achieving the goal of transforming itself into a post-Fordist industry through the infusion of foreign capital. The foreign ownership of American film studios, however, did not necessarily facilitate the "internationalization" of American cinema. The purchase of Columbia Pictures by Sony or the acquisition of MCA and Universal by Matsushita Corporation did not prompt these studios to inject their films with elements of Japanese national culture. The importance of the foreign ownership of Hollywood studios lies in the fact that transnational corporations provide Hollywood with a hitherto unprecedented amount of capital, with which film studios can keep making one blockbuster after another; moreover, those corporations incorporate Hollywood into massive media conglomerates, which now own not only film studios but also television networks, cable and satellite businesses, publishing and recording houses, consumer electronics companies, etc. In other words, the industrial restructuring of old Hollywood has been accomplished through its merger with transnational media conglomerates, which are the driving forces of global image culture.

The image is the basic commodity in the global economy. According to

Brian Massumi, the image promotes a new capitalist dynamic motivating consumption for its own sake. In his reformulation of Marx's theory, Massumi argues that "C-I-C' (replication of a commodity-object that has use-value on the basis of an image or model of it: production of production) becomes I-C-I' (the elision of use-value in the movement from one commodity-image to the next: self-turnover, production of consumption for consumption's sake). The commodity has become a form of capital with its own motor of exchange . . . and cycle of realization."[23] But what C-I-C' or I-C-I' stands for is not so clear since a commodity is not directly exchanged for an image, nor can we purchase a commodity with an image. Instead, as commodities become commodity-images, new cycles of consumption and capital accumulation emerge: I-M-I (circulation of commodity-images) and M-I-M (circulation of money). One of the implications of these new formulas is the following: in the age of global image culture, it is not only money but also image that circulates without being consumed. While in C-M-C, the starting and end points of the cycle are qualitatively different, in I-M-I, as in M-C-M, that difference becomes merely quantitative. Capital now accumulates not only through the circulation of money but also through the circulation of images without end. As money begets money, images also bring forth more images.

As Marx has shown, the circulation of capital is not a smooth process; that is, in the M-C-M cycle, there is a disequilibrium between M-C (the purchase) and C-M (the sale). A critical point which can potentially create a crisis in the movement of capital is neither production nor consumption; instead, it is the act of selling (C-M). While with money one can always buy commodities, there is no guarantee that one can always sell commodities. Credit was invented to minimize the risks that accompany the act of selling.[24] Credit—deferment or virtualization of the sale—accelerates the circulation of capital, and delayed payment enables capitalists to make a new investment; that is, unless they continue investing, they cannot settle accounts. At this point, the circulation of capital truly becomes an endless process of virtualization[25] in which capital emerges as a "body without organs" (Deleuze and Guattari), that is, a network of pure virtual systems[26] to which global image culture belongs.

Notes

1   Christian Metz, *The Imaginary Signifier: Psychoanalysis and the Cinema*, trans. Celia Britton, Annwyl Williams, Ben Brewster, and Alfred Guzzetti (Bloomington: Indiana University Press, 1982), p. 3.

2 Timothy Corrigan, *A Cinema without Walls: Movies and Culture after Vietnam* (New Brunswick: Rutgers University Press, 1991), pp. 4–5.

3 See, for instance, Joseph J. Tobin, ed., *Re-Made in Japan: Everyday Life and Consumer Taste in a Changing Society* (New Haven: Yale University Press, 1992); and Mitsuhiro Yoshimoto, "The Postmodern and Mass Images in Japan," *Public Culture* 1, no. 2 (1989): pp. 8–25.

4 Ien Ang, "Hegemony-In-Trouble: Nostalgia and the Ideology of the Impossible in European Cinema," in *Screening Europe*, ed. Duncan Petrie (London: BFI, 1992), pp. 21–31; and Mitsuhiro Yoshimoto, "Images of Empire: Tokyo Disneyland and Japanese Cultural Imperialism," in *Disney Discourse: Producing the Magic Kingdom*, ed. Eric Smoodin (New York and London: Routledge, 1993).

5 For the problematic of national cinema studies, see Mitsuhiro Yoshimoto, "The Difficulty of Being Radical: The Discipline of Film Studies and the Post-Colonial World Order," in *Japan in the World*, ed. Masao Miyoshi and H. D. Harootunian (Durham, N.C.: Duke University Press, 1993), pp. 338–353.

6 Brian Rotman, *Signifying Nothing: The Semiotics of Zero* (Palo Alto, Calif.: Stanford University Press, 1987), p. 2.

7 Paul Virilio, *The Vision Machine* (Bloomington: Indiana University Press, 1994), p. 64.

8 Timothy Binkley, "Refiguring Culture," in *Future Visions: New Technologies of the Screen*, ed. Philip Hayward and Tana Wollen (London: BFI Publishing, 1993), pp. 92–105.

9 Virilio, *Vision Machine*, p. 63.

10 Ibid., p. 68.

11 Ibid., p. 47.

12 Gilles Deleuze and Félix Guattari, *Anti-Oedipus: Capitalism and Schizophrenia*, trans. Robert Hurley, Mark Smith, and Helen R. Lane (Minneapolis: University of Minnesota Press, 1983), pp. 222–240.

13 This, of course, does not include a desire for accumulating capital.

14 Karl Marx, *Capital*, trans. Ben Fowkens (New York: Vintage, 1977), vol. 1, p. 256.

15 Marx, *Capital*, p. 256.

16 Ibid., p. 253.

17 Brian Massumi, *A User's Guide to Capitalism and Schizophrenia: Deviations from Deleuze and Guattari* (Cambridge: MIT Press, 1992), p. 200.

18 Jonathan Crary, "Capital Effects," *October* 56 (Spring 1991): 121–131; and Lawrence Grossberg, *We Gotta Get Out of This Place: Popular Conservatism and Postmodern Culture* (New York: Routledge, 1992), pp. 346–347.

19 Marx, *Capital*, p. 256.

20 I draw information on Taylorism, Fordism, and flexible accumulation mainly from Harvey's *The Condition of Postmodernity* (Cambridge: Basil Blackwell, 1989). See particularly part 2, pp. 121–197.

21 Richard Peet, *Global Capitalism: Theories of Societal Development* (London: Routledge, 1991), p. 154.

22 Lester Thurow, *Head to Head: The Coming Economic Battle among Japan, Europe, and America* (New York: William Morrow, 1992), pp. 11–25.

23 Massumi, *User's Guide*, p. 200.

24 Félix Guattari, "Regimes, Pathways, Subjects," *Zone 6: Incorporations* (Cambridge: MIT Press, 1992), pp. 26–27.

25 "The existence of such a transmission mechanism—information and telecommunication machinery—can be explained in terms of capital's imperative to circulate, its capacity to change form as quickly as possible. Marx saw these possibilities when he pointed out that the 'tendency of capital is *circulation without circulation time* . . . .' Capital, in other words, seeks to make each moment of its circulation ideal, irreducibly symbolic but abstract, in order to generalize its space of operation" (Richard Dienst, "Image/Machine/Image: On the Use and Abuse of Marx and Metaphor in Television Theory," in *Classical Hollywood Narrative: The Paradigm Wars*, ed. Jane Gaines [Durham, N.C.: Duke University Press, 1992], p. 319).

26 Massumi, *User's Guide*, p. 129.

PHOBIC SPACES AND LIMINAL PANICS:

INDEPENDENT TRANSNATIONAL

FILM GENRE

Hamid Naficy

●

We are living in an increasingly global media environment. Access to multiple channels and types of transnational media is problematizing our received notions of, and demanding new approaches to, questions of national cultures and identities, national cinemas and genres, authorial visions and styles, and audience reception and ethnography. This paper takes as its point of departure Arjun Appadurai's forceful statement that "The image, the imagined, the imaginary—these are all terms which direct us to something critical and new in global cultural processes: *the imagination as social practice.* . . . The imagination is now central to all forms of agency, is itself a social fact, and is the key component of the new global order."[1] In this essay I attempt to identify and theorize "something critical and new" in current global media practices by proposing a genre of "independent transnational cinema," a genre which cuts across previously defined geographic, national, cultural, cinematic, and meta-cinematic boundaries. I will develop two aspects of this genre here: transnational filmmakers as interstitial authors and configuration of claustrophobic spaces as one of the chief iconographies that characterizes this genre.

The important contribution that transnationals, exiles, émigrés, refugees, and expatriates have made to the literatures and cinemas of the West is undeniable. Indeed, "foreigners and émigrés" have dominated the pinnacles of modern English literature.[2] Filmmakers from Eastern Europe and Russia in the early part of this century to those from Germany in the second to the fifth decades, dominated both the studio system and the master genres of Hollywood cinema. Despite acknowledging their contributions, however, little sustained and systematic attention has been paid to theorizing the expatriate or exile genre, particularly in cinema. Recent shifts in the global configuration of capital, power, and media, however, have made such an attempt necessary. In addition, vast global economic and structural changes since World War II have ushered in the postmodern era characterized in part by massive displacement of peoples the world over, creating a veritable "other worlds" of communities living outside of their places of birth and habitus. Transnational filmmakers not only have given expression to these other worlds but also have enriched the cinemas of their home and adopted lands.

How films are conceived and received has a lot to do with how they are framed discursively both in their production and exhibition. The films that transnationals have made are usually framed within the "national cinemas" of their host countries or the traditional and established cinematic "genres." Thus, the films of F. W. Murnau, Douglas Sirk, George Cukor, Vincent Minnelli, Jacques Tourneur, Fritz Lang, and Alfred Hitchcock are usually considered as exemplars of the classical Hollywood cinema or of such genres as melodrama, noir, and spy-thriller. Of course, the works of these and other established directors (such as Andrey Tarkovsky) are also discussed under the rubric of "auteurism." Alternatively, many independent transnational filmmakers who make films about their homelands and its peoples, cultures, and politics (such as Abid Med Hondo, Michel Khleifi, Fernando Solanas, and Ghasem Ebrahimian) are often marginalized as merely "ethnic," "national," "third world," or "third cinema" filmmakers, unable to reach mainstream audiences in either their country of residence or origin. Others, such as Jonas Mekas, Mona Hatoum, and Trinh T. Minh-ha, are placed within the "avant-garde" category.

While these classificatory categories are important methods for framing and positioning films to target markets, distributors, exhibitors, reviewers, and academic studies, they also serve to overdetermine and delimit the films' potential meanings. Genres are not neutral structures but are "ideological constructs masquerading as neutral categories."[3] The undesirable consequences of overdetermination of meanings and ideological structuration are particularly grave for films made in diaspora. By classifying these films into one of the established categories, the very cultural and political foundations which constitute them are limited, negated, or effaced altogether. Such traditional schemas also tend to lock the filmmakers themselves into "discursive ghettos" which fail to adequately reflect or account for the filmmakers' personal evolution and stylistic transformations over time. Once labeled "ethnic" or "ethnographic," transnational filmmakers remain so even long after they have moved on.

Like all genres, of course, the independent transnational genre also attempts to reduce and channel the free play of meanings in certain predetermined manners. But, in this task, the genre is driven by its sensitivity to the production and consumption of films in conditions of transnationality, liminality, multiculturality, multifocality, and syncretism. This new generic designation will allow us to classify certain hitherto unclassifiable films. It will also allow us not only to classify new transnational films but also to reclassify and thereby to reread certain existing films by loosening them from their traditional generic moorings. Thus, Jonas Mekas's massive film *Lost, Lost, Lost* (1976), which has been variously classified as documentary, avant-garde, or diary film will yield new insights if reclassified as transnational cinema. Transnational films are here considered as: (1) belonging to a genre of cine-writing and self-narrativization with specific generic and thematic conventions and (2) products of the particular transnational location of filmmakers in time and place and in social life and cultural difference. By linking genre, authorship, and transnational positioning, the independent transnational genre allows films to be read and reread not only as individual texts produced by authorial vision and generic conventions, but also as sites for intertextual, cross-cultural, and translational struggles over meanings and identities.

One of the values of such an undertaking is that it forces us to reconcile three different approaches to film studies that are usually kept separate for fear of contaminating one other: generic, auteurist, and cultural studies. By problematizing the traditional generic and authorial schemas and representational practices, such an approach blurs the distinction, often artificially maintained, between types of films: fictional, documentary, ethnographic, and avant-garde. Because it considers the relationship of all types of cinemas to their filmed subjects to be one of representation not presentation, the independent transnational cinema is an inclusive and integrative genre, encompassing various types of films. More, this genre considers the relationship of the transnational filmmakers to their subjects to be a relationship that is filtered through narratives and iconographies of memory, desire, loss, longing, and nostalgia. Memories are fallible, playful, and evasive, and the narratives and iconographies that they produce—in whatever type of film—are palimpsestical, inscribing ruptures, fantasies, and embellishments as well as ellipses, elisions, and repressions.

To delimit the topic and to differentiate the current moment of transnationality and its cinematic figuration from previous moments in this century, my examination of the transnational film genre is focused on the films made in the last two decades by transnational filmmakers who live and/or make their films in Europe and the United States. By and large these filmmakers are from the so-called Third World, and they operate independently, that is, outside the studio systems and the mainstream film industries of the host countries. As a result, they are presumed to be more prone to tensions of exile, acculturation, and transnationalism, and their films should and do encode these tensions. These are important factors that set apart recent transnational filmmakers from European filmmakers who emigrated to the United States from the 1920s to the 1940s and who were often absorbed by the studio system and were in fact instrumental in its consolidation as a hegemonic transnational cinema of another kind.

Now, what kinds of generalizations can one make about the films produced by the late-twentieth-century liminars, transnationals, and exiles? First of all, this: each of their films is a product of the particular location of its maker in time, place, and culture. As such, each is a new and different film, a product of authorial vision, contextual politics, and cinematic practices. Yet, each expresses the personal vision and "location" of its maker in terms of themes and styles that are indicative of the independent transnational genre as a whole. There is a reciprocal relationship between genre formation and society. Each epoch creates its own narratives about itself and its own genres, and each act of self-narrativization and generic formation influences the perception of the age and the formation of its cultures. Transnationality and its shared features are experienced through and are expressed as never before via the mass media that span the globe and penetrate all communities, necessitating the formulation of not only one but a series of transnational genres.

We could define a genre as the recurring patterns in a film of expectations and their frustration and fulfillment. Such recurring patterns must be repeated in a number of films to form the corpus of the genre. Genres are not immutable *systems,* however; they are *processes* of systematization, structuration, and variation which function to produce regularized variety.[4] Further, a one-to-one relationship between genre and reality does not exist. As such, genres are not reflections of reality; rather, they are a means of processing and structuring reality through narrative conventions, industrial practices, and authorial decisions.

In genre cinema, spectatorial pleasure is not derived entirely from newness but from the play, or the slippage, between the old and the new. Pleasure is obtained from the familiarity and comfort of repetition and from the recognition of the conventions and deviations from them. However, since it is impossible to bridge the gap between repetition and difference, the desire to repeat in hope of obtaining pleasure does not exhaust itself. In theory exhaustion occurs only when bliss or death is reached! In practice, exhaustion occurs when over a period of time the formulae are repeated with only minor differentiations or slippages (such as was the case with the western in the last couple of decades). Difference and slippage, however, are essential to generic economy, and they are inscribed by filmmakers not only as authorial visions or stylistic variations but also as markers of ethnic, gender, national, racial, or class differences.

Genre cinema thus rests on the existence of an implied contract among four parties: filmmakers/authors, film texts, individual spectators and interpretive communities, and the film industry and its practices. In the remainder of this essay, I will explore two of the terms in this quadruple contract: the transnationals as filmmaking authors and one aspect of the transnational film texts, the claustrophobic configuration of space in films made in exile by Turkish and Iranian filmmakers.

Transnational Filmmakers as Authors

Traditionally, exile is taken to mean banishment by governments for a particular offense, with a prohibition of return, either for a limited time or for life. Depending on the location to which one is banished, it could be called "internal" or "external" exile. If internal exile were to be defined as "isolation, alienation, deprivation of means of production and communication, exclusion from public life,"[5] then many intellectuals, women, artists, religious and political figures, and even entire communities have suffered from it within their own countries. These deprivations may be social or economical, and they may be sought by the exiles themselves or imposed upon them by the state. To this constellation of deprivations and repressions, literary critic Paul Ilie applied the term "deculturation," which on the surface appears apt but by implying no culture, it posits the state of being in internal exile as an empty space.[6] In fact, however, many filmmakers flourish under internal constraint and deprivation and fail to prosper in their absence.[7] Since the "fall" of communism, for example, many successful east-central European filmmakers have began to covet the restrictions (on what they can say) and the incongruities (between private life and public propaganda) of the communist era which drove them to develop personal "auteurist" styles and hermeneutically rich texts. In the absence of such restrictions and incongruities, they now find themselves "dislocated, unable to complete projects, even abandoning filmmaking altogether."[8] Of course, this withdrawal may be temporary as new restrictions and incongruities—of the free market system—will emerge, forcing them to develop fresh themes and styles appropriate to their new realities. Under communism in Hungary, for instance, political repression inspired a rich symbolic and satirical cinema that made fun of the regime that financed it. Now, deprived of "paymaster and punching bag," Hungarian cinema must struggle to find other ways of telling stories that compete with Hollywood films and appeal to a broad spectrum of audiences—not just to the local elite or festival audiences.[9] The tremendous toll that internal restrictions, deprivations, and various forms of censorship prevalent in totalitarian countries have taken on filmmakers has been widely publicized. What has been acknowledged less is the way such constraints become loyal and reliable oppositions against which many filmmakers define themselves and develop their style. The continued creativity of some of the filmmakers who stay in repressive societies (such as Bahram Baiza'i of Iran) must be partly sought in the inspiration and certainty that these harsh conditions provide.

In the age of internationalized capital and tourism and exposure to globalized mass media and electronic links, it is not necessary to leave home to enter the spaces of liminality and transnationality. In this way, not only filmmakers but people the world over are always already transnational.[10] However, those filmmakers who journey beyond their homelands constitute more fully the type of exilic transnationals whom I have in mind. While most definitions of external exile consider it to be a dystopic and dysphoric experience, stemming from some form of deprivation, exile must also be defined by its utopian and euphoric possibilities, driven by wanderlust or, better yet, by what in German is called *fernweh,* which means not only wanderlust but also a desire to escape from one's own homeland. In its Germanic sense, for those in their homeland this wanderlust for other places is just as insatiable and unrealizable as is the desire for return to the homeland for those who are in exile.

To be in transnationality is to belong to neither of the two modes of dystopia or utopia. The authority of transnationals as filmmaking authors is derived from their position as subjects inhabiting transnational and exilic spaces, where they travel in the slip-zone of fusion and admixture.[11] What results is an agonistic liminality of selfhood and location which is characterized by oscillation between extremes of hailing and haggling. This turns exile and transnationalism into a contentious state of syncretic impurity, intertextuality, even imperfection. They become moments of dialectical vision, of sameness in difference, of continuity in discontinuity, of synchronicity in diachronicity. Emotionally, they are characterized by zeniths of ecstasy and confidence and nadirs of despondency and doubt. Finally, exile and transnationality are highly processual, discursive, and ambivalent.[12]

For exilic transnationals the descent relations with the homeland and the consent relations with the host society are continually tested. Freed from old and new constraints, they are "deterritorialized." Yet, they continue to be in the grips of both the old and the new, the before and the after. Located in such a zone, they become interstitial creatures, liminars suffused with hybrid excess. On the one hand, Like Derridean "undecidables" they can be "both and neither": the pharmakon, meaning both poison and remedy; hymen, meaning both membrane and its violation; the supplement, meaning both addition and replacement.[13] On the other hand, they could aptly be called, in Rushdie's words, "at once plural and partial."[14] As partial subjects and undecidable multiple objects, these filmmakers are capable of producing ambiguity and doubt about the absolutes and taken-for-granted values of their home or host societies. They are also capable of transcending and transforming their own individual, cultural, and other affiliations in order to produce hybrid, syncretic, or virtual identities. If Rushdie himself were to be taken as an example of exilic hybridity, F. M. Esfandiary may be considered to be an example of exilic virtuality. Esfandiary wrote novels in the 1960s from exile about the horror of life in his home country but in the late 1980s changed his name to FM-2030 and developed the concept of transhumanism which, in the interest of discontinuity and provisionality, dismissed all usual markers of continuity and identity—such as descent, homeland, religion, language, nationality, ethnicity, race, and gender.[15] To be a transhuman is to be a universal "evolutionary being."[16]

Not all transnationals, of course, savor fundamental doubt, strive toward hybrid self-fashioning, or reach for utopian or virtual imaginings. However, for those who remain in the enduring and endearing crises and tensions of transnational migrancy, liminality becomes a passionate source of creativity and dynamism that produces in literature and cinema the likes of James Joyce and Margaret Duras, Joseph Conrad and Fernando Solanas, Ezra Pound and Trinh T. Minh-ha, Salman Rushdie and Andrey Tarkovsky, García Márquez and Atom Egoyan, Vladimir Nabakov and Raúl Ruiz.

Transnational cinema is concerned with the output of filmmakers who not only inhabit interstitial spaces of the host society but also work on the margins of the mainstream film industry. As a result, these filmmakers are multiple not only in terms of their identity and subjectivity but also in the various roles they are forced to play in every aspect of their films. As independent filmmakers, they have to search for financing and cofinancing from national and international institutions and from private (particularly ethnic, religious, and nationalist) sources, state agencies, and television companies. What this means is that like many independent filmmakers in the Third World, they are forced often to write their own scripts and even act in a principal role in them in order to control the film and keep the cost down.[17] By editing their own films, many transnational filmmakers not only save money but also control the film's vision and aesthetics. And, after the film's completion, these filmmakers must either spend extra effort to distribute their films themselves or be satisfied with limited distribution in art-house cinemas or TV transmission at non-prime-time hours. A large audience for their films is not a given; they must be created and sought after. One consequence of the difficulties of making and exhibiting films under conditions of transnationality is the very meager output of most transnational filmmakers. Sometimes, years pass without a new film being made: Argentinean filmmaker, Fernando Solanas, made his second film in exile (*Tangos: Exile of Gardel*, 1986) eight years after his first (*The Sons of Fierro*, 1975–78). Iranian filmmaker, Parviz Sayyad, made his second film in the United States (*Checkpoint*, 1987) only four years after his first (*The Mission*, 1983). However, now, six years later, he has yet to make his third. Another accomplished Iranian director, Amir Naderi, emigrated to the United States in 1986 to make films. But it took him seven years to produce his first English language film (*Manhattan by Numbers*, 1993), which he directed, wrote, and edited. Likewise, despite constant efforts, Marva Nabili has directed only one feature film (*Nightsongs*, 1984) in the past dozen years in her adopted land. Sometimes it takes years to shoot a single film: Mauritanian exile filmmaker Abid Med Hondo relates how it took him a year and a half to film *Soleil O* (Sun Oh) and three and a half years to film *Les Bicots-Nègres, Vos Voisins* (The Nigger-Arabs, Your Neighbors).[18]

For transnational filmmakers, thus, the dream of transcendence and transformation that their liminality promises must constantly be checked against the realities of fierce competition in the free market. Some of their output is entertaining even though ironically and parodically critical of the host society. But as artists who often make distressing and dystopian films, transnational filmmakers inhabit a realm of incredible tension and agony, as Iranian exile filmmaker in Germany, Sohrab Shahid Saless, has sarcastically noted:

> People like us who make somber and hardly entertaining films are not fortunate. They write letters, come up with treatments, put together scripts that are never filmed and once in a while a good soul appears, gestures to them and says—just like in Kafka—: it's your turn now. You too can have a chance.[19]

Straddling more than one culture, sometimes transnational filmmakers are in a position to play funding agencies from different countries against each other to receive financing. Sometimes, transnational filmmakers attempt to get ahead by cashing in on the newsworthiness of their country of origin. Such efforts pay off more when newsworthiness is based on positive attributes, but they can back-fire badly if negative connotations are involved. The case of *Veiled Threat* (1989), made by Iranian-American filmmaker Cyrus Nowrasteh may be cited briefly. The film was scheduled to premiere at the American Film Institute's Los Angeles International Film Festival in April 1989, but the festival organizers canceled the screening on account of a bomb threat. Much furor ensued and many issues such as responsibility for public safety and First Amendment rights were discussed, but it was difficult to sort out definitively the real reasons behind the bomb threat itself or the cancellation of the show. The festival director claimed that the producers had brought on the threat themselves as a publicity stunt by publicly linking their film and its anti-Islamist content to the Ayatollah Khomeini's *fatwa* against Salman Rushdie. The producers, on the other hand, claimed the threat was real enough for the FBI to take it seriously. This low-budget, low-velocity, lowbrow thriller finally opened in Los Angeles theaters to dismal reviews and attendance. Trying to recoup their loss by down-playing its Islamic connotations, the producers dropped the "veil" from the title.[20]

The Kafkaesque situation that Shahid Saless speaks about is certainly real, and it becomes more personally painful when it comes to national representation in festivals, raising anew for transnational filmmakers such questions as: which country do they belong to and which "national cinema" do they represent? Since the 1973 military coup, Chilean exile filmmakers have produced over 250 feature and documentaries—far more films than were produced in Chile itself up to 1973.[21] Much of this work constituted a "Chilean cinema of resistance." The classification excluded certain films made in exile, for example, the works of Raúl Ruiz after *Dialogue of Exiles* (1974), which critiqued the exiles.[22] The politics of exilic filmmakers, which is usually against their government at home, often force them into painful positions which highlight both the liminal-ity of their status as exiles and the problematic of their national identification as artists. For example, the Turkish government revoked Yilmaz Güney's citizen-ship after he escaped his country to complete his film *Yol* (The Way, 1982), which powerfully critiqued the Turkish society under military rule. Thus, the most famous Turkish filmmaker and a very popular actor could not represent his own country abroad. Sayyad, too, could not enter in Cannes Film Festival as an Iranian product *The Mission* (1983), a sharply anti-Islamic Republic film. Unwillingly, he entered it as a U.S. production.[23] By doing so, he was forced in effect to admit that he did not represent Iran and Iranians. This was a painful admission for him who, like many Iranian exiles, claimed the clerics were destroying the "true" Iranian culture at home and who faced increasing social hostility in their adopted land. Unable to represent his own and unwilling to represent the host country, he was in essence made "homeless."[24]

It is this homelessness and unbelonging and the filmmakers' split subjectivity and multiple involvements in every aspect of production that turns them from "auteur directors" (implying benefiting from mainstream institutions of cinema) to "filmmaking authors" (implying individual efforts and involvement at all levels of production and distribution). As authors of their texts (and to some extent of their lives), their biography is not just implicitly coded in their films. Often autobiography and self-reflexivity are the forces that drive the narratives and the tropes through which the films are conceived and structured.[25] Any cultural space such as the transnational liminality described here is capable of generating films that inscribe at a fundamental level their makers' station in life and their location in culture, marking their films with narrative and iconographic hybridities, doublings, and splittings.

Space in Transnational Cinema

Genres are often spatially overdetermined by gender and sexuality. From Elsaesser to Mulvey,[26] melodrama has been considered to be a feminine and domestic genre, characterized by "emotion, immobility, enclosed space, and confinement." Such a configuration is postulated in opposition to a masculine space which is outside and is characterized by "adventure, movement, and cathartic action."[27] Generically, this masculine space most defines the American western. Every society and social condition creates its own space. In the transnational cinema genre, the inside and outside spaces express not only gendered subjectivity but also often national or ethnic imaginings and longings. Western critics have associated the domestic, enclosed spaces with women and heralded the disappearance of nature. However, many non-Western and preindustrialized civilizations still live in nature and although they often confine women to inner quarters, they associate the external, particularly the wilderness and the sea, with the female and the maternal. Transnational filmmakers bring to their films these different styles of spatial inscription. In addition, they further destabilize the traditional gendered binarism of space since in transnationality the boundaries between self and other, female and male, inside and outside, homeland and hostland are blurred and must continually be negotiated. Moreover, spatial configuration in their films is driven not only by structures of identification and alienation but also by eruptions of memory and nostalgia and the tensions of acculturation. The inside and outside spaces are thus not only, as it were, transnationalized but also nationalized and ethnicized.

It has been noted that the emotional high and low points of many classic Hollywood melodramas are staged against the vertical axis of the staircase, where the staircase becomes the site not only for the presentation but also the representation of emotional extremes.[28] In transnational genre, it is the enclosed claustrophobic spaces, often in the form of prisons, which both express and encode the (melo)drama of transnational subjectivity. These phobic spaces are often played off of spaces of immensity. Space in transnational cinema, therefore, mediates between cosmos (order) and chaos (disorder).

To examine the dynamics of the closed and open spaces, I must take a moment to bring in the allied concepts of agoraphobia and claustrophobia—only in so far as they have a bearing on the configuration of space in this genre. My intention here is not to establish a pathology of transnational cinema or of its spaces but to use the medical language and paradigms suggestively and heuristically to discover the specificities of the experiential and allegorical uses of space in this genre.

In 1871 a Berlin neurologist, Carl F. O. Westphal, described three male patients who shared common symptoms which he termed agoraphobia.[29] All three became extremely anxious when crossing empty streets or large open spaces. Today, agoraphobia is understood to be a complex complaint, involving fear and avoidance of public places whether mobile (trains, elevators, buses, and subways) or stationary (streets, tunnels, movie houses, restaurants). It is also associated with "panic attacks" consisting of breathlessness, air hunger, heart palpitation, and fear of going insane or of dying. Other symptoms germane to this context include fear of being away from home and from familiar places and people who provide psychological comfort and security.[30] Light aggravates agoraphobias as does social interaction. Finally, agoraphobia also usually involves claustrophobia, dread of enclosed places—which most of the public places noted above are.

Although the first patients characterized as agoraphobic by Westphal were all men, the majority of agoraphobes today are women. The onset of agoraphobia is often preceded not by a single trauma but by "excessive adverse life events," among them relationship disruptions, loss, bereavement, and separation anxiety.[31]

To gain control over these clusters of fearful symptoms, agoraphobes withdraw to "safe zones" by confining themselves to their place of residence or sometimes to a single room or even to their bed. They draw comfort not only from "housebondage" but also from the company of "phobic partners" such as a trusted person or an object (such as an umbrella and a suitcase). They prefer dark places and when they venture outside they tend to wear dark glasses. Erecting such physical and visual barriers and withdrawing to confining places, of course, can aggravate their claustrophobia. Thus, the affected individual may oscillate between agoraphobia and claustrophobia, between feeling secure or trapped.

Such contradictory states have been linked by sociocultural critics such as Simmel and Kracauer to the pathology of living in modern cities.[32] Other social critics have written treatises on various enclosed spaces of urban excess and commerce—from arcades to shopping malls—which engender both agoraphobia and claustrophobia and recuperate them in the service of increasing consumption.[33] With the onset of postmodernism and the postindustrial global economies, such enclosed spaces of economic, social, and psychic excess have become practically universal.[34] In addition, "societies of control" have gradually replaced the old "disciplinary society" about which Foucault theorized.[35] If the disciplinary society was characterized by central institutions such as prisons that molded "individuals," the new societies of control are dispersed networks of domination that serve to modulate "dividuals." Thus, schools are replaced with perpetual training, watchwords by passwords, discipline with control, and factories with corporations—all in the interest of "universal modulation."[36]

For many transnationals, the voluntary or forced separation from homelands, the state of seemingly permanent deterritorialization, and the pervasive controlling modulations which postmodernist late capitalism has engendered may constitute sufficiently "excessive adverse life event" to lead us to expect to see in their films agoraphobic and claustrophobic spatiality. As independent, even marginal, filmmakers, they are less apt to follow the conventions of established genres or the styles of dominant cinemas than to inscribe in their films their own experience of liminality and multifocality. The inscription of phobic spaces, which is often based on their own experience of incarceration in their indigenous disciplinary societies, also reflects the conflicting and confining social and political conditions in their homelands. Such phenomenological and allegorical inscriptions of space may serve therapeutic as well as strategic purposes. They not only express the psychic tensions of transnationalism (thus therapeutic) but also assist transnationals in working out new individual and collective identities in the new societies (hence strategic).[37]

Phobic Spaces and Liminal Panics

A sense of claustrophobia pervades the worldview, mise-en-scène, shot composition, and plot development of many transnational films.[38] These are films of liminal panic, of retrenchment in the face of what is perceived to be a foreign, often hostile, host culture and media representation. This perceived (and at times very real) threat is dealt with by invoking confining but comforting claustrophobic spaces. A variety of strategies are used to create such spaces, including the following: closed shot compositions, tight physical spaces within the diegesis, barriers within the mise-en-scène and the shot that impede vision and access, and a lighting scheme that creates a mood of constriction and blocked vision. Often many of these strategies are condensed in the site in which the film unfolds. Such locations are self-referential, but since at the same time they refer to other places, they are also symbolic.

Turkish Transnational Films

A review of films made by Turkish filmmakers in Europe shows that for them the key spatial symbol seems to be the prison. One of the ironies of transnationalism is the way in which key symbols are manipulated by political adversaries of the nation-states and by transnationals themselves. This is the case with prison as a key symbol for Turkey. According to Turkish film critics, no film has damaged the public image of Turkey as a nation more than did Alan Parker's powerful but hysterical and ethnocentric prison movie, *Midnight Express* (1978).[39] And yet, it is the image of the prison that Yilmaz Güney deployed in his film *Yol* to critique his own society. In fact, from his prison cell in Turkey, Güney obtained permission to direct this film by proxy under the pretext of combating the negative portrayal of *Midnight Express* by focusing on the liberal Turkish prison policies, including a furlough program.[40] The film was shot on his behalf by his associate Şerif Goren.[41] Afterward, Güney escaped from prison (and the country) using the very furlough program depicted in *Yol*. He edited the film in Switzerland. The film tracks the harrowing stories of five prisoners released on a five-day leave from their small jail cells into the larger prison of the Turkish society, where the modern military and bureaucratic apparatuses and the traditional feudal patriarchy keep relentless check on all citizens. In this film the space of the nation becomes a claustrophobic, repressive panopticon dispersed throughout the country transforming Turkey from a disciplinary society into societies of control. By highlighting the stories of a woman—wife of the main protagonist—and a Kurd—a significant minority in Turkey (20 percent of the population)—Güney genders and ethnicizes his spaces and emphasizes the double oppression of women and ethnic minorities in his homeland. Because of a sexual relation with another man during her husband's absence, the wife is held captive by his family. Awaiting certain death, she is confined to a dark, damp barn where she is chained and starved. The most confining metaphors are reserved for the woman while the most liberatory is reserved for the Kurdish prisoner on furlough. Himself a Kurd, Güney portrays the Turkish army's ruthless massacre of the Kurdish rebels caught in their walled village homes and alleys. But in the midst of these claustrophobic spaces of the village and the dominating spaces of the state's assertion of Turkish nationalism, Güney introduces a new space of immensity which he encodes as the space of the longed-for Kurdish homeland achievable by means of exile. These points are underscored by the Kurdish prisoner who, wooed by love for a Kurdish girl and passion for a Kurdish nation, decides to join the rebels in the hills beyond Turkey's borders.

With the release of this scathing film, Güney was sentenced in absentia in Turkey to twenty additional years in prison and all his films (including those he directed and scripted and those in which he acted) were confiscated and banned.[42] Understandably, Güney never returned home. A year after Yol, with financial aid from the French government, he directed his last film, The Wall (Duvar, 1983). About a prison in Turkey, it is shot entirely within the walls of a single prison, itself divided into other walled prisons housing women, boys, and anarchists. In a more insightful and nuanced way than Midnight Express, this film demonstrates the Foucauldian structures of vision and division so necessary for coercion and control. However, perhaps because of the specific microeconomics of control and the cultural characteristics of Turkish society, the prisoners are not totally atomized and neutralized. There is much life and happiness even though these moments are tinged with irony and tragedy. A male and a female prisoner awaiting execution are prepared by other prisoners for an elaborate wedding. They are wed but also shot, with the palm-print of the bride's hennaed hand on the prison wall the only reminder of their moment of joy. There is an uprising by anarchists, ironically not to be freed, but to be transferred to another prison which turns out to be no better than the one they left. Although there is reference to the Kurdish aspiration for political independence, this theme is muffled in the interest of returning to the metaphor of Turkey as a total phobic space. The meticulous portrayal of life's routines (including a birth), the wide spectrum of social strata incarcerated, and the high angle shots that dramatically capture the entire prison system with its subdivisions—all these work together to turn the diegetic prison into a metaphor of Turkish society itself as a total prison.

As is true of all key symbols, Güney's relation to prison was complex and appears to have hardened with the militarization of his homeland and his own exile. When he was imprisoned before the military coup in 1981 on the charge of murdering a judge, he appeared to have had a benign view of prisons and, indeed, the prison system itself was benign to him. When film director Elia Kazan interviewed Güney in prison in 1979, jail did not represent to Güney just a brutal and traumatic confinement but also a place of security, where he was given a study from which he was able to run his successful production company, directing by proxy at least three features. At the time, the prison rules were so lax that Güney could have escaped but, as he told Kazan, he felt safer where he was.[43] The military takeover at home and exile seem to have transformed this rather mild view into a totally pessimistic one, disallowing any possibility of escape or change. In a short on-camera statement which appears at the beginning of the print of Yol in distribution in the United States, he says that some people are imprisoned by the state but all are prisoners of their own mind.

In Güney's case we can observe the dynamics of the transnational genre at work, where the filmmakers' liminal subjectivity, their own memories and biographical experiences at home, and the genre's spatial configuration intersect. For Güney the prison was partly an allegorical rumination on the real stifling social conditions of his homeland, especially under military rule. It also expressed and reworked Güney's own life experiences before exile, so much of it spent in jail: of the twenty years he had been active in cinema, he spent twelve in jail, two in the military service, and three in exile.[44] Finally, creating phobic spaces and safe zones for Güney was also a reaction against exilic deterritorialization and chaos (and possibly against the surveillance of European societies of control, especially against the "undecidable" guestworkers). An inflexible vision of the homeland as a total prison may be appealing when caught in the flux of transnationality and when you are not there in the belly of the beast, so to speak, where you might be forced to consider other tainted options involving compromise.

Güney is the most celebrated of the Turkish filmmakers abroad (he died of cancer in France in 1984). There are, however, a number of others whose collective output can be said to have created a kind of Turkish cinema in exile. These directors include Tunç Okan, Erden Kiral, Tuncel Kurtiz, and Tevfik Başer. To demonstrate that claustrophobic spaces, especially prisons, are not just an authorial preoccupation of Güney but also a feature of transnational location and subjectivity, I will examine briefly three films made in Europe over a period of a dozen years by two of the directors named above.[45] Unlike Güney's exile films which deal with Turkish society and are "located" at home, these three films each deal with Turkish immigrants living in Europe. Yet, despite the shift in location, the metaphor of encapsulation and the key symbol of imprisonment are equally strong and pervasive in them. *The Bus* (Otobüs, 1977), directed by Tunç Okan, deals with a group of Turkish migrant workers who, swindled by a Turkish con man, are abandoned without passport, food, or money in their battered bus in the middle of a square in Stockholm. Although comic at times, the metaphor of prison is grimly multilayered here. At one layer, the bus—a means of mobility, even freedom, and a safe haven for the migrants who fear the foreign society—is transformed into its opposite—an immobile and confining edifice. At another level, those who venture out of the bus discover that the host society which they feared is not always hostile; more often, it is just indifferent to their presence. The claustrophobic space in *The Bus* is parasitically transnational in that a Turkish microorganism (the bus and its inhabitants) is inserted under the skin of the Swedish body politic. As an encysted ethnic organism, this foreign body must be expelled, symbolized by the demolishing of the bus at the film's end.

In Başer's two films made in Germany, the claustrophobic space of Turkish immigrants is inscribed not so much as ethnic or national but as feminine. *40 Meter² Germany* (40 m² Deutschland, 1986) portrays a wife who is literally locked by her cruel and distraught husband inside their apartment every day that he goes out to work. Her access to Germany is limited to what she sees and hears from her window. Her strategy of denying herself to the man by refusing to speak or show emotions reduces her space even further. She possesses neither 40 meters *of* Germany nor 40 meters *in* Germany.[46] All she has is the space of her own body and her memories of her childhood home.[47] In this film, the closed space is totally gendered and, although both man and wife practice denial against each other, it is the woman who is its chief victim. As a victim, however, she is empowered with subjectivity, able to escape the gendered confinement by imagining spaces of childhood's immensity. For many transnationals, especially poor migrant workers, men and women alike, the phobic personal space of the body here and now is enlarged by the nostalgia for and the memories of the elsewhere and other times. Together, claustrophobia and immensity constitute the space of transnationality.

In his *Farewell to a False Paradise* (Abscheed vom Falschen Paradies, 1988),

Başer puts a different spin on his meditation on confinement and control. In most of the transnational films I have seen, closed spaces are coded negatively, as prisons that trap individuals. In this film, the coding is reversed, turning the prison into a haven. The protagonist is serving a jail term in Germany for killing her abusive husband, but as her release becomes imminent, the fear of what freedom means engulfs her. The film posits that for Turkish immigrants, particularly women, confinement to a prison in Germany and protection by German laws are preferable to life outside the prison in either Germany or Turkey. Prison provides for women a safe haven from the racist attacks of German neo-Nazis and the severe patriarchal retributions should they return home. In insisting on the security of confined spaces, this film echoes an Iranian director's film, *Utopia*, also made in Germany (see below).

Iranian Transnational Films

The configuration of closed spaces in the Iranian transnational cinema is similar to the Turkish exile cinema, yet there are certain key differences which are driven by national, historical, and individual differences. Iranian transnational filmmakers have been among the most active in the last two decades, completing over two dozen feature fictional films in Europe and North America.[48] Here I will focus on a few outstanding examples that deal with configuration of closed spaces. Parviz Sayyad's last film in Iran, *Dead-end* (Bonbast, 1977), was completed a year before the revolution which drove him into exile to the United States.[49] In this film—a treatise on the stifling prerevolution conditions—a young girl is pursued by a man she thinks is a suitor but who turns out in the end to have been a security agent tailing her brother. The man, dressed in a dark suit, always watches from across the street the girl's house which is located in a cul-de-sac. Looking out of her window, she (mis)reads with disastrous consequences the surveying gaze of the state police as the desirous look of a potential suitor. The film's structure of confinement is both national and gendered. It is national because the girl is posited as a metaphor for all Iranians condemned to live in a panoptic disciplinary society; it is gendered because the girl's confinement to a room overlooking the dead-end alley is itself a haunting metaphor for women's lives in Iran. While her window promises freedom, the cul-de-sac suggests an obstacle to freedom.[50]

Most of the story in Sayyad's second film made in the United States, *Checkpoint* (Sarhad, 1987), takes place in a bus during the so-called Iranian "hostage crisis" (1979–81) when Americans were held hostage in their own embassy in Tehran. Although the specific circumstances of this Iranian bus are very different from that of the Turkish bus discussed earlier, as an allegory of exilic liminality they are nearly identical. The bus is carrying Iranian and American students on a field trip to Canada. While there, President Carter, in retaliation for hostage-taking, revokes the student visas of all Iranians in the United States. Attempting to reenter the United States, the bus is caught in a spatial and legal no-man's land at the Canadian-U.S. border. The passengers can neither return to Canada nor pass into the United States. The liminal place of the border and the claustrophobic space of the bus produce a tremendous emotional flare-up among the passengers. The transnational space in this case is interstitial in that the bus is caught in between and astride two liminal zones, the physical Canadian-American border and the discursive Iranian-American politics. In this interstitial location, the phobic space of the bus provides neither security nor comfort. They are obtained only when the bus is allowed to return to the United States and the students gather at the home of one of the passengers, an Iranian-American. The sympathetic portrayal of this Iranian, who has moved from exilic liminality into ethnic stability, appears to recuperate all tensions and differences in the interest of acculturation.

Jalal Fatemi's video feature, *The Nuclear Baby* (1990), is a futuristic work about a postnuclear holocaust world, where a woman on the run gives birth to a child in a desert. Much of the story, however, unfolds in the claustrophobic spaces of her memories and the nightmare narrative created by a nightmare-mercenary hired by the Ministry of Nightmares. Not only the narrative but also the mise-en-scène is extremely claustrophobic. In several protracted sequences, characters wear terribly confining face masks. The girl—given birth to in the desert—is never seen without her mask. Here again the claustrophobic space is gendered, but it is also encoded with a humanist Iranian nationalism and an ironic reading of American society.

For Iranian exiles, cage and suitcase have become "phobic partners" and confinement to them has taken on the symbolic value of exile.[51] This confinement is often gendered, as in the film *The Suitors* (Ghasem Ebrahimian, 1989) where several parallels are drawn between a captured sheep being readied for slaughter, a Persian cat confined to an airline carrying cage, and the female protagonist caught in the snare of persistent suitors. The suitcase is a potent symbol of exilic subjectivity because it contains souvenirs from the homeland, denotes travel and living a provisional life, and connotes a pervasive sense of being closed in, profound deprivation, and diminution of one's possibilities in the world. It became a multifaceted symbol of national, transnational, and gendered subjectivity for Iranians as a result of a tragic and sensational event in the early 1980s involving a young Iranian couple. The husband was a permanent U.S. resident but his wife, who was in Europe, was not. Unsuccessful in obtaining a visa for his wife, the desperate husband attempted to smuggle her into the United States inside a suitcase. Upon discovering in the San Francisco airport that she was asphyxiated and crushed to death, he committed suicide. This story became a cause célèbre in the exile media, and years later it was restaged, albeit with a different ending, in the The Suitors. As the suitcase containing the woman is being carried by a conveyor belt in its slow and seemingly inevitable journey toward the aircraft, the screen goes black. We are inside the suitcase and can hear her troubled breathing and her quiet desperation, which builds into a panic. At that point, few exiles would fail to grasp the connotations of constriction and diminution that exile spawns. Just before being loaded into the cargo bay of the plane, the woman unzips the suitcase and steps out. The last shot shows her from above, flagging a cab, heading not toward constriction and claustrophobic spaces but toward the full immensity of American society, with the multiple choices and the uncertainties it offers.

Amir Naderi's visually stunning film, *Manhattan by Numbers,* picks up where *The Suitors* leaves off. It deals with the widening uncertainty and the deepening homelessness and panic of an unemployed journalist, George Murphy, in New York City. Having lost his wife, child, and job and having pawned or sold most of his belongings, he has become practically deterritorialized in his own country. To forestall his certain eviction from his apartment, he begins a search for a moneyed friend, a journey which carries him first through a Kafkaesque residential building where none of the rooms are numbered or bear any names and later from one end of Manhattan to another.[52] The filming strategy inside Murphy's apartment and in the streets tends to emphasize the sense that the world is closing in—physically, psychologically, and discursively. Telephoto shots collapse large physical places into compressed visual spaces, turning trains into eerily undulating caterpillars and high-rises into ominous steel and glass canyons and craters. Much of Murphy's search is conducted underground, where the ever-speeding and overcrowded subway trains create classic claustrophobic and agoraphobic conditions. Overground, he travels from the physically decrepit buildings and neighborhoods of Harlem to the impersonal splendor of Wall Street. Psychologically, he traverses in the opposite direction. As he passes through each overcrowded or desolate neighborhood without finding his friend, his desperation surges into visible moments of panic, resembling Westphal's description of his patients' panic attacks in 1871. The attacks are exacerbated by posters, giant video screens, billboards, neon signs, and huge advertisements everywhere which create a discursive consumerist claustrophobia, from which he finds no escape.[53] Almost sick with panic, blurred vision, and disorientation, Murphy resorts to the safety of a wall as a phobic partner—only to have the camera careen across it and ominously turn the corner, leaving him behind. To be sure, *Manhattan by Numbers* is a "city symphony" film not only in its deft orchestration of images and sounds but also in the way it is propelled forward in movements. However, in its dystopic vision it differs from almost all the other exuberant and renowned exemplars of the genre—from Paul Strand's *Mannahatta* (1921) to Alberto Cavalcanti's *Only the Hours* (Rièn Que les Heures, 1926), from Walther Ruttmann's *Berlin: Symphony of the City* (Berlin: Sinfonie der Grosstadt, 1927) to Dziga Vertov's *Man with the Movie Camera* (Chelovek s Kinoapparatom, 1929), and from Ralph Steiner and Willard Van Dyke's *The City* (1939) to Francis Thompson's *N.Y., N.Y.* (1958).[54]

That claustrophobic spaces, narratives, and aesthetics are informed by the conditions of exile and not just by the subject matter or place of production is evident when similar claustrophobic tendencies are noticed in the Iranian transnational films which are not about Iranian topics and are not made in the United States. Sohrab Shahid Saless's despairing and powerful film *Utopia* (1982), made in Germany, takes place in the confining spaces of a house of prostitution run by a ruthless male whoremaster. Although the life of the female prostitutes inside the house is miserable and demeaning, they are bound to it and when one of them dares to leave to experience the outside, she returns disappointed. The security that confinement represented for her far surpassed the choice that freedom posed. Claustrophobia both expresses and for a time being constitutes life itself in exile. That which encloses is a womblike haven promising security. Yet, as I have tried to show, in transnational cinema the enclosed space is more often than not inscribed as a prison, trapping the individual. In a sardonic short write-up, Shahid Saless calls cinema a "whore's milieu," one that does not do "much for one's potency."[55] If *Utopia* is read through this comment, the analogy of transnational filmmakers as whores working in a society in which they do not fully belong and from which they cannot truly escape becomes more poignant (the option of going back is closed to many of them).

In the unipolar, postmodern world of today, globalized capital, deterritorialization, fragmentation, and uncertainty are all immanent and imminent. Under such circumstances nations and communities everywhere seem to be involved in creating an other(s) against whom they can best (re)define themselves. The ideologies and practices of a "United Europe," "American firstism," Serbian "ethnic cleansing," "Islamic fundamentalism," and what we might call "heimatism," following Morley and Robin's formulation,[56] are all instances of not only (re)creating actual, material borders but also of drawing new discursive boundaries between the self and its others. Transnationals living in postindustrial societies are constantly in the process of redefining themselves against encroaching abstraction and semiotic manipulation which the reduction of all life's spheres to sign systems promises. Under such circumstances, space becomes untrustworthy. Place, however, becomes attractive and emplacement a viable option. The emphasis on negatively coded phobic spaces in transnational cinema is perhaps part of transnationals' attempts to turn the abstraction of the space in their lives into the concreteness of the place in their representation. It is an attempt to create ontological security and a place-bound identity. When in place, the space is mine—even if it is only 40 m².

Capitalism continually reterritorializes its liminars and transnationals through strategies of assimilation and co-optation, transforming them into ethnic subjects and productive citizens. By barricading themselves, however, these liminars reterritorialize themselves as exiles, as refusniks—psychically and socially. As a result, they become neither the society's others against whom its overarching identity could be formed nor its full citizens who could be pressed into servicing its values. Proactive psychic denial and social refusal and insistence on inscribing phobic spaces differ from passive alienation and the production of alienating spaces ascribed to modernity. They are part of the transnationals' strategies of haggling with and against the hailing efforts of the prevailing capitalist imperium. Ultimately, however, refusal and emplacement may reveal themselves to be forms of entrapment. It is then that the space of liminal panic described here may give way to the space of paranoia—so characteristic of the postmodern science fiction—or of liberation—so promised in third cinema.

Notes

I thank Melissa Cefkin for her comments on parts of this paper. I also appreciate Kathryn Milun sharing with me her thoughts on agoraphobia and modernity.

1   Arjun Appadurai, "Disjuncture and Difference in the Global Cultural Economy," *Public Culture* 2, no. 2 (1990): 1–24.

2   Terry Eagleton, *Exiles and Emigrés: Studies in Modern Literature* (London: Chatto & Windus, 1970), p. 9.

3   Rick Altman, *The American Film Musical* (Bloomington: Indiana University Press, 1989), p. 5.

4 Stephen Neale, *Genre* (London: BFI, 1983), pp. 48–50.

5 William Rowe and Teresa Whitfield, "Thresholds of Identity: Literature and Exile in Latin America," *Third World Quarterly* (January 1987): 233.

6 Paul Ilie, *Literature and Inner Exile: Authoritarian Spain, 1939–1975* (Baltimore: Johns Hopkins University, 1980), p. 19.

7 For the potential cultural richness of internal exile films, see Coco Fusco, *Internal Exiles: New Films and Videos from Chile* (New York: Third World Newsreel, 1990).

8 Catherine Portuges, "Border Crossings: Recent Trends in East and Central European Cinema," *Slavic Review* 51, no. 3 (1992): 531.

9 Carol J. Williams, "New Picture for Hungary's Filmmakers," *Los Angeles Times,* March 3, 1992, p. F5.

10 See, for example, Lazlo Santhás's film, *Inner Movie,* in which Hungarian movie lovers recount and display the power of American films over their imagination and individual identity. See also Hamid Naficy, "Autobiography, Film Spectatorship, and Cultural Negotiation," *Emergences* 1 (1989): 29–54, which examines the self-othering power of Western films for Third World audiences.

11 Indeed all great authorship is predicated on taking a distance, in essence banishment and exile of sort, from the larger society. The resulting tensions and ambivalences produce the complexity and multidimensionality so characteristic of great art. In the same way that sexual taboo permits procreation, transnational banishment encourages creation.

12 I have incorporated these and other attributes of otherness and alterity to formulate a paradigm of exile and transnationality. See Hamid Naficy, *The Making of Exile Cultures: Iranian Television in Los Angeles* (Minneapolis: University of Minnesota Press, 1993).

13 Zygmunt Bauman, "Modernity and Ambivalence," in *Global Culture: Nationalism, Globalization and Modernity,* ed. Mike Featherstone (London: Sage, 1991), pp. 145–146.

14 Salman Rushdie, *Imaginary Homelands: Essays and Criticism 1981–1991* (London: Granta, 1991), p. 15.

15 In his *The Identity Card* (1966), the protagonist, an expatriate, loses his identity card on returning to his homeland, Iran. Unable to prove who he is, he feels imprisoned in a society he does not belong to and cannot leave.

16 FM-2030, *Are You a Transhuman?* (New York: Warner Books, 1989), p. 205.

17 Lizbeth Malkmus and Roy Armes, *Arab & African Film Making* (London: Zed Books, 1991), p. 60.

18 Abid Med Hondo, "The Cinema of Exile," in *Film & Politics in the Third World,* ed. John D. H. Downing (New York: Praeger, 1987), p. 75.

19 Sohrab Shahid Saless, "Culture as Hard Currency, or, Hollywood in Germany (1983)," in *West German Filmmakers on Film: Visions and Voices,* ed. Eric Rentschler (New York: Holmes and Meir, 1988), p. 56.

20 For more on the controversy surrounding this film, see Nina J. Easton, "Threats Spur Police Aid for Film Maker," *Los Angeles Times,* April 4, 1989, part 6, p. 1. On the impact on Latin American exile films of the politics of the home front, see Zuzana M. Pick, "The Dialectical Wandering of Exile," *Screen* 30, no. 4 (1989): 48–64.

21 Richard Pena, "Images of Exile: Two Films by Raoul Ruiz," in *Reviewing Histories: Selections from New Latin American Cinema,* ed. Coco Fusco (New York: Hallwalls, 1987), p. 137.

22 Zuzana M. Pick, "Chilean Cinema in Exile (1973–1986)," *Framework* 34 (1987): 41.

23 The ambivalent and often negative attitude of Iranian exile filmmakers toward the American foreign policies vis-à-vis Iran since the 1950s has prevented some of them from wanting to identify their films as products of the United States. Yet, as filmmakers needing recognition and wide exhibition of their films, they have little choice but to do so.

24 This kind of homelessness, of course, is not limited to Third World films. A recent European example is Angieszka Holland's *Europa, Europa* (Hitlerjunge Solomon, 1991) made in Germany. The German Export Film Union refused to nominate the film for an Academy of Motion Picture Arts and Science foreign film Oscar, claiming it was too "international." According to the Union the film's Polish director, French cofinancing, and Russian assistance disqualified it as a German entry. Critics, however, felt that the Germans were uncomfortable with the film's depiction of a young Jew who opportunistically survives in the Hitler Youth. For more on the controversy, see Karen Breslau, "Screening Out the Dark Past," *Newsweek,* February 3, 1992, p. 30, and Joseph McBride, "Foreign Oscar Hopeful Tongue-Tied," *Variety,* October 28, 1991, p. 3.

25 Good examples of transnational autobiographies are *Lost, Lost, Lost, The Great Sadness of Zohara* (Nina Menkes, 1983), *Measures of Distance* (Mona Hatoum, 1988), and *Manhattan by Numbers.*

26 Thomas Elsaesser, "Tales of Sound and Fury: Observations on Family Melodrama," in *Film Theory and Criticism: Introductory Readings,* ed. Gerald Mast, Marshall Cohen, and Leo Braudy 4th ed. (New York: Oxford University Press, 1992). Laura Mulvey, "Pandora: Topographies of the Mask and Curiosity," in *Sexuality and Space,* ed. Beatriz Colomina (Princeton: Princeton University Press, 1992).

27 Mulvey, "Pandora," p. 55.

28 Elsaesser, "Tales of Sound and Fury," p. 528.

29 For an English translation of Westphal's original article, see Ted Curmp, "Westphal's Agoraphobia," *Journal of Anxiety Disorders* 5 (1991): 77–86.

30 Diane L. Chambless, "Characteristics of Agoraphobia," in *Agoraphobia: Multiple Perspectives on Theory and Treatment,* ed. Diane L. Chambless and Alan J. Goldstein (New York: John Wiley & Sons, 1982), p. 2. Issac M. Marks, *Fear, Phobias, and Rituals: Panic, Anxiety, and Their Disorders* (New York: Oxford University Press, 1987), pp. 323–324.

31 Marks, *Fears, Phobias, and Rituals,* p. 360; Chambless, "Characteristics," p. 3; and Maryanne M. Garbowsky, *The House without the Door: A Study of Emily Dickinson and the Illness of Agoraphobia* (Rutherford: Fairleigh Dickinson University Press, 1989), p. 58.

32 Anthony Vidler, "Agoraphobia: Spatial Estrangement in Georg Simmel and Siegfried Kracauer," *New German Critique* 54 (Fall 1991): 31–45.

33 On the arcade (*passage*) and the allied concept of the strolling spectator (*flaneur*), see Susan Buck-Morss, *The Dialectics of Seeing: Walter Benjamin and the Arcades Project*

(Cambridge: MIT Press, 1990). On the relationship between shopping malls and cinema, see Anne Friedberg, *Window Shopping: Cinema and the Postmodern* (Berkeley: University of California Press, 1993).

34 The following scholars have fruitfully elaborated on this topic: David Harvey, *The Condition of Postmodernity: An Enquiry into the Origins of Cultural Change* (Cambridge and Oxford: Blackwell, 1992); Henri Lefebvre, *The Production of Space*, trans. Donald Nicholson-Smith (Oxford: Blackwell, 1991); Fredric Jameson, *The Geopolitical Aesthetic: Cinema and Space in the World System* (Bloomington: Indiana University Press, 1992); Edward Soja, *Postmodern Geographies: The Reassertion of Space in Critical Social Theory* (London: Verso, 1989).

35 Michel Foucault, *Discipline and Punish: The Birth of the Prison*, trans. Alan Sheridan (New York: Vintage, 1979).

36 Gilles Deleuze, "Postscript on the Societies of Control," *October* 59 (Winter 1992): 7.

37 Some feminists have argued that the higher incidents of agoraphobia among women and the act of women secluding themselves are both symptoms of patriarchy and resistance against its restrictions on women: see Garbowsky, *House without the Door*, p. 133, and Chambless, "Characteristics," p. 3.

38 In exile literature, we have a number of powerful inscriptions of phobic spaces. In Esmail Fassih's *Soraya in a Coma*, the Soraya of the title is an Iranian patient who remains in a coma in a Paris hospital throughout the novel. In Kafka's *Metamorphosis*, Gregor Samsa is trapped in the body of a beetle, forced to crawl under the couch and hide in the interstitial spaces of an enclosed room. In Ariel Dorfman's *The Last Song of Manuel Sendero*, all the unborn children decide not to be born as a protest against the world adults have created. For a similar reason, in Gunther Grass's *Tin Drum* Oscar decides not to grow physically, trapping himself inside his three-year-old body. In Albert Camus's *The Plague*, whole sections of the town are closed off and many people confined to rooms in order to prevent spread of the disease. However, such denials and phobic configurations are not all innocent protests, they are also skewed by ideological and political projects of their authors. Fassih uses the girl in the coma as a metaphor to condemn Iranians who after the Islamic revolution went into exile in Europe. Kafka denounces the modernist bureaucratization of the unconscious. Although the protest of Dorfman's children is against an unnamed country, it is clear that the country is to be read as the author's homeland, Chili under Pinochet. Oscar's protest against Nazism may be read as Grass's warning against the reemergence of a reconfigured form of Nazism. Although, Camus's protest may be construed as a humanist voice against modernist alienation. However, as Edward Said has noted ("Narrative Geography and Interpretation," *New Left Review* 180 [1990]: 81–97), the staging of the plague in Algeria (Camus's place of birth and rearing) makes the author complicit with French colonialism.

39 Atilla Dorsay made this remark during a conference on images of the East in Western films, Hawaii International Film Festival, December 1992. A similar point is made by Mehmet Basutcu, "The Power and Danger of the Image," *Cinemaya*, nos. 17–18 (1992–93): 16–19.

40 John Wakeman, ed., *World Film Directors, Volume II, 1945–1985* (New York: H.W. Wilson Company, 1988), p. 407.

41 Clandestine filming or filming by proxy is not unknown in the Third World. A celebrated example is Miguel Littin's four-hour film *Acta General de Chile* (Chile: A General Record, 1986), shot by five foreign film crews, each entering Chile under the guise of filming innocuous documentaries. Littin himself, as the head of one crew, entered Chile incognito as a businessman, and he appears as such in the film.

42 Ersan Ilal, "On Turkish Cinema," in *Film & Politics in the Third World*, ed. John D. H. Downing (New York: Praeger, 1987), p. 125.

43 Elia Kazan, "The View from a Turkish Prison," *New York Times Magazine*, February 4, 1979.

44 Roy Armes, *Third World Film Making and the West* (Berkeley: University of California Press, 1987), p. 271.

45 That the closed configuration of space is also not limited to cinema is indicated by the confrontational performances of the Turkish-German-American choreographer, Mehmet Memo Sander, who calls himself "HIV+ and Queer choreographer from Istanbul" (Lewis Segal, "Young Turk," *Los Angeles Times Calendar*, July 12, 1992, p. 52). He constructs relentlessly oppressive and claustrophobic physical processes and spaces that test his own and his dancers' endurance, even survival skills. In one dance, Sander is confined within a 6-by-8-foot box, where he climbs the walls, eventually emerging on top. In other dances, a dancer is found hanging inside a wooden box or squeezed within a transparent plastic cube. Sander's use of phobic spaces may be due not only to his transnational status but also his activist queer politics. For gays, being inside the closet or coming out of the closet always entails and unleashes claustrophobic and agoraphobic spatialities and sensibilities. The film *Agora* (Robert and Donald Kinney, 1992), about a gay agoraphobe paralyzed by fear of being found out, represents gayness as agoraphobia. The film also demonstrates that coming out of the closet often forces gays and lesbians to hole themselves in the undesirable interstices of society.

46 The choice of the forty meters may be a reference to Islam and to Turkish cultural beliefs vis-à-vis women. In some traditions in Turkey, women are to remain indoors for forty days after giving birth.

47 In *Passages* (1992), directed by Yilmaz Arslan, a Turkish-born filmmaker with polio, confinement is also mapped onto the body. However, the actors in this semi-documentary, which takes place in a German rehabilitation center, are confined to incomplete, missing, or mutilated bodies. Their limitation is not just metaphorical, but also real.

48 See Naficy, "Autobiography," 1993.

49 This film and Güney's *Yol* demonstrate that external exile is often preceded by a form of internal exile.

50 Jamsheed Akrami, "The Blighted Spring: Iranian Cinema and Politics in the 1970s," in *Film & Politics in the Third World*, ed. John D. H. Downing (New York: Praeger, 1987), p. 147.

51 For Iranian exiles, the caged bird as a metaphor of imprisonment and exile appears in songs, TV programs, and films. That this type of imagery might be associated with clinical agoraphobia is indicated by the prevalence of metaphors of cage and prison in the poetry of Emily Dickinson who suffered from agoraphobia and was housebound for the last twenty-five years of her life.

52 The protagonist's search for money can be read as a powerful metaphor for all independent filmmaking, but particularly for filmmakers of the transnational genre, who spend much of their time in such searches.

53 The film *Agora* insightfully links agoraphobia to fear of not only the public marketplace but also of consumerism itself. Labels for consumer products dominate the public sphere and the screen and colonize the dreams and consciousness of the gay male agoraphobe.

54 In the case of Iranians, too, as with the Turkish exiles, it can be demonstrated that closed spatiality is not limited to transnational cinema or to the confinement of only straight women. The powerful theatrical performances of Iranian-American director Reza Abdoh may be cited. In one recent confrontational, in-your-face production, *Bogeyman* (1993), the audience witnesses through the windows of a three-story apartment house violent discussions and activities among various gay and other sexually "transgressive" people. Soon, the entire front of the building is lifted away to reveal the disturbing interiors of these little confining worlds. What comes across strongly is the explosive desire to break out of the socially predefined spatial, gendered, and sexual categories and roles. The lifting of the building's facade can be read as a metaphor for coming out of the closet to face and to expose oneself to a hostile homophobic world.

55 Shahid Saless, "Culture as Hard Currency," p. 56.

56 David Morley and Kevin Robins, "No Place like Heimat: Images of Home(Land) in European Culture," *New Formations* 12 (1990): pp. 1–23.

FROM THE IMPERIAL FAMILY TO THE TRANS-NATIONAL IMAGINARY: MEDIA SPECTATORSHIP IN THE AGE OF GLOBALIZATION

Ella Shohat and Robert Stam

●

Since all political struggle in the postmodern era necessarily passes through the simulacral realm of mass culture, the media are absolutely central to any discussion of multiculturalism, transnationalism, and globalization. The contemporary media shape identity; indeed, many argue that they exist close to the very core of identity production. In a transnational world typified by the global circulation of images and sounds, goods and populations, media spectatorship impacts complexly on national identity, political affiliation, and communal belonging. By facilitating a mediated engagement with "distant" peoples, the media "deterritorialize" the process of imagining communities. And while the media can destroy community and fashion solitude by turning spectators into atomized consumers or self-entertaining monads, they can also fashion community and alternative affiliations. Just as the media can exoticize and "otherize" cultures, they can also promote multicultural coalitions. And if dominant cinema has historically caricatured non-European civilizations, the media today are more multicentered, with the power not only to offer countervailing representations but also to open up parallel spaces for alternative transnational practices.

The Ambiguities of the Local and the Global

The dispersed nature of the globalizing process, and the global reach of the contemporary media, virtually oblige the cultural critic to move beyond the restrictive framework of the nation-state. Within this transcultural logic, "First World" and "Third World" trajectories are not separate but closely interlinked. Most contemporary nation-states are "mixed" in ethnic as well as political-economic terms. A country like Brazil, arguably Third World in both racial terms (a *mestizo* majority) and economic ones (given its economically dependent status) is still dominated by a Europeanized elite and by transnational corporations. The United States, a First World country, which always had its Native American and African American minorities, is now becoming even more "Third Worldized" by waves of postindependence migrations. Contemporary U.S. life intertwines First and Third World destinies. The song "Are My Hands Clean?" by Sweet Honey in the Rock, traces the origins of a blouse on sale at Sears to cotton in El Salvador, oil in Venezuela, refineries in Trinidad, factories in Haiti and South Carolina. Thus there is no Third World, in Trinh T. Minh-ha's pithy formulation, without its First World, and no First World without its Third. The First World/Third World struggle takes place not only between nations but also within them.

The term "globalization" usually evokes a complex realignment of social forces engendering an overpowering wave of global political, cultural, and economic interdependency.[1] In its more euphoric versions, it evokes the mobilization of capital, the internationalization of trade and tariffs, a salutary "competitiveness" on the part of labor, and the transformation of the world into a seamlessly wired global village. The term evokes a cybernetic dance of cultures, "one planet under a groove," the transcendence of rigid ideological and political divisions, and the worldwide availability of cultural products and information, whether it be CNN, world beat music, American serials, or Brazilian *telenovelas*. The more dystopian view of globalization, in contrast, evokes the homogenization of culture and annihilation of political autonomy for the relatively disempowered and, ultimately, ecological catastrophe, as an untenable consumerist model is spread around a globe that can ill afford it. The theoretical challenge, however, is to avoid the twin pitfalls of euphoria and melancholy. The globalization thesis, as a group of Australian analysts has recently put it, often descends into teleological assumptions of global integration and uniformity or into unidirectional accounts of cultural imperialism and obliteration. There is a corresponding tendency among those who assert the primacy of the local to mythologize independence from international power structures and to romanticize indigenous cultural forms.[2]

The old imperial hegemonies, many argue, are now more "dispersed"[3] and "scattered."[4] But even within the current situation of dispersed hegemonies, the historical thread or inertia of Western domination remains a powerful presence. Although direct colonial rule has largely come to an end, much of the world remains entangled in neocolonialism, that is, a conjuncture in which direct political and military control has given way to abstract, semi-indirect, largely economic forms of control whose linchpin is a close alliance between foreign capital and the indigenous elite. Partially as a result of colonialism, the contemporary global scene is now dominated by a coterie of powerful nation-states, consisting basically of Western Europe, the United States, and Japan. This domination is economic ("the Group of Seven," the IMF, the World Bank, GATT), political (the five veto-holding members of the UN Security Council), military (the new "unipolar" NATO), and techno-informational-cultural (Hollywood, UPI, Reuters, France Presse, CNN).[5] Neocolonial domination is enforced through deteriorating terms of trade and the "austerity programs" by which the World Bank and the IMF, often with the self-serving complicity of Third World elites, impose rules that First World countries would themselves never tolerate.[6]

Despite the imbrication of "First" and "Third" worlds, furthermore, the global distribution of power still tends to make the First World countries cultural "transmitters" and to reduce most Third World countries to the status of "receivers." (One by-product of this situation is that First World minorities have the power to project their cultural productions around the globe.) While culture is produced everywhere, only some locales enjoy the power to project their cultural products around the world. In terms of the cinema, few people in the First World realize that Hollywood, despite its hegemonic position, contributes only a fraction of the annual worldwide production of feature films.[7] The cinemas of Africa, Asia, and Latin America clearly constitute the majority cinema of the world, just as people of color form the majority population. The cinematic productions of countries now designated as "Third World" would include the major traditional film industries of countries like India, Egypt, Mexico, Argentina, and China, as well as the more recent postindependence or postrevolution industries of countries like Cuba, Algeria, Senegal, Indonesia, and scores of others. What we now call Third World cinema did not begin in the 1960s as is often assumed. Brazil's cinematic *bela epoca,* for example, occurred between 1908 and 1911, before the country was infiltrated by American distribution companies in the wake of World War I. In the 1920s, India was producing more films than Great Britain. Countries like the Philippines were producing over 50 films a year by the 1930s, Hong Kong was producing over 200 films a year by the 1950s, and Turkey was producing almost 300 films a year in the early 1970s. (One interesting feature of early Third World production is the presence of women directors and producers: Aziza Amir in Egypt, Carmen Santos and Gilda de Abreu in Brazil, Emilia Saleny in Argentina, and Adela

Sequeyro, Matilda Landeta, Candida Beltran Rondon, and Eva Liminano in Mexico.) Third World cinema, taken in a broad sense, far from being a marginal appendage to First World cinema, actually produces *most* of the world's feature films. If one excludes made-for-TV films, India is the *leading* producer of fiction films in the world, producing between 700 and 1,000 feature films a year. Asian countries, taken together, produce over half of the yearly world production. Burma, Pakistan, South Korea, Thailand, the Philippines, Indonesia, and even Bangladesh produce over fifty feature films a year. "Standard" film histories, and the media generally, unfortunately, rarely engage this filmic cornucopia.

Although arguably the majority cinema, Third World cinema is rarely featured in cinemas, video stores, or even in academic film courses. The yearly Oscar ceremonies inscribe Hollywood's arrogant provincialism: the audience is global, yet the product promoted is almost always American, the "rest of the world" being corralled into the restricted category of the "foreign film." In this sense, the cinema inherits the structures laid down by the communication infrastructure of empire, the networks of telegraph and telephone lines and information apparatuses which literally wired colonial territories to the metropole, enabling the imperial countries to monitor global communications and shape the image of world events. In the cinema, this hegemonizing process intensified shortly after World War I, when U.S. film distribution companies (and secondarily European companies) began to dominate Third World markets, and was further accelerated after World War II with the growth of transnational media corporations. The continuing economic dependency of Third World cinemas makes them vulnerable to neocolonial pressures. When dependent countries try to strengthen their own film industries by setting up trade barriers to foreign films, for example, First World countries can threaten retaliation in some other economic area such as the pricing or purchase of raw materials. Hollywood films, furthermore, often cover their costs in the domestic market and can therefore be profitably "dumped" on Third World markets at very low prices.

While the Third World is inundated with North American films, TV series, popular music, and news programs, the First World receives precious little of the vast cultural production of the Third World, and what it does receive is usually mediated by transnational corporations. One telling index of this global Americanization is that even Third World airlines program Hollywood comedies, so that a Thai Air jet en route to India, packed with Muslims, Hindus, and Sikhs, screens *Honey, I Shrunk the Kids* as the airlines' idea of "universal" fare. Another index of this phenomenon is that Brazilian popular music, widely recognized as among the world's most vibrant musical traditions, is rarely heard on radios in the United States, while American top-forty music is constantly heard on radios in Brazil. These processes are not entirely negative, of course. The same multinational corporations that disseminate inane block-busters and canned sitcoms also spread Afro-diasporic music such as reggae and rap around the globe. The problem lies not in the exchange but in the unequal terms on which the exchange take place.

At the same time, the media imperialism thesis needs drastic retooling in the contemporary area. First, it is simplistic to imagine an active First World simply forcing its products on a passive Third World. Second, global mass culture does not so much replace local culture as coexist with it, providing a cultural lingua franca. Third, the imported mass culture can also be indi-genized, put to local use, given a local accent. Fourth, there are powerful reverse currents as a number of Third World countries (Mexico, Brazil, India, Egypt) dominate their own markets and even become cultural exporters. The Indian TV version of the *Mahabharata* won a 90 percent domestic viewer share during a three-year run,[8] and Brazil's Rede Globo now exports its *telenovelas* to more than eighty countries around the world. One of the biggest TV hits in the new Russia is a venerable Mexican soap opera called *Los Ricos Tambien Lloran* (The Rich Also Cry). We must distinguish, furthermore, between the ownership and control of the media—an issue of political economy—and the specifically cul-tural issue of the implications of this domination for the people on the receiv-ing end. The "hypodermic needle" theory is as inadequate for the Third World as it is for the First: everywhere spectators actively engage with texts, and specific communities both incorporate and transform foreign influences. For Appadurai, the global cultural situation is now more interactive; the United States is no longer the puppeteer of a world system of images, but only one mode of a complex transnational construction of "imaginary landscapes." In this new conjuncture, he argues, the invention of tradition, ethnicity, and other identity markers becomes "slippery, as the search for certainties is regularly frustrated by the fluidities of transnational communication."[9] Now the central problem becomes one of tension between cultural homogenization and cul-tural heterogenization, in which hegemonic tendencies, well-documented by Marxist analysts like Mattelart and Schiller, are simultaneously "indigenized" within a complex, disjunctive global cultural economy. At the same time, we would add, discernible patterns of domination channel the "fluidities" even of a "multipolar" world; the same hegemony that unifies the world through global networks of circulating goods and information also distributes them according to hierarchical structures of power, even if those hegemonies are now more subtle and dispersed.

Some of the paradoxes of the global/local become manifest in the recent practices of "indigenous media," that is, the use of audiovisual technology (camcorders, VCRs) for the cultural and political purposes of indigenous or "fourth world" peoples. The phrase itself, as Faye Ginsburg points out, is oxymoronic, evoking both the self-understanding of aboriginal groups and the vast institutional structures of TV and cinema.[10] Within "indigenous media," the producers are themselves the receivers, along with neighboring communities and, occasionally, distant cultural institutions or festivals.[11]

Indigenous media is an empowering vehicle for communities struggling against geographical displacement, ecological and economic deterioration, and cultural annihilation.[12] Although occasionally supported by liberal governments or international support groups, these efforts are generally small-scale, low-budget and locally based. Indigenous film and video-makers confront what Ginsburg calls a "Faustian dilemma": on the one hand, they use new technologies for cultural self-assertion, and on the other they spread a technology that might ultimately only foster their own disintegration. Analysts of indigenous media such as Ginsburg and Terence Turner see such work not as locked into a bound traditional world but rather as concerned with "mediating across boundaries, mediating ruptures of time and history," and advancing the process of identity construction by negotiating "powerful relationships to land, myth and ritual."[13] At times, the work goes beyond merely asserting an existing identity to become "a means of cultural invention that refracts and recombines elements from both the dominant and minority societies."[14] Indigenous media thus bypasses the usual anthropological hierarchy between the "local" object of study/spectacle, on the one hand, and the global/universal anthropologist/filmmaker, on the other. At the same time, "indigenous media" should not be seen as a magical panacea either for the concrete problems faced by indigenous peoples or for the aporias of anthropology. Such work can provoke factional divisions within indigenous communities and can be appropriated by international media as facile symbols of the ironies of the postmodern age.[15]

Among the most media-savvy of the indigenous groups are the Kayapo, a Go-speaking people of central Brazil who live in fourteen communities scattered over an area roughly the size of Great Britain. When a documentary crew from Granada Television went to Brazil to film the Kayapo in 1987, the Kayapo demanded videocameras, VCR, monitor, and videotapes as the quid pro quo for their cooperation. They have subsequently used video to record their own traditional ceremonies, demonstrations, and encounters with whites (so as to have the equivalent of a legal transcript). They have documented their traditional knowledge of the forest environment and plan to record the transmission of myths and oral history. For the Kayapo, as Turner puts it, video media have become "not merely a means of representing culture . . . but themselves the ends of social action and objectification in consciousness."[16] The Kayapo not only sent a delegation to the Brazilian Constitutional Convention to lobby delegates debating indigenous rights, but also videotaped themselves in the process, winning international attention for their cause. Widely disseminated images of the Kayapo wielding videocameras, appearing in *Time* and the *New York Times Magazine,* derive their power to shock from the premise that "natives" must be quaint and allochronic; "real" Indians don't carry camcorders. In the Granada Television documentary *Kayapo: Out of the Forest* (1989), we see the Kayapo and other native peoples stage a mass ritual performance to protest the planned construction of a hydroelectric dam. One of the leaders, Chief Pombo, points out that the dam's name (*Kararao*) is taken from a Kayapo war cry. Another, Chief Raoni, appears with the rock star Sting in a successful attempt to build on his global appeal in order to capture international media attention. A Kayapo woman, in a remarkable reversal of colonialist ecriture, tells the spokesman to write down her name, reminding him that she is one of those who will die because of the dam. The spectator enamored of "modernity" comes to question the reflex association of hydroelectric dams with an axiomatically good "progress." But this site-specific activism becomes translocal when representatives of the Kayapo go to Canada and meet the Cree indians, threatened by a similar hydroelectric project, and make common cause on the basis of a pan-indigenous valorization of ancestral land.

The Antecedents of Globalization

It is often forgotten that "globalization" is not a new development, that it must be seen as part of the much longer history of colonialism. Although colonization per se preexisted European colonialism, having been practiced by Greece, Rome, the Aztecs, the Incas, and many other groups, what was new in European colonialism is its planetary reach, its affiliation with global institutional power, and its imperative mode, its attempted submission of the world to a single "universal" regime of truth and power. The 500-year-long colonial domination of indigenous peoples, the capitalist appropriation of resources, and the impe-

rialist ordering of the world formed part of a massive world-historical movement—colonialism and imperialism—that reached its apogee at the turn of the
century. Globalization theory, in this sense, goes back to what J. M. Blaut calls
the "diffusionist" view of Europe spreading its people, ideas, goods, and political systems around the world. Colonialist diffusionism transmuted into "modernization" theory in the late 1940s and 1950s, the idea that Third World nations
would achieve economic takeoff by emulating the historical progress of the
West.

Indeed, it is very significant that the beginnings of cinema coincided with
the giddy heights of the imperial project, with a time when Europe held sway
over vast tracts of alien territory and hosts of subjugated peoples. (Of all the
celebrated "coincidences"—of the beginnings of cinema with the beginnings of
psychoanalysis, with the rise of nationalism, with the emergence of consumerism—it is this coincidence with the heights of imperialism that has been least
studied.) The first film screenings by Lumiere and Edison in the 1890s closely
followed the "scramble for Africa" that erupted in the late 1870s, the Battle of
"Rorke's Drift" (1879) which opposed the British to the Zulus (memorialized in
the film *Zulu*, 1964), the British occupation of Egypt in 1882, the Berlin Conference of 1884 that carved up Africa into European "spheres of influence," the
massacre of the Sioux at Wounded Knee in 1890, and countless other imperial
misadventures.

The most prolific film-producing countries of the silent period—England,
France, the United States, Germany—also "happened" to be among the leading
imperialist countries, in whose clear interest it was to laud the colonial enterprise. The cinema emerged exactly at the point when enthusiasm for the imperial project was spreading beyond the elites into the popular strata, partially
thanks to popular fictions and exhibitions. For the working classes of Europe
and Euro-America, photogenic wars in remote parts of the empire became
diverting entertainments, serving to "neutralize the class struggle and transform class solidarity into national and racial solidarity."[17] The cinema adopted
the popular fictions of colonialist writers like Kipling for India, Rider Haggard,
Edgar Wallace and Edgar Rice Burroughs for Africa, and absorbed popular
genres like the "conquest fiction" of the American southwest. The cinema
entered a situation where European and American readers had already devoured Livingston's *Missionary Travels* (1857), Edgar Wallace's "Sanders of the
River" stories, Rider Haggard's *King Solomon's Mines* (1885), and Henry Morton
Stanley's *How I Found Livingston* (1872), *Through the Dark Continent* (1878) and
In Darkest Africa (1890). English boys especially were initiated into imperial

ideals through such books as Robert Baden-Powell's *Scouting for Boys* (1908), which praised:

> the frontiersmen of all parts of our Empire. The "trappers" of North America, hunters of Central Africa, the British pioneers, explorers, and missionaries over Asia and all the wild parts of the world . . . the constabulary of North-West Canada and of South Africa.[18]

The practical survivalist education of scouting, combined with the initiatory mechanisms of the colonial adventure story, were designed to turn boys, as Joseph Bristow puts it, into "aggrandized subjects," an imperial race who imagined the future of the world as resting on their shoulders.[19] While girls were domesticated as homemakers, without what Virginia Woolf called a "room of their own," boys could play, if only in their imaginations, in the space of empire. For white male heroes, the benighted colonial regions offered "charismatic realms of adventure" free from "the complexities of relations with white women."[20] Adventure films, and the "adventure" of going to the cinema, provided a vicarious experience of passionate fraternity, a playing field for the self-realization of the white European male. Just as colonized space was available to empire, and colonial landscapes were available to imperial cinema, so was this expansive space available, as a kind of psychic lebensraum, for the play of the virile spectatorial imagination. Empire, as John McClure puts it in another context, provided romance with its raw materials, while romance provided empire with its "aura of nobility."[21]

The cinema, as the world's storyteller par excellence, was ideally suited to relay the projected narratives of nations and empires. National self-consciousness, generally seen as a precondition for nationhood, that is, the shared belief of disparate individuals that they share common origins, status, location, and aspirations, became broadly linked to cinematic fictions. In the modern period, for Benedict Anderson, this collective consciousness was made possible by a common language and its expression in "print capitalism."[22] Prior to the cinema, the novel and the newspaper fostered imagined communities through their integrative relations to time and space. Newspapers—like TV news today—made people aware of the simultaneity and interconnectedness of events in different places, while novels provided a sense of the purposeful and relational movement through time of fictional entities bound together in a narrative whole.

The fiction film also inherited the social role of the nineteenth-century realist novel in relation to national imaginaries. Just as nationalist literary fictions inscribe onto a multitude of events the notion of a linear, comprehensible destiny, so films arrange events and actions in a temporal narrative that moves toward fulfillment, and thus shape thinking about historical time and national history. Narrative models in film are not simply reflective microcosms of historical processes; they are also experiential grids or templates through which history can be written and national identity created. Like novels, films can convey what Bakhtin calls "chronotopes," materializing time in space, mediating between the historical and the discursive, providing fictional environments where historically specific constellations of power are made visible. In both film and novel, "time thickens, takes on flesh" while "space becomes charged and responsive to the movements of time, plot and history."[23] There is nothing inherently sinister in this process, except to the extent that it is deployed asymmetrically, to the advantage of some national and racial imaginaries and to the detriment of others.

The national situation described by Anderson becomes complicated, we would argue, in the context of an imperial ideology that was doubly global and transnational. First, Europeans were encouraged to identify not only with their single, local European nations but also with the global racial solidarity implied by the imperial project as a whole. Thus English audiences could identify with the heroes of French Foreign Legion films, Euro-American audiences with the heroes of the British Raj, and so forth. Second, the European empires (what Queen Victoria called the "imperial family") were themselves conceived paternalistically as providing a "shelter" for diverse races and groups, thus downplaying the national singularities of the colonized themselves. Given the geographically discontinuous nature of empire, cinema helped cement both a national and an imperial sense of belonging among many disparate peoples. For the urban elite of the colonized lands, the pleasures of cinema-going became associated with the sense of a community on the margins of its particular European empire (especially since the first movie theaters in these countries were associated with Europeans and the Europeanized local bourgeois).[24] The cinema encouraged an assimilated elite to identify with "its" empire and thus against other colonized peoples.

If cinema partially inherited the function of the novel, it also transformed it. Whereas literature plays itself out within a virtual lexical space, the cinematic chronotope is literal, splayed out concretely across the screen and unfolding in the literal time of 24 frames per second. In this sense, the cinema can all the more efficiently mobilize desire in ways responsive to nationalized and imperialized notions of time, plot, and history. The cinema's institutional ritual of gathering a community—spectators who share a region, language, and culture—homologizes, in a sense, the symbolic gathering of the nation. Anderson's sense of the nation as "horizontal comradeship" evokes the movie audience as a provisional "nation" forged by spectatorship. While the novel is consumed in solitude, the film is enjoyed in a gregarious space, where the ephemeral communitas of spectatorship can take on a national or imperial thrust. Thus the cinema could play a more assertive role in fostering group identities. And unlike the novel, the cinema was not premised on literacy. As a popular entertainment it was more accessible than literature. While there was no mass reading public for imperial literary fictions in the colonies, for example, there *was* a mass viewing public for imperial *filmic* fictions.

The dominant European/American form of cinema not only inherited and disseminated a hegemonic colonial discourse, but also created a powerful hegemony of its own through monopolistic control of film distribution and exhibition in much of Asia, Africa, and the Americas. Eurocolonial cinema thus mapped history not only for domestic audiences but for the world. African spectators were prodded to identify with Cecil Rhodes and Stanley Livingston against Africans themselves, thus engendering a battle of national imaginaries within the fissured colonial spectator. For the European spectator, the cinematic experience mobilized a rewarding sense of national and imperial belonging, on the backs, as it were, of otherized peoples. For the colonized, the cinema (in tandem with other colonial institutions such as schools) produced a sense of deep ambivalence, mingling the identification provoked by cinematic narrative along with intense resentment, for it was the colonized who were being otherized.

While the novel could play with words and narrative to engender an "aggrandized subject," the cinema entailed a new and powerful apparatus of the gaze. The cinematic "apparatus," that is, the cinematic machine as including not only the instrumental base of camera, projector, and screen but also the spectator as the desiring subject on whom the cinematic institution depends for its imaginary realization, not only represents the "real" but also stimulates intense "subject effects." The cinema stimulated an overpowering impression of reality, combining the phenomenological realism of analogical images and sounds with an apparatus that disposed spectators to lose themselves in the fiction. For Metz, the cinematic apparatus fosters narcissism, in that the spectator identifies with him/herself as a "kind of transcendental subject."[25] By prosthetically extending human perception, the apparatus grants the spectator the illusory ubiquity of the "all-perceiving subject" enjoying an exhilarating sense of visual power.

From the Diorama, the Panorama, and the Cosmorama up through NatureMax, the cinema has amplified and mobilized the virtual gaze of photography, bringing past into present, distant to near. It has offered the spectator a mediated relationship with imaged others from diverse cultures. We are not suggesting that imperialism was inscribed either in the apparatus or in the celluloid, only that the context of imperial power shaped the uses to which both apparatuses and celluloid were put. In an imperial context, the apparatus tended to be deployed in ways flattering to the imperial subject as superior and invulnerable observer, as what Mary Louise Pratt calls the "monarch-of-all-I-survey." The cinema's ability to "fly" spectators around the globe gave them a subject position as film's audiovisual masters. The "spatially mobilized visuality"[26] of the I/Eye of empire spiraled outward around the globe, creating a visceral, kinetic sense of imperial travel and conquest, transforming European spectators into armchair conquistadors, affirming their sense of power while making the inhabitants of the colonies objects of spectacle for the metropole's voyeuristic gaze.

Spectatorial Displacements

Although film spectatorship can shape an imperial imaginary, as we have seen, there is nothing inherent in the cinema that makes spectatorship *necessarily* regressive. The strong "subject effects" produced by narrative cinema are not automatic or irresistible, nor can they be separated from the desire, experience, and knowledge of historically situated spectators, constituted outside the text and traversed by sets of power relations such as nation, race, class, gender, and sexuality. Media spectatorship forms a triated plurilogue between texts, readers, and communities existing in clear discursive and social relation to one another. It is thus a negotiable site, an evolving scene of interaction and struggle, seen, for example, in the possibility of "aberrant" or resistant readings, as the consciousness or experience of a particular local audience generates a counter pressure to globally dominant representations.

In its quasi-exclusive focus on sexual as opposed to other kinds of difference, and in its privileging of the intrapsychic as opposed to the intersubjective and the discursive, film theory has often elided questions of racially, culturally, and historically inflected spectatorship. And although recent media theory has productively explored the sociologically differentiated modes of spectatorship, it has rarely done so through a multicultural or transnational grid. The culturally variegated nature of spectatorship derives from the diverse locations in which films are received, from the temporal gaps of seeing films in different historical moments to the conflictual subject-positionings and community affiliations of the spectators themselves. The colonial situation in which colonized Africans and Asians went to European-owned theaters to watch European and Hollywood films, for example, encouraged a kind of spectatorial schizophrenia or ambivalence in the colonized subject, who might on the one hand internalize Europe as ideal ego and on the other resent (and often protest) offensive representations. Some of the major figures articulating anticolonial and postcolonial discourse symptomatically return in their writing to colonial spectatorship as a kind of primal scene. The "cinema stories of fabulous Hollywood," writes Kwame Nkrumah:

> are loaded. One has only to listen to the cheers of an African audience as Hollywood's heroes slaughter red Indians or Asiatics to understand the effectiveness of this weapon. For in the developing continents, where the colonialist heritage has left a vast majority still illiterate, even the smallest child gets the message.[27]

The Martiniquian revolutionary theorist Frantz Fanon, the Ethiopian-American filmmaker Haile Gerima, and the Palestinian-American cultural critic Edward Said have all registered the impact of *Tarzan* on their impressionable young selves. Gerima recalls the "crisis of identity" provoked in an Ethiopian child applauding Johnny Weissmuller as he cleansed the "dark continent" of its inhabitants: "Whenever Africans sneaked up behind Tarzan, we would scream our heads off, trying to warn him that 'they' were coming."[28] In *Black Skin, White Masks,* Fanon too brings up *Tarzan* to point to a certain instability within cinematic identification:

> Attend showings of a Tarzan film in the Antilles and in Europe. In the Antilles, the young negro identifies himself de facto with Tarzan against the Negroes. This is much more difficult for him in a European theatre, for the rest of the audience, which is white, automatically identifies him with the savages on the screen.[29]

Fanon's example points to the shifting, situational nature of colonized spectatorship: the colonial context of reception alters the very process of identification. The consciousness of the possible negative projections of other spectators triggers an anxious withdrawal from the film's programmed pleasures. The conventional self-denying identification with the white hero's gaze, the vicarious performance of a European selfhood, is short-circuited through the awareness of being looked at in a certain way, as if one were being "screened" or "allegorized" by a colonial gaze within the movie theater. While feminist film theory has spoken of the "to-be-looked-at-ness" (Laura Mulvey) of female screen performance, Fanon's example calls attention to the "to-be-looked-at-ness" of spectators themselves, who become slaves, as Fanon puts it, of their own appearance: "Look, a Negro! . . . I am being dissected under white eyes. I am *fixed*."[30]

On the other hand, spectators can also return the gaze through critical comments or hostile looks. An active exchange of words and looks, whether in the movie theaters of colonial Egypt, India, or in Times Square, turns public spectatorship into a discursive battle zone, where members of the audience actively negotiate "looking relations" (Jane Gaines) between communities. In *Alexandria Why . . . ?* the movie theater literally becomes a space of ideological combat between an Australian soldier and Egyptian nationalists, while the Egyptian protagonist is lost in a Hollywood dream, watching a sequence (Helen Powell's "Red, White, and Blue" staged in front of battleship guns aimed at the camera/spectator) that encodes its own nationalist agenda. Social contradiction, as such cases make clear, is alive not only in media texts but also within the audience. James Baldwin in the 1970s contrasted his own experience of watching Hollywood films, where almost no one looked like he did, with his attendance at Harlem performances of Orson Welles's all-black *Macbeth* (1936), where Macbeth was "a nigger, just like me" and "where I saw the witches in church, every sunday."[31] Baldwin also recounts the racially differentiated reaction to *The Defiant Ones* (1958), a film that for him was rooted in a profound misunderstanding of the nature of racial hatred. Recounting the reaction of a Harlem audience, Baldwin wrote:

> It is this which black audiences resented about *The Defiant Ones*: that Sidney was in company far beneath him, and that the unmistakable truth of his performance was being placed at the mercy of a lie. Liberal white audiences applauded when Sidney, at the end of the film, jumped off the train in order not to abandon his white buddy. The Harlem audience was outraged, and yelled "Get back on the train, you fool!"[32]

Sidney jumps off the train, Baldwin concludes, in order to delude white people into thinking that they are not hated. The film's "liberal" gesture of inverting the imperial and masculinist rescue trope (here the black man rescues the white), its proposal of a utopia of interracial male camaraderie, still maintains the black in a subservient space. It fails to imagine the historical depths of a black consciousness unimpressed by such "heroism." Audience reactions thus can divide along racial lines, as in cases where a historical film (e.g., *Ganga Zumba*) shows a black rebel killing a slave driver, where it is not uncommon for black spectators to applaud, while whites (even radical whites) hold back. In such cases, the socially differentiated reactions of spectators become obvious. Applause, sighs, gasps, and other expressions of audience affectivity render palpable the visceral feelings that lurk behind abstract phrases like "spectatorial positioning."

Neither text nor spectator is a static, preconstituted entity; spectators shape and are shaped by the cinematic experience within an endless dialogical process. Cinematic desire is not only intrapsychic; it is also social and ideological. In this sense, Stuart Hall's class- and ideology-based notion of "negotiated readings" might be extended to issues of race and ethnicity. Here too we might speak of *racially* "dominant" readings, *racially* "negotiated" readings, and *racially* "resistant" readings.[33] We would add that a "resistant" reading on one axis (e.g., class) might go hand in hand with a "dominant" reading on another axis (e.g., race), along all the permutations of social identity and affiliation. David Morley, complicating Hall's tripartite schema, argues for a discursive approach that would define spectatorship as the "moment when the discourses of the reader meet the discourse of the text."[34] Any comprehensive ethnography of spectatorship must distinguish multiple registers of spectatorship: (1) the spectator as fashioned by the text itself (through focalization, point-of-view conventions, narrative structuring, mise-en-scène); (2) the spectator as fashioned by the (diverse and evolving) technical apparatuses (movie theater, domestic VCR); (3) the spectator as fashioned by the institutional contexts of spectatorship (social ritual of moviegoing, classroom analysis, cinematheque); (4) the spectator as constituted by ambient discourses and ideologies; (5) the actual spectator as embodied, raced, gendered, and geographically and historically situated. Text, apparatus, discourse, and history, in sum, are all in play and in motion. The analysis of spectatorship must therefore explore the gaps and tensions among the different levels, the diverse ways that text, apparatus, history, and discourse construct the spectator and the ways that the spectator as subject/interlocutor shapes the encounter.

Nor is there a perfect match between alternative spectator and alternative text: here too there are fault lines and tensions over class, gender, sexuality, and ideology. Indeed, we would argue against the notion of any racially, culturally or even ideologically circumscribed essential spectator—*the* white spectator, *the* black spectator, *the* Latino/a spectator, *the* resistant spectator. First, the categories themselves are sociologically imprecise, suppressing the heteroglossia characteristic of all communities. Is the "Latino/a spectator" a wealthy Cuban businessman, a Salvadorean refugee, or a Chicana domestic worker? Second, the categories repress the heteroglossia within spectators themselves. Spectators do not have single monolithic identities but are involved in multiple identities (and identifications) having to do with gender, race, nation, region, sexual preference, class, and age. Third, socially imposed epidermic identities do not strictly determine personal identifications and political allegiances. It is not only a question of what one is or from which locale one is coming, but also of what one desires to be, where one wants to go, and with whom one wants to go there. Within a complex combinatoire of spectatorial positions, members of an oppressed group might identify with the oppressing group (Native American children being induced to root for the cowboys against the "Indians," Africans identifying with Tarzan, Arabs with Indiana Jones), just as members of privileged groups might identify with the struggles of oppressed groups. Spectatorial positioning is relational: communities can identify with one another on the basis of a shared closeness or on the basis of a common antagonist. The spectator, in sum, inhabits a shifting realm of ramifying differences and contradictions.

Thus spectatorial positions are multiform, fissured, even schizophrenic. The view of spectatorial identification as culturally, discursively, and politically discontinuous suggests a series of gaps; the same person might be crossed by contradictory discourses and codes. The spectator comes to the cinema psychically disposed and historically positioned. The viewer of hegemonic cinema might consciously support one narrative or ideology, yet be subliminally seduced by the other fantasies proffered by the text. Thus we cannot posit a simple polarity between ceaselessly resistant, politically correct spectators on the one hand and cultural dupes on the other. Even politically correct spectators are complex, contradictory, unevenly developed. On one level this "uneven development" has to do with the contradiction between the charismatic charm and power of the apparatus, of narrative, of performance, on the one hand, and the degree of the spectator's intellectual or political distance from that charm and power on the other. Bertolt Brecht's account of his reaction to a classic imperialist film, George Stevens's *Gunga Din* (1939), is revelatory in this regard:

In the film *Gunga Din* . . . I saw British occupation forces fighting a native population. . . . The Indians were primitive creatures, either comic or wicked: comic when loyal to the British, and wicked when hostile. . . . One of the Indians betrayed his compatriots to the British, sacrificed his life so that his fellow country-men should be defeated, and earned the audience's heart-felt applause. My heart was touched too: I felt like applauding and laughed in all the right places. Despite the fact that I knew all the time that there was something wrong, that the Indians are not primitive and un-cultured people but have a magnificent age-old culture, and that this Gunga Din could also be seen . . . as a traitor to his people.[35]

Even the theorist of distantiation, then, could not distance himself emotionally from the powerful mythmaking machines of empire.

That the spectator is the scene of proliferating differences and contradic-tions does not mean that an opposite, agglutinative process of cross-racial and cross-cultural identifications and alliance imagining does not also take place. Amending Raymond Williams, we would argue for the existence, in life as in spectatorship, of "*analogical* structures of feeling," that is, for a structuring of filmic identification across social, political, and cultural situations, through strongly perceived or dimly felt affinities of social perception or historical experience. Spectatorship is not sociologically compartmentalized; diverse communities can resonate together. In a context where one's own community goes unrepresented, analogical identifications become a compensatory outlet. A member of a minority might look for him/herself on the screen, but failing that, might identify with the next closest category, much as one transfers alle-giance to another sports team after one's own team has been eliminated from the competition. Larry Peerce's *One Potato, Two Potato* (1964), a film about interracial marriage, offers a poignant narrative example of this analogical process. The black husband in the film, enraged by a series of racially motivated slights, attends a western in a drive-in movie theater. Projecting his anger, he screams out his support for the Indians, whom he sees as his analogues in suf-fering, and his hatred for the cowboys. Reading "against the grain" of the west-ern's colonialist discourse, he is thrown into the imaginative space of alliance.

Far from being essentially regressive and alienating, the space of media spectatorship is politically ambivalent. The theories of the apparatus and of dominant cinema first developed in the 1970s were rightly critiqued as being monolithic, even paranoid, failing to allow for progressive deployment of the apparatus, or for resistant texts, or for "aberrant readings." The very word "apparatus" evokes an overwhelming cinema-machine, imagined as a monstrous operation or *engrenage,* in which the spectator is denied even a Chaplinesque *Modern Times*-style subterfuge. But real-life spectatorship is more complex and overdetermined. Anyone who has been part of or witnessed a combative audience given to hisses, insults, ironic laughter, and satiric repartee is unlikely to portray spectators as the passive objects of an all-powerful apparatus. In communities given to impromptu verbal improvisation, the audience comments to the screen (and to each other) affirming the existence of the community itself.[36] At times a full-scale dialogue breaks out; the film loses its diegetic hold as the spectacle is displaced from screen to audience. Paralinguistic expressions, such as hisses or applause, create a distantiating effect; audience participation modifies the experience of the film.

Media Culture and Community Identity

The same cinematic apparatus that creates blockbusters can also provide alternative films to audiences. While adventure films can nourish imperial narcissism, other films flatter the subjects of less retrograde ideologies. Nor are Hollywood films monolithically reactionary. Even hegemonic texts have to negotiate diverse community desires—Hollywood calls it "market research." As Fredric Jameson, Hans Magnus Enzensberger, Richard Dyer, and Jane Feuer have all argued, to explain the public's attraction to a text or medium one must look not only for the "ideological effect" that manipulates people into complicity with existing social relations, but also for the kernel of utopian fantasy reaching beyond these relations, whereby the medium constitutes itself as a projected fulfillment of what is desired and absent within the status quo. Symptomatically, even imperialist heroes like Indiana Jones and Rambo are posited not as the oppressors but as the liberators of subject peoples. Films can nourish dreams of upward mobility or encourage struggle for social transformation. Altered contexts, meanwhile (for example alternative films screened in hospitals, union halls, and community centers) also generate altered readings. The confrontation is not simply between individual spectator and individual author/film—a formulation that recapitulates the individual-versus-society trope—but between and among diverse communities within diverse contexts viewing diverse films in diverse ways.

   A purely cognitive approach to film reception allows little space for such differences. It does not explore how spectators can be made to identify with tales told against themselves. Privileging denotation over connotation, a cognitive model has little room for what one might call *racialized schemata or eth-nically inflected cognition,* that is, the fact that the appearance of a white police-man in a film, for example, might trigger feelings of ease and protectedness in some "interpretive communities" and bitter memories and feelings of menace in others. Different reactions to films are symptomatic of different historical experiences and social desires. How do we account for orientalist films screened in the Middle East, where the spectator is simultaneously pleasured by lux-uriant Western fantasies and irritated by a distorting specularity? And through what displacements of identification is *Rambo* received in anti-U.S. Lebanon not as a product of American imperialism but as an exemplum of soldierly courage?

Perception itself is embedded in history. The same filmic images or sounds provoke distinct reverberations for different communities. For the Euro-American, shots of Mount Rushmore might evoke fond memories of patriotic father figures; for the Native American they might evoke feelings of dispossession and injustice. What does it mean, for a reservation-based Native American, to hear the lyrics from the theme song to *Oklahoma!*—"We know we belong to the land/and the land we belong to is grand"? A shot of a familial visit to church, a character crossing himself, or the sound of church bells to an-nounce a marriage or a death all address themselves to an interlocutor pre-sumed to be, if not Christian, at least familiar with Christian culture. But images which for one spectator evoke a reassuring norm, for another might just as easily provoke a sense of exclusion, and in the specific case of Jewish culture even come burdened with overtones of oppression. (In Jewish poetry, for ex-ample, church bells often signify danger.)[37] If communities respond differently to symbolically charged events like national holidays ("Thanksgiving" for Na-tive Americans) and religious rituals (Christmas for Jews, Muslims, Buddhists), they should respond no differently to mediated representations. A multi-cultural audiovisual pedagogy, in this sense, would render explicit hidden as-sumptions about address, problematizing the text's "universal" norms.

Resistant readings, for their part, depend on a certain cultural or political preparation that "primes" the spectator to read critically. In this sense we would question the more euphoric claims of theorists, such as John Fiske, who see TV viewers as mischievously working out "subversive" readings based on their own popular memory. Fiske rightly rejects the "hypodermic needle" view that sees TV viewers as passive drugged patients getting their nightly fix, reduced to "couch potatoes" and "cultural dupes." He suggests that minorities, for exam-ple, "see through" the racism of the dominant media. But if it is true that disempowered communities can decode dominant programming through a resistant perspective, they can do so only to the extent that their collective life and historical memory have provided an alternative framework of understanding. In the case of the Persian Gulf war, for example, the majority of American viewers, including many people of color, lacked any alternative grid to help them interpret events, specifically a view rooted in an understanding of the legacy of colonialism and its particular complexities in the Middle East. Primed by orientalist discourse and by the sheer inertia of the imperializing imaginary, they gave credence to whatever views the administration chose to present. Thus even some victims of racism within the United States were persuaded by the media to buy into an imperialist narrative, made to forget the linked analogies between colonial/international and domestic/national forms of oppression.

In an increasingly transnational world, characterized by nomadic images, sounds, goods, and peoples, media spectatorship impacts complexly on national identity, communal belonging, and political affiliation. To a certain extent, a negotiation with diverse national desires is built into cinema, in that most film industries, especially those without strong domestic markets, have to take into account the possible reactions of other nationalities. At times, collective memories and desires encounter one another in a kind of transcultural rendezvous. Film, television, and video allow immigrants, refugees, and exiles to luxuriate in the landscapes of their lost homeland, to bathe in the sounds of their childhood language. The media and exile interact in what Hamid Naficy calls a space of "liminality" involving "ambivalences, resistances, slippages, dissimulations, doubling, and even subversions of the cultural codes of *both* the home and host societies."[38] Arabic, Hindi, and Farsi videotapes (unsubtitled) are sold in local grocery stores in the United States, reinforcing a community imaginary and sometimes suggesting a desire for insularity, a denial of "being here." Iranian exile TV programs such as *Parandush* nourish nostalgia for the homeland through maps, landscapes, and poetry, invoking the paradigm of exile as it has traditionally functioned within Iranian culture. The viewer's glance takes in TV programming from the standpoint of an interior crowded with ethnically coded souvenirs, carpets, flags, aromas, and handicrafts.[39] For Arab Jews (Mizrahim) in Israel, marginalized by official hostility toward the "Orient," watching Egyptian, Turkish, Indian, and Iranian films releases a communal nostalgia, disallowed in the public sphere, for their Middle Eastern and North African countries of origins. Transnational spectatorship can also mold a space of future-oriented desire, nourishing the imaginary of "internal émigrés," actively crystallizing a sense of a viable "elsewhere," giving it a local habitation and a name, evoking a possible "happy end" in another nation. Given the inequitable distribution of power among nations and peoples, such movements are often one-directional, and the desire for an elsewhere is often frustrated by the law of green cards and border patrols. Cross-cultural spectatorship, in other words, is not simply a utopian exchange between communities, but a dialogue deeply embedded in the asymmetries of power.

The ethnically hybrid character of most world metropolises, meanwhile, turns cinemagoing into a revealing multicultural experience: screenings of "foreign" films for mixed audiences in New York or London or Paris, for example, can create a gap between cultural "insiders," who laugh at the jokes and recognize the references, and the "outsiders" who experience an abrupt dislocation. Not conversant with the culture or language in question, they are reminded of the limits of their own knowledge and indirectly of their own potential status as foreigners. Thus First Worlders in their own countries come to share an experience common to dislocated Third World and minoritarian audiences; the feeling that "this film was not made for us."

If spectatorship is on one level structured and determined, on another it is open and polymorphous. The cinematic experience has a ludic and adventurous side as well as an imperious one; it fashions a plural, "mutant" self, occupying a range of subject positions.[40] One is "doubled" by the cinematic apparatus, at once in the movie theater and with the camera/projector and the action on screen. And one is further dispersed through the multiplicity of perspectives provided by even the most conventional montage. Cinema's "polymorphous projection-identifications" (Edgar Morin) on a certain level transcend the determinations of local morality, social milieu, and ethnic affiliation.[41] Spectatorship can become a liminal space of dreams and self-fashioning. Through its psychic chameleonism, ordinary social positions, as in carnival, are temporarily bracketed.

Contemporary spectatorship and media pedagogy must also be considered in the light of the changing audio-visual technologies. These technologies make it possible to bypass the search for a profilmic model in the world; one can give visible form to abstract ideas and improbable dreams. The image is no longer a copy but rather acquires its own life and dynamism within an interactive circuit. Electronic mail, meanwhile, makes it possible for a community of strangers to exchange texts, images, video sequences, thus enabling a new kind of transcommunitarian media culture. Computer graphics, interactive technologies, and "virtual reality" carry the "bracketing" of social positions to unprecedented lengths. Within cybernetic paraspace, the flesh-and-blood body lingers in the real world while computer technology projects the cybersubject into a terminal world of simulations. Such technologies expand the reality effect exponentially by switching the viewer from a passive to a more interactive position, so that the raced, gendered sensorial body could be implanted, theoretically, with a constructed virtual gaze, becoming a launching site for identity travel. Might virtual reality or computer simulation be harnassed, one wonders, for the purposes of multicultural or transnational pedagogy, in order to communicate, for example, what it feels like to be an "illegal alien" pursued by the border police or a civil rights demonstrator feeling the lash of police brutality in the early 1960s? Yet it would be naive to place exaggerated faith in these new technologies, for their expense makes them exploitable mainly by corporations and the military. As ever, the power resides with those who build, disseminate, and commercialize the systems.[42] All the technological sophistication in the world, furthermore, does not guarantee empathy or trigger political commitment. The historical inertia of race, class, and gender stratification is not so easily erased. Nor should an antiracist pedagogy rely on empathy alone. A person might "sample" oppression and conclude nothing more than: "C'est la vie" or "Thank God it wasn't me!" The point is not merely to communicate sensations but rather to advance structural understanding and promote change.

Within postmodern culture, the media not only set agendas and frame debates but also inflect desire, memory, fantasy. By controlling popular memory, they can contain or stimulate popular dynamism. The challenge, then, is to develop a media practice by which subjectivities may be lived and analyzed as part of a transformative, emancipatory praxis.[43] The question of the political "correctness" of texts is ultimately less important than the question of mobilizing desire in empowering directions. The question then becomes: How can we transform existing media so as to mobilize adversary subjectivity? Given the libidinal economy of media reception, how do we crystallize individual and collective desire for emancipatory purposes? In this sense, media culture must pay attention to what Guattari calls the "production machines" and "collective mutations" of subjectivity. As right-wing forces attempt to promote a superegoish "conservative reterritorialization" of subjectivity, those seeking change in an egalitarian direction must know how to crystallize individual and collective desire.

Since cultural identity, as Stuart Hall has pointed out, is a matter of "becoming" as well as "being," belonging to the future as well as the past,[44] multicultural media could provide a nurturing space where the secret hopes of social life are played out, a laboratory for the safe articulation of identity oppressions and utopias, a space of community fantasies and imagined alliances. Media culture of this kind joins and parallels the realm of "indigenous media" as a means for "reproducing and transforming cultural identity among people who have experienced massive political, geographic, and economic disruption."[45] Alex Juhasz, extending Ginsburg's conception to First World alternative media, sees AIDS activist video as a form of "indigenous media," where people who have experienced "massive disruption" counter their oppression.[46] Speaking of the camcorder activism of the Kayapo in Brazil, Terence Turner stresses how their video work concentrates not on the retrieval of an idealized precontact past but on the processes of identity construction in the present. The Kayapo use video to communicate between villages, to record and thus perpetuate their own ceremonies and rituals, to record the official promises of Euro-Brazilian politicians (and thus hold them accountable), and to disseminate their cause around the world, in what Turner calls a "synergy between video media, Kayapo self-representation, and Kayapo ethnic self-consciousness."[47] Just as people all over the world have turned to cultural identity as a means of mobilizing the defense of their social, political, and economic interests, multicultural media activism might serve to protect threatened identities or even create new identities, a catalyst not only for the public sphere assertion of particular cultures but also for fostering the "collective human capacity for self-production."[48] We might see media in this sense as exercising a tribalizing power, as potentially increasing a community's *ache* (Yoruba for "power of realization"), with media art as participating in the creation of an emergent transcultural community.

Notes

1   See, for example, A. D. King, ed., *Culture, Globalization and the World-System* (London: Macmillan, 1991).

2   See David Rowe, Geoffrey Lawrence, Toby Miller, and Jim McKay, "Global Sport? Core Concern and Peripheral Vision," *Media, Culture and Society* (London) 16 (1994): 661–675.

3   A similar concept, "scattered hegemonies," is advanced by Inderpal Grewal and Caren Kaplan who use the phrase in their "Introduction: Transnational Feminist Practices and Questions of Postmodernity," *Scattered Hegemonies: Postmodernity and Transnational Feminist Practices* (Minneapolis: University of Minnesota Press, 1994).

4   See Inderpal Grewal and Caren Kaplan, Introduction, *Scattered Hegemonies*.

5   See Heinz Dieterich, "Five Centuries of the New World Order," *Latin American Perspectives* 19, no. 3 (Summer 1992).

6   See Jon Bennet, *The Hunger Machine* (Cambridge: Polity Press, 1987), p. 19.

7   Needless to say, we use the term "Hollywood" not to convey a knee-jerk rejection of all commercial cinema, but rather as a kind of shorthand for a massively industrial, ideologically reactionary, and stylistically conservative form of "dominant" cinema.

8   See Mark Schapiroo, "Bollywood Babylon," *Image* (June 28, 1992).

9   Appadurai posits five dimensions of these global cultural flows: (1) ethnoscapes (the landscape of persons who constitute the shifting world in which people live); (2) technoscapes (the global configuration of technologies moving at high speeds across previously impermeable borders); (3) financescapes (the global grid of currency speculation and capital transfer); (4) mediascapes (the distribution of the capabilities to produce and disseminate information and the large complex repertoire of images and narratives generated by these capabilities); and (5) ideoscapes (ideologies of states and counterideologies of movements, around which nation-states have organized their political cultures). See Arjun Appadurai, "Disjunction and Difference in the Global Cultural Economy," *Public Culture* 2, no. 2 (Spring 1990): 1–24.

10   See Faye Ginsburg, "Aboriginal Media and the Australian Imaginary," *Public Culture* 5, no. 3 (Spring 1993).

11   The three most active centers of indigenous media production are native North American (Inuit, Yup'ik), Indians of the Amazon Basin (Nambiquara, Kayapo), and Aboriginal Australians (Warlpiri, Pitjanjajari). In 1982, the Inuit Broadcasting Corporation (IBC) began broadcasting regularly scheduled TV programs in order to strengthen the culture of the Inuit spread across Northern Canada. In Kate Madden's account, Inuit programming reflects Inuit cultural values. The news/public affairs program *Oagik* ("Coming Together"), for example, departs dramatically from Western norms and conventions by avoiding stories that might cause a family pain or intrude on their privacy and by eschewing any hierarchy between correspondents and anchors. See Kate Madden, "Video and Cultural Identity: The Inuit Broadcasting Experience," in *Mass-Media Effects Across Cultures,* ed. Felipe Korzenny and Stella Ting-Toomey (London: Sage, 1992).

12   Indigenous media have remained largely invisible to the First World public except for occasional festivals (for example the Native American Film and Video Festivals held regularly in San Francisco and New York City, or the Latin American Film Festival of Indigenous Peoples held in Mexico City and Rio de Janeiro).

13   Faye Ginsburg, "Indigenous Media: Faustian Contract or Global Village?" *Cultural Anthropology* 6, no. 1 (1991): 94.

14   Ibid.

15   For a critical view of the Kayapo project, see Rachel Moore, "Marketing Alterity," *Visual Anthropology Review* 8, no. 2 (Fall 1992), and James C. Faris, "Anthropological Transparency: Film, Representation and Politics," in *Film as Ethnography,* ed. Peter Ian Crawford and David Turton (Manchester: Manchester University Press, 1992). For an answer by Turner to Faris, see "Defiant Images: The Kayapo Appropriation of Video," Forman

Lecture, RAI Festival of Film and Video in Manchester 1992, forthcoming in *Anthropology Today.*

16 See Terence Turner's account of his long-standing collaboration with the Kayapo in "Visual Media, Cultural Politics, and Anthropological Practice," *The Independent* 14, no. 1 (Jan.–Feb. 1991).

17 See Jon Pietersie's chapter on "Colonialism and Popular Culture" in *White on Black* (New Haven: Yale, 1992), p. 77.

18 Robert Baden-Powell, *Scouting for Boys*, quoted in Joseph Bristow, *Empire Boys: Adventures in a Man's World* (London: HarperCollins, 1991), p. 170.

19 Joseph Bristow, *Empire Boys: Adventures in a Man's World* (London: HarperCollins, 1991), p. 19.

20 Patrick Brantlinger, *Rule of Darkness: British Literature and Imperialism 1830–1914* (Ithaca: Cornell University Press, 1988), p. 11.

21 See John McClure, *Late Imperial Romance: Literature and Globalization from Conrad to Pynchon* (London: Verso, 1994).

22 Benedict Anderson, *Imagined Communities* (New York: Verso, 1983), pp. 41–46.

23 For more on the extrapolation of Bakhtin's notion of the chronotope, see Robert Stam, *Subversive Pleasures: Bakhtin, Cultural Criticism, and Film* (Baltimore: Johns Hopkins, 1989); Kobena Mercer, "Diaspora Culture and the Dialogic Imagination," in *Blackframes*, ed. Mbay Cham and Claire Andrade-Watkins (Cambridge: MIT, 1988); and Paul Willemen, "The Third Cinema Question: Notes and Reflections," in *Questions of Third Cinema*, ed. Jim Pines and Paul Willemen (London: BFI, 1989).

24 Movie theaters in the colonized world were first built only in urban centers such as Cairo, Baghdad, Bombay. For early responses to the cinema in Baghdad, Ella Shohat has conducted series of interviews with Baghdadis from her own community, now dispersed in Israel/Palestine, England, and New York.

25 Christian Metz, *The Imaginary Signifier: Psychoanalysis and the Cinema* (Bloomington: Indiana University Press, 1982), p. 51.

26 For more on the "mobilized gaze" of the cinema, see Anne Friedberg's discussion in *Window Shopping: Cinema and the Postmodern* (Berkeley: University of California Press, 1993).

27 Kwame Nkrumah, *Neo-Colonialism: The Last Stage of Imperialism* (London: Nelson, 1965), p. 246.

28 Haile Gerima, interview with Paul Willemen, *Framework*, nos. 7–8 (Spring 1978): 32.

29 Frantz Fanon, *Black Skin, White Masks* (New York: Grove Press, 1967), pp. 152–53.

30 Ibid., pp. 112–116.

31 James Baldwin, *The Devil Finds Work* (New York: Dial, 1976), p. 34.

32 Ibid., p. 62.

33 Stuart Hall, "Encoding/Decoding," in *Culture, Media, Language* (London: Hutchison, 1980), p. 136.

34 See David Morley, *The "Nationwide Audience": Structure and Decoding* (London: British Film Institute, 1980).

35 John Willet, ed., *Brecht on Theatre* (London: Hill & Wang, 1964), p. 151.

36 Christian Metz makes a similar point about audiences in provincial Spain. See *The Imaginary Signifier.*

37 In *Singin' in the Rain,* to take a counterexample, Gene Kelly and Donald O'Connor, as they sing "Moses," wrap themselves with lined curtains reminiscent of Jewish prayer shawls (*talith*), a visual allusion that Jewish spectators are more likely to appreciate.

38 Hamid Naficy, *The Making of Exile Cultures: Iranian Television in Los Angeles* (Minneapolis: University of Minnesota, 1993), p. xvi.

39 Ibid., p. 106.

40 See Jean-Louis Schefer, *L'Homme Ordinaire du Cinema* (Paris: Gallimard, 1980).

41 See Edgar Morin, *Le Cinema ou L'Homme Imaginaire* (Paris: Gonthier, 1958).

42 Anne Friedberg, *Les Flaneurs du Mal(l): Cinema and the Postmodern Condition* (Berkeley: University of California Press, 1992).

43 See Rhonda Hammer and Peter McLaren, "The Spectacularization of Subjectivity: Media Knowledges, Global Citizenry, and the New World Order," *Polygraph,* no. 5 (1992).

44 Stuart Hall, "Cultural Identity and Cinematic Representation," *Framework* 36 (1989).

45 Faye Ginsburg, "Indigenous Media," p. 94.

46 Alexandra Juhasz, "Re-Mediating AIDS: The Politics of Community Produced Video" (Ph.D. diss., NYU, 1991).

47 Terence Turner, "Defiant Images."

48 Terence Turner, "What is Anthropology that Multiculturalists Should Be Mindful of It?" unpublished paper, presented at the American Anthropological Association, San Francisco, 1992.

II LOCAL CONJUNCTIONS

FLIRTING WITH THE FOREIGN: INTERRACIAL SEX IN JAPAN'S "INTERNATIONAL" AGE

Karen Kelsky

●

Introduction

Since the late 1980s, a small population of young Japanese women has become the subject of intense controversy within Japan and abroad for its allegedly aggressive sexual pursuit of white, black, Balinese and other non-Japanese (or *gaijin*) males.[1] The activities of these women—labeled "yellow cabs" (*ierō kyabu*) in a racist, sexist slur coined by their foreign male conquests and appropriated by the Japanese mass media—have inspired best-selling novels, television documentaries, films, and, in the early 1990s, a heated debate in the major popular magazines. Anthropologist John Russell has observed of the phenomenon (which has tended to particularly sensationalize the role of black males), "what was once a taboo subject—the relations between black [men] and Japanese women—[has] suddenly become a topic fit for open discussion, sensational serials in Japanese magazines, late-night television debate, and underground cinema."[2] These women are interesting not only for the controversy that they have engendered in Japan, but also because they defy standard Western Orientalist understandings of the Asian-Western sexual encounter, typically based on the *Madame Butterfly* trope of Western male power over and victimization of the Oriental women. In the standard yellow cab narrative, it is wealthy and leisured young Japanese women who travel to exotic locales to pursue these sexual liaisons; it is the Japanese women who themselves pay for the expenses of initiating and maintaining the liaisons; and it is Japanese women who, along with Japanese men, have developed a thriving industry at home devoted to commentary upon and evaluation of the gaijin male as lover—a commentary entirely independent of the foreigner himself.

The term "yellow cab" is a slur that implies that Japanese women are "yellow," and that, like a New York taxi, "they can be ridden any time."[3] The persistent use of the term encapsulates the hysterical response of the male-dominated Japanese media (as well as of the foreign men who originally coined the term) to the specter of sexually aggressive and transgressive Japanese females. However, within the Japanese media there are competing voices, as the "yellow cabs" themselves, as well as female commentators and writers, proffer their own interpretations of the women's behavior. In fact, the graphic, semi-pornographic novels on the topic of black male-Japanese female sex which have comprised perhaps the most important element in this sensational media discussion have been written by two young women writers, Yamada Eimi and Ieda Shōko,[4] who are notorious for flaunting their preference for black men and black culture. These novels are not only best-sellers, but Yamada's work has been nominated for the Naoki and Akutagawa literary prizes—the most prestigious in the Japanese literary world.

In this essay I will examine the contradictions and negotiations which accompany the yellow cab phenomenon. I will show that critical Japanese male representations are countered and resisted by the women, who demonstrate their own active goals in choosing gaijin lovers. I argue that the goals and behavior of the so-called yellow cabs are in fact of considerable theoretical significance for a Western audience, for they constitute not only a coherent, although indirect, critique of Japanese patriarchy, but also an instance of the increasingly shifting and contested grounds of encounter between Japan and the West and, finally, the emerging local/global continuum along which both people and theories must now be tracked.

The intersections of race, gender, nationalism, and sexuality have come under increasing interrogation by Western scholars who are seeking to problematize the dark and obscure associations between "love of country," imperial will, and erotic longing. Much of this work has been concerned to show the extent to which "Oriental" and other nonwhite women have suffered from a unique brand of sexual colonization at the hands of Western men, not shared by their male counterparts. This line of research is necessary and valuable, and the various planes of continuing Western male power over the non-Western woman—particularly in the still obscure areas of sexual encounters and sex tourism—must be further explored. However, just as Appadurai and Breckenridge have argued that "old images that we associate with neo-colonialism" do not exhaust all that is happening within "new forms of transnational, cosmopolitan cultural traffic,"[5] so, it must be kept in mind, old images of the victimized native woman do not exhaust all the possibilities of contemporary Asian female-Western male sexual encounters. In the age of *M. Butterfly,* things are not so simple. Japan refuses to be contained by Western tropes and academic theories, and Japanese women (although this point seems scarcely recognized) in many ways defy the Western-set gender dichotomy between public powerlessness and private influence. For one thing, they refuse to be, echoing Appadurai, "incarcerated" in their native land. Japanese women—particularly young, single, "pink-collar" women—are perhaps the most enthusiastic and committed travelers of any demographic group in the world; they are also, arguably, one of the wealthiest, with an expendable income over twice that of the typical Japanese male and with an average expenditure in a vacation locale like Hawaii almost three times that of any other individual tourist. Thus Japanese women embody to a large degree what Clifford has called the new global "cosmopolitanism," which is marked, more than anything else, by the postmodern idiom of "travel" and the crossing (and inhabiting) of borders. This essay begins with the notion of culture as travel (as well as its inverse, "travel as culture") to interrogate the meanings of a population of young Japanese women who travel to post/neocolonial borderlands to pursue sexual encounters with non-Japanese men. By probing the competing Japanese female and male discourses on the yellow cab, I will show how the travel of this population of young Japanese women enacts and resists, defies and maintains, Japanese cultural norms of gender, race, and sexuality. My goal, however, is not thereby to draw conclusions about a timeless, bounded, and coherent entity called "the Japanese culture," but rather to set these local discourses against a global backdrop of increasingly complicated and interconnected transnational flows of people and power in order to show the circumstances of flux, confrontation, resistance, and displacement that mediate the global/local nexus of Japan in the world.

Without question "yellow cabs" are a small, marginal group, and the term itself is highly contested. Even the women who engage in such behavior would certainly not apply the term to themselves, for it has become a rhetorical weapon used by Japanese men to discredit a form of female behavior that they find threatening and disturbing and by foreign men to maintain hierarchies of power over Asian women. There are many Japanese women, including a group founded in New York City by Japanese professional writers called the Association to Think About Yellow Cabs (*ierō kyabu wo kangaeru kai*), who reject the term outright, alleging that no such women exist, and that the whole media phenomenon is the invention of Japanese men to undermine the activities of all

Japanese women abroad.[6] Indeed, as time has passed, the yellow cab controversy has begun to have a deleterious influence on the reputations of Japanese
women living abroad for any reason, first in Japan, but later even in the United
States, where the term and its meaning has slowly dispersed to parts of the
American male population. The anguish and humiliation at being labeled "yellow cabs" experienced by serious professional women residing overseas to pursue careers is undoubtedly great, and their consternation is understandable;
however, to censor and/or deny yellow cab reality is not an adequate solution.
Any such efforts to negate their existence and experience run the risk of reinscribing patriarchal systems' hostility toward and rejection of women as
sexual actors.

Connoisseurs of the West

However few their numbers, the women come in large part from the ranks of
"office ladies" (OLs): young, unmarried clerical officer workers who, through
the strategy of living with their parents, enjoy a larger expendable income than
any other group of people in Japan.[7] The OL has virtually no chance for upward
mobility within the company, and for this reason has been almost universally
branded, by Western observers, a victim of oppressive gender discrimination.
What is too little recognized, however, is the degree to which the OLs have
employed their considerable financial resources to construct a vital, vibrant
subculture of their own in the interstices of the male-dominated Japanese
business world. The very circumstances that are marks of the OLs' inferior
professional status—lack of serious responsibilities, shorter working hours,
flexibility to quit uncongenial jobs—are the same circumstances which leave
these women free to pursue a substantially independent lifestyle devoted to
shopping, hobbies, gourmet dining, overseas travel, and the satisfaction of
purely personal leisure desires.[8] Many observers have remarked that only the OL
is truly enjoying the fruits of the Japanese economic miracle.

    The OL lifestyle and subculture depend more than anything upon compli-
cated and sophisticated patterns of consumption and demand a single-minded
commitment to commodity ethics and aesthetics that goes beyond mere purchasing or appreciation, but instead enters the realm of connoisseurship. While
this consumption has undoubtedly declined since the bursting of the 1980s
"bubble economy" and extended recession, it still outpaces anything seen in
Western countries in many years. In fact, OL connoisseurship has long since
exhausted the resources of native or Japanese products and has in the last ten

years expanded to encompass the goods, services, experiences, and opportunities of the entire globe—in particular, the West. Many OLS have traveled so widely, and shopped so extensively, that they are satisfied with nothing less than the finest the West has to offer, including diamonds and gemstones, haute couture fashion, Club Med vacations, French perfumes, and designer goods of all types. Things Western are not merely coveted, however; that was the case for earlier generations for whom foreign goods were seductively exotic. Now, Western goods are contained as signifiers within a largely self-sufficient OL universe of style and status; the West has been "domesticated," to the extent that it is Japan itself that is now, for this generation, exotic and alien.

As Tobin has noted, Japan "now has the desire, wealth and power to import and consume passion in many forms from the West."[9] Thus the stage is set for a few of these cosmopolitan young women—these connoisseurs of the West and citizens of the (late capitalist) world—to cross Japan's borders in search of the "gaijin lover," the exotic sexual experience that represents the final frontier of the foreign left to consume.

Postcards from the Edge

The locations in which young women so inclined may seek out a gaijin male are many and varied, but are concentrated, within Japan, in the fashionable Roppongi district of Tokyo, Yokohama, Kōbe, and the U.S. military bases of Yokosuka, Yokota, Misawa, Iwakuni, Sasebo, and Okinawa. Outside of Japan, they include Hawaii, Bali, Saipan, New York, and the U.S. West Coast. Not coincidentally, each of these locations is a border region, inhabited by a highly transient, ethnically, racially, and culturally mixed population. Even the regions within Japan are not really of Japan. The American military bases are, of course, U.S. real estate; Yokohama and Kōbe are historically the centers of foreign presence in Japan; and the Roppongi district—commonly known as the "gaijin ghetto" of Tokyo—is a kind of dreamlike (or nightmarish) liminal region of bars and nightclubs in which Japanese and non-Japanese mingle freely. Each of these locations is geopolitically ambiguous, caught within the post/neocolonialist regimes of U.S. military presence abroad, Japanese investment, mass tourism, international labor flows, and commodification of the "native." As such, they are obvious places to seek out the foreign erotic, for the foreign men in these locations are themselves often wanderers from Europe and the mainland United States, gravitating to the borderlands of Asia and the West in search of the "erotic Orient."[10] In Hawaii these men are known locally as "playboys," and they form a bounded and mutually recognizable population which roams the streets of Waikiki daily, seeking out and accosting Japanese female tourists for money and sex. Likewise, every weekend night in Roppongi, the clubs are packed with foreign men hoping to encounter their "Roppongi girl" for the evening.

Once in these locations, the young women, extending the consumer patterns that dominate their lives elsewhere, pay for the company of foreign males. This is not an institutionalized prostitution, but rather falls within the rubric of *mitsugu,* an old Japanese word—defined in the dictionary to mean "to give financial aid to one's lover"—that has taken on new life in this transnational context. The practice of *mitsugu* of foreign males includes extension of loans (which may go unreturned), coverage of the foreign male's rent, upkeep, and outstanding debts, payment of all costs associated with the affair, and finally, material gifts including cars, designer goods, watches, and jewelry. It is understood by both parties that both inside and outside of Japan, Japanese women, as possessors of the strong yen, are likely to be in the financially superior position. As one "playboy" in Waikiki told me, "they know if they want us they have to pay for everything." Women have here usurped the traditionally male prerogative of purchasing sex in pleasure districts at home and abroad. Some women, in fact, assert that "it was Japanese men, with their sex tours, who taught us how to behave like this." As we shall see, however, Japanese men disclaim all responsibility for yellow cab behavior.

Deviance, Deception, and Defense of the State

The intensity of the public outcry surrounding this yellow cab behavior suggests that it has indeed struck a nerve, particularly among Japanese men. The response of Japanese male journalists to the specter of the yellow cab can be described very simply: it is reactionary, conservative, and prurient. Devoted to the reassertion and reinscription of all elements of Japanese national/racial/ sexual identity, and of traditional power hierarchies between Japanese men and women, men's representations derive their primary rhetorical force from the use of derogatory labels: not just yellow cab, but also *"burasagarizoku"* (armhangers), referring to the sight of diminutive Japanese women hanging on the arms of tall foreign men; *"sebun-irebun"* (seven-eleven), meaning that the women, like the stores, are "open twenty-four hours"; and *"eseburakku"* (fake blacks), referring to those who imitate "black" hairstyles, fashion, and mannerisms. Each of these labels draws attention to the ways in which "proper" racial/

gender boundaries have been violated. Yellow cab and *sebun-irebun* imply that the women's sexuality has become abandoned, out of control; *burasagarizoku* and *eseburakku* suggest that critical racial distinctions—tall foreigner/short Japanese, blackness/Japaneseness—are threatened. The use of these terms thus reinscribes the racial and gender boundaries deemed vital to the proper maintenance of the Japanese nation-state. At the same time, these boundaries are also interchangeably transgressive—and therefore doubly threatening. That is, historically, Japanese women are always already deeply associated with the foreign, and foreign men are always already highly sexualized. Thus, the foreign men also imperil sexual boundaries, and Japanese women also jeopardize national/racial ones. These two themes, then, combine together into one hypersexualized, hostile, and prurient male discourse that depends upon master narratives of oversexed foreign men and duplicitous Japanese women. "It's the Japanese girls who can be found dancing on the tables at discos, with their underpants showing for all to see. . . . They live in Waikiki hi-rises . . . that their daddies pay for."[11] "The temperature of Narita Airport goes up each time a planeload of girls returns from their trips overseas . . . and on outbound flights, they all may pretend to be little ladies, but actually, in their hearts, each one wants to be the first to get a gaijin to bed."[12]

Even the prose of highly regarded novelist and columnist Tanaka Yasuō (author of the popular cult novel *Nantonaku Kurisutaru* [Somehow, Crystal]), degenerates into a hostile diatribe on the subject of yellow cabs: "Of course, they have no use for Japanese men, and this shows on their faces. . . . They try to pretend that they're intellectuals, [but] people who know laugh at them. . . . These girls may seem delicate, but they're actually tough as nails."[13] Tanaka is clearly as disturbed by the women's deceptiveness as by their sexual transgressions. This fear of the "traitor in disguise," reveals the male linking of female sexual duplicity and national honor. This linking is most explicitly achieved in popular writer Ishikawa Miyoshi's recent suggestion that "Japanese women spread their legs a little wider for the sake of U.S.-Japan relations."[14]

Within this male rhetoric, AIDS takes on a dire significance. Through the specter of AIDS, Japanese men may at once paint the foreign male as not just an oversexed animal, but a diseased oversexed animal; the Japanese woman as treacherous and dirty; and themselves as innocent victims whose lives and health are endangered because of female duplicity. Again and again in the Japanese media, yellow cabs are targeted as the most high-risk group in Japan for HIV infection, while the men's sex tours to Thailand, Korea, and the Philippines go unmentioned. In fact, only a fraction of Japanese female heterosexual

HIV-positive individuals contracted the disease overseas, compared to heterosexual Japanese males. However, statistics cannot compete against a self-righteous male hysteria which culminated in one man plastering the walls and sidewalks of Waikiki with small, xeroxed notes that read: "Aloha Japanese girls . . . all men in Hawaii have AIDS. If you go with them, they will give you liquor and drugged cigarettes, and while you are sleeping, you will be raped, and have everything taken."[15] Writers such as Yamada Eimi and Ieda Shōko cannily feed into this hypersexualized hysteria by dwelling ostentatiously and obsessively in their novels on themes of black male sexual appetites and genital size. The works themselves are nothing more than soft-core pornographic novels which capitalize on the very worst racist notions of black male sexuality and racial inferiority:

> Nuzzling his chest hair with my lips, I inhaled his body odor. I recognized the smell as the sweetish stink of rotten cocoa butter. . . . His smell seemed to assault me, like some filthy thing. But it also made me feel, by comparison, clean and pure. His smell made me feel so superior. It was like the smell of musk that a dog in heat sends out to attract his bitch.[16]

> Jean stood over me as I lay naked on the bed, holding his heavy dick in his left hand and swinging it back and forth. I'm not usually so eager, but all I could think about was being wrapped in Jean's powerful body. . . . I was crazy with lust. . . . While he toyed with it, his copper-colored "thing," which had been dangling in his left hand, swelled. It seemed as if it reached to his navel. I can only say, it was a wonderful sight.[17]

Yet by taking this line, Yamada and Ieda are guaranteed not just good sales, but even critical acclaim and literary accolades from Japanese male reviewers.

Good Gaijins/Gaijin Goods

Women other then Yamada and Ieda, however, offer an entirely independent interpretation of the foreign male as lover—one that is, compared to the monotonous rantings of male commentators, varied, subtle, and complex. On one level, women's accounts are concerned with issues not of identity and morality, but of commodity and value. For what distinguishes the rhetoric of women is its shrewd and insistent contrast between Japanese and gaijin men—a kind of "comparison shopping" that carefully weighs the advantages of individual men on the basis of race and nationality.

The comparative advantages of the foreign male range widely, but include foremost an alleged "kindness" (*yasashisa*). It is in fact a virtual stereotype that foreign men are kind (*yasashii*), with many women offering contrasts like this one: "American men have been trained by their mothers since childhood to respect women—in a 'ladies first' kind of atmosphere. . . . But in Japan, women are always below men" (graduate student, University of Hawaii). Other women dwell on the good looks of foreign men, as in "A Japanese man's got to be dressed up to look good, but a gaijin looks good even when he looks bad." Foreign males' native English ability is often mentioned as an attraction. As one source stated, succinctly, "It's faster, cheaper, and more fun than going to English classes." Finally, of course, there is the allegedly superior sexual skill of the foreign male:

> Americans know how to enjoy sex! It's fun, natural, wonderful. Japanese men treat it like something dirty or bad.

> The thing that black guys have in bed that other guys don't is strong thrusting motion and a sense of rhythm.[18]

This sexual dimension is deemphasized, however, by others who claim that in the sexual act itself foreign men are the same as or inferior to Japanese men in skill. Such women argue that it is *yasashisa*, both in and out bed, that sets gaijin males apart. The glibly racist novels of Yamada Eimi and Ieda Shōko have, of course, made foreign male sexuality—in particular black male sexuality—a cause célèbre in Japan today.

The praise that is heaped upon the foreign male, however, is in most respects the praise given to a serviceable commodity object. Ieda states, "Girls know what they want!" "Chanel, Louis Vuitton bags, Hermes scarves, and gaijin men!"[19] Another woman, a habitué of Roppongi, suggests, "Gaijins are fun . . . but not if you fall in love . . . so it's better to just keep him around for awhile, to show off . . . like a pet."[20] Once again turning to the works of Yamada Eimi, we can see that the gaijin male is, in many ways, merely a "stand-in" for his penis. "[Spoon's] dick was not at all similar to the reddish, disgusting cocks of white guys. It was also different from the sad and pathetic organs of Japanese men. . . . Spoon's dick shone before my eyes like a living thing. It reminded me of the sweet chocolate candy bars I love."[21] Here it is the male genitals that are made into marketable commodities, and rated, by race, according to their serviceability.

When it comes to the question of marriage, some women are blunt: "I'll never marry a hairy barbarian [*ketō*]. I'll marry a Japanese even if he's terrible in bed and ugly. At least he's stable." A young woman interviewed on a television special entitled, "The Real Truth About 'Resort Lovers'" informed an aghast male interviewer that "In a few years I'll wash my hands of this whole gaijin business, and return to Japanese men." An English student I spoke with was even more direct: "For marriage we want a Japanese guy; for playing around we want gaijins." The gaijin male's serviceability, then, is only in the capacity of escort/lover, and the reason lies in his rarity—or "*mezurashisa.*"

> I have to admit we have a weakness for gaijins. The reason is, there aren't too many of them in Japan, so they're rare [*mezurashii*]. (English student, Hawaii)

> Why do we like blacks? 'Cause there aren't any in Japan [*nihon ni nai desho*]. (Tourist in Hawaii)

Apparently racial preferences shifted toward black men in the late 1980s based on the relative rarity of different racial types: "Two years ago everybody was going out with whites . . . but then, white guys weren't rare [*mezurashii*] anymore, so, right now everyone's going out with black guys" (English student). The commodity cycle continues to evolve as tastes more recently move toward Asian immigrant laborers. In men, as in other things, rarity brings status. This status is coveted, and its effect calculated. As *Cosmopolitan Japan* gushed in 1988, "We'd all like to be seen walking down the street arm in arm with a gaijin boyfriend, wouldn't we, girls?" A tourist in Hawaii explained, "We can walk a little taller. We think '*you* go out with men from the same country, but *I* go out with men from a different country.'" Complete objectification has been achieved: "Being with a gaijin feels good. . . . When another Japanese comes up and asks me 'what language is that?' I feel pretty proud, you know? So, he's an accessory. From that point of view, any gaijin will do, even Sankhon."[22]

Race and Reflexivity[23]

The primary characteristic of women's discourse on the foreign male is its insistent contrast between Japanese and gaijin men. The attractions of the foreigner are attractive precisely because those qualities—kindness, sexiness, English ability—are claimed to be lacking in the Japanese male. It is clear, then, that the Japanese male is the invisible but central point of reference in this female discussion. Intricately interwoven into the discourse on the "attractions of the gaijin" is a parallel discourse of frustration against the Japanese male. This discourse, although indirect, amounts to a coherent gender critique of Japanese society and Japanese men. Nearly every female statement from the previous two sections depends for its rhetorical force upon a critical contrast with the Japanese male: "But in Japan, women are always below men." "A Japanese guy would never do that." "Japanese men treat sex like something dirty."

Perhaps nowhere so much as in the realm of kindness (*yasashisa*) is the Japanese male felt to be deficient. As one source writes, poignantly, "[My black boyfriend] treated me like a lady after I'd been treated like trash by Japanese men." Another offers, "When I go to visit a British or Italian guy, they always . . . serve food and drinks themselves. But when I go to a Japanese guy's place, . . . he tries to make me clean his room and cook his dinner!"[24] Some women disparage the appearance of Japanese men: a tourist in Hawaii told me, "Gaijins are more masculine than skinny, unhealthy-looking Japanese men." And with exceptional virulence women can be heard criticizing the sexual behavior of their male counterparts: "Even in sex, I mean, if a gaijin is really telling you 'I want you, I need you, I want you,' you get in the mood, right? Not like with some stone-faced Japanese guy who tries to push you into a hotel all of a sudden."[25] As mentioned above, however, other women contest this emphasis on sexuality, arguing in some cases that Japanese men are actually better at "technique," but lack "emotional availability" or "the ability to create a romantic atmosphere."

Perhaps the most explicit summarization comes from the pen of journalist Kudō Akiko in the women's magazine *Fujin Kōron*:

> The reasons Japanese women reject Japanese men are *not just physical*. . . . Women evaluate them badly in all areas—"they are childish and disgusting," "they have a bad attitude toward women," "they are fake and dishonest," "they are narrow-minded," "they are bad-mannered," "they can't take care of themselves," "they can't do housework." . . . Japanese men are the opposite of the Japanese GNP—they are the lowest in the world![26]

In this passage the writer confronts the sexualized focus of the yellow cab controversy in order to deny that the attractions of the foreign male are "just physical." To the contrary, I would argue that the attractions of the foreign male are whatever the female speakers and writers feel is lacking in the Japanese male. For Kudō and others clearly imply that the gaijin male is *not* childish and disgusting, is *not* fake and dishonest, is *not* narrow-minded, and loves to do housework. Yet, do they truly believe this?[27] I argue that, rather, they attribute these traits to the gaijin for exclusively rhetorical purposes. The foreign male becomes a reflexive symbol in an indirect discourse of complaint; a mirror against which the Japanese women can reflect back the deficiencies of Japanese men as lovers, husbands, and friends. He enables a coherent, albeit indirect, gendered critique. We can interpret the yellow cab encounters, then, not, as the Association to Think About Yellow Cabs seeks to claim, as a conspiracy perpetrated by Japanese men, but rather as a locus of potent and influential negotiations between some Japanese women and men over present-day and future gender relations in Japan.

As we have seen, the foreign male in reality may not be remotely kind, good-looking, or sexy; these facts are irrelevant. What is important is merely that he is not-Japanese. He is seen as an inert and harmless object, inherently *yasashii*, infinitely separate, entirely Other, by virtue of Japanese racial ideologies, and therefore endlessly malleable to the pursuit of female aims and agendas. That the gaijin may have any agendas of his own, in the pursuit of which the Japanese (or other Asian woman) is merely a tool, is not recognized or perhaps even imagined. The consequences of this ignorance can, however, be serious. Time and again young Japanese women in Waikiki are raped, impregnated, or, at the very least, taken advantage of financially and physically by the local population of "playboys." My playboy informants were blissfully convinced of their power over Japanese women, bragging about the sums of money they had extracted from them, and the abusive, humiliating, and degrading sexual acts they had compelled the women to perform. The Western men, then, are hardly passive and inert.[28]

However, circumstances conspire against women's recognition of the real nature of the Western male partner. The fantasy of *yasashisa*, Japanese racial ideologies of separateness and "alien"ation, commodity aesthetics and commodity ethics, Japanese consumer power over the West—all these lead to the gaijin male being objectified and commodified, seen and treated in a manner that fails to recognize his agency and power.[29] Women have appropriated the gaijin males as reflexive symbols by which they construct an image of Japanese men as they are, and as they wish them to be. Yet for all his deficiencies, it is the Japanese man who, in the end, retains the status of legitimate marital partner. These "flirtatious commodities" (in a stunning illustration of Haug's argument) are, and must be, described in terms that communicate to Japanese women peers, and to Japanese men, that they are no more than discursive symbols through which genuine matters of power and status are discussed and negotiated.

Conclusion—Gender and (Trans)National Sexualities

Yellow cabs challenge prevailing stereotypes of many things: of the passive and victimized Japanese woman, of the Madame Butterfly trope, of the "proper" relations between Japan and the West. In conclusion I will trace the meanings of their challenge to understandings of Japan and the transnational moment.

The yellow cabs challenge us to consider the new meanings that cultural marginality takes on in a transnational world. Ivy writes that in the cultural imaginary of Japan, men are associated with the native/authentic and women with the foreign: "images of fictionality and authenticity waver between the poles of the feminine and the masculine—the non-native and the native."[30] Women's impurity, derived from menstruation, childbirth, and household "dirty work," puts them forever at odds with the purity of blood and body required by Japanese racial ideologies. In the past, this marginality put Japanese women at a grave disadvantage, rendering them "inauthentic," unreliable, and unqualified to participate in many ritual and institutional practices. In the transnational world, however, such hierarchies are increasingly destabilized, even reversed. It is precisely because young Japanese women are marginalized professionally and culturally that they have both the leisure and the inclination to travel or reside abroad, to intensively study foreign languages, and consequently to enjoy ever more intimate relations with the foreign(er). And it is precisely because they enjoy an intimate association with the foreign/global that women gain discursive leverage in their domestic gender struggles and in their local dialogues with Japanese men.[31]

Thus Japanese women, through their very marginality, possess knowledge of gender alternatives and options, without which they could not criticize and challenge Japanese male norms and values so consistently and effectively. The benefits for women of foreign associations are clearly parallel to the changing status of the *kikokushijo* (returnee children) in Japan. Once viewed as contaminated from "too much" foreign experience, the *kikokushijo* are now often seen as possessors of an "elite 'cultural' or 'symbolic' capital" which guarantees them entry into some of the finest universities and most prestigious jobs.[32]

We can find then, in these and other examples in Japan, ways that the transnational "refracts and shapes 'the local.' "[33] The yellow cabs demonstrate the necessity of taking a transnational perspective in ethnographic analysis;

their behavior is simply not comprehensible within the confines of a bounded and essentialistic notion of "Japanese culture." The yellow cabs are who and what they are precisely because they negotiate the borders between cultures, races, nations, browsing among the wares of the (masculine) world. The yellow cabs act and speak in the places of "betweenness," of "hybridity and struggle, policing and transgression,"[34] in which flows of people and power meet and interact, creating new forms of encounter and behavior. The degree of policing and struggle that characterize such locations (both spatial and cultural) is revealed in the insulting labels with which this group of women has been branded by Japanese and foreign men. The price of transgression is condemnation. Eluding the "border police," however, women continue to flirt with the foreign in their desire to disturb and recreate the Japanese.

But what is recreated? Are the discursive strategies employed by the yellow cabs effective in changing Japanese male nativist behavior? Japanese men's response has not been to embrace women's demands but to exaggerate the threat they represent: to precipitate a crisis. An example of male inability to cope constructively with the challenge of the yellow cabs and of women's demands can be found in a "Public Debate" on the subject of kissing in public, staged by a popular magazine between female novelist Kajiwara Hazuki and male columnist Ikushima Jirō. Kajiwara begins by arguing passionately that Japanese males' ability to express affection is "the worst in the world." She continues, "Because of that, recently the women whose desires for physical warmth and affection are not being satisfied find what they're looking for overseas, and end up being called 'yellow cabs.' "[35] Ikushima, however, responds in this way: "Japanese people are fundamentally poor at [public displays of affection]. They are a shy race. As proof, Japanese males may say 'I like you,' or 'I'm crazy about you,' but they find it difficult to say 'I love you.' . . . Women may say that easily, and demand that men say it too, but Japanese men will not say it if they can avoid it."[36] Kajiwara concludes her side of the debate by asserting, "I think the time has come for busy Japanese men to start changing. . . . [A]ny country that will go as far as 'exporting' women's frustration is just not right."[37] But Ikushima, it is clear, cares only to avoid confronting Japanese women's call for change; to reiterate essentialistic, nativist, and male-centered representations of "Japanese culture"; and to compel Japanese women to conform to such representations. It is as though Japanese men, confronted with an unflattering reflection in the mirror held out by women, have responded by turning away their eyes, to gaze instead upon women themselves as examples of female treachery, unbound sexuality, and cultural inauthenticity.

The men co-opt the women's voices, and in their highly influential media accounts, twist this discourse on gender into a discourse on sex and nation.

The dialogue between Kajiwara and Ikushima represents in microcosm the growing tensions in Japan between the much-touted boom in internationalization (*kokusaika*) and the equally conspicuous rise of neonationalist sentiments. Some believe that the two sides do in fact represent opposing opinions and desires, that there is a faction in Japan that seeks genuine internationalization. Others are not so sanguine. Yoshimoto argues instead that neonationalism and internationalization in Japan are merely two sides of the same coin and that "both are necessary to construct a model of the world at the center of which Japan is situated."[38] Similarly, I suggest that what is "recreated" within the yellow cab phenomenon is not a brave new world of female empowerment and international intimacy, but rather old racism in a new guise. Women transform the foreigner into a signifier whose primary purpose is to further their domestic agendas. Japanese men respond to the challenge by reinscribing inalienable boundaries of race and nation. And foreign males permit themselves to be "bought" only to recreate, indeed relive, ancient Western male fantasies of sexual access to and manipulation of the Oriental woman.

For these reasons, the example of the yellow cabs finally challenges us to be unfailingly alert to the shifting, cross-cutting, and mutually contradictory—indeed incommensurate—claims of race, gender, desire, and sexual fetish in the transcultural border regions.[39] Too eager an embrace of the Bakhtinian carnivalesque, too gleeful a celebration of titillating possibilities of sexual "inversions," will result in our overlooking the local negotiations made of and through these sexual encounters and the way in which these encounters may obscure persistent inequalities, exploitations, and separations on a number of different planes simultaneously. Torgovnick has observed that "the essence of carnivalesque is that one cannot tell male from female, rich from poor, black from white . . . everything is possible."[40] But as we have seen everything is not possible, and the contact with the Other can just as easily depend on maintaining those differences between male and female, rich and poor, Japanese and black and white. Furthermore, an irresponsible fetishization of, for example, a highly marginal case of Japanese women's sexual objectification of the white male runs the risks of furthering the historical eroticization of the Oriental female ("she can never get enough") and inadvertently serving as "justification" for continued Western male sexual exploitation of Asian women.[41]

This failure of the carnivalesque should be kept in mind when evaluating other interracial sexual encounters, such as those increasingly glorified within the Bennetton-esque multicultural carnival of the contemporary United States. White America's eagerness to appropriate "lovers of color" simultaneously enacts and masks efforts to employ them as signifiers within a self-serving agenda of white liberalism and/or postmodern chic. Regarding this trend, bell hooks has written, "Getting a bit of the Other, in this case engaging in sexual encounters with non-white females, [is now] considered a ritual of transcendence. . . . White males claim the body of the colored Other instrumentally, as unexplored terrain, a symbolic frontier. . . . They see their willingness to openly name their sexual desire for the Other as affirmation of cultural plurality."[42] The increasingly common construction of the Asian woman as appropriate, even ideal, partner for white men must always be considered in light of a sexual economy which still permits (encourages?) the publication of essays such as: "Oriental Girls: The Ultimate Accessory."[43] We have entered a new era of race relations, in which sexual contact is often constructed as "a progressive change in white attitudes toward non-whites."[44] But in the age of *M. Butterfly,* things are not so simple. All too often the white men and women who see their foreign/nonwhite lovers as evidence that they are nonracist, liberal, sensitive, and culturally aware are "not at all attuned to those aspects of their sexual fantasies that irrevocably link them to collective white racist domination."[45] It behooves us to remember that on all points of the global sex map, capital and the forces of commodification can dominate even as they liberate desire. We must recognize this domination, and acknowledge the overdetermined agendas that underlie the exhilarating encounters (sexual and otherwise) of the transnational borderlands.

Notes

This research was supported by grants from the National Science Foundation, the East-West Center, and the Japan Foundation Doctoral Dissertation Fellowship. My gratitude goes to Takie S. Lebra, Alan Howard, Iwata Tarō, Martha Mensendiek, and John Russell for their close and penetrating readings of earlier drafts. I particularly want to thank Rob Wilson for his encouragement, generosity, and stimulating criticisms of this and other work. Finally, I would like to thank the many Japanese women who offered me their insights on and analyses of the yellow cabs.

1   In the interests of economy, throughout this paper the term *gaijin* will be used to refer to all non-Japanese men, although in actual Japanese usage the term (literally meaning "outsider") is sometimes restricted to Caucasian foreigners.

2   John Russell, "Race and Reflexivity: The Black Other in Contemporary Mass Culture," *Cultural Anthropology* 6, no. 1 (February 1991): 21.

3   The etymology of the term yellow cab is itself a remarkable example of the ebb and flow of transnational cultural tides. Ieda claims that the term originated in the United States, among certain black and white men in New York City and Hawaii who coined it to refer to Japanese women who were, from their perspective, "easy." Ieda made the term the focus of controversy by claiming that it is well-known in the United States as a slur on "loose Japanese women." When her work grew popular in Japan, the male-dominated Japanese media took it up as a catchall insult for "disreputable" Japanese women abroad. Women (including the New York-based Association to Think About Yellow Cabs) objected, claiming, rightly, that for the vast majority of Americans the term "yellow cab" has no meaning other than the name of a New York taxi company. Eventually, however, foreigners living in Japan and American journalists got involved in the fray, and as the controversy grew, the term and the debate around it did indeed flow back to the United States, where more men have now begun to use it. Since 1993, however, a new trend has emerged in which some young Japanese women have reappropriated the term in a gesture of pride and defiance against Japanese men. In 1993 a young female writer Iizuka Makiko published a book entitled *The Guys Who Can't Even Ride Yellow Cabs*, in which she argues that as low as some women's standards may be, they are still too high for "selfish, ugly, sexist" Japanese men to reach.

4   All Japanese names are written surname first, given name last.

5   Arjun Appadurai and Carol Breckenridge, "Editors' Comments," *Public Culture: Bulletin of the Project for Transnational Cultural Studies* 1, no. 1 (Fall 1988): 2.

6   This association has pursued a vigorous media campaign against the work of Ieda Shōko, so fierce that it has earned the name "Ieda Bashing" and has left Ieda's reputation seriously damaged. While Ieda's work is certainly of questionable reliability, it appears that she was also used as a scapegoat to bear women's rage over the yellow cab controversy.

7   This research is based on ethnographic fieldwork conducted over an eighteen-month period (January 1991–July 1992) in Honolulu, Hawaii. For an ethnographic account of the data, please see Karen Kelsky, "Sex and the Gaijin Male: Contending Discourses of Race and Gender in Contemporary Japan," ASPAC Occasional Papers No. 5 (1993). All translations, unless otherwise noted, are my own.

8   There is no question that many OLS experience real victimization in the form of thwarted career goals, demeaning work, sexual harassment, and corporate paternalism. Nevertheless, I feel it is important to respect the voices of those OLS who assert that equality with men is not a particularly appealing prospect and that they have no desire to compete with or emulate "male corporate drones."

9   Joseph Tobin, "Introduction: Domesticating the West," in *Re-Made in Japan: Everyday Life and Consumer Taste in a Changing Society*, ed. Joseph Tobin (New Haven: Yale University Press, 1992), p. 11. The most recent form this imported passion takes is J-Club, a wildly popular male strip club in Tokyo, in which eight muscular foreign male dancers, dressed variously as American hillbillies, fifties rockers, cowboys, and trenchcoated film noir P.I.s, gyrate and disrobe to a background of American rock music

before a screaming female audience. As the climax of the performance women may tuck fake U.S. dollar bills (¥1000 for three bills) into the fluorescent G-strings of the foreigner of their choice in exchange for a kiss.

10 An exception are the "beachboys" of Bali, Indonesian men, often from poverty-stricken regions of Java, who look upon Japanese women less as "exotic Oriental women" than as economic benefactors.

11 Anonymous, "Hawaii Nihon ryūgakusei no gōka naru benkyōburi" (Japanese overseas students extravagant 'pretend study' abroad), *Shūkan Gendai* (August 1989): 151.

12 Anonymous, "OL, Joshidaisei kaigairyokō no seika hōkoku" (OL, girl college students overseas travel sex report), *Shūkan Hōseki* (August 1988): 218.

13 Tanaka Yasuo, "Otoko ni sukareru kao, kenkyū repōto" (Research report on the kind of face men like), *An An* (September 1988): 81.

14 John Russell, personal communication.

15 Japan is of course not the only country in which AIDS stands in as a metaphor for a host of other social ills. See Susan Sontag, *AIDS and Its Metaphors* (New York: Farrar, Straus and Giroux, 1989). Also, drugging and raping as described in the note is, according to the local police, actually one consistent pattern of Japanese female abuse in Waikiki.

16 Yamada Eimi, *Beddotaimu Aizu* (Bedtime eyes) (Tokyo: Kawade Shobō Shinsha, 1985), p. 13.

17 Ieda Shōko, *Ore no hada ni muragatta onnatachi* (The women who flocked to my skin) (Tokyo: Shōdensha, 1991), p. 14.

18 Both quotes from Kudo Akiko, "Gaijin no otoko denakereba sekkusu dekinai onna" (The women who can only have sex with foreigners), *Fujin Kōron* (June 20, 1990): 409, 410.

19 Ieda, *Ore no hada ni muragatta onnatachi*, p. 5.

20 Quoted in Katsuhira Ruika, "Roppongi gyaru" (Roppongi gals), in *Sekkusu to iu oshigoto* (The job of sex), ed. Ito Shinji (Tokyo: JICC, 1990), p. 215.

21 Yamada, *Beddotaimu Aizu*, p. 15.

22 Quoted in Katsuhira, "Roppongi gyaru," p. 215. Ousemann Sankhon is a Senegalese businessman turned Japanese TV personality; he is noted in the Japanese media for his "peculiar" and "amusing" African looks.

23 This phrase is borrowed from Russell, "Race and Reflexivity," p. 3.

24 Quoted in Kudo, "Gaijin no otoko denakereba sekkusu dekinai onna," p. 408.

25 Quoted in Murota Yasuko, "Kanaami ni karamitsuita kanashii yokubō" (Sad desires entangled by wire fences), *Asahi Journal*, November 13, 1987, p. 7.

26 Kudo, "Gaijin no otoko denakereba sekkusu dekinai onna," p. 411.

27 Subsequent research has shown that many Japanese women do hold a markedly idealized image of Western (white) men. The white male is often described as a "knight in shining armor" or "prince charming" (lit. prince on a white horse, *hakuba ni notta ōjisama*) who is unfailingly chivalrous yet treats women with perfect equality. John Russell has called this image of the white male the "Messianic Mystic," and it is in some ways parallel to the Western male image of "Madame Butterfly," in that both serve as

indirect efforts at sexual control by acting as cautionary reminders to the opposite sex within the race/nation of the existence of competition.

28 See the works of Boye De Mente, especially the 1964 and 1991 editions of his classic guidebook *Bachelor's Japan* for a blunt exposition of this Western male power fantasy.

29 For a discussion of these racial ideologies and the "alien"ation of the foreigner, see Karen Kelsky, "Intimate Ideologies: Transnational Theory and Japan's 'Yellow Cabs' " *Public Culture* 6, no. 3 (Spring 1994): 465–478.

30 Marilyn Ivy, "Discourses of the Vanishing" (Ph.D. diss., University of Chicago, 1988), p. 49.

31 See Karen Kelsky, "Postcards from the Edge: The 'Office Ladies' of Tokyo," *U.S.-Japan Women's Journal (English Supplement)* 6 (March 1994): 3–26.

32 See Roger Goodman, "Deconstructing an Anthropological Text: A 'Moving' Account of Returnee Schoolchildren in Contemporary Japan," in *Unwrapping Japan: Society and Culture in Anthropological Perspective,* ed. Eyal Ben-Ari et al. (Honolulu: University of Hawaii Press, 1990).

33 Akhil Gupta, "The Song of the Nonaligned World: Transnational Identities and the Reinscription of Space in Late Capitalism," *Cultural Anthropology* 7, no. 1 (February 1992): 63.

34 James Clifford, "Traveling Cultures," in *Cultural Studies,* ed. Lawrence Grossberg, Cary Nelson, and Paula Treichler (London: Routledge, 1992), p. 109.

35 Kajiwara Hazuki, "Kōron shuron—Hitomae de no kisu" (Debate—kissing in public), *AERA,* August 6, 1991, p. 58.

36 Ikushima Jirō, "Kōron shuron—Hitomae de no kisu" (Debate—kissing in public), *AERA,* August 6, 1991, p. 59.

37 Kajiwara, "Koron shuron," p. 58.

38 Yoshimoto Mitsuhiro, "The Postmodern and Mass Images in Japan," *Public Culture* 1, no. 2 (Spring 1989): 22.

39 See also Anna Tsing, *In the Realm of the Diamond Queen* (Princeton: Princeton University Press, 1993), pp. 213–229 for a nuanced discussion of this complexity and its implications for the ethnographic encounter.

40 Marianna Torgovnick, *Gone Primitive: Savage Intellects, Modern Lives* (Chicago: University of Chicago Press, 1990), p. 40.

41 One entirely unforeseen consequence of this research has been the large number of white Western male scholars and academics who have personally approached or contacted the author with the apparently self-therapeutic goal of explaining, justifying, rationalizing, or otherwise attempting to absolve themselves for a variety of unhappy personal relationships with Japanese women. I have been quite disturbed to find my research used to promote an identity as abused and misunderstood victim among white male academics; I have the odd, unpleasant sense of, in Lisa Yoneyama's words, "entertaining those I do not wish to entertain." At the same time, however, this latest, somewhat surreal, twist in the yellow cab saga has been instrumental in alerting me both to the ongoing issues of politics and agenda in academic work (whose purposes is it

serving? Is it serving purposes that I do not intend?) and to my own culpabilities and responsibilities as ethnographer of such global sex "trades."

42   bell hooks, *Black Looks: Race and Representation* (Boston: South End Press, 1992), p. 23–24.

43   Tony Rivers, "Oriental Girls: The Ultimate Accessory," *Gentlemen's Quarterly (British Edition)* (October 1990): 39–44.

44   hooks, *Black Looks,* p. 24.

45   Ibid.

DESIRING THE INVOLUNTARY: MACHINIC ASSEMBLAGE AND TRANSNATIONALISM IN DELEUZE AND *ROBOCOP 2*

Jonathan L. Beller

●

The fate of the flesh in the context of transnationalization may be understood as the preoccupation of the contemporary cyborg film. Indeed the question of the relation between mind and "meat," to use William Gibson's neuromanic phrase for what used to be called "the body," emerges with increasing intensity as multiplex technologies (from literature to modems to fighter planes) perform what Paul Virilio designates in *Speed and Politics* as the "boarding of metabolic vehicles."[1] That culture and technology, as general forms of mediation which utilize human bodies for the working out of their logics, find expression in the popular and elsewhere in the myriad production of cyborgs forecasts the cyborg as one of the coming figures for the preoccupations of the transnational age. The production of cybernetic concepts alongside the production of the cyborg itself holds open various possibilities for the rethinking of that historical collection of phenomena (and that phenomenology) known as modernization. Such a project suggests that modernization and its historical outcomes or consequences have at their crux the development of ever more corporeally encompassing machine-body interfaces. Furthermore, the ramified inroads made by capitalized technology into the land of the body and the mind all have the capacity to organize labor time and extract surplus value. Where the meat meets the machine, a worksite is born. Thus the cyborg is not merely a figure for the transnational age, but for transnational capital, that is, capitalism.

The word "cyborg" is itself, to borrow from the technophilic vocabulary of Gilles Deleuze and Félix Guattari, a machinic assemblage of the words "cybernetic" and "organism." These words sprout from the Greek roots *kubernetes* and *organon* meaning "governor" and "instrument," respectively, or, together, "governing instrument," or again, and perhaps most tellingly, "instrumental governance." The production of the concept of the cyborg as such, that is, as a *form* of instrumental governance, illuminates questions common to the body, history, power, and technology. It produces a concept of historical flux that is first and foremost technological, foregrounding the hardware of social organization throughout history as this hardware articulates the functions and possibilities of the flesh and hence consciousness, literature, and the arts. These latter viruses, which themselves invade the flesh, giving it new dispensations, might also be considered as technologies, interfaces of sorts.[2]

The cybernetic organism is to a certain extent on the trajectory of all disciplines concerned with governance and the state. In today's cyborgs converge the interests of consumers as well as multinational companies along with academic departments as varied as history, social studies, literature, art history, and linguistics, not to mention the "hard" sciences, medicine and engineering. Indeed the cyborg, along with the related systems of artificial intelligence and virtual reality, is rapidly becoming an *objet petit a* for many departments in a typical graduate school of arts and sciences. In addition to its fascination for the academic world, the figure of the cyborg is also becoming that obscure object of desire of the academy's "real world" counterparts: the "organic" intellectual apparatuses of television, cinema, the military, computer engineering, and popular discourses of several varieties. This latter aspect of the cybernetic fetish is manifest in the cyberneticization of language apparent not only in the mass media and the popular press, in books on the subject and museum exhibitions, but in philosophers such as Deleuze and Guattari, Virilio, Baudrillard, etc., and more generally in what is in this volume being called the transnational imaginary. Those who would be on the cutting edge of progress, development, and innovation all find themselves confronting the questions and possibilities of cybernetics. As the concepts concerning the integration of the flesh and characteristics of the flesh with the machine gain currency, it should inevitably turn out that the cyborg has been, in one form or another, a structural preoccupation endemic to modernization, that is, a desire at the edge of reason, for some time. Although we have the gothic novel and futurism and Fritz Lang as precedents, this desire for the active integration of human agency with machinic technology becomes especially clear after the work of child prodigy and mathematician Norbert Wiener on antiaircraft guidance systems during World War II[3] and, presently, from a cursory survey of Hollywood's box office hits during the last ten years. In certain respects the cyborg is the absolute limit-figure for the conjunction of the global and the local—the intersecting of the human being from anywhere in the world (but, in the movies, usually from the metropolitan service sector) and the technology (military, industrial, and informational) endemic to transnational capitalism. The cathexis of cultural attention onto the cyborg marks an intense anxiety/fascination about the matrix of international forces that circulate over and through the body.

Though the concept of the cyborg lifts out a certain web of relationships in all discourses concerned with human meaning precisely because it takes exchanges between flesh and machines (machinic production) as events, this essay forgoes a general discussion of concepts such as war, technology, mass media, cinema, sexuality, gender, and the city, with respect to the formation of cybernetic organisms, even though all such concepts (and practices) entail the deterritorialization of the body (and to some greater or lesser degree a reterritorialization of it). Each of the above concepts and their related practices could well be understood as an interfacing of human flesh and a techno-mechanico-logistics of one sort or another. War, as Elaine Scarry has shown, cuts culture into the body through the engineering of pain,[4] while cinema and television, as I have shown elsewhere, burrow into the body in order to mine it of productive value.[5] Simon de Beauvoir wrote in 1949 that "one is not born a woman, one becomes one," already suggesting that gender and subjectivity generally were introjections from that machine known as social life. What I would like to do here is to examine the nature and economy of body-machine interfaces in *Robocop 2* in order to register the expression of their intensities on the skin of the film and on our own skins. The film, though not especially remarkable, was at once popular, violent, and elegantly imagined in its own way. Like any other thirty-million dollar investment, it has a lot of the world manifest within it. Also, I saw it one afternoon on a tremendous screen in New York City, where, by chance, I was the only one in the entire theater (a necking couple having left after the first five minutes), and the willful thrashing about of the monstrous machines seemed not to take my presence into account whatsoever. By the end of the film I felt that their spectacular indifference to my existence was an essential part not only of the film proper, but of the postmodern sublime, that is, precisely the sublime affect of transnational capitalism. The infinite swiftness and scale of the social machines, driven by international finance and the military industrial complex, along with the attendant (and strangely pleasurable—it is this which we will have to investigate) quashing of individual ego seems to me to be the paradigmatic experience of postmodernism.[6] For me this particularly intense and somewhat traumatizing encounter with the film became a concentrated moment emblematic of one important strain of my experience of society.

Also I should say in advance that my analysis of *Robocop 2* forms a longish preamble to an interrogation of Deleuze and the politics of the machinic assemblage, of becoming machine(s). An avowedly political discussion of the work of Deleuze must necessarily be alternately direct and oblique because the standard frames of evaluation desiring to register the progressive or reactionary significance of Deleuzian transformation along with the trajectories of human, sociological, and technological movement he projects, collapse as it becomes manifest that forms of the flesh, and of consciousness itself, are together undergoing drastic deterritorialization. In other words, the presuppositions of the political categories for the evaluation of theory and practice are, in the work of Deleuze, undermined by the very phenomena that they would judge. Such also are the characteristics of the shifting political terrain in which the cybernetic organism is found. Where the cyborg appears, a crisis for politics inheres. Indeed the deterritorialization brought about by the cyberneticization of the flesh can be said to be the impetus of the work of Deleuze and Guattari. The conjunction of the terms "global" and "local," which in many ways can be understood to be the historical conditions of possibility of Deleuze and Guattari's work, emerges precisely at the moment when each term is being radically destabilized by the other. The so-called local is coming to exist in a globalized space and hence acquires a global circulation that displaces the very idea of locality, while the global that erupts in various localities is less a geographical index (as in global warfare) than the name for new technico-economic capacities of spatial and corporeal access. The significance of these transformations are experienced at the sites in which they interpenetrate with bodies and effect their constitutions. Such a reconfiguration of space, time and corporeality has interdependent and cofunctioning equivalents in philosophy (the crisis of the subject) and politics. In this context, the political discourse of "progressive and reactionary," that is, of good dog/bad dog politics, finds itself in crisis at the moment when its presuppositions—the subject, and hence, logically, democracy, along with the nation and space (the nation as subject, the nation as space), the body, and the sensorium—assume what has been called "the condition of postmodernity."[7] Though it is easy and obvious to say that the imposition of export-oriented economies by the IMF and the World Bank on Third World nations generally ends by taking value out of these countries and impoverishing them further relative to the world power which their labor generates for others, many of us find ourselves less ready to pass a verdict on the technologies which make these forms of "aid" possible and which have grown out of precisely such "aid": satellite telecommunications, computing, global news networks, air transport, etc. I find Benjamin's idea that when evaluating a situation politically, one must split the situation into its progressive and reactionary elements and then take the reactionary elements and split them again in order to find the utopian strains within them useful here.

Once one has the concept of cybernetics in mind, it becomes a useful tool with which to rethink not only present orchestrations of bodies with technology, but certain historical formations. In, for example, Marx's famous injunction from the *Communist Manifesto,* "Workers of the world unite," chains are already a machinic figure for the condition of human flesh in the capitalist system that intensify the question of agency. A suffering proletariat composed of human flesh is at once produced and enslaved by the machinations of capital logic. Marx's slogan, like so many others, posits a revolutionary situation characterized by the unity of the body and consciousness. To put it another way, the slogan expresses the utopian longing for the unity of the Gibsonian "meat" and desire, a historical solution to the mind-body split, an end to the continued alienation of subjectivity in the production of an objectified world which confronts us as something alien. In the case of Marxist-Leninist revolution, a radical (necessarily violent) reappropriation of the body by the consciousness of the proletariat is the key to self-determination.[8]

In any case, the problem of agency has been a question for revolutionaries, capitalists, psychoanalysts, philosophers, literary critics and filmmakers alike, to name a nearly arbitrary few. The question of agency has at root marked the contest between the volition of concrete bodies and the historical forces acting on those bodies. Complexes such as consumer spending, party politics, perception, will, and aesthetic reception are often made to fall under the rubric of "agency." Various antitheses of subjective and collective agency have also been objects of inquiry, not to mention de facto social formations, and have been expressed by concepts ranging among ideas such as coercion, ideology, slavery, domination, fate, capital, and nature. These categories or systems which crush the agency of certain social groups are perceptible from above, as it were, as concepts, that is, from a sociological or systems-analysis point of view and yet are able to exert control via an underside as well, a logistics of domination that is their working surface: each has certain points and methods where it touches the human animal with the aim of controlling it. These undersides, which are the machinic manipulation of human bodies may be figured in their subjective reception by the term "involuntary." Such involuntary forces break the integrity of the subject or, at times, impose it.[9]

Deleuze, taking up the modernist obsession with cinema, the city, and "the liquidation of the traditional value of the cultural heritage"[10] (i.e., the nineteenth century) that gives rise to new forms of consciousness and therefore new relations of the involuntary to consciousness, writes of Proust in his 1964 *Proust and Signs,* "Proust's critique touches the essential point: truths remain arbitrary and abstract, so long as they are based on the good will of thinking. . . . The truths of Philosophy are lacking in necessity, and the mark of necessity. As a matter of fact, the truth is not revealed, it is betrayed; it is not communicated, it is interpreted; it is not willed, it is involuntary."[11] From this work, which is really a meditation on the beautiful and the sublime (two more expressions of the involuntary) in the face of the crisis of the modern subject (the crisis that *is* the modern subject), a completely new vocabulary for the terms of consciousness will emerge in the capitalism and schizophrenia books, *Anti-Oedipus* and *A Thousand Plateaus,* and also in *Dialogues, Cinema 1,* and *Cinema 2.*

> The great theme of Time regained is that the search for truth is the characteristic adventure of the involuntary. . . . The truthseeker is the jealous man who catches a lying sign on the beloved's face. He is the sensitive man in that he encounters the violence of an impression. He is the reader, the auditor, in that the work of art emits signs which will perhaps force him to create, like the call of genius to other geniuses. The communications of garrulous friendship are nothing compared with a lover's silent interpretations. Philosophy, with all its method and its good will, is nothing compared with the secret pressures of the work of art (*Proust,* 139–40).

Present in this analysis of Proust are the seeds of Deleuze's "abstract machine," "the overcoding machine," "desiring machines," "the machinic assemblage" and "the line of flight." In the later work of Deleuze, "the secret pressures of the work of art" give way to the secret and the explicit pressures of the machine. The work of Deleuze (including the cinema books) manifests the mechanization of the relations which in an earlier period were considered to be cultural, philosophical, and aesthetic relations; the *machine aesthetic* that pervades the work of Deleuze is central to his return to a modernist ethos. As the cyborg film demonstrates, the conjunction of machinic and aesthetic experience is, however, no longer, or at least not only, particular to philosophers or amusement parks but indicates a historical shift which, in the generalized production of the *concept* of the cyborg that emerges from the deepening cybernetization of consciousness through the mass dissemination of the image of the cyborg, enables new forms of history, philosophy, and aesthetics to be written and hence new processes to emerge. The affects produced by our watching representations of cyborgs in action at once gives the world system new entry points into our bodies and allows for the creation of the concepts adequate to that experience. Our experience in the cinema is not only a scene of systemic events, but a scene for the formulation of the concepts of these events.

Deleuze's wonderful postmodern figures (the machinic assemblage, etc.), his names for formulation, are expandable categories with the versatility to frame events ranging in scale from a momentary impression to a world historical movement. They emerge at the termination of the sustainability of the category of the subject (although Deleuze himself would reject that formulation because it implies *one particular* narrative for the history of the subject). These assemblages are abstract figures (technologies of figuration) that remove a philosophical dilemma that is already being removed in practice, in spite of ourselves, specifically, the division between inside and outside, between consciousness and the world. Though this breakdown process is as old as history itself (in other words the flow across membranes is also a process of construction), the intensity with which it today occurs seems to be qualitatively different. In fact the new and multiple assemblages produced in Deleuze (but also in the world) mark a radical deterritorialization of the reified subject and impute animism (animation) or agency to all social products. Thus the social formation that produces the subject in the first place is an instance of an abstract machine. Furthermore it is an overcoding machine in as much as it overdetermines the meanings and limits the possibilities of consciousness. Assemblages of signs that like "the call of genius to other geniuses" force the truthseeker to create become figured in *Anti-Oedipus* as desiring machines. The call of genius becomes the line of flight, and creation is the creation of the machinic assemblage. These terms have the virtue of being able to factor in causality (process) without partaking of an anal cathexis on the subject, that is, without presupposing that a unified subject is the seat of consciousness, the registrar of the life force. This, of course, is in keeping with the Marxist analysis of commodification, that is, that the object-ive world is frozen and alienated subjectivity. The products of congealed human labor, as expropriated subjectivity exercise in the work of Deleuze, but again, also in the world, their own agency, in their own way, and according to their own laws.

In *Robocop 2*, the state in crisis is, like the modern subject and contemporary philosophy, in the process of rejecting its own organization. The state is contending with new forms, new speeds, new spaces, war machines that unweave its organization, that destabilize its field of stratification. The global extension of state power, which is one of the trademarks of postmodernism and multinational capital, marks the moment when the Other as enemy to *state* expansion is no longer outside, but within a world system. The so-called post-colonial result of the total capitalization of the globe is that the Other can no longer be convincingly figured as such without straining the state to the point of self-contradiction, precisely because state power has incorporated others all over the planet. The term "postcolonial," since it marks an intensification of the colonizing *process*, is itself an indicator of this contradiction, and hence a form of double think. It arises because the Other, as the force opposing the full capitalization of the globe, can no longer be convincingly figured as such. The Other, if her or his existence is still allowed at all, has dropped below the threshold of perception. The expanding state only meets with the resistance of former versions of itself.

The proclamation of the end of the category of "nation" by "postcolonial" intellectuals and *Business Week* alike is an example of the effacement of the Otherness of which I am speaking. In one view the celebration of the end of the nation abets imperialism because dominant nations at once establish national borders and then deny their existence, all the while using the real force of these imaginary lines as a means of control.[12] The struggle for representational terrain takes place among already enfranchised groups with common interests: the many capitals within Capital. This paper, despite the reality that more than one half of the globe lives in nations with a per capita income of less than one thousand dollars (U.S.) per year, somewhat masochistically, accepts the terms of the fantasy of the ultimate corrosion of national boundaries and the total capitalization of the globe in order to intensify the dynamics of this fantasy and produce an understanding of how it articulates itself to itself. We must find the internal limits to the postmodern claim to global universality. I seek to show how otherness in the transnational is coming to mean the self-contradiction of a systemic logic. For this reason, we occupy the text of *Robocop 2*.

The situation of the global expansion of capital is represented as achieved in *Robocop 2*. Such expansion is, following Marx, posited from the beginning of capital and capital logic and is indeed the very presupposition of capitalism. Those who labor under the strain of capital can never consume all that they are to produce if surplus value is extracted (as it must be for capital investment to realize itself at a profit) during each of the cycles of capital investment. Commentators on Marx have argued, as did Marx himself, that the falling rate of profit inherent in capital expansion and the finite size of the globe would necessarily throw capital into its ultimate crises because, at a certain point, it would have nowhere to expand. In my view the capitalization of cultural interstices seems, for the moment at least, to provide a negative forecast for this "inevitability." As I have argued elsewhere, capital expands not only geographically, but, through media, burrows into the body—seeking new work sites, extracting labor power, and mining the body of value, hence overcoming the falling rate of profit by forcing consumers to build the new pathways of circulation with their own labor time. On this view, all television viewers can be thought to work in a type of cottage industry, where they manufacture value for the media as well as retool themselves to meet the shifting protocols of flexible production.[13] Daily we form new synapses and new links with the outside world as we produce our own (and others') social cooperation. Since the essence of the media is the management of crisis, and the central crises of our time have been fomented by capital's search for self-valorization, the role of media as a new structure for the generalized extraction of surplus value during "leisure time" begins to emerge. Historically, it has been precisely crisis, that is, the destruction of form, that has marked the growing pains of an economy becoming progressively more and more multinational.

As long as the Other could be figured as being outside of "our" system, as precisely a reality that our own reality involuntarily bumped up against during its continuing expansion, state-slaughter occurred in more or less predictable ways.[14] That is, those who were within the system more or less found the destruction of those outside necessary and logical. Ultra-violence had specific targets. As capital materially "thought" its own expansion and came across a pocket of resistance, precisely there it encountered the involuntary and became aware of its limits (as did the occupants of that "other" pocket or enclave of reality soon to be overrun and "re-programmed," but this, from the standpoint of the dominant at least, in a less intelligible and sometimes unintelligible way).[15] The coming into awareness (yet again) of the encroaching but, to date, momentary limitations of capital extension manifests itself on the "home" terrain as crisis (recession, depression, the threat of the end of "the American way of life," the call to arms, etc.) and inevitably results in certain deployments of force on the "away" field: either legislative, police, or military power is deployed to subjugate that which momentarily falls outside of capital logic to that logic itself: Native Americans, black nationalism, Sandinistas, Iraqis, etc. This formulation is an abstract and simplified expression of the history of imperialism, labor movements, modern global warfare, and failed revolutions. Revolution and the refusal of the terms of Euro-American capital has always been the effort to consolidate value and value production in a manner external to the circulatory pathways of Western capitalism.

The domestic scene portrayed in *Robocop 2* depicts capital formations competing within a fully capitalized universe. One could argue that with the "dissolution" of national boundaries violence is ubiquitous to the point of arbitrariness, not only from the standpoint of "the other," but now from the standpoint of "the self." This marks the impinging disenfranchisement of everyone. This schema, that of the postmodern state, more adequately describes the system, potentially everywhere connected but with no individual connections guaranteed (and over which presides no single master), than did the older scenario (described above) of capitalist expansion blazing its way through otherness within the modernist fantasy of imperialism. Thus the domesticity of capital as portrayed in *Robocop 2* may be understood in a multinational framework. In *Robocop 2* the contradictions of global capitalism manifest themselves in downtown Detroit. For this reason alone *Robocop 2* is a "postmodern" film.

Although competition has always been central to capitalism, the configuration of the state in *Robocop 2* differs from the older imperialism, the so-called "highest stage of capitalism," because *the primary struggle is among different corporations for different media and modes through which the architectonics of capital logic may play itself out.* That is, the struggle in *Robocop 2* is for the subordination of matter to one or another of the developing circulatory pathways. The "democratic" state, championed by the machinic assemblage called Robocop (assembled from the brain stem and nerve endings of ex-officer Murphy and several million dollars of high-tech war equipment, plus research, human labor, and the history of the machine) finds itself confronted by what is represented as two forms of organized crime: (1) The corporate world of private ownership and (2) the highly organized drug ring. Each of these represents a competing logic of material appropriation, and hence of expression, and hence a competing worldview.

As the city of Detroit fights its "war on crime," the corporation, represented by OCP (Omni Consumer Products: "the only choice") and its new enforcement device Robocop 2, wages economic warfare on the city (as entity) and, incidentally, on its people. The film makes clear that it believes itself to be in a later stage of capitalism because the opposition between labor and capital is here neither fundamental nor perhaps "real." The actual decentering of the opposition between labor and capital occurs because capital itself no longer presents a unified front against labor, nor is it primarily in competition for labor power. *Mediation, not labor, is visible as the primary resistance force to capital circulation.* The organization of the body under the concept of labor has, at least in the fantasy that informs *Robocop 2*, been effectively overcome. Because poverty has been won, there is an unlimited supply of extras. Today, capital wages war along its own flanks in competition for media, pathways, forms of circulation. Human attention is one such medium. Human flesh is another. Capital logic can extend its force along either, and this in a variety of ways.[16]

OCP, who has contracted to run Detroit's police force, has absolutely no interest in appeasing or replacing its own striking workers, the police officers, since it is precisely their intransigence that makes Detroit unable to repress the "criminal" activities of its urban poor and therefore unable to manage itself. In the postmodern state even crime, human suffering, and the strike become immediately productive for capital, instead of only recuperatively so. In *Robocop 2*, corporate-induced "malfunctions"—crime, unemployment, strikes, etc.—undermine the city's credit. OCP, having banked upon the city's mismanagement and loss of credit due to dropping investor confidence, calls on an overdue note owed from the city and begins to foreclose on the city's assets, that is, its properties, its neighborhoods. These properties, once confiscated, will be open to the corporate circulatory system and become integrated with its body. The extension of the nervous system (the system that regulates circulation) of the corporate body into urban property allows the corporation to incorporate urban space into its own body and to materialize its social vision: "towers of steel and glass" built right on top of urban squalor and policed by robocop enforcement units.

OCP's arbitrage on Detroit is complicated when a third corporation, now under the leadership of a brilliant and fast-talking fourteen-year-old boy, jockeys for control of the new metropolis. The drug ring challenges OCP's lean on the democratic state by offering to bail out the city with 50 million dollars of drug money in exchange for the city's taking the "heat" off of the drug ring's principal product: "Nuke." Nuke, an addictive narcotic, is a machinic assemblage, a form of material consciousness similar, in many respects, to the robocops—it forms an active matrix of technology and flesh that embodies certain logics and trajectories, certain desires. Nuke is, in short, a medium of circulation and control, a mode of production—with its own investors, networks of production, distribution, and financing—that, like other cyborgs tied inexorably to capital logic, lives on human flesh and appropriates its function for what could be called its own interests: capital expansion along the nuclear pathway, a syntax that regulates the extraction and disbursement of surplus value. The Nuke family of users, producers, and distributors has clearly replaced the nuclear one. The plot of *Robocop 2* turns on the struggle among the three principal cyborgs of the film and the struggle among their "intellectuals": Robocop, Robocop 2, and Nuke, machinic assemblages constructed by the overcoding *machines* of the so-called democratic state, private enterprise, and the drug cartel/family, respectively.

With impeccable logic the drug ring's child-leader puts the argument to the mayor that he, with the economic help of the drug cartel, could be the mayor who won the war on crime: "Why do people commit crimes? Drugs. Let the people have what they want. We're finding ways to make Nuke cheaper and safer, and with you off our backs distribution will cost even less. You'll be the mayor who cleaned up Detroit."

Where the distinction between the inside and outside of a world system becomes obsolete, as it has in *Robocop 2*, the image and function of an involuntary that forces consciousness to "discover . . . and attain its own limits" (*Proust,* 141) is transformed. In other words the system will, for lack of a better expression, come up against self and not other. This is the situation portrayed in *Robocop 2:* the capitalist system is many overlapping systems struggling to mediate the same materials, that is, running on the same medium: human flesh—a fact that is not without consequences. In general, the figure of the involuntary in a given discursive system is also a metaphysics, a concentrated image for the *weltanschauung* or worldview informing the work, because it locates the territory that belongs to knowledge and the limits of that territory. The figure of the involuntary yearns to depict that which falls outside the purview of consciousness and thus expresses an outer limit, an outside, a context that frames and inflects phenomenological consciousness. For example, the involuntary appears as the "Real" in Lacan, "Ideology" and the "Ideological State Apparatus" in Althusser, and as "History" in Jameson.[17] In *Robocop 2*, the involuntary, or to put it most basely that which happens to the *flesh* (now, because of the shift of consciousness to machinic continuity, considered the minimal unit, the cipher of humanity, that which is left when everything else is taken away), comes not from outside of the system, for (according to its ideology) there is no outside, but is the system. This system, whether through sheer force, ubiquity, or sheer speed, perpetrates itself on the flesh according to its own laws and its own laws of chance. One is tempted to say that this short circuit is an emblem of totalitarianism, but such a label risks simplification because we think we know what the word "totalitarianism" means.

Totalitarianism, in the orthodox Marxism of Georg Lukács, meant the equivalent of the dictatorship of (by) the proletariat. It reflected the utopian aspiration for a scientific, rational, and democratically planned society. In its worst sense, totalitarianism has translated into Stalinism or the Orwellian dystopia that involves the linguistic impossibility of even expressing, and hence of even thinking, discontent—it is a version of Baudrillard's America.[18] However, at base, dystopias of this sort are theories of a state which does violence to *individuals*. At its deepest level, and perhaps in the American way, discontent becomes impossible to think because of the incessant policing of language (mediation) and the resultant reconfiguration of the brain's pathways. Thus, without the Western ideal of the Individual as the context and background of Orwell's *1984*, the inability to express and hence "know" oppression would be Utopian. To love Big Brother is to be happy. I is the loss of individuality that generates pathos in dystopias. It is precisely the intensification of this loss, that is, the drama of the subject's annihilation, that produces the interest in a thinker such as Baudrillard.

Such a scene of individual annihilation is portrayed in *Robocop 2*, except the individual (ex-officer Murphy) who receives the violence offered by the state can no longer be considered as an individual. When OCP's Dr. Fax, the ruthless psychologist in charge of finding a brain for Robocop 2 (she ultimately chooses the brain of Cain, the schizophrenic murderer who originally led the drug cartel), reprograms Robocop, she attempts to program into his circuitry a series of public service clichés: "Thank you for not smoking," "A stitch in time saves nine," etc., in an effort to improve OCP's public image. During the re-programming session, what is left of Robocop/Officer Murphy refuses to take the programming stating, when asked who he thinks he is, that he is "Officer Murphy." Fax responds with disdain: "You take away the plastic and wires and you're just a couple of chunks on a coroner's table; you're not even a corpse." After delivering this apt image for what remains of the integrity of the human body and its unaccommodated function in late capitalism, she types into her computer. Robocop dutifully responds in a throaty monotone, "I am the Robo-cop law enforcement unit." As Fax types she says, "I type it you think it." Robocop responds, "You type it, I think it." Fax: "You're really very lucky. What would have taken years of psychiatric treatment takes only moments with you." Robocop: "I'm really very lucky." Fax: "You are free. No worries, no doubts, no puzzling questions." Robocop: "I am free."

In his account of the Enlightenment as the dissolution of the precapitalist modes of production during capital expansion, Marx notes in the *Grundrisse*, that human beings become "free" precisely at the moment in which they have no value.[19] As Fax frees Murphy, she tells the technician, "Load up the program, he's ready." Then, using her most sincere corporate voice, she says to Robocop, "I'm so glad we had this chance to dialogue." This discursive situation in which, in the name of communication, the individual is crushed and channeled along the logic of a capital intention, is an extremely useful figure for mediation in general. Geographically speaking, this figure has its equivalent in the desire of transnational corporations to incorporate more and more of the globe as "the free world," manifest, for example, in what Rob Wilson has called "the ongoing transformation of the Pacific Ocean into a kind of dematerialized cyberspace linking Southern California to postmodern Japan."[20] This tremendous shattering of space which is the subjugation of place(s) to a new informational web is the geographical equivalent of the human subjective annihilation attendant in late capitalism.

Deleuze and Guattari, grappling with the involuntary and the attempt to think beyond the periphery of thought, which in the postmodern situation crops up more and more only to announce the eternal return of the same process (that is, the rationalization of the arbitrary), write in *A Thousand Plateaus*, "In short we think that one cannot write sufficiently in the name of an outside."[21] Thus, it is not surprising that the vocabulary invented by Deleuze and Guattari to describe the existential territory of thought aptly describes the world portrayed in *Robocop 2* since each system struggles with the local incidence of intercalated elements of what can no longer properly be considered an outside. Robocop, for example, may at once be thought as "machinic assemblage," "war machine," and "body without organs." Though these terms function somewhat differently to describe Robocop or Nuke, the ease with which they translate from *A Thousand Plateaus* to *Robocop 2*, brings up certain philosophical and political questions concerning the *revolutionary force* of Deleuzian thought or, conversely, the revolutionary potential (or absence thereof) of popular culture.

The assemblage is, for Deleuze, "a multiplicity which is made up of many heterogeneous terms and which establishes liaisons, relations between then, across ages, sexes and reigns—different natures. Thus the assemblage's only unity is that of its cofunctioning: its symbiosis, a 'sympathy.' It is never filiations which are important, but alliances, alloys; these are not successions, lines of descent, but contagions, epidemics, the wind."[22] The assemblage is, for Deleuze, machined by desire. Not the desire of a desiring subject, or desire arising from lack, but desire itself. "Desire: who except priests would call it lack? Nietzsche calls it the 'Will to Power. . . .' Desire is not at all easy, but this is precisely because it gives instead of lacks."[23]

For Deleuze desire is productive, positive, collective. "Even individuality, the constructing of the plane, is a politics, it necessarily involves a 'collective,' collective assemblage, a set of social becomings."[24] The assemblage, since it is both constructed by and constructing desire may potentially yield the plane of consistency, or the plane of organization. The former allows for the flow of desire and is associated with the rhizome, the monad, and the body without organs. The latter blocks what Deleuze calls minoritarian desire, producing a field of stratification. Indeed these planes (the plane of consistency and the plane of organization) are in one sense reversible, that is, the plane of consistency and the plane of organization may be understood as two sides of a membrane. The plane of consistency, like the body without organs, effects the possibility of the free flow of desire along its surface, in short, it is the space of the line of flight. The plane of consistency is rhizomatic, not, like the plane of organization, arborescent. Rhizomes are molecular, minoritarian; arborescence is molar, major, statist. Deleuze assembles language in such a way that he animates different "standpoints" that deterritorialize the state. He produces philosophical events (not, properly speaking, concepts) that attempt to reveal and counter the functions of the state. Thus there is a certain correspondence between the Hecceity (singularity), the line of flight, the plane of consistency, multiplicity, molecularity, desire, the nomad, the rhizome, the body without organs, and the war machine. These are different figures for the constructive pragmatics of desire expressed in different dimensionality and temporality that oppose various forms of the desire-impeding state: arborescence, plane of organization, field of stratification, molarity, totality, the organized body, institutional gods, Marx and Freud. Robocop/Murphy can be found on the membrane between these two sets of terms which I have rather violently culled from *A Thousand Plateaus.*

Though Deleuze defines the war machine as being "exterior to the state apparatus,"[25] we must be wary of the reversibility of his terms. That is why it is possible to think of Robocop as at once the machinic assemblage of the state par excellence, functioning in *Robocop 2* to make the case for the state, and procuring identification (for Deleuze the most reactionary of activities) from the audience, and conversely acting as war machine that unweaves state consciousness. As war machine, Robocop can be understood to be minoritarian. Indeed, Robocop/Murphy speaks, as Deleuze and Proust say we must, like "a foreigner in his own tongue," a spirit fleeing from overcoding: at once straining to escape the confines of the machine and escaping previous determinations of the flesh.

The question of whether or not these takeovers (attempted in different ways by Robocop, Robocop 2, and Nuke) would be revolutions against the state is echoed in the reversibility of the political valence of certain Deleuzian categories, that is, by the fact that his categories do not *guarantee* the politically progressive character of becoming. Though at times the Deleuzian categories seem as if they do indeed promise a radical position with respect to the state (which is why Deleuze, like creative writing jobs in academe, sometimes seems to provide a last refuge for thoughtful white guys), they are reversible. Such reversibility has important consequences for the intensities produced by Deleuze's texts, for this reading of *Robocop 2* and, ultimately, for any theory of social transformation that desires in some way, however elliptical, to feel itself "good," that is, to feel itself within the framework of morality. The political paradox may be grasped clearly in the section of *Dialogues* where the definition of man is taken as "deterritorialized animal."

> When they say to us that the hominoid removes its front paws from the earth and that the hand is at first locomotor, then prehensile, these are the thresholds or the quanta of deterritorialization, but each time with a complementary reterritorialization: the locomotor hand as the deterritorialized paw is reterritorialized on the branches which it uses to pass from tree to tree; the prehensile hand as deterritorialized locomotion is reterritorialized on the torn-off, borrowed elements called tools that it will brandish and propel. But the "stick" tool is itself a deterritorialized branch.[26]

This formulation, were it not concerned with multiplicities, that is, many logics in their proliferation as opposed to one logic in its teleological extension, would be dialectical. In the image of the cyborg it expresses the paradox of Deleuzian formulation: that of the potential symmetry of de-/reterritorialization or the reversibility of the terms. In this view, which is fast becoming *reductio ad absurdum,* all movement is at once revolutionary and reactionary. Desire travels along a membrane between the state and what lies outside of it, the "steppe." Simply put, Robocop may be understood, depending on the standpoint, as either the deterritorialization of the flesh and technology, the machinic assemblage of "the wasp and the orchid," or the reterritorialization of the flesh and technology by the new state. However, the Deleuzian polemic is against the adaptation of any "standpoint" that implies such an ethical frame. Rather than sit and consider this, we should prepare for the nonfascist life. But how, when the drama of de-/reterritorialization holds us rapt as spectacle, and when the spectacle is itself the playing out of that drama in our own bodies?

The Deleuzian prohibition against the either/or and the urge to the "and," factors desire back into the symmetrical relation antiseptically and simplistically (and fascistically?) described by me above. Assemblages are not hollowed out forms, sterile architectures that exist without force; they are constructed, animated by desire. The question is, as it always is, what is done with the terms of the assemblage, how are they deployed? Their very deployment is an expression of desire. Deleuze accomplishes with the concept of deterritorialization and reterritorialization what Haraway claims for the cyborg. "The cyborg skips the step of original unity, of identification with nature in the Western sense."[27] This at least provides an unstable situation, a disequilibrium of mind in which the forces that will distribute the outcome are not understood in advance. In this, there is immanence that forces a new situation. However, the contemporary spectacle, rather than providing an either/or situation or an and situation, might indeed create a "Duh!" situation—an outcome, not known in advance, which is achieved precisely through contemplation, but of a mindless sort. The visceral excitation of the drama of late capitalist annihilation addicts many of us to its spectacle while leaving us with the addict's quiescence.

Critiquing Marxist and conspiracy theory, Deleuze writes, "What a sad and sham game is played by those who speak of a supremely cunning Master, in order to present themselves as rigorous, incorruptible, and 'pessimist' thinkers" (*Dialogues*, 146):

> Instead of gambling on the eternal impossibility of the revolution and on the fascist return of a war machine in general, why not think that *a new type of revolution is in the course of becoming possible,* and that all kinds of mutating, living machines conduct wars, are combined and trace out a plane of consistency which undermines the plane of organization of the World and the States? For, once again, the world and its States are no more masters of their plane than revolutionaries are condemned to the deformation of theirs. . . . The question of the future of the revolution is a bad question because, in so far as it is asked there are so many people who do not *become* revolutionaries, and this is exactly why it is done, to impede the question of the revolutionary-becoming of people, at every level, in every place.[28]

This formulation is a rejection of moralism as a form of metacommentary. In the milieu of *Robocop 2,* blood spills at all moments, lubricating every frame and the very movement of the machine. Death is deployed arbitrarily; because the social machines strike not at individuals, for they are irrelevant as such, but at each other. As Robocop and Robocop 2 battle it out on the screen with their machine guns and extraordinary destructive force, not only do they emblematize the struggle between the two competing megalogics that they are the articulations of: the battle between the "democratic" state and private ownership, but they shed human blood continuously. Because the central attraction is the battle among machines, blood is shed at the edge of the frame, in the margins. Arbitrarily, death is dealt to bystanders, the extras who are the audience's real counterparts in the film. The trend toward the absolute marginalization of the flesh indicates the end of the possibility of humanistic subjective identification. This, incidentally, is the project of Deleuze. This suggests that *Robocop 2* and *A Thousand Plateaus* accomplish similar intensifications of the dominant contradictions in order to achieve their deterritorialization.

Robocop as protagonist of *Robocop 2* is at once main character and no longer human. As such he reveals the truth of all cinema, and indeed of all representation: our identification with the so-called other, the protagonist, is our identification with a figure from the machine, a figure of the machine, that achieves one of its highest expressions in the cinematic apparatus. Marlon Brando, Jimmy Dean, on the cover of a magazine, Grace Kelly, Fred Astaire, Ginger Rogers, dance on air, Madonna, even movie-Mom and Dad are never really present for fleshy communion in mass mediation, but exist as precisely what Robocop is represented as: machinic assemblages, singing machines, dancing machines, killing machines, cyborgs, assemblages of technology, flesh, and desire. As the illusion of continuity given to an assemblage of fragments shows when it is dismantled from the standpoint of production, that is, when the fragments are grasped as fragments, filmic characters are partial characters and as such elicit the identification of partial subjects. We, as members of the audience are these partial subjects. Our fragments dance with their fragments in the shadow play of fractured subjectivity.

As Robocop enters a Nuke warehouse, he encounters an Elvis reliquary collected by the first drug lord, Cain. The Elvis archive demonstrates that Elvis was Robocop's precursor, perhaps the first postmodern cyborg. Elvis himself was a machine: glitter suits, musical instruments, bones and a pelvis all working in tandem with the mass media. The bones of Elvis resting in their garments in an elaborate coffin stand in sharp contrast to the poster that frames his still glittering image. Understood as cyborgs, cinema protagonists and stars are denatured, as is the cultural milieu in which our meanings circulate. Therefore, identification with cultural icons is denatured as well because the productive apparatuses are laid bare. The machinic reality of consciousness and of flesh in its machinic interrelations and identifications is present to be revealed as a formation of collective and historical desire. The fact that our disaffection should lead us to desire our own deterritorialization is perhaps the occasion for the capitalist appropriation of late capitalist despair. Such a desire is potentially revolutionary, but when it feeds capital, it produces doomed revolutions. In short, as a member of the audience in *Robocop 2* and, more generally, as a member of the audience in postmodernism, we have available the experience of the cancellation of ourselves as subjects, not only through the deconstruction of the protagonist-subject, but also (and this is the necessary corollary) through the cinematic (and televisual, architectural, etc.) experience of ultra-violence (death, blood, screams of agony, exploding bombs, the mammoth scale of power, televised—and therefore ubiquitous—disaster and assassination) that is attendant to the implosion of subjectivity along with the implosion of the imperialist state. The vector of imperialistic violence, that reinforced the maintenance of a state ego by being directed from "self" to other has been intensified to the point of its own fragmentation and therefore the simultaneous rupture of the self-other dichotomy. Such ego cancellation, the psychoanalytic expression of a situation of ubiquitous and arbitrary violence, the aesthetic expression known as the sublime, presents new possibilities for experience that fall under the category of the postmodern sublime. On this view, postmodern sublimity results from the intensification of the forces that negate humanistic (read also imperialistic) thought. This however no way implies any decrease in violence, nor, for that matter, in imperialism, simply a change of its quality and of its terms.

Deleuze says as much concerning the potential effects of all postwar cinema when in *Cinema 2* he refers to the viewer as a "spiritual automaton." Likewise, Benjamin's cinematic "distraction" held revolutionary potential for him precisely because subjectivity in its statist form (contemplation) could be negated. This for him was a kind of de-reification because distraction, the state in which one perceived cinema (and architecture) was a visceral event, a material-perceptual praxis (which, for architecture at least, the signature buildings of contemporary architecture that construct the building as spectacle rather than as machine for living may well be changing). What might be done with distraction, however, remained and remains to be seen. So far, I'm sorry to report, I see little cause for rejoicing. What the virtual realists (the engineers of virtual reality) call haptic visualization may well approximate a pragmatics of distraction which functions through the rewiring of the normative circuits of thought and perception. Another approximation may well be the postmodern sublime itself. Each effects the release of desire through intensification. However, the question remains: "What is it released into, and what does its release accomplish?"

Though in *Cinema 2* a certain crypto-Hegelianism regarding Deleuze's views of cinema/consciousness may be noted, his conflation of cinema and consciousness liberates new forces of becoming. As pure consciousness cinema dissolves the subject/object paradigm along with logocentrism and dialectics. "Man is in the world as if in a pure optical and sound situation."[29] This insight marks in effect, for Deleuze, the end of idealism and the project of philosophy. "What cinema advances is not the power of thought, but its impower, and thought has never had any other problem."[30] For Deleuze, cinema forces thought's encounter with itself, and in that moment checkmates it. As evidence, he cites George Duhamel's rejection of the medium, "I can no longer think what I want to think, the moving images are substituted for my own thoughts,"[31] and conceives of Artaud's answer to Eisenstein, "If it is true that thought depends on a shock which gives birth to it (the nerve, the brainmatter), it can only think one thing, *the fact that we are not yet thinking*."[32]

Again quoting Artaud, Deleuze writes: "It is indeed a matter . . . 'of bringing cinema together with the innermost reality of the brain,' but this innermost reality is not the Whole [as in Eisenstein], but on the contrary a fissure, a crack."[33] This fissure appears as a crack in the state functions of consciousness. "The cinema must film, not the world, but belief in this world, our only link."[34] Thus for Deleuze, cinema and its consciousness offers the possibility of the restoration of immanence. Belief is multiple, becoming, in short, desire. A desire for the world as other than it appears in representation, other than it is as it negates us. A desire that potentially constructs a line of flight.

To put it positively, cinema can be thought to be nomadic in relation to the state, a war machine, an agent for the deterritorialization of state consciousness. For some, *Robocop 2* might deterritorialize component aspects of consciousness by providing consciousness with the involuntary encounter that intensifies the limits of bureaucratized thought concerning such reified concepts as gender, sexuality, media, memory, the flesh, and the public sphere, to name but a few.[35] All this activity might take place even as the cybernetic unit of film and viewer reinscribes certain bourgeois and/or transnational ideologies. "Artaud is a forerunner from a specifically cinematographic perspective . . . because he points to 'real psychic situations' between which trapped thought looks for a way out."[36] As "Godard said, about his film *Bande a part*: 'These are people who are real and it is the world that is a breakaway group.'"[37] Paradoxically it is cinema that forces the world to seek a line of flight from the icons it projects.

I am well aware of the upbeat sound of that last sentence, and therefore I want to qualify it and distinguish it from certain odious American-centric forms of postmodern celebration. Also, the revolutionary potential of mediation should be distinguished from what may today be called the native utopianism of a Vertov or an Eisenstein, who each in his own way believed that technology, under the guidance of the gifted intellectual, would scientifically work the revolutionary transformation of the world. Cinema, the abstract form, has no necessary truck with humanistic concepts such as freedom, self-determination, science, or dialectics. It potentially creates attitude, what Deleuze calls "the right to desire." This "right," though clearly a strategy of liberation for individuals and perhaps for groups supplies little in the way of protection for those without such rights. Though Deleuze seems correct to discount the needs of crusaders to go about liberating others and places the onus of liberation on the assemblage, this, we should note, reflects precisely the laissez-faire system of capital. Such a pronouncement is a dialectic critique of Deleuze and would be the reason for Deleuze's disavowal of dialectics.

We could add that Deleuze's moviegoers, today's "spiritual automatons," fleshy nodes in the circuits of mass mediation, have most in common with the masochist as they "choose" their stimulation. What of it? For Deleuze, "the masochist uses suffering as a way of constituting a body without organs and bringing forth a plane of consistency of desire."[38] It is just possible that ultraviolence in the cinema (and elsewhere?) forces an achieving of the plane of consistency. As we witness the deterritorialization of gender, media, flesh, memory, the public sphere, and sexuality itself in a cyborg film such as *Robocop 2*, we submit our senses to a program similar to the masochist's:

> PROGRAM . . . At night, put on the bridle and attach my hands more tightly, either to the bit with the chain, or to the big belt right after returning from the bath. Put on the entire harness right away also, the reins and the thumbscrews, and attach the thumbscrews to the harness. My penis should be in a metal sheath. Ride the reins for two hours during the day, and in the evening as the master wishes. Confinement for three or four days, hands still tied, the reins alternately tightened and loosened. The master will never approach her horse without the crop and without using it. If the animal should display impatience or rebelliousness, the reins will be drawn tighter, the master will grab them and give the beast a good thrashing. (*ATP*, 155)

For Deleuze, the masochist destroys "the instinctive forces" in order to replace them with transmitted forces.[39] "In fact," he says, "it is less a destruction than an exchange and circulation ('what happens to a horse can also happen to me')."[40] In the scene above, two forms of overcoding, that of the horse's lot and that of the masochist's, play across each other in a becoming animal that opens the flow of desire in the body without organs by deterritorializing the masochist. The body loses its "proper" organization by pushing overdetermination to the limit. Like Haraway in her "Manifesto for Cyborgs," Deleuze desires the monstrous to bring an end to stratification, organization, formations of priests and the state. "Inevitably there would be monstrous crossbreeds. The plane of consistency would be the totality of all bodies without organs, a pure multiplicity of immanence, one piece of which may be Chinese, another American, another medieval, another petty perverse, but all in a movement of generalized deterritorialization in which each person takes and makes what she or he can, according to tastes she or he will have succeeded in abstracting from a Self (Moi), according to a politics or strategy successfully abstracted from a given formation, according to a given procedure abstracted from its origin."[41] New forms of circulation interrupt and rechannel dominant circulation.

This is an alternative to morality, Marx, and Freud, all of which continue to fail us, even yesterday as our deterritorialized parts waged war in the Persian Gulf. Only the body without organs can register the enormity of the catastrophe of the present and generate the nonbureaucratic, nonstatist, non "outcome known in advance," nonfascist revolution that exists never in transcendence, but only in immanence. Or not. Though it may appear lame to end here on the antinomial structure of postmodernism, that is, the ostensible dead end of the opposition between, for example, identity and deterritorialization or between distraction and subjective consolidation or between the cyborg as a good thing or the cyborg as apocalypse, the fact and the stating of this undecidability may in time do its work. Like Kierkegaard's philosophers who sit down together in order to plan a spontaneous event, the present aporia may lead us beyond ourselves in unexpected ways. For the time being, however, we may want to remember Deleuze's definition of ethics: to be worthy of what happens to us.[42]

Notes

1   Paul Virilio, *Speed and Politics: An Essay on Dromology*, trans. Mark Polizzoti (New York: Semiotext[e]), 1977.

2   This is already the idea which informs Mikhail M. Bakhtin's, *The Dialogic Imagination* (Austin: University of Texas Press, 1981). Unitary discourse, for example, that language which comes from outside of us and does the work of the state by suppressing polyph-

ony and dialogism, is already conceived by Bakhtin as a *technology* of control. See especially chap. 4, "Discourse in the Novel."

3   For a riveting account of the philosophy and practice informing the origins of cybernetics, see Norbert Weiner, *The Human Use of Human Beings: Cybernetics and Society* (Garden City: Anchor Books, 1954).

4   Elaine Scarry, *The Body in Pain: The Making and Unmaking of the World* (New York: Oxford University Press, 1985).

5   See my essay, "Cinema, Capital of the Twentieth Century," in *Postmodern Culture* 4, no. 3 (May 1994).

6   Somehow, when there's not pleasure involved in the crushing of human-scale imagination, these latter forms of violence and violation are not counted as among the postmodern. One of my tasks here is to counter this aspect of postmodernism as a cultural ideology by endeavoring to show the continuity between the aesthetics of large-scale violence and the practice of more traditional violence. This is not an argument based on causality, that is, violent TV causes violence (although, in a qualified way, it probably does) but something more complex: violence is central to technologies of expression and control under capital and is therefore manifest at every level of the capitalist articulation of neurophysiological possibility.

7   For a detailed examination of some of these characteristics, see David Harvey, *The Condition of Postmodernity: An Enquiry Into the Origins of Cultural Change* (Cambridge, Mass.: Blackwell, 1990).

8   This insight is taken to its conceptual extreme in Lukács's *Reification and the Consciousness of the Proletariat,* where it is argued that the proletariat's entry into the self-consciousness that it is the subject-object of history marks the dissolution of the capitalist order. See Georg Lukács, "Reification and the Consciousness of the Proletariat," in *History and Class Consciousness* (Cambridge, Mass.: MIT Press, 1971).

9   I think here of Althusserian interpellation in all of its possible forms, that is the internal consolidation of the subject in response to the hail of ideology. See "Ideology and Ideological State Apparatuses" in Louis Althusser, *Lenin and Philosophy* (New York and London: Monthly Review Press, 1971).

10 See Walter Benjamin in *Illuminations* (New York: Schocken Books, 1969), p. 221. It would seem that Deleuze owes a large and unacknowledged debt to Benjamin.

11 Gilles Deleuze, *Proust and Signs,* trans. Richard Howard (New York: G. Braziller, 1972), pp. 138–139.

12 For this insight as well as many of the others that inform my discussion of nationalism, I am indebted to Neferti Xina M. Tadiar.

13 Elsewhere I have argued that cinema marks the colonization of the visual field by industrial practices. Indeed, assembly line production, which entails the cutting and editing of matter/capital is a proto-cinematic process, while the circulation of commodities was itself a form of proto-cinema—images, abstracted from the human world and flowing just out of reach. Cinema is the movement of these relationships into the visual field and inaugurates the emergence of a visual economy in which relations of

capitalist production take on an increasingly abstract and immaterial dimension. In addition to "Cinema, Capital of the Twentieth Century," cited above, see my essay "The Circulating Eye," in *Communication Research* 20, no. 2 (April 1993): 298–313, for the basics. For further elaboration, see my dissertation, *The Cinematic Mode of Production*.

14 For a fascinating if markedly unphilosophical registration of this crisis of identification, see Robert Reich's "Who is Them?" in the *Harvard Business Review*, March–April 1991, pp. 77–88.

15 This dynamic between an encroaching cultural logic and a cultural enclave is a dominant feature of the Latin American fiction known in the United States as "magical realism."

16 With the claim that it is the media that is the involuntary, a careful definition of mediation becomes necessary. Suffice it to say that at the extreme limits of the concept, *nothing escapes mediation*. All movement, from the trucking of vegetables to high-tech cinema to conversation to the growing of grass is mediation. Mediation will, in short, replace our concept of flux because it understands the priority of circulation. The various hardwares that move are the media. The software through which they move (flesh, the brain) are forms of mediation. Likewise, hardware is mediated and organic systems are media. Precisely the distinction between media and mediation is on the brink of vanishing. As it is no secret that all things are in motion, then it becomes clear that as soon as they move for profit, as soon as they move through the information grid of capitalism, they are at once mediated and a media for the flow of value. All life passes across the screen of value at one moment or another in the dynamic of interchangeability. Rather then going back to Bergson and elliptically building a case for the ontology of flux, as Deleuze does, let us say that a point of view is becoming possible which allows the apprehension of the (potential) interconnectedness of all thought, and hence of all material reality. Furthermore, it is becoming apparent that this mediation in general is itself mediated by incontestably technological forms of mediation. Put simply, this idea is precisely the philosophical description of mind that, for better and for worse, allies itself with the concept of the world system.

17 Before thinking implosion as a figure for the involuntary, our century produced various other forms of the involuntary. The figure of the Real in Lacan, Ideology and the Ideological State Apparatus (ISA) in Althusser, and History in Jameson each import a tropological system that expresses the involuntary through the precise manner in which the limits of knowledge are observed. These expressions, tropological systems that distribute metaphor, can be understood at once to construct and betray the ideologies of the schools of thought from which they emerge (see Hayden White's Introduction to *Metahistory*).

In the case of Lacan, the Real is in effect outside the access of discourse, though it informs the symbolic order and at times radically and violently realigns its momentary conditions in what is called "the encounter with the Real." However, Lacan proposes such lack (of the immanence of the Real) as the very condition of language. In effect this presupposition naturalizes human suffering. In this respect Lacan is a tragic thinker whose bourgeois equation of fulfillment runs as follows. All desire arises from lack that results from castration and the entry into the symbolic order. "Love is not only a recognition of desire, but a desire for recognition." When one says "I love you," what one is really saying is "You are the one who cannot satisfy me." Fulfillment is forever blocked. Alongside the depoliticization of desire in Lacan via the naturalization of lack, fulfillment becomes ontologically impossible.

Althusser's figure of Ideology and the ISA and Jameson's figure of History, as different as they are, each depend, like the Lacanian real on some echo of an inside/ outside dipole inasmuch as they are both forms of phenomenology. Simply put, "inside" there is mind, while "outside" there is event, and also there is the becoming conscious interaction between the two. Both Jameson and Althusser attempt to theorize the problem of consciousness and knowledge through the registration of what is signaled beyond the purview of consciousness and knowledge. Both figure consciousness as falling prey to that which was and partially remains exterior to it, for Althusser it is the omnivorous state that is outside, and for Jameson it is the seething but dialectical flux of History, "what hurts." Althusser, with his structural ISAs depicts the primal scene of subjectification, the instantiation of the subject through interpellation. This figure for consciousness is preeminently political, as it becomes the obverse of the state machine. In this conception, he posits the ISA as a site of political struggle. However, this scenario is unable to reckon with temporality or the subtleties of narrative because the theory configures consciousness itself as a form of reification.

Jameson's "History" is a figure for world flux that spans the voluntary and involuntary effects of and on consciousness, that is, the tension between volition and determinism within the specificity of a particular historical conjuncture: relationships among micro- and macropolitical structures. The figure of History and the imperative to Historicize politicizes all phenomenon. Jameson, who stresses the importance of producing "the concept of History" in literary and social analysis, relies ultimately on hermeneutics to produce the intellectual as the self-conscious subject of history. Historicizing texts produces interpretations that politicize phenomena and brings their interconnections up over the threshold of ideology. The involuntary is that which provides both the subjective and objective conditions of interpretation and, to Jameson's credit, the necessity of interpretation.

18 Jean Baudrillard, *America,* trans. Chris Turner (London: Verso, 1988).

19 See Karl Marx and Frederick Engels, *Complete Works,* vol. 28 (New York: International Publishers, 1975), p. 218.

20 See Rob Wilson's "*Goodbye Paradise:* Global/Localism in the American Pacific," in this volume.

21 Gilles Deleuze and Félix Guattari, *A Thousand Plateaus,* trans. Brian Massumi (Minneapolis: University of Minnesota Press, 1987), p. 23.

22 Gilles Deleuze and Claire Parnet, *Dialogues,* trans. Hugh Tomlinson and Barbara Habberjam (New York: Columbia University Press), p. 69.

23 Deleuze and Parnet, *Dialogues,* p. 91.

24   Ibid., p. 91.

25   Deleuze and Guattari, *A Thousand Plateaus*, p. 351.

26   Deleuze and Parnet, *Dialogues*, p. 134.

27   Donna Haraway, "A Manifesto for Cyborgs," in *Coming to Terms: Feminism, Theory, Politics*, ed. Elizabeth Weed (New York and London: Routledge, 1989), p. 175.

28   Deleuze and Parnet, *Dialogues*, p. 147.

29   Gilles Deleuze, *Cinema 2*, trans. Hugh Tomlinson and Robert Galeta (Minneapolis: University of Minnesota Press, 1989), p. 172.

30   Ibid., p. 166.

31   Ibid.

32   Ibid., p. 167.

33   Ibid.

34   Ibid., p. 172.

35   These are suggestions for thinking the film but would require a close reading of particular scenes to be substantiated. As space is limited I offer only one brief example.

When the brain of Cain has been implanted in Robocop 2, the Cain-cyborg encounters his old female lover while on a murder spree. The armor plating around the head opens up and Cain's face appears imaged on a television monitor. As the ex-lover recognizes Cain, the machine extends a claw. Tentatively she reaches up to touch the massive hand. The machinic arm and the human arm fill the screen like the arms of God and Adam on the Sistine Chapel ceiling. This is the new creation myth. As the woman touches the cyborg's metallic claw, she runs her hand along a pressed metal rivulet, saying: "It'll take some getting used to," and then, smiling seductively up at the machine, "but I like it." Instantly a much larger arm lashes out from the machine, taking her by the head and beating her repeatedly against the walls. So perhaps, this might be one sexuality of the new flesh. Clearly, not all deterritorializations, not all cyborgs are good cyborgs—for everyone, at least.

36   Deleuze, *Cinema 2*, p. 169.

37   Ibid., p. 171.

38   Deleuze and Guattari, *A Thousand Plateaus*, p. 155.

39   Ibid.

40   Ibid.

41   Ibid., p. 157.

42   This was cited by E. San Juan Jr., in a talk given at Duke University on Nov. 7, 1994.

IN WHOSE INTEREST? TRANSNATIONAL
CAPITAL AND THE PRODUCTION OF
MULTICULTURALISM IN CANADA

Katharyne Mitchell

●

[T]he discourse and practice of multiculturalism have been integral to the process of administrative normalization within the framework of the . . . state. Because fundamentally *different* traditions are described as necessarily *contradictory* (and therefore in need of regulation), state power extends itself by treating them as norms to be incorporated and coordinated.[1]

The job facing the cultural intellectual is therefore not to accept the politics of identity as given, but to show how all representations are constructed, for what purpose, by whom, and with what components.[2]

In the past two decades, new forms of flexible production and financial deregulation have encouraged vast movements of people, capital, and commodities across international borders. For industrial workers, union organizers, and community activists, this transnational flexibility has spelled a debilitating loss of local control. In the face of increasing cross-border movements and general deterritorialization, proponents of localism defensively call for greater state and regional regulation, even as the evidence mounts of governmental unwillingness and increasing inability to impose effective restrictions on transnational flows of any kind. At the same time as the warnings sound, however, numerous culture-workers point to the increasing opportunities that they believe have also arisen in the new spaces of advanced capitalism. They argue that greater flexibility enables the renegotiation of formerly static meanings and metanarratives and opens the possibilities for new subject positionings. Furthermore, new global-local intersections produce important new cultural forms—forms which are able to celebrate the mobile, marginal, and hybrid nature of their births and ongoing metamorphoses.

In this spirit, anthropologists such as Clifford have introduced the concept of the informant as traveler, where the relations of movement and displacement are foregrounded over those of dwelling and local, confined knowledge.[3] Here "the 'chronotope' of culture (a setting or scene organizing time and space in representable whole form) comes to resemble as much a site of travel encounters as of residence, less a tent in a village or a controlled laboratory or a site of initiation and inhabitation, and more like a hotel lobby, ship, or bus." Culture is rethought in terms of mobility rather than boundedness, of plural identities rather than those fixed in place. Similarly, Arjun Appadurai's concerns about the previous privileging of the local and the representational in Western analyses of "native" peoples (1988) has drawn him toward a celebration of deterritorialization in his discussion of disjuncture and difference in the new cultural mediascapes of late capitalism.[4] Here he seeks to escape the "metonymic freezing" of peoples' lives in Western anthropological discourse through an emphasis on historical mobility and ongoing displacement.

Other efforts to celebrate the positive implications of transnationalism have centered on the notions of hybridity and pluralism. Culture-workers interested in questions of identity and the constitution of subjectivity herald the ways in which new cross-border movements have facilitated the production and reworking of multiple identities, dialogic communications, syncretic cultural forms, and seemingly emancipatory multicultural ideologies. For some, the increased awareness of cultural hybridity and the promulgation of a multicultural ethic by state and institutional leaders are perceived as inherently progressive movements toward more tolerant and just societies worldwide.

In this paper, through a critical examination of the appropriation of the liberal rhetoric of multiculturalism by Canadian business interests, I join with those who believe this kind of abstract celebration of travel, hybridity, and multiculturalism to be premature.[5] In numerous celebratory representations of these "new" transnational cultures and hybrid subject positions, the powerfully oppressive socioeconomic forces underlying the changes are neglected, as are many of the people caught within them. As bell hooks has noted of Clifford's somewhat playful evocation of travel and "hotel lobby" culture, the actual, terrorizing experience of border crossings for many people of color is effectively elided.[6] On-the-ground experiences are relegated to a secondary position—if included at all—in the general rush to proclaim the beneficial potential of hybrid forms and state-sponsored drives toward increasing cultural diversity and mutual tolerance. In an era of global capitalism, the heralding of subject positions "at the margins" too often neglects the actual marginalization of subjects. And positive readings of the forces of deterritorialization inadequately address "the powerful forces of oppression unleashed by them."[7]

In addition, the abstract promotion of liberal tenets such as multiculturalism neglects the numerous ways in which liberal cultural projects are always at risk of appropriation. The concept of culture as a "way of life" and a manifestation of national identity has a historical legacy that Williams traces to the English social critics of the nineteenth and early twentieth centuries.[8] He argues that the idea of culture in the modern sense, as the daily practices and everyday life of a whole people, emerged during the formation of industrial liberal society. Attempts to define culture as a way of life are linked to an effort to politicize and harness all aspects of life in the context of a rapidly changing and increasingly fragmented "modern" industrial society. By controlling the meaning of culture and broadening it to include the minutiae of everyday existence, the process of hegemonic production, as outlined by Gramsci and others, can be initiated and extended into the very fabric of social life.[9]

Thinking of culture as "our common life" allows lifestyle and the habits of everyday life to be normalized and reconstructed by the state and by social institutions through the process of ideological production. In this paper I look at how the image of multiculturalism as the correct Canadian "way of life" becomes manipulated in this cultural project during the period of hypermodernity of the late 1980s.[10] In particular, I examine how this concept has been politically appropriated, normalized, and reconstructed by the Canadian state and by private institutions to facilitate international investment and capitalist development in Vancouver, British Columbia. In this manner, I hope to show how terms like multiculturalism are not *naturally* emancipatory, but must be constantly monitored and interrogated—especially with regard to their symbiotic relationships with the transnational movements of capital.

Vancouver's Integration into the Global Economy

In the 1980s, Vancouver's increasing integration into the global economy had many negative effects for urban residents and led to new types of resistance to transnational capitalist ventures. During this time, an increasing number of business ventures and agreements were occurring between Canadian businessmen, government bureaucrats, and wealthy Pacific Rim players, particularly those operating out of Hong Kong. These connections became highly visible in December 1988, when buyers in Hong Kong purchased 216 luxury condominiums on the south shore of False Creek in downtown Vancouver. The condominiums were marketed exclusively in Hong Kong and sold out within a period of three hours. The sale prompted a tremendous outcry among Vancouver residents and fueled major anti–Hong Kong sentiment in the city. Members of various political parties became involved in the fray, as did representatives from international business centers, universities, multicultural institutes, and neighborhood organizations.

Politicians who spoke scathingly of the condominium sales included Committee of Progressive Electors (cope) councillor Harry Rankin. Rankin, a progressive leftist, said at the time, "The basic issue is to give Canadians the first and only chance to buy: that means Canadian residents or landed immigrants. No offshore people should be allowed to speculate in this market."[11] Michael Goldberg, chairman of the Vancouver International Financial Centre (a nonprofit society acting as conduit between government and business to promote Vancouver as an international business center) responded by dismissing negative reactions such as those of Rankin's as fueled by racism and fear of change. "People who experience change . . . look for a bogeyman to blame. Now it is really easy to blame foreigners, especially visible minorities for these changes. If the same units had been marketed in London, I suspect the outcry would have been much less."[12]

In the preceding remarks by Rankin and Goldberg, the age-old theme of globalism versus localism emerges. This theme has been part of an ongoing debate in Vancouver since the late 1960s and has recurred with each successive period of prosperity and renewed urban development. Most frequently the politicians who have aligned themselves on the side of localism and slow-growth development have been members of left or liberal parties such as cope. Believing that uncontrolled international investment and rapid development often produce major, unacceptable dislocations within the city, these politicians and parties have fought (usually unsuccessfully) for more stringent local controls over land and urban form over the past quarter century.

This is an old story. But the twist introduces a new dimension to this pervasive development conflict. When Goldberg accused Rankin of inhibiting international capitalism, he accused him of being a racist at the same time. This new strategy, involving the political manipulation of the meanings of race and racism, has had profound repercussions for political and economic alliances, consciousness formation, and urbanization in Vancouver. Capitalists and politicians seeking to attract Hong Kong Chinese investment target "localists" as racist and endeavor to present themselves and the city as nonracist. Their willingness to attract foreign capital and to advertise the city as "open for business" is deliberately conflated with a willingness to engage with Chinese immigrants and businesspeople in the spirit of racial harmony.

Racism, particularly against the Chinese, has been a long-standing problem in British Columbia, that has been addressed seriously only in the past decade. As racism hinders the social networks necessary for the integration of international capitalisms, it has been targeted for eradication. Multiculturalism has become linked with the attempt to smooth racial friction and reduce resistance to the recent changes in the urban environment and experiences of daily life in Vancouver. In this sense, the attempt to shape multiculturalism can be seen as an attempt to gain hegemonic control over concepts of race and nation in order to further expedite Vancouver's integration into the international networks of global capitalism.

Vancouver's urban environment has been shaped by several periods of capital investment, following the boom cycles of the economy. The most recent period of rapid transformation prior to the late 1980s, occurred two decades earlier, when mammoth glass office buildings began to crowd the city skyline.[13] The most recent changes introduced by international investment are thus part of an ongoing cycle, but reflect the shock of the new in a particularly acute manner owing to the intensity and speed of the transformations. Statistics on Vancouver's rapid growth and internationalization in the past decade have been documented in a number of places[14] as have the city's increasing links to the Pacific Rim and shift to a more service-oriented economy.[15] Increasingly high-profile trade with Asian countries has been crucial for Vancouver's growth and establishment as the primary commodity gateway for the U.S. market since the final settlement of the North American Free Trade Agreement (NAFTA) in 1993.

In the early 1980s, there was a determined effort by municipal and provincial representatives and businesspeople to attract offshore Asian capital into Vancouver. In the hopes of enticing some of the wealthy Hong Kong elite to make investments in advance of 1997, there was a campaign to "sell" Vancouver as a secure, profitable and livable city in which to do business and reside.[16] This campaign crossed political divides and led to unlikely alliances between liberals and conservatives; it was advocated by B.C. Premier Vander Zalm of the Social Credit (Socred) party throughout his term of office, and is currently a major concern of Premier Harcourt of the New Democratic party (NDP). Harcourt visited Hong Kong as mayor of Vancouver and returned to reassure Hong Kong residents of his ongoing loyalty to the city one month after his election as premier.[17]

The major reason for the heightened interest in attracting Hong Kong capitalists to Vancouver is quite simple: there is a lot of money there. Estimates of the actual amounts of capital flowing between Hong Kong and Vancouver vary widely and figures are not documented by statistical agencies connected with either city government. At a private banking conference in Geneva in 1990, however, president-elect of the Swiss Private Banker's Association, Pierre Mirabaud, was quoted as saying that people in Hong Kong and Taiwan transfer about a billion Canadian dollars a month to Canada.[18] How much of this capital stays in Canada, how much goes to Vancouver, and how much flows to the United States, back to Hong Kong or elsewhere is impossible to even estimate. One more specific measure of capital flow between Hong Kong and Vancouver, although still highly approximate, is through the business immigration program statistics. The category of business immigration was initiated in Canada in 1984 and was targeted for the Hong Kong elite diversifying their portfolios in advance of the 1997 changeover to Chinese communist control. The category includes investors and entrepreneurs who are required to bring a certain amount of money into Canada and are then given higher processing priority for immigration. As of 1991, the total amount required for investors in British Columbia was a minimum personal networth of C$500,000 with a promise to commit C$350,000 to a Canadian business over a three-year period.

The business immigration program set up by the Canadian federal government attracted a great proportion of wealthy immigrants from Hong Kong during the late 1980s. From 1984 through 1991, Hong Kong led as the primary source country under the program, jumping from 338 landed immigrants in 1984, to 6,787 by 1990.[19] Although Vancouver is second to Toronto in the preferred destination for most of these immigrants, the amount of estimated funds brought to British Columbia in 1988 (most of the funds brought into the province wind up in Vancouver) was nearly one and a half billion Canadian dollars, three hundred million dollars more than to Ontario.[20] Figures from 1989 show an approximate capital flow of C$3.5 billion from Hong Kong to Canada, of which C$2.21 billion or 63 percent was transferred by the business migration component.[21] I consider these figures quite conservative. Most applicants underdeclare their actual resources by a significant margin for income tax purposes. Bankers and immigration consultants I interviewed in Hong Kong put the overall figure as high as C$6 billion being transferred from Hong Kong to Canada in the late 1980s and early 1990s. Of that amount, over one-third would be destined for British Columbia.[22]

Banking networks between the cities have grown tremendously in order to accommodate and encourage the financial activity. The Hong Kong and Shang-hai Banking Group (Hongkong Bank), the largest non-Japanese bank in Asia has, through rapid expansion in the past two decades, incorporated many wholly owned and subsidiary firms in Canada. For example, the Hong Kong Bank of Canada was founded in 1981 as a small branch of the international giant. In 1986 the bank acquired the assets of the Bank of British Columbia for C$63.5 million, and in 1990 it bought out Lloyds Canada. By 1991 the bank had the largest consumer presence of any foreign-owned bank in Canada and had opened 107 offices—including sixteen which specialized in Asian banking. Twenty-five percent of its retail deposits (totaling over C$5 billion) originated from Asian customers.[23]

Socioeconomic Power and Transnational Mobility

New forms of capitalism, involving the intensification and acceleration of global linkages and local fragmentations, have led to new experiences of modern life and to new forms of consciousness. In examining consciousness formation, however, it is necessary to emphasize the various hierarchies of power that affect each individual's experience. If the social relations of power are not acknowledged, it becomes possible to offer a somewhat apocalyptic and universalistic vision of modern life as a fragmented and schizophrenic experience where "the truth of (the) lived experience no longer coincides with the place in which it takes place."[24] In Jameson's vision, for example, the new global realities of late capitalism are "inaccessible" to any individual subject; individuals, who are trapped in a kind of "monadic relativism" cannot negotiate the disorienting new spaces that have become both fragmented and compressed owing to the insidious saturation of voids, the suppression of distances, and the barrage of immediacy.[25] Although this depiction may be accurate for many, it does not correspond with the practices and consciousness of the people I interviewed who are living, traveling, and doing business in both Hong Kong and Vancouver.

The transnational elite, professionals, and businesspeople living and working in several global sites, and involved in the control of capital and information flows between these sites, negotiate the new spaces of "late capitalism" to their supreme advantage. One highly successful real estate agent spoke of the efficacious use of the fifteen-hour time difference between Hong Kong and Vancouver. With an immediacy of communication juxtaposed with a real time lag, she is able to maintain nearly continuous buyer-seller information and connections. As a result of this "postmodern condition," she obtains market information from Hong Kong and sells Vancouver real estate twenty-four hours a day. She is also occasionally able to get a jump on the local market for her Hong Kong clients depending on the time of day that the Vancouver office buildings are made available. She said in a February 1991 interview:

> From a real estate perspective, if a transaction happens over here—something as spectacular as the Campbell building getting sold—because of the time zones, we can phone back to Hong Kong and say, "guess what . . . ?" At six thirty at night or whatever, it's at the beginning of their day, it's only nine-thirty, and that means that "Yes, the market is still there, and if you want to look at that other stuff. . . ." So they have the whole day to digest, they phone you back at home, it goes through my lawyer the next day and boom! you've got something happening.[26]

Several businesspeople in Hong Kong spoke to me of the strategic location of their children in universities in Canada, the United States, and England in order to acculturate them to different areas of the world in which there might be the potential to live or do business. This move is partly an effort to safeguard the family's wealth and well-being in the case of negative ramifications after 1997, but also represents a desire to extend the family network spatially. Parents and children travel and communicate easily and on a frequent basis. The socioeconomic *power* involved in the ability to control the experience of travel, transcultural communication, habitation, education, and business thus produces a completely different experience of late capitalism than that described by Jameson. It also leads to new and different forms of cultural identity, and to a need for new ideological meanings of race and nation in the context of the growing economic ties as international capitalisms become intertwined.

A frequent interviewee and friend in Hong Kong operates in the spaces of "late modernity" quite easily and profitably. Susan Liu was educated in English from the first year of primary school and went to secondary school in England. She is the wife of a prominent surgeon in Hong Kong, and the daughter of a wealthy Shanghai businessman who emigrated to Hong Kong in the 1940s. She is currently educating one son at Eton and one at Dartmouth. Susan has recently obtained a green card from the United States and is pondering a move to either the United States or Canada, depending on her husband's job and business opportunities. She often told me that she considered herself an "internationalist" or "global citizen" when I asked her questions about personal identity. She has friends all over the world, speaks several languages, travels frequently, and feels comfortable in many different cultures. Her "national" allegiance is based on a special familiarity with the *culture* of Hong Kong, not with a "racial" allegiance. She said in an interview: "Hong Kong is always home. Hong Kong is in a way my country. I don't have an allegiance to China. I don't understand them, I don't know them. I don't want to know them. I would feel more at home with an American or British or Canadian than mainland Chinese."[27]

Another friend and informant in Hong Kong is also a member of the transnational or "internationalist" camp. She and her husband are considering a move to Canada or England as a result of the 1997 transition to Communist control. Lucy was born and raised in Trinidad until the age of eleven. After her father's death, her mother moved the family to England, where she was educated at convent and grammar school. She and her husband studied dentistry in England and now practice in Hong Kong. Her two oldest children were educated in medicine at Cambridge University, and her youngest has just graduated from Oxford. When I asked Lucy about her Chinese heritage and feelings about personal identity, she responded that she felt Chinese, but that her values and beliefs, her "form of consciousness" was a complete mix:

> K: After living in so many different environments, how do you feel about Western and Chinese values and ways of living?
> L: I feel that I'm so mixed and assimilated that I cannot distinguish one from another. And that I . . . it's kind of instinctual that when I meet up with somebody who's western in their values it doesn't strike me as being strange or unusual. . . . And I think it's because I've just been living and brought up in a western world for so long that nothing strikes me as being unusual. Likewise I think with Chinese cultures. Because I'm sort of just in it. You know, absorbed.[28]

These two women, new "global citizens," members of a transnational elite, expressed some of the multiple experiences around issues of cultural and national identity that are being formed and reformed in the context of the recent joining of global capitalisms. Their feelings about the experiences of modernity are important for politicians and capitalists in Canada because of the desire to entice them and people like them to invest in Canadian society. In Gilroy's examination of race and nation in Britain, he demonstrates the ways in which race and culture have been conflated to legitimate the exclusion of "blacks" from "being British."[29] The linking of race and culture and the naturalized sense that white culture is equivalent to British culture has positioned black culture and black people permanently outside the possibility of national belonging. In Vancouver, in contrast, the desire to attract members of the transnational elite, powerful individuals like Susan and Lucy, who have global connections as well as global capital to invest, has initiated efforts of an opposite nature. Although culture is still conflated with race, the intent of this linking is one of inclusion and attraction. The contemporary message of Canadian identity and nationhood is the message of multiculturalism. Rather than one culture (white) being identified with the essence of the nation, as in Britain, all cultures together will form the essence of what it means to "be Canadian."

Race and National Identity in Canada:
Powerful Interests and High Stakes

Meanings of race and nation are particularly delicate in the Canadian context because of the country's early colonial history. Divisions between the two charter groups, the French and the British (who were believed to be different racial groups), as well as territorial struggles with indigenous peoples has made the search for common symbols and meanings of community and nationhood hazardous at best. Early efforts to increase a unified spirit of nationalism heightened English and French antagonisms and threatened to break the federal system apart. Yet the growing threat of U.S. hegemony and the fear of being absorbed into American culture and the American economy was and continues to be felt by both sides. In this context, the production of meanings of race and national identity have been bound up with the necessity of placating those of different "races," yet avoiding the use of American symbols, such as the melting pot. Cultural pluralism, the ethnic mosaic, and the multiculturalism were the original, celebratory examples of the state-led attempt to forge a unique "Canadian" identity.

Although the "interested" and contextual nature of race construction has been stressed by numerous scholars,[30] the understanding of the nation and nationalism as a similar process and production is less well articulated. National identity is often presented as a cultural relationship or pact shaped over time; incipient problems of acculturation stem from the alien-ness of immigrants and their inability to share in the "deeply grounded and active social identities" of the common working man.[31] What this image elides is the element of power and material gain implicated in the production of national identity. As with race and racism, the production of categories and meanings around this concept is neither static nor innocent. When the meanings of race and nation are articulated, as they are in the ideology of multiculturalism in Canada, it is necessary to interrogate that joining as a process that is imbricated in historically and geographically specific networks of power.

In examining race and nation in Vancouver in the past decade, the social relations of power involved in the struggles over meaning become immediately apparent. Those who perceive Vancouver's integration into the global economy as a positive move facilitate the transition by presenting the issues of progress, growth, internationalism, world-class cities, Pacific Rim investment, and racial diversity in a positive light. Those who believe integration to be harmful emphasize concepts of conservation, environment, nationalism, localism, neighborhood, and control. Interrogating *who* is claiming *what* becomes imperative to discover some of the motives and rationale behind each particular skirmish. When Libby Davies, a cope city councillor and a proponent of localism, told a newspaper that she was displeased with Victor Li's marketing strategy of the Expo luxury condos in 1990, her position was immediately attacked as racist.[32] Davies said in an interview:

> Racism became very much the scapegoat and it kind of worked both ways. Progressive people also got caught by it. Because *we* got characterized that way. There's been an issue about the sale of condos on the north shore of False Creek as to whether or not they're marketed exclusively in Hong Kong or here. When it was found out that they *were* marketed exclusively in Hong Kong, there was an outcry—people were really mad. Carole Taylor met with Victor Li and made a deal that they would agree that they would be marketed first in Vancouver so that local people would have an opportunity. Then the next set of sales came up and the Sun phoned me and said do you know that they're doing the same thing again and I said, well then they've broken the deal, that's not what they promised. I don't control the media . . . there was this horrible headline: "Davies' Claims Concord Pacific Breaks" and then there were two or three letters to the editor saying I was a racist for dealing with this issue. And I was upset. I didn't respond to it. But it did upset me because you see my criticism of this developer and how I felt that they really weren't handling their marketing in the public interest became racist. So it's been a very hard issue to deal with.[33]

The ideologies in contestation are not monolithic nor are they necessarily instrumental or oppressive, but they are always bound up with power. Davies, like Rankin, was labeled racist despite her legitimate concern about unacceptable dislocations and the loss of a "quality" of life and her professed aims of local, neighborhood protection and slow-growth development. Although she contests the label for herself, she acknowledges that the issue of local neighborhood protection has, in fact, served as an alibi for some Vancouver residents with decidedly racist agendas.[34] She said, "I did get racist phone calls, particularly from older, white people—people who were born in Vancouver and from the west-side who would say, goddamn Chinese, it's the Chinese moving into our neighborhood." The presence of Vancouver residents with an active racist motivation for "protecting" their neighborhoods from change elucidates the difficulties that Davies and Rankin face in disentangling their agendas and beliefs from actual racists and underscores the inherent strength of the attack against them. Since many of the ideological contestations in Vancouver spring from a multiplicity of sites impossible to pinpoint clearly, the manipulation of meanings of race and nation in the interests of international capitalism has been particularly well camouflaged and efficacious.[35]

Race and Place

Racism, like capitalism, is an old story in Vancouver. The power of definition over what constitutes race and racism is central to the forms it takes over the years. White Vancouverites' conceptions of "Chineseness" have often been bound to these definitions and also to the construction of an Anglo-Canadian identity through this process of othering. The identities that have been constructed along racial lines for Chinese Canadians and Anglo-Canadians have been historically tied to place in Vancouver, with Chinatown and Shaughnessy exemplifying two contrasting neighborhoods with formerly rigid racial boundaries and class distinctions.[36]

Until recently, wealthy Anglo neighborhoods in Vancouver's west-side, like Shaughnessy, were almost completely homogeneous. The symbols of distinction in these neighborhoods were predicated on the links to a British aristocratic past, one that expressed both class and racial separateness. Recent expressions of racism against wealthy Hong Kong Chinese immigrants, which have increased in number in the past decade,[37] often become manifest in struggles over boundary protection and land control in these areas. These struggles reflect an anxiety about the loss of both economic and symbolic control over the defining and marking of place.

Some long-term, white residents fear exclusion from the business practices of the Hong Kong entrepreneurs, whom they perceive as directing or channeling their capital and opportunities along racial, regional, or family lines. Much of the anger and resentment at the 1988 marketing of the Vancouver Regatta condominiums in Hong Kong stemmed from this fear of exclusion. At the same time, media articles, popular books, jokes, and anecdotes from the late 1980s also emphasized the threat of engulfment. Words relating to water, such as tide or wave, were used frequently in reference to the new business activities and immigration of the Hong Kong Chinese.[38] Floods and tides of destruction had been evident in images of "Asian" takeovers in earlier years as well, with Lothrop Stoddard's postwar treatise, *The Rising Tide of Color*, a popular book in Vancouver in the 1920s. In this book, Stoddart wrote of the vulnerability of "white race-unity" and the "very imminent danger that the white stocks may be swamped by Asiatic blood."[39]

Other conflicts centered on the transformation of the urban environment. In the late 1980s, demolitions, "monster" houses, and the destruction of trees and gardens were the source of greatest strife. The monster house is a term that is used for recently constructed houses that are especially large in the context of Vancouver neighborhoods on the west-side of the city.[40] The original, smaller houses, built on Canadian Pacific Railroad land in the 1920s, were demolished to make space for the new monster houses, which often extend to the extreme edges of the lots. Before the demolitions began in the early 1980s, one long-term resident of Kerrisdale described his west-side neighborhood as "one of the most conservative, fossilized landscapes in the province."[41]

Many of the new houses are perceived as ugly and cheap by the older, white residents, who are drawn primarily from the ranks of the upper middle class and wealthy.[42] Although the new houses are much larger than most of the buildings that were there formerly, the general neighborhood impression of these houses is that the quality of materials is poor, the architectural style is boxy and clumsy, the landscaping is unappealing, and the entire package is noncontextual. Residents spoke to me frequently about the loss of ambience, tradition, and heritage in their neighborhoods, bemoaning the new buildings' lack of "character." Implicit in many of the statements was a perceived threat to an established way of life, a way of life predicated on the symbols, values, and distinction of a white, Anglo tradition.[43] One person wrote in a letter to Vancouver City Council, April 10, 1990:

> I grew up in Shaughnessy, on Balfour Street, and have watched closely the changes happening within it. I am saddened and disgusted when I walk through it today to see so many of the trees and houses gone, only to be re-

placed by hideous monster houses!! . . . I talked to a construction worker who was working on one of these new atrocities they call a house . . . he said, and I quote, "the house is a piece of shit, and will probably be falling to pieces in ten years." So, is this what Shaughnessy is to become? . . . We need assurances that the character of the neighborhood will be maintained!

In addition to the actual physical changes in the landscape, there have been extreme economic changes as well. The most prominent real estate company in Vancouver, Royal LePage, shows average prices for an executive detached two-story in the west-side, rising from C\$185,000 in 1979 to C\$500,000 in 1989. The price for a detached bungalow doubled in just four years, from C\$200,000 in 1985 to C\$400,000 in 1989.[44] Forecasts by real estate agents for the future show prices soaring to C\$700,000 in 1995 and C\$800,000 by the year 2000 for the average Kerrisdale home.[45] Word-of-mouth stories and newspaper accounts depict far more acute price changes, including stories of houses that were flipped for great profit three or four times within a single year.[46]

The association of the influx of wealthy immigrants from Hong Kong with the aesthetic and economic changes in neighborhoods like Shaughnessy and Kerrisdale was made both directly and obliquely in letters to the Vancouver City Council, letters to the editor, and in interviews with me. The anxiety surrounding the loss of a way of life was often expressed as a concern about individual and national identity as well as a concern about urban change. One person wrote in a letter to the editor: "Canadians see monster housing as an arrogant visible demonstration of the destruction of Canadian culture. Yes, we have a Canadian identity and Canadians should beware of persons who say we don't while they try to rebuild Canada in a different mould for their own purpose and profit."[47]

The reference to profit is a direct jab at the Hong Kong Chinese, who are perceived as responsible for house price escalation as a result of using homes for profit through the practice of speculation, rather than as places to live. For wealthy white residents, investing in "tasteful" or "high" culture in Vancouver society, which includes the home where one lives, secures profit yet *does not have to be pursued as profit.* Living in an established and wealthy area such as Shaughnessy purportedly because the character of the neighborhood "feels right," allows the homeowners to profess ignorance and innocence of any cynical or mercenary motives such as profit, yet establishes their fundamental connection to the underlying systems that generate it.[48]

Although the letter refers to the destruction of a national identity, the concern over social identity is implicit; profit-generating development in Vancouver's east-side and outlying areas is rarely contested, nor are those areas (which are far more economically and racially mixed) defended on the grounds of preserving heritage, tradition, character, or identity of any kind. The violence of the reaction against the aesthetic and economic changes in Kerrisdale and Shaughnessy betrays the profound fear that the symbols and meanings of the established and dominant Anglo group are being eroded, and with them the chance of appropriating and naturalizing the appropriation of the rare rights and assets that are dependent upon one's position in social space as well as the distribution of those assets in geographical space.[49]

The repercussions of these economic, morphological, and social changes in west-side neighborhoods have been extreme. Many people living in areas such as Kerrisdale have expressed a twofold anxiety: first, that the quality of the neighborhood that they are living in is being eroded through the imposition of large and "ugly" buildings and the influx of people with different tastes and values and, second, that because of the fantastic price leaps in housing, their children will not be able to live in the same area where they grew up.[50] The anxiety expressed is that an elite lifestyle, represented largely through both the choice of neighborhood and the style of house and gardens within that neighborhood, can no longer be reproduced in succeeding generations.

Although the rise in house prices and the construction of the monster houses may derive from a number of causes, including intraprovincial migration and demographic shifts, there is a general feeling among many residents of these neighborhoods that the Hong Kong Chinese are largely responsible for the changes. Some residents I spoke with felt that the cultural differences, the different practices of daily life that they envisaged as the norm for people in Hong Kong, were changing the patterns of daily life in Vancouver. Here the conflation of race and culture operates in an insidious way to legitimize the exclusion of the Hong Kong Chinese from west-side neighborhoods. Residents invoked cultural difference as the reason that they felt uncomfortable with the new immigrants and were thus able to mobilize resistance to the changes on relatively neutral grounds. One woman in her fifties, a resident of Vancouver who had been born and raised in England, said of the changes in her Kerrisdale neighborhood:

A: It's a shame because we have many friends . . . I hate to single out one race but you're particularly thinking about one race . . . but we have many friends and they're fine people. But I just think their way of life is so totally different.

K: So assimilation is difficult?

A: It's very difficult. The very thought of having an apartment lot would make my husband sick. Whereas to a Chinese, it's great. It's business. It's just so different. This is the thing that's interesting. We put our house up for sale and it's quite big and I love it; I think it's a beautiful house. This lady came in and looked around and looked around and walked out. And the real estate lady said, she probably doesn't even know what color your drapes are. She's going to knock it down.

K: Is this a Chinese woman?

A: Yes. And so, we're just so completely different.[51]

Spatial Integration and the Circulation of Capital

Other urban changes that affected Vancouver in the late 1980s included declining vacancy rates for apartments, the demolitions of apartment buildings where many elderly resided, the loss of single-resident occupancy hotels, and the gentrification of some neighborhoods surrounding the former Expo lands.[52] As mentioned before, some (although certainly not all) of the dissatisfaction with these urban changes was associated with the entry of the wealthy Hong Kong immigrants into the Vancouver real estate market. Most of the resistance to the changes, however, became embodied in urban social movements focusing on local control of development, zoning, rental agreements, and the provision of public housing. Tenant action groups attempted to stop the demolitions of viable apartment buildings, while zoning control groups aimed at controlling the size and style of new houses.

One neighborhood movement resulted in a new amendment to control the zoning of property in a small area of south Shaughnessy. John Pitts, a Shaughnessy resident, spent C$15,000 to draft a bylaw to rezone nearly 200 houses between 37th and 41st and Granville and Maple streets. The zoning law, labeled the Pitts-Stop by city planners,[53] was approved by the city council in June 1990. The law reduces floor-space ratio and sets out stringent property setbacks specifically designed to end the construction of monster houses in the neighborhood. Harry Rankin of COPE said of the new bylaw, "This is going to be the start of a lot of other neighborhoods wanting to protect the integrity of their neighborhoods. That is a reasonable demand." Gordon Price, an NPA member of the city council, objected to the idea of putting the neighborhood "in formaldahyde."[54] He felt that there would be negative consequences for other areas of the city if the bylaw were implemented and blamed the political left for helping to increase local area power for political purposes. He said in a February 1991 interview: "The left and the right have both bought into it [restrictive zoning]. In fact, the left is more aggressive in supporting the Pitts because COPE sees their opportunity to build a constituency on the west-side and undermine the traditional NPA constituency."

The Pitt-Stop, or "Preservation District 1," social movement outlined above demonstrates both the growing local resistance to change in Vancouver and also the disparate reactions to that resistance by city council representatives. The fears of the NPA, prodevelopment representative, Gordon Price, concern the potential loss of a political constituency to the opposition, but also touch on the wider threat of a loss of "rational" control over land use and land exchange by the city bureaucracy.[55] The rationalized, systematic control of urban space is crucial for the free flow of capital through the city. If local groups are able to wrest control away from city government and "freeze" or remove neighborhood districts from the ravages of rapid development the circuit of goods and capital will be hindered, reducing profit and perhaps driving investors from future projects within the city.

For capital to operate effectively in a city, physical barriers to its circulation must be reduced to a minimum. Local control of particular spaces within a city increases bureaucratic, physical, and social frictions, which then cause an increase in transaction times. The increased friction caused by local barriers increases the costs of circulation and may render the city a less profitable site for investment than a competing city without barriers. City officials interested in development and in attracting international investment thus seek to aid the circuit of capital by reducing the chaotic or unsystematized local control of specific neighborhood districts. Following the passing of the Pitts zoning law in June 1990, several other urban social movements were formed with the similar intent of protecting specific neighborhoods from unwanted change. The city attempted to block these movements by increasing bureaucratic entanglements and fees and by proposing new, stricter citywide zoning laws of its own.[56]

As the reduction of physical and social barriers to capital flow increases the overall value of the city, so too does Vancouver's spatial integration into the global economy. With the alteration of space relations comes an alteration in value; in general, the higher the degree of spatial integration on any number of levels—neighborhood, city, region, Pacific Rim—the higher the value of the city as a site for international capital investment.[57] As in the case of Haussman's

Paris 1850–1870, the planners and administrators of Vancouver increased the potential value of the city by increasing spatial integration and aiding the circuit of capital; this was accomplished in both cities with the freeing up of land and property values, increasing land speculation, opening to international competition, and increasing immigration.[58]

The contradictions and problems inherent in the attempt to integrate Vancouver on so many different levels have been manifold. As Harvey has noted, corporate and political hierarchies require complex coordinations and articulations, and "the problem of integrating local with global requirements always remains a thorny problem for any administration."[59] Racism, as an autonomous process linked in complex ways with capitalism; localism, featuring the attempt to preserve and reproduce an established standard and quality of life; and patriotism, focusing on the search for a "true" (Anglo) Canadian national identity are all processes that have hindered Vancouver's spatial integration both locally and internationally. The growing anti–Hong Kong sentiment in Vancouver is a complex mix of all of these processes, varying by place and person but uniformly antithetical to the interests of multinational capitalism.

Multiculturalism and Capital Accumulation: Whose Interest?

In the following section I will examine some of the strategies that have been taken to combat racism, localism, and patriotism in the context of Vancouver's integration in the global economy. The ongoing attempt to influence and guide the production of meanings and the new articulations of race and nation are directly implicated in the production of a multiculturalist rhetoric in Canada. This rhetoric, in turn, is implicated in the strategy of spatial integration and the articulation of international capitalisms. The multiculturalist ideology has been produced and contested by many groups and individuals in Vancouver, but I will focus in particular on the role of the state and on one private institution.

Cultural pluralism has been promoted in Canada in different forms and with different meanings since the time of Sir Wilfrid Laurier's term in office.[60] At the time that he was elected in 1896, Canada was experiencing an economic boom, and Laurier saw his mission as prime minister to be one of easing "racial" tensions so that the country could expand geographically and economically without the drag of conflicting sentiments from the two charter groups. For most of the twentieth century, government policy initiatives around the concept of cultural pluralism functioned as a relief valve for growing tensions with Quebec and as a framework for a national discourse on the possible reconstitution of Canadian society and Canadian identity.[61]

The term "multiculturalism" became common after Prime Minister Trudeau's speech in October 1971, in which he introduced a new plan for the country called, "multiculturalism within a bilingual framework." The specific "multicultural" programs that were funded and the types of conferences that were convened in the first decade after this speech did not deviate much from the earlier initiatives, which had focused on general questions of Canadian national identity and on the reduction of animosity with the Québécois. Critics of multicultural policy in the early 1980s noted that the weakest policy programs were those that were aimed at reducing racial and ethnic discrimination, and that aside from a noisy rhetoric, the general effort by the government was minimal at best. The budget allocated for the implementation of multicultural programs in 1980 was a miserly C$10.8 million, and relatively little labor or energy was expended by government agencies—aside from a cursory interest in producing a few films and a couple new radio programs.[62]

In the mid 1980s, however, the emphasis began to shift. The early concern about identity in the context of friction with Quebec became more widespread and all-encompassing. Canadian national identity was no longer just manifested in expressive instances of multicultural unity and harmony, it was explicitly linked in language and law to the multicultural ethic. At the same time, the policy initiatives of the government shifted from interest in the maintenance of cultural language and heritage (which had been primarily focused at the French Canadians) to a far more extensive and stronger commitment to the improvement of what it terms "race relations." Government funding nearly tripled between 1980 and 1991, with a far greater proportion of federal money allocated to programs dedicated to the improvement of race relations (see table 1).

Alongside the increase and shift in government funding, there were concrete moves toward the entrenchment of multiculturalism in the constitutional and statutory levels of government. The 1982 Canadian Charter of rights and Freedoms included two provisions that were related to multiculturalism; Section 27 explicitly linked the interpretation of the charter as consistent with the "preservation and enhancement of the multicultural heritage of Canadians." The Canadian Multiculturalism Act of 1988 was even more direct in its affirmation of the cultural diversity of Canada and the role of the government in "bringing about equal access for all Canadians in the economic, social, cultural and political realms."[63]

Table 1   Multiculturalism Expenditures under Three Federal Programs,
1984–85 to 1990–91

	Race relations (%)	Heritage culture (%)	Community participation (%)	Total ($ millions)
1984–85	—	50	50	18.4
1985–86	—	46	54	16.1
1986–87	—	48	52	17.8
1987–88	—	40	60	19.6
1988–89	14*	37	49	22.1
1989–90	24	37	38	27.1
1990–91	27*	22	51	27.0

Source: Based on data from Canada, *New Faces in the Crowd: Economic and Social Aspects of Immigration* (Ottawa: Minister of Supply and Services, 1991).
*Figures exclude one-time payments of $12 million to the National Association of Japanese Canadians in 1988–89 and $24 million to the Canadian Race Relations Foundation in 1990–91.

With the commitment to multiculturalism enshrined in the Constitution Act of 1982, and entrenched in the nation's statutes with the Multiculturalism Act of 1988, yet with a clear emphasis on maintaining the privileging of the English and French languages, the first steps in the nation-building of a new Canadian order were taken. The language used in reference to the new act is explicit in the linking of multiculturalism with identity, nationhood, and progress. The connection of a new Canada with a new world order involving international cooperation and increased economic prospects is similarly categorical. David Crombie, the secretary of state of Canada and the minister responsible for multiculturalism, wrote in 1987:

> Dear fellow Canadians,
> I am pleased to introduce a Bill which, upon passage, will become the world's first national Multicultural Act. It contains the government's new policy respecting multiculturalism, an essential component of our Canadian identity. . . . Its intention is to strengthen our unity, reinforce our identity, improve our economic prospects, and give recognition to historical and contemporary realities. . . . Multiculturalism has long been fundamental to the Canadian approach to nation-building. . . . Canadians are coming to realize that substantial social, economic and cultural benefits will flow from a strengthened commitment to multiculturalism.[64]

Crombie's words echoed the sentiments of Prime Minister Brian Mulroney, who had emphasized the potential economic benefits of multiculturalism in 1986, at a conference called, appropriately enough, "Multiculturalism Means Business." In his speech, Mulroney is unequivocal about the pragmatic reasons for promoting a new multiculturalism. He makes the link between Canada's need for export markets and increased trading opportunities with a more nurturing, progressive stance of government vis-à-vis the nation's ethnic members who might perhaps have links to "other" parts of the globe. The changing patterns of immigration into Canada make it more than likely that the "other" parts of the globe to which Mulroney refers will be located in Asia. The gamble for increased business opportunities with the booming Pacific Rim countries through the particularist ties of well-coddled Asian-Canadians is unambiguous and unapologetic, couched as it is in the lingo of humanitarianism and the entrepreneur spirit:

> We, as a nation, need to grasp the opportunity afforded to us by our multicultural identity, to cement our prosperity with trade and investment links the world over and with a renewed entrepreneurial spirit at home. . . . In a competitive world, we all know that technology, productivity, quality, marketing, and price determine export success. But our multicultural nature gives us an edge in selling to that world. . . . Canadians who have cultural links to other parts of the globe, who have business contacts elsewhere are of the utmost importance to our trade and investment strategy.[65]

The connection between the government's promotion of better race relations and human rights and the increasing immigration of wealthy Asian investors is made in several government publications, albeit indirectly. In a statement by the Economic Council of Canada in 1991, called "New Faces in the Crowd," the authors juxtapose statistics showing the decline of British immigration and growth of Asian immigration, discussions of the economic impact of the immigrant investor category, and government expenditures showing increases in funding for multiculturalist programs engaged with group acceptance and tolerance and improved race relations.[66] The interconnections are implicit but fairly clear: the government has embarked on a new ideological strategy involving the mitigation of racial tensions surfacing around the increase of wealthy Asian immigrants into the society. Two new bills and a national campaign in 1989 and 1990 were directly engaged with defusing racial animosity and educating people about racial discrimination.[67] It cannot be entirely coincidental that the national public education campaign to mark the International Day for the Elimination of Racial Discrimination was organized less than a month after the following two articles appeared in Canada's major daily newspaper, the *Globe and Mail:*

> What, for Vancouver, is tomorrow?
> The answer: to call what is taking shape here startling is an understatement. Vancouver, barely past its 100th birthday, is going to become an Asian city.[68]

> The Hong Kong immigrants are of a different breed from the usual new arrivals: they're rich. . . . Choice blocks of condominiums are being built that are sold only to Hong Kong buyers. Old houses are being bulldozed and replaced by unattractive megahouses for Hong Kong buyers. Hong Kong investment—about $800 million a year in the province, most of it in Vancouver—is gobbling real estate.[69]

The set of beliefs around what multiculturalism is and should be reflects private concerns as well as those of government agents. In addition to a flourishing of government organizations in Vancouver in 1989 and 1990 such as the Hastings Institute and the Affiliation of Multicultural Societies and Services Agencies of B.C. (AMSSA), there have been some key private institutions involved in promoting multicultural understanding, particularly between Vancouver and Hong Kong. The Laurier Institute, headquartered in Vancouver, is the most prominent and well-financed of these organizations.

The Laurier Institute came into existence legally in the middle of 1989 but, according to the executive director, was operational for a year prior to that time. The goals of the institute are quoted in a number of brochures and publications. In short, they are "to contribute to the effective integration of the many diverse cultural groups within Canadian society into our political, social and economic life by educating Canadians of the positive features of diversity."[70] Orest Kruhlak, the executive director of the institute, specifically mentioned the attempt to defuse potential racial friction as an important principle of the organization. He cited the organization's worry about future problems arising as a result of the increase in immigration and the growing racial diversity of Vancouver. "Nobody seemed to be looking at the long-term implications of increased diversity. What we wanted to do was say how can we start working with some of the issues that might come forward in the future with the idea of trying to get ahead on the issue and do research and educational programming to try and prevent the problems that we have come to understand were going to be major problems in the future."[71]

One of the first projects that was commissioned by the institute was a study on real estate price increases in Vancouver. According to Kruhlak, this study had not been planned but was in response to "a growing and emerging problem." In the report, entitled "Population and Housing in Metropolitan Vancouver: Changing Patterns of Demographics and Demand," the author's results seemed to indicate that the rising house prices were a product of demand from the aging postwar baby boomers. The author of the report, David Baxter wrote in the executive summary: "Regardless of the level of migration assumed (none, normal, or high) and regardless of the level of household headship rates assumed (constant or increasing), it is the demographic process of the aging of the postwar baby boom into the 35 to 44 age group (1986 to 1996) and then into the 45 to 54 age group (1991 to 2006) that will determine the characteristics of changes in housing demand in metropolitan Vancouver in the future."[72]

Although this paragraph is fairly general, seeming to indicate that demographic change is at least partially responsible for changes in housing demand in Vancouver (with the implication of increasing house prices), the following paragraph in the summary demonstrates the persuasive rhetorical strategy that is at the heart of the study. In this section, Baxter makes it clear that the report is not so much concerned with showing the possible reasons for price increases as showing what are *not* possible reasons. What is not possible and not acceptable in the dictates of multiculturalism and the Canadian way would be to label and identify and otherwise pinpoint a particular group. In an avuncular, warning tone, he writes: "If we seek someone to blame for this increase in demand, we will find only that the responsible group is everyone, not some unusual or exotic group of residents or migrants. In fact, there is no one to blame: the future growth in housing demand is a logical and normal extension of trends in the nation's population."

The findings of Baxter's report, part of a series of joint research projects sponsored by the Canadian Real Estate Research Bureau and Bureau of Applied Research (at the Faculty of Commerce and Business Administration at the University of British Columbia) as well as the Laurier Institute, were picked up and commented on by nearly all of the major newspapers in Canada. The effect of Baxter's warning statement on the media was immediate, and immediately conveyed to the public. The *Vancouver Sun* and the *Globe and Mail*, still recovering from the accusations of racism in articles written on Hong Kong and Vancouver in 1988 and early 1989, made the connection between Baxter's statement on "unusual or exotic groups" with wealthy immigrants from Hong Kong. This connection, although implied, was not explicitly mentioned anywhere in the text. The media, in an ecstasy of self-flagellation and expiation for former sins, printed the story with explicit reference to Hong Kong. The *Globe and Mail* wrote in November 1989, "Aging baby boomers, not foreign immigrants, are the main reason Vancouver housing prices are rising, a study says. . . . [The study] was prompted by public complaints that home-buying by affluent Hong Kong immigrants had been forcing up Vancouver home prices."[73]

The other Laurier project reports, all focused in some way on housing and real estate in Vancouver, were also broadcast nationally in several forums. Professor Hamilton's study, entitled, "Residential Market Behavior: Turnover Rates and Holding Periods," claimed the immigration levels did not contribute to speculation (flipping) in the housing market. The *Vancouver Sun* declared soon after in headlines, "Foreign buyers absolved."[74] And the local Vancouver paper, the *Courier,* wrote in April 1990, "Home speculation not immigrants' fault."[75] A study by Dr. Enid Slack on the impact of development cost fees charged by municipalities (the fourth in the series) showed that the levies on developers (for financing water supply systems, sewage treatment plants, etc.) are often passed on to new home buyers in increased house prices. The *Real Estate Weekly* in Vancouver wrote of these findings, "Slack's report is part of a major study commissioned by the Laurier Institute to determine whether any basis exists for suggestions that Chinese immigrant buyers are driving up Vancouver real estate prices. So far, the Institute has found, 'in fact there is no one to blame. . . . [T]he responsible group is everyone.' "[76]

The continual reiteration of Baxter's statement that no one is to blame appears to operate like a mantra for warding off the evil spirit of racism. But in fact, the statement operates on a number of levels. In denying that blame for the specific results of higher real estate prices can be pinned on anyone in particular, the proponents of this belief achieve two results: first, those who disagree with this belief are not joining in the valiant effort to defeat racism, and thus can be seen as somewhat suspect in this area; and second, since everyone is responsible and no one to blame, there is no obligation and no need to uncover and demask the agents or systems involved in the process that has, in fact, led to higher prices. The workings of capitalism thus remain opaque, the agents involved in capital transfer remain faceless, and the spatial barriers and frictions that may disrupt the free flow of capital over and through municipal and international borders are eradicated.

The implications of Dr. Slack's report go one step further. Not only is no one to blame for the unfortunate (for house buyers) rise in house prices, but if anyone should be held accountable, it is city government. Although house prices have doubled and tripled in a single year, adding hundreds of thousands of dollars to house prices in certain neighborhoods, Slack's findings focus on the development costs imposed by *municipalities* on new housing projects. These costs (which only affect new houses, not those that are the main source of the controversies discussed earlier) range from about C$1,500 for new homes in Burnaby to about C$12,000 for a new home in Richmond. Furthermore, the costs are not imposed in many communities in Vancouver or North Vancouver. Nevertheless, Slack's report was commented on in the *Vancouver Sun* with the headline: "Study finds extra charges placing heavy burden on new home buyers."[77] Here, it is the extra charges that are to blame; the charges, levied by the municipalities, are forcing people to pay more. Too much government obviously throws the whole supply and demand system off, and developers are naturally forced to pass off these onerous tax burdens onto the buyer. If anyone is to blame it is an overly controlling and paternalistic city government.

Why would the Laurier Institute, an organization whose express mission and role is to "promote cultural harmony in Canada" and "encourage understanding among and between people of various cultures" commission these particular reports? Although my sources indicate that the Laurier Institute was founded by "a group of businessmen," the organization's brochures do not identify the founders by name. The list of the board of directors of the institute in 1990 included thirteen people and their positions. Of this group there are four lawyers in major law firms, three executives in large corporations, two investment and management counselors, and one real estate executive. Of the corporations or firms represented, nine are directly or indirectly involved with Hong Kong business or investment. Of the seven founding donors (donating C$25,000 or more), there is a similar overlap with Hong Kong business concerns.[78]

The role of the Laurier Institute to provide guidance through the education of the benefits of multiculturalism has been expressed in a number of areas, including a video and curriculum guide for use in the schools called, "Growing Up Asian and Native Canadian."[79] The dissemination of general information from studies that educate and persuade readers about "what is really happening" is made public and broadcast via the media. In addition, the information generated from commissioned research is offered to companies who become corporate members of the institute. In seeking to attract corporate members, one brochure enumerates the advantages of having insider information on changes regarding cultural diversity in Canada that may be economically fruitful. Like Mulroney's speech quoted earlier, the emphasis on the economic potential of contributing to the multicultural ideology is clear:

> The cultural diversity of Canada's population has brought, and continues to bring, significant change to the Canadian workforce and the Canadian marketplace. Companies which recognize the potential of this diversity and act accordingly will have enormous advantage over those who do not. Membership in The Laurier Institute offers assistance in terms of both recognizing the potential and implementing programs which will deliver that advantage.[80]

Other corporate members and major supporters of the Laurier Institute include the Bank of Nova Scotia, the Canadian Maple Leaf Fund Ltd., Concord Pacific Developments, Grand Adex, Hong Kong Bank of Canada, Pacific Canadian Investment and the Royal Bank of Canada. All of these corporations have major stakes in Hong Kong and in the continued flow of people and capital from Hong Kong into Canada. Those who helped to fund the real estate reports mentioned earlier, plus sponsoring a number of Laurier Institute events and conferences, include the major real estate companies and foundations in Vancouver, most of whom have profited enormously as a result of the increased connections with Hong Kong over the past decade.

Reclaiming Multiculturalism

Is it possible then to reclaim multiculturalism as a possible counterpublic sphere?[81]

In *Political Power and Social Classes,* Poulantzas describes how the dominant discourse of bourgeois ideology presents itself as innocent of power, often through the concealment of political interests behind the objective facade of science.[82] In the production and promotion of multiculturalism in Canada, the particular configurations of power remain similarly concealed, but in this case, behind the facade of national identity and racial harmony. The struggle over ideological formation, such as the language and meaning of race and nation, resonates as an effort to shape a dominant discourse for specific *material* ends. Culture-workers who ignore the socioeconomic elements involved in this struggle run the risk of celebrating new voices and cultural opportunities, just as those voices risk being appropriated and/or extinguished.

In Vancouver, for example, increasing global connections and rapid urban development have been accompanied by an influx of wealthy "Asian" immigrants and by several high-profile development projects by Hong Kong investors. Tensions around city transformation have reflected anger toward the unacceptable dislocations occasioned by rapid capitalist development, as well as increased antagonism toward Hong Kong Chinese investors, who are often represented as invaders flooding the city on a tidal wave of capital. As tensions have grown, resistance to change has become more vociferous, culminating in several local attempts to halt "flows" of any kind. In this context, the reworking of multiculturalism as an ideology of racial harmony and bridge-building in the city operates as both a localized effort at damage control in a specific situation and part of a much broader strategy of hegemonic production in the interests of multinational capitalism.

By identifying the production of multiculturalism on the ground rather than heralding it in the abstract, it is possible to recognize sites of resistance as well as sites of control. When examining *who* is saying *what* and *why* about multiculturalism, one can identify the ways in which representations are made and appropriations are occurring. Unmasking the individuals and institutions responsible for these appropriations is the first step in contesting and reclaiming meaning. Despite the difficulties of disentangling agendas and interrogating material gain, it is only through this process that more positive interpretations of liberal concepts like multiculturalism can be won.

Notes

Portions of this chapter have appeared in the journal *Antipode*. In addition to the original acknowledgments, I would like to thank Matthew Sparke for his editorial comments on this revision.

1   Talal Asad, "Multiculturalism and British Identity in the Wake of the Rushdie Affair," *Politics and Society* 18, no. 4 (1990): 465.

2   Edward Said, *Culture and Imperialism* (New York: Alfred Knopf, 1993), p. 314.

3   James Clifford, "Traveling Cultures," in *Cultural Studies*, ed. L. Grossberg, C. Nelson, and P. Treichler (New York: Routledge, 1992), p. 101.

4   See Arjun Appadurai, "Putting Hierarchy in its Place," *Cultural Anthropology* 3, no. 1 (1988): 36–49, and "Disjuncture and Difference in the Global Cultural Economy," *Public Culture* 2, no. 2 (1990): 1–24.

5   See Anne McClintock, "The Angel of Progress: Pitfalls of the Term 'Post-Colonialism,'"

Social Text 10, nos. 2–3 (1993): 84–98; Gayatri Chakravorty Spivak, "Neocolonialism and the Secret Agent of Knowledge: An Interview," *Oxford Literary Review* 13, nos. 1–2 (1991): 220–51; Ella Shohat, "Notes on the 'Post-Colonial,' " *Social Text* 10, nos. 2–3 (1992): 99–113; Sneja Gunew, "Denaturalizing Cultural Nationalisms: Multicultural Readings of 'Australia,' " in *Nation and Narration,* ed. H. Bhabha (New York: Routledge, 1990); and Asad, "Multiculturalism."

6   bell hooks, "Representing Whiteness in the Black Imagination," in *Cultural Studies,* ed. L. Grossberg, C. Nelson, and P. Treichler (New York: Routledge, 1992).

7   Kamala Visweswaran, *Fictions of Feminist Ethnography* (Minneapolis: University of Minnesota Press, 1994), p. 109.

8   Raymond Williams, *Culture and Society, 1780–1950* (Harmondsworth: Penguin Books, 1961), p. 285.

9   Antonio Gramsci, *Selections from the Prison Notebooks* (London: International Publishers, 1971).

10 The term "hypermodernity" is used by Allan Pred and others to emphasize both the chronic and ongoing symptoms of modernity and capitalist development as well as their acute acceleration in the past two decades. See Allan Pred and Michael Watts, *Reworking Modernity: Capitalisms and Symbolic Discontent* (New Brunswick: Rutgers, 1992).

11 *Vancouver Sun,* "Reaction to Sale of Condominiums Felt Fuelled by Fear of Change, Racism," December 19, 1988.

12 Ibid.

13 For a discussion of this earlier period of development, see Donald Gutstein, *Vancouver, Ltd.* (Toronto: James Lorimer and Co., 1975). I am indebted to David Ley for pointing out the historical nature of these real estate booms.

14 See, for example, *Vancouver Trends,* City of Vancouver, May 1990; *Vancouver Perspectives,* Province of British Columbia Ministry of Regional Development, 1991.

15 See, for example, Thomas Hutton and H. Craig Davis, *Vancouver as an Emerging Centre of the Pacific Rim Urban System,* U.B.C. Planning Papers, Comparative Urban and Regional Studies, no. 19 (August 1989); David Edgington and Michael Goldberg, "Vancouver and the Emerging Network of Pacific Rim Global Cities," paper presented at the North American Meetings of the Regional Science Association, Santa Barbara, Calif., Nov. 10–12, 1989, revised August 1990; David Ley, "Liberal Ideology and the Postindustrial City," *Annals of the Association of American Geographers* 70, no. 2 (June 1980): 238–258.

16 Pamphlets in B.C. Government offices in Hong Kong are full of details on how to invest in Canada; Canadian and Hong Kong banks also provide information on the transferal of funds, tax holidays through the offshoring of funds, and general services for individuals moving from Hong Kong to Canada. See, for example: "Invest Canada: The Magazine of Canadian Opportunity"; "Prospectus Canada" (in Chinese); "Your Future is in British Columbia: A Guide to Business Immigration"; "Gateway to Canada: Canadian Imperial Bank of Commerce" (in Chinese).

17   Harcourt said in a speech at a British Columbia reception for the Hong Kong trade and investment community on November 21, 1991: "As British Columbia's new premier, I am committed to strengthening and expanding BC's ties with Hong Kong." *Canada and Hong Kong Update* (Winter, 1992): 10. See also "Asia's Big Money Players Get Some Political Reassurance," *Vancouver Sun,* November 23, 1991.

18   Jack Moore, "Swiss Banker Estimates Billions Pouring into Canada from Hong Kong, Taiwan," *Courier,* June 17, 1990.

19   Diana Lary, "Trends in Immigration from Hong Kong," *Canada and Hong Kong Update,* Fall 1991, p. 6.

20   Employment and Immigration Canada, "Immigration to Canada: A Statistical Overview," November 1989.

21   Alan Nash, "The Emigration of Business People and Professionals from Hong Kong," *Canada and Hong Kong Update,* Winter 1992, p. 3.

22   My estimate, based on interviews with nine immigration consultants and five high-level bankers in Hong Kong, is far lower than one given by Hong Kong economist and businessman Simon Murray, who believed that Hong Kong lost HK$2.25 billion per month to Vancouver in 1989. In Canadian dollars, this comes to nearly C$4 billion per year being transferred from Hong Kong to Vancouver. See F. Wong, "Confidence Crisis Costing Billions," *Hong Kong Standard,* September 21, 1989.

23   *Globe and Mail,* August 5, 1991.

24   Jameson uses this spatial image to describe the disorienting effects of the period of monopoly capitalism for the individual. He believes the experience of the individual to be even more fragmented and disoriented in late capitalism. See Fredric Jameson, "Cognitive Mapping," in *Marxism and the Interpretation of Culture,* ed. C. Nelson and L. Grossberg (Chicago: University of Illinois Press, 1988), pp. 349–350.

25   Jameson, "Cognitive Mapping," p. 351.

26   Interviews were conducted in Vancouver and Hong Kong between September 1990 and December 1991. Ninety formal, open-ended interviews and numerous informal interviews were conducted. The names of private citizens have been changed to protect privacy. Names of public officials have not been changed.

27   Interview with Susan Liu, September 26, 1991.

28   Interview with Lucy Wei, November 26, 1991.

29   Paul Gilroy, *'There Ain't No Black in the Union Jack': The Cultural Politics of Race and Nation* (Chicago: University of Chicago Press, 1991).

30   Stuart Hall and others in the Centre for Contemporary Cultural Studies at the University of Birmingham have done several important studies emphasizing the historical and geographic specificity of race and racism. See, in particular, Stuart Hall, "Race Articulation and Societies Structured in Dominance," in *UNESCO 1980,* and CCCS, *The Empire Strikes Back: Race and Racism in 70s Britain* (London: Hutchison, 1982).

31   Raymond Williams, *Towards 2000* (London: Chatto and Windus: Hogarth Press, 1983), p. 195; see also Gilroy, *'There Ain't No Black,'* pp. 49–50, for a critique of this perspective.

32   One person wrote in a letter to the editor, "It is simply good business sense to promote

the condos aggressively in Hong Kong, emphasizing the location of 900 Cambie in relation to the rest of the city. . . . Ald. Libby Davies has a bias against this development so it's not surprising to see her try to get some political mileage out of the issue. Unfortunately, her views come across as racist." See *Vancouver Sun,* "Letters," December 11, 1990. See also *Vancouver Sun,* "Hong Kong Condo Ads Draw Fire," November 28, 1990.

33 Interview with Libby Davies, February 14, 1990.

34 Mike Davis, *City of Quartz* (New York: Verso, 1991) notes a similar phenomenon in the case of Los Angeles's "homegrown revolutions."

35 While the use of race and racism to divide opposition to capitalist development is certainly not a new phenomenon, the present case is distinctive in the tenor and focus of the attack. Not only have those supporting expansion taken the moral high ground, they have also been largely successful in positioning politicians and other opponents generally perceived as "left" or "politically progressive" on the defensive.

36 See Kay Anderson, *Vancouver's Chinatown: Racial Discourse in Canada, 1875–1980* (Montreal: McGill-Queen's University Press, 1991) for an insightful look at these processes as they apply to the construction of Vancouver's Chinatown.

37 According to Lydia Chan, a coordinator at SUCCESS (United Chinese Community Enrichment Services Society), incidents of racism against Chinese Canadians have risen markedly in the late 1980s, but rarely involve physical violence. She said in an interview, "The reception here has changed. I guess now some people feel that there are too many Chinese people, too many Asian immigrants . . . and that's why we feel that the racial tension is there." Interview, October 1990. See also, *Equity,* "Racism Is an Ugly Word," June 1989.

38 A few examples include: *China Tide* (Toronto: Harper and Collins, 1989), a popular book by Margaret Cannon chronicling Hong Kong investment in Vancouver; "Asian Capital: The Next Wave" from *B.C. Business,* July 1990; "Tidal Wave from Hong Kong," *B.C. Business,* February 1989; "Flippers Awash in Profits," *Vancouver Sun,* February 8, 1989; and "Hong Kong Capital Flows Here Ever Faster," *Vancouver Sun,* March 21, 1989. The metaphor of destruction and engulfment by water has been shown by authors like Theweleit, in his study of the German Freicorps, to have been a symptom in writing and fantasy that related to deep fears about dissolution and the transgression of boundaries. These anxieties were largely related to concerns about the wholeness and stability of identity and masculine sexuality. See Klaus Theweleit, *Male Fantasies,* Volume 1, *Women, Floods, Bodies, History,* trans. Stephen Conway (Minneapolis: University of Minnesota Press, 1987).

39 Lothrop Stoddart, *The Rising Tide of Color* (New York: Charles Scribner's Sons, 1920), p. 301. Quoted in Anderson, pp. 109–110.

40 Extra large houses have also been built in east-side neighborhoods, but these have been called "Vancouver Specials" by the local populace.

41 Interview, February 1992.

42 In 1986 average family income for residents of the Kerrisdale area was C$76,451 per

year (with a standard error of C$2,522) and approximately C$96,034 for residents of Shaughnessy—with over 67 percent earning over C$50,000 per year, according to census statistics. (The Economic Council of Canada defined "middle-income families" as those with an income between C$33,800 and C$56,400 in 1990.) See *Vancouver Local Areas, 1986*, City of Vancouver Planning Department, June 1989.

43 Duncan and Duncan discuss the instrumental use of pastoral symbols to evoke an image of a romanticized (aristocratic) English past in the west-side suburb of Shaughnessy. See James Duncan and Nancy Duncan, "A Cultural Analysis of Urban Residential Landscapes in North America: The Case of the Anglophile Elite," in *The City in Cultural Context*, ed. J. Agnew, J. Mercer, and D. Sopher (Boston: Allen and Unwin, 1984). Prior to the 1980s, most west-side neighborhoods were composed almost exclusively of white residents, most of British heritage. In 1914, 80 percent of the social register of Vancouver was composed of members who resided in Shaughnessy Heights.

44 From the 1991 Royal LePage Survey of Canadian House Prices.

45 C. Smith, "Prime Time," *Equity*, March 1990.

46 See, for example, "City Housing Market Flipping Along," *Business*, September 1, 1989; "Flipping Is Hong Kong Game," *Vancouver Sun*, March 20, 1989; "Flippers Awash in Profits," *Vancouver Sun*, February 8, 1989.

47 *Western News*, July 26, 1989.

48 Bourdieu writes that legitimating culture as a second nature allows those with it to see themselves as disinterested and unblemished by any mercenary uses of culture. See Pierre Bourdieu, *Distinction: A Social Critique of the Judgement of Taste* (Cambridge: Harvard University Press, 1984), p. 86.

49 Bourdieu, *Distinction*, p. 124.

50 A housing survey in 1991 showed that 96 percent of Vancouver residents said that their children will not be able to afford to live where they were raised. *Vancouver Sun*, November 9, 1991. In the expressed anxiety about the "ugly" buildings and erosion of the neighborhood, what is often left unstated is the anxiety felt about the difference in race of the people moving into the neighborhoods. In this case, the emphasis on cultural values and taste can be seen to operate as an alibi or "screen-allegory" for a foreclosing of the broader narrative of racism. See Gayatri Chakravorty Spivak, "Can the Subaltern Speak?" in *Marxism and the Interpretation of Culture*, ed. C. Nelson and L. Grossberg (Chicago: University of Illinois Press, 1988), p. 291.

51 Interview, October 11, 1990.

52 Statistics on all these changes are available in a number of sources. On declining vacancy rates, see "Apartment Vacancy Rates, 1976–1992," *Vancouver Monitoring Program*, City of Vancouver, August 1992; on the demolitions of apartment buildings see Demolitions and Permits, City of Vancouver Planning Department; for information on gentrification in areas adjacent to the Expo lands, including the loss of SROs, see the numerous publications from the Centre for Human Settlements, University of British Columbia.

53 The sarcastic title is part of a history of struggle over the naming of the newly zoned

area. Pitts wanted it called Preservation District 1, but the city declined. From an interview with John Pitts, February 8, 1991.

54 Quoted in J. Lee, "Rezoning Idea has a Permanent Air," *Vancouver Sun,* May 16, 1990.

55 In this scenario the conflicting pressures and dilemmas on the political right become more apparent. The prodevelopment forces on council are torn between acceding to the slow-growth demands of its electoral heartland in west-side neighborhoods and the demands of international capitalists for unrestricted access and development opportunities.

56 The city's RS-1 zoning bylaws were amended in 1986, 1988, and 1990. The increase in bureaucratic entanglements was felt by organizers of the Granville-Kerrisdale neighborhood movement. President Rick Smith said of his fight, "People are trying to outthink other people. Even right now with our proposal they (City Council) want to go through a horrendous process. They say we have to advise the people and we have to give them information . . . and I say, look, 'the people' are the ones who are *right here,* who have signed these petitions." Interview January 23, 1991.

57 David Harvey, *The Limits to Capital* (Oxford: Basil Blackwell Publisher, 1982), pp. 413–445.

58 David Harvey, *Consciousness and the Urban Experience* (Baltimore: Johns Hopkins University Press, 1985), chap. 3.

59 Harvey, *Limits to Capital,* p. 423.

60 Laurier was Canada's seventh prime minister and first French-Canadian prime minister.

61 Jean Elliot and Augie Fleras, "Immigration and the Canadian Ethnic Mosaic," in *Race and Ethnic Relations in Canada,* ed. Peter Li (Toronto: Oxford University Press, 1990).

62 Ronald Wardhaugh, *Language and Nationhood: The Canadian Experience* (Vancouver: New Star Books, 1983), p. 201; Evelyn Kallen, "Multiculturalism: Ideology, Policy, and Reality," *Journal of Canadian Studies* 17, no. 1 (1982): 55.

63 Canada, *The Canadian Multiculturalism Act: A Guide for Canadians* (Ottawa: Minister of Supply and Services, 1990).

64 Canada, *Multiculturalism . . . being Canadian* (Ottawa: Minister of Supply and Services, 1987), pp. 1–2.

65 Quoted in Elliot and Fleras, "Immigration," p. 67.

66 Canada, *New Faces in the Crowd: Economic and Social Aspects of Immigration* (Ottawa: Minister of Supply and Services, 1991).

67 Canada, *Working Together Towards Equality: An Overview of Race Relations Initiatives* (Ottawa: Minister of Supply and Services, 1990).

68 *Globe and Mail,* "Face of Vancouver to be Radically Altered," February 20, 1989.

69 *Globe and Mail,* "Is Vancouver Trading Furs for Beads?" March 1, 1989.

70 *The Laurier Institute,* Newsletter/Announcement.

71 Interview, January 3, 1991.

72 David Baxter, "Population and Housing in Metropolitan Vancouver: Changing Patterns of Demographics and Demand," unpublished manuscript, 1989.

73   *Globe and Mail,* "Study Says Baby Boomers Behind Home Price Surge," November 16, 1989.

74   B. Constantineau, *Vancouver Sun,* March 28, 1990.

75   B. Truscott, "Home Speculation Not Immigrants' Fault," *Courier,* April 22, 1990.

76   *Real Estate Weekly,* "Burb Buyers Hit with Levies," April 6, 1990.

77   B. Constantineau, "Foreign Buyers Absolved," *Vancouver Sun,* April 18, 1990.

78   The founding donors are Lieutenant-Governor Dr. and Mrs. David C. Lam, Asa Johal, Dr. Peter Lee, Milton K. Wong, the Chan Foundation, the Bank of Montreal, and the Pacific Canadian Investment Group.

79   *The Laurier Institute,* letter to potential members, November 2, 1991.

80   Laurier Institute, "Corporate Member Benefits, Cultural Harmony through Research, Communication, and Education."

81   Sneja Gunew, "Denaturalizing Cultural Nationalisms: Multicultural Readings of 'Australia,'" in *Nation and Narration,* ed. H. Bhabha (New York: Routledge, 1990), p. 114.

82   Nicos Poulantzas, *Political Power and Social Classes,* trans. Timothy O'Hagan (London: NLB and Sheed and Ward, 1973), p. 217.

III GLOBAL/LOCAL DISRUPTIONS

●

GLOBALISM'S LOCALISMS

Dana Polan

●

In the first narrative sequence of *Mr. Baseball,* the hero, on-the-decline baseball player Jack Elliot (Tom Selleck), wakes up in the bed of a college coed. Sneaking out of the bed in the nude, he picks up a fluffy pillow and covers his crotch with it. Later in the film, Jack is invited to take a Japanese bath with the young Japanese woman he has been getting interested in. As he gets into the scalding water and as she begins the rubdown that will turn into kisses (and into a visually elided scene of lovemaking), Jack takes a small towel and again covers his crotch with it.

Several times in *Iron Maze,* the heroine, Chris Sugita (Bridget Fonda), slips away from her Japanese businessman husband to engage in sex with Barry (Jeff Fahey), a former steelworker whose rundown mill Mr. Sugita is proposing to turn into an amusement park. Each time Chris and Barry make love, they are either fully clothed or posed in such a way that we see no nudity. At another moment, Sugita breaks in on Chris in the shower, wanting to make love to her, and his desire almost turns into marital rape. Though Chris is naked in the shower, and though she and her husband struggle violently for several moments, again no details of nudity are visible.

No doubt there are lots of local, contingent reasons for the lack of nudity in the films I have mentioned: the need to have child and youth appeal for the baseball film; the desire of big stars to avoid nude scenes; the restrictions of the rating system (the "R" category has gotten more limiting in recent years). But the very fact that, like the Japanese comics that censor sexual organs but then render them essential by obvious blank spaces on the page, *Mr. Baseball* goes out of its way to signal the presence of the very thing it renders absent strikes me as significant.

In his already classic *Imagined Communities: Reflections of the Origin and Spread of Nationalism*, Benedict Anderson suggests that the large-scale social organizations that are nations find one source of cohesion in a move from the realm of the physical and immediate contact to the mediations of discourse. As he says, "The pre-bourgeois ruling classes generated their cohesions in some sense outside language, or at least outside print-language. . . . [A]n illiterate bourgeoisie is scarcely imaginable. Thus in world-historical terms bourgeoisie were the first classes to achieve solidarities on an essentially imagined basis."[1] Small-scale groups find unity in direct interaction, but nationhood needs symbolic structure. In a seeming throwaway line, Anderson sums up the distinction: "To put it another way, one can sleep with anyone, but one can only read some people's work."[2]

Now, as I emphasize, Anderson's contrast of sleeping with/discoursing with is offered up in a seemingly throwaway line, a cute and quotable aphorism. One perhaps should not push it too far. The line is interesting nonetheless as one of the few places where sex enters into Anderson's argument. Simultaneously, the binary opposition is intriguing and problematic. Intriguing: Anderson's emphasis on imagining allows him to avoid the standard discussion of nations as just economic or statist or diplomatic (discussions that then come to confine discussion of nations to the concerns of "hard" social science disciplines like political science or international relations). For Anderson, nations are not only things negotiated but also images that are lived, myths that reach out for imaginings rooted in assent or dissent. His book offers one bridge between social theory and cultural study by encouraging us to think of the physical and discursive investments one might make in a nation.

Problematic: for the most part, although Anderson is trying to place the imagination in the center of thinking about nationhood (as in the very title of his study), his is a book not about such factors as the unconscious, as desire, as gender and difference, as the everyday activities of bodies. Concentrating on other moments in his text, Eve Kosofsky Sedgwick has argued cogently that *Imagined Communities*'s overall lack of interest in matters of sex and desire means that the few moments when the book does touch upon such matters have especial significance.[3] Sedgwick looks in particular at an earlier phrase from Anderson's book: "In the modern world, everyone can, should, will 'have' a nationality, as he or she 'has' a gender."[4] In Sedgwick's analysis, it is the very rarity but also the surety of such an enunciation that enables Anderson to build sex and gender into the variant givens that then other things can be measured against. As Sedgwick notes, not everyone "has" a gender in any easy and automatic way, and it is only by ignoring (whether consciously or not) a whole literature in the variabilities of gender definition that Anderson can collapse gender into biology and take it as a given that nationhood can be measured against.

Similarly, the contrast of sleeping with/discoursing with only works unambiguously if one assumes an ease and evidence and, most especially, a concreteness of sex relations against which national discourse offers the advantage of a relative autonomy. Just as in this assumption sex is sex (and gender is gender), there is a concreteness of prenationalist discourse that will be undone by nationalism's freeing of the signifier: as Anderson puts it very early in the book, "If the sacred silent languages were the media through which the great global communities of the past were imagined, the reality of such apparitions depended on an idea largely foreign to the contemporary Western mind: the non-arbitrariness of the sign."[5]

For all his awareness of the semiotic nature of social being, for all his probable agreement with the Derridean contention that "there is no *hors-texte*," it seems to me that there is a symptomatic slippage in Anderson from a notion that social practices are discursive in shape to one that assumes they are specifically linguistic, having their sole embodiment in common language practices (like the newspaper or the bourgeois novel, which Anderson sees as essential tools in the rise of nationhoods). In other words, it seems to me that to say that to imagine nationhood is to live it is not necessarily the same as saying, or is not reducible to saying, that it is thereby lived in specifically linguistic media. Just as Lacan's dictum that the unconscious is structured "comme une langue" frequently gets mistranslated to imply that it is a "langue," so does the notion that nationhood is lived discursively slide confusedly into one that takes nationhood to be little other than the specific discourses that give it embodiment in this or that particular (and limited) case.

This pan-semiosis, convinced that modern power works through a freeing of the signifier, brings with it some other assumptions, as we can see from the sleeping with/discoursing with distinction. Even though such pan-semiosis claims that nothing is not not textual, it obviously assumes that some things are more or less textualized and others more or less concretized. In particular, for our purposes here, it seems to me to encourage a setting of the two terms of our symposium in an epistemological and ontological opposition. Globalism is the realm of the abstract, of an irreal circulation (of economy, of signs); localism is the realm of the lived, of the physical, of the grit and grime of day-to-day existence. Not for nothing does Jean-François Lyotard's famous declaration in *The Post-Modern Condition* that "The Trilateral Commission is not a popular pole of attraction"[6] have an echo in another throwaway phrase of Anderson, "Who would willingly die for Comecon or the EEC?"[7] In fact, I could easily imagine gripping narratives being generated to promote adhesion to multinational projects and practices.

In the following arguments, I want to offer modifications of Anderson's binary assumptions; while, as Sedgwick convincingly argues, Anderson skews his historical argument by basing it on an (unsurfaced) assumption about the givenness of sexuality and the very different givenness of modern media, nonetheless I think we can make use of Anderson's oppositions if we rewrite them as historical practices or strategies. It is not that there is sex and in opposition to it media, but that a particular culture produces a particular representation of sex to which it contrasts particular media constructions. I want to suggest that the putting of an abstract globality into binary opposition with a concrete localism needs deconstruction; in particular, I argue that where the assumptions behind this opposition often lead to a dubious politics—as in the new consumerist cultural studies (John Fiske, Henry Jenkins, etc.) where local users subvert dominant ideology to their own, immediate ends—we need to rethink both dominance and opposition if we conceive of localism as the specific way in which the global is lived. Globalism is not an abstraction but a concrete activity whose mode of being has its effect on the local body. Even if it is represented in abstract terms, globalism's mode is embodied, and its embodiment occurs locally. To take a minor example, speaking of local steelworkers' perception of high-level union and management decisions, John Hoerr notes in his *And the Wolf Finally Came: The Decline of the American Steel Industry* that such perceptions imagined power as simultaneously and necessarily abstract and embodied:

> The sense that a remote, all-knowing authority held ultimate power over the mills and their workers is reflected in expressions used by employees in the [Mon] valley. . . . When the workers struggle to form a union in the 1930s, mill managers avoid settling their grievances by sending their complaints to "City Office," where they vanish in a "bottomless pit." In the 1970s and 1980s, workers in the valley used the equally impersonal term "Pittsburgh" to refer to U.S. Steel headquarters. Frequently heard comments were, "Pittsburgh says . . ." or "Pittsburgh wants . . . ," usually accompanied by a shrug of shoulders.[8]

In the pages that follow, I'll make not infrequent reference to firms and texts from the local Pittsburgh context. But I intend no privilege with this "site-specific intervention." In a discussion of cross-cultural analysis, "The Difficulty of Being Radical: The Discipline of Film Studies and the Postcolonial World Order," Mitsuhiro Yoshimoto cautions against attempts to imagine that knowledge is some sort of free-floating force that can be applied indifferently to diverse cases: "The question is whether cross-cultural analysis can really contribute to a cultural exchange between two different cultures on an equal basis, to the understanding of the Other without making it fit the underlying assumptions of the analyst's own culture, or simply, to a non-dominating way of knowing and understanding the Other."[9] One "solution" for the analyst is to examine not the Other but the cultures of domination that themselves constitute the Otherness. But if I put "solution" in quotation marks, it is to indicate, and hopefully renegotiate, some of the dangers of site-specific intervention. First of all, there is the temptation to assume that what is going on in the culture of domination is then what is going on in other cultures—dominated or not. For example, it may be that we need to revise, or even discard, the notion of dominant ideology which assumes a sharing of beliefs across frontiers of class, sex, race, and ethnicity. Second of all, it is easy to turn site-specific intervention or analysis into a form of apologetics: to paraphrase Popeye, site-specificity declares, "I am where I am," and in doing so can conclude the impossibility of being anywhere else. I think, for example, of Richard Rorty's famous essay, "Solidarity or Objectivity?" where the philosopher's pragmatism leads him to assume that because one is in situation, one can take up no position other than that given by the situation.[10] But, against Rorty, it might be argued that one is not in situation, but in situations, and one is not "one," but a number of different identities for different situations. The sum total of these may also have its limits, but it is easy to cut off self-definition and context-definition too early in the process: I remember, for example, a conference on Cultural Studies at my home university at which, in response to Gayatri Spivak's opening call for eschewing grand theory for site-specific analysis, several men ("male feminists") responded by announcing their agreement and then manifesting this as confessional declarations ("I'm a middle-aged white sexist male") that both pinpointed a situation but then seemed to assume its inevitability (and therefore appeared to excuse the men for their limitations).

The assumptions that guide me in my work here are several: first, as I've just mentioned, that situations and identities are both specific and multiple. Second, but as a complementary inverse of the first, that all specificities are in their own ways replays or reworkings of the totality of social reality. This is what I mean by the idea of "globalism's localisms"—each and every local case is readable as, in Jamesonian terms, "symbolic response" to the global. (But, then, just as the local is no one thing, we need to understand that the global is no one thing, but an asynchronous assemblage: as Immanuel Wallerstein puts it in *Geopolitics and Geoculture,* "Rather than representing simply abstract ideological expressions, then, nationalism and internationalism represent political and ideological tendencies with a variable class content which is derived from the continuous efforts on the part of capital and labor to respond to the structural conditions engendered by capitalist production.")[11] The argument then is simultaneously theoretical and historical. Theoretical: Sartrean in inspiration (in my case), it assumes that there is a unity to the human experience, that there is an overall totalization in which each local case is what Sartre calls "une totalisation en cours" (a totalization-in-process). Historical: the argument assumes there is no necessary form by which the local case dialectically enacts the total context. Sartre has been rightly criticized (by Claude Lévi-Strauss, among others) for the specific content he attributes to the "human adventure"—as Lévi-Strauss notes, Sartre's anthropology refuses historicity to "premodern" cultures—and it is necessary to distinguish between the theoretical unity of all human experiences and the particular ways partial unities are offered up to this or that globality—the global in Mike Featherstone's terms as "the generative frame within which diversity can take place."[12] For example, the global media village may express one image of universality (yet only for those in fact who are in the informational loop), but it can also be challenged by other such images which bring out its various partialities.

How then do some new American films negotiate their global context? In the following pages, I want to argue the emergence of a new globalist practice in recent American cinema. But where we assume too readily that emergent modes tend as such to be progressive, I want to argue that the case here is more complicated: the opening up of American cinema to the global has as much to do with accommodations of representation to new multinational political and economic concerns as with ostensible deconstructions of American ideology.

As in the case of *Mr. Baseball* at least, one might have argued with facility that the film narrativizes its visual desexualizing of the male to transcend it and thereby reinvigorate older myths. The film easily lends itself to an Oedipalized reading. If in the first scene Jack finds himself in a girl's dorm where he has to cover over his masculinity, it should be noted that he has just woken up from a nightmare in which pitchers keep striking him out as he swings his big bat in powerlessness. The narrative of *Mr. Baseball* would then be one of those stories of "remasculinization," to use Susan Jefford's term to describe American post-

Vietnam narratives, popular especially in the Reaganite eighties, in which fallen man redeems himself by a rediscovery of masculine prowess. Jack learns to recover his powerful swing, he manages to gain the admiration of his girlfriend's father (who happens also to be his coach), and he manages to win the girl (who had hesitated about going off with him to the United States).

And yet, there seems equally to me to be something postsexual and post-Oedipal going on in such a film. Although Jack's relation with his girlfriend is obviously sexual, the visual representation of it and the narrative dynamic around it suggest that sex and love are only one part of their relationship: what they are building together is less corporeal than corporate. The editing of both films is significant. *Iron Maze* borrows its overall narrative inspiration from film noir—a rich married woman has an affair with an earthy guy and seduces him into thinking about killing her husband—and the film adheres to the noir way of dealing with the woman. If not literally destroyed as in classic noir, the woman here is absented from the story: all the men come to expel her from their world. At the end of the film, a surrogate, postsexual, new family is imaged on the screen: Mr. Sugita, Barry, and the young boy Barry has taken under his wing all get together at the construction site for the new amusement park and engage in good, old masculine contests of throwing rocks at targets. The two adults and the boy image a postfamilial corporate rearticulation of the family.

The ending of *Mr. Baseball* is even more explicit about such rearticulation. Jack has been wanting the relationship with his girlfriend to solidify. She knows, however, that he also wants to return to the United States, and she realizes this will force her to give up her career in Japan (in keeping with other ways in which the film is about a global economy centered in services—especially sports and entertainment—rather than goods, she is an advertising executive). The last scene offers a good postindustrial solution. The last scene shows Jack back in the United States as a team coach. As he teaches batting technique to a new generation of ballplayers, we cut to his girlfriend (now wife) watching him admiringly from the bleachers with other young women. But before we can assume she's become just one more sports groupie to the remasculinized sports hero, she whips out a portable phone and makes a business call in which she reminds someone to send her a needed fax. What enables Jack and the woman to come together is not so much their love as their perfect professionalism in the new corporate world. These two films about Japanese-American relations, and about the concretizing of such relations in heterosexual couplings, downplay the body, minimize the physicality of inter-national mediations, and suggest the building of new relations that transcend sex. They are films of a new globalism in which one relates to others as potential partners, not lovers.

Furthermore, *Mr. Baseball* gives striking figuration to Benedict Anderson's argument that the imaginings in emergent forms of community (such as, for him, nationhood or, here, globalism) require the mediations of new forms of communication. For Anderson, imagined communities are communities created even in the face of distance: each person is a member of a collective whose other members he/she does not know directly. To this argument we might add Sartre's suggestion in the *Critique of Dialectical Reason* that the way modern media build community out of the serialization of the crowd into isolated monads has less to do with any specific content of media representations than with the fact that media, themselves are forms that multiple and dispersed audiences can participate in across space and time. As both Sartre and Anderson argue, the very fact that we read or watch, with the background assumption that others are doing the same thing, builds up an imagining of community out of serialized anonymity. *Mr. Baseball* renders such communalizing of seriality in numerous scenes of a range of Japanese watching or listening to Jack Elliot's baseball exploits: it is his actions (and their replay in the montage of the film that intercuts among these Japanese) that brings a country together, that totalizes it. If the scenes of Jack's (non)nudity suggest that he is not a fully constituted subject in his own right, one goal of the film will be less to show how Jack's remasculinization leads to new subjectival coherence (significantly, he does not get a chance at film's end to prove his batting prowess) than to imply that he is a mutable signifier around which others—the others of a national identity—can gain the coherence of imagined community. As befits subjectivity in a postsubject age, Jack indeed matters less for what he "is" than for what he represents—literally so insofar as he is an image on TV screens or a description on the radio (and in a revealing moment, we see the commercial that Jack's girlfriend makes him shoot—one in which his identity varies between that of American and Japanese, between that of baseball player and samurai or suma wrestler). As Mitsuhiro Yoshimoto writes in "Real Virtuality," his essay in this volume:

> In a new global capitalist formation, it is increasingly becoming clearer that capitalism does not require any substantial supposition of a subject, either as the liberal autonomous individual of a capitalist entrepreneur (the United States) or as the centralized bureaucratic state of "totalitarianism" (the Soviet Union). Thus, so-called "Japan Inc." is a misleading label

since it posits a mythical "Japan" as a unified subject coordinating every economic activity from a rational, centered point of perspective. The dynamic of Japanese capitalism is not motivated by the centralized State with its autonomous will but by the overdetermined, decentered corporate networks.[13]

In these films, and in other recent cultural production I'll be discussing, I think we can see marks of the emergence of a new global-American culture. This cultural production is globalist in several motifs that interconnect: a concern with movement and the ease of crossing fluid frontiers (whether these be the geopolitical limits between nations or the cybernetic limits between the human cogito and the computer networks in which the subject enters); an emphasis on service occupations; the representation of human interaction as mediated forms of communication (faxes, portable telephones, computer links, television, and so on); a fascination with prostheses, as if to suggest that human corporeality extends into the network of cybernetic interaction through the interface of cyborg body parts; a relative downplay of the passions of the flesh (and also, often, of plots centered on bodies in violent action or sexual activity); plots that are themselves about the mediation between various subcultures of the global economy; consequently, the directing of narrative movement toward end-of-story glimpses of new postsubject forms of agency (whether these be the figurations of new postfamilial collectivities as in *Iron Maze* or the suggestion that subjectivity itself will break up and mutate—as in *The Fly* with its scientist-hero merging at the end with hi-tech machinery in a dramatic rendition of the cybernetization of the self). These cultural productions both are about and are themselves in their production figurations of the five forms of border crossing that Arjun Appadurai sees as defining the complexities of the global cultural economy: ethnoscape (the transport of people); technoscape (the transport of technologies); finanscape (the movement of monies); mediascape (the movement of information-forms themselves); ideoscape (the floating of stereotypes, social images and concepts—for example, the regulative ideal of sexual equality at the end of *Mr. Baseball*).[14] But, as Appadurai reminds us, there can be all sorts of disjunctions in and between each form of global transport: for example, insofar as a film like *Mr. Baseball* is both about equality (men and women both have the right to a career) and about finance (only those at the top of the service economy have the privilege to cross borders while maintaining control of information), the film limits the representation of equality to the well-off, suggesting they literally can afford to be progressive.

We can see this hierarchized globalism more directly if we look at some of the context for a film like *Iron Maze*. As is well known, the American steel industry falls apart in the 1970s. Looking at the industry in 1982, John Hoerr can observe, "The industry is now operating at only slightly more than 30 percent of capacity, close to the record of the Depression."[15] But the end of the 1980s and the beginning of the 1990s will see a globalist rewriting of the story now with a happy ending. With a macho remasculinization and corporatist optimism, Richard Preston can subtitle his 1991 *American Steel* "Hot Metal Men and the Resurrection of the Rust Belt."[16] As with *Iron Maze*, Preston's story is a masculine one: steel mill foremen who spend their days off in target practice with rapid firepower handguns, company presidents who speed around in big cars, wives who fade into the background (the steel company's safety expert is a woman, but she is given much less attention than the metal men). Locally and globally, *American Steel* tells of ways a new steel industry sets out post-Fordist solutions to the overly expansive tendencies of the past. At the local level, the tactics are insistently localist: moving away from the massive mills of the past, the new mode of production tends toward the creation of mini-mills—smaller operations out in the country. In a nice irony, the mini-mills cut short the original steps in the process of steel production: instead of producing steel from mined ore, the mini-mills reprocess old steel—especially all the mangled or corroded detritus of the Rust Belt thrown into the furnaces and melted down for a new start. Away from urban influence, the new mini-mills are often nonunion and nonspecialist, employing local farmers who have been rendered available by the downturn in agriculture. And the smallness of the mini-mill also offers the chance of deliberate impermanence: one of the discoveries of post-Fordism is the advantage of floating factories that can be easily retooled if one industry flops or that can themselves be moved elsewhere if need be. The smallness and specialization of the mill also enables top-level management to diversify with greater ease: companies like the wonderfully named U.S.X. (formerly "U.S. Steel") now only devote a moderate portion of their work to steel production.

But all this local retooling requires transnational capitalizing and researching. In the case of Nucor's Crawfordsville, Indiana mini-mill, the particular plant whose retooling Richard Preston traces out in *American Steel*, this means an alliance with German companies, and one of the set-piece macho scenes has the American team going to Germany and signing contracts after bonding around many games of bowling and many high-speed drives in souped-up cars through city streets and, especially, ingestion of many potent

German schnapps. (This real-life scene has an uncanny fictional antecedent in the 1986 film *Gung Ho* about American workers trying to revive their factory under disciplined Japanese ownership. In a first major moment of male-bonding that is also an allegory of international cooperation, the Japanese engineer and the American foreman go to a bowling alley and get stinking drunk. In this activity, each will learn to appreciate the comparative advantages of the other, and each will learn necessary compromises. Like Preston's *American Steel, Gung Ho* is very much a story of men: in an early scene, the hero will feel guilty for having told his girlfriend to "shut up" when she remains behind at a dinner table meeting after all the Japanese wives have left; later, though, in what will be her last scene in the film, the girlfriend will voluntarily absent herself when the American foreman and the Japanese engineer rebond by splashing around in the Monongehela River.)

Such local (and, in their emphasis in "hot metal men" bonding virulently, residual) glimpses of a more global geopolitical process are given official sanction. Take, for instance, several symptomatic situations of 1992. First, on May 14, U.S. Vice-President Quayle and the Japanese minister of international trade and industry sign in Tokyo the MTI (the Manufacturing Technology Initiative) designed to "provide the opportunity for American private sector manufacturing personnel to share practical work experience with Japanese personnel in Japanese corporations for extended periods of time. During this time they will have the chance to build long-term bonds of friendship and cooperation mutually beneficial to both nations."[17]

Interestingly, Quayle's own comments at the ceremony suggest that the official view does not simply see the initiative as a way of forming bonds but as a practical decision as to comparative advantage and means of trading off competencies in a globalist situation:

> There is no doubt that the United States and Japan will continue to be technological leaders in the twenty-first century. Both of our countries have strong economies thanks to the hard work and creative ability of our people. We each have unique strengths. For example, Japan's corporations are investing in research and development at a high rate. U.S. corporations conduct world-leading basic research and American factories have the highest level of productivity in the world. The Japanese people and industry have long understood the importance of learning about foreign technology. You have come to the United States and attended our universities, worked in our businesses, invested in our economy, and studied develop-

ments in the United States. We have and will continue to welcome you to our country. It is time that we in the United States do more here in Japan.[18]

(The last sentence is interesting in its ambiguities: the suggestion is simultaneously that the United States and Japan work together but that the particular advantage in the hierarchy should be to the United States.) Responding to a question about Japan-bashing, Quayle distinguishes official policy from bashing: "You'd have to ask the Japan-bashers that question ['do you think that agreements like this are going to be enough to trim the Japan-bashing that's been going on in the United States?']. I'm not one of them. I underscore the importance of this relationship. This relationship is critical to peace, stability, prosperity, not only in the Pacific, but it has a great deal of importance for global stability." (The progressions in this last sentence are significant. One could even read them as mininarratives: on the one hand, an achieving of peace out of prior existing conditions, a conversion of this into narrative stability, and a necessary emergence from this steady-state into the happy ending of financial benefit; on the other hand, a spatial expansion that moves from the Pacific to spread its effects over the globe.)

Significantly, such large-scale bondings have their resonances at the local level. For example, in Pittsburgh, two universities—the University of Pittsburgh and Carnegie Mellon University—have been chosen together as two of the four sites for MTI training (and here again what are often competitors find a way to bond): as the *Pitt News* (November 17, 1992) explains,

The University of Pittsburgh and Carnegie Mellon have received a $2.6 million grant from the U.S. Air Force Office of Scientific Research to train Americans in the Japanese style of management of sciences and technology. Susie Brown, CM director of special projects and planning, said she hopes that both universities can combine their strengths and make this two-year project a success. "Pitt offers a very good language and cultural training, while CMU is famous for its technology," Brown said. "By combining the two, we can hopefully find out why Japan has been doing so well in the past two to three decades."[19]

Complementary to the MTI is another initiative, an attempt to promote the necessary transformation of the American steel industry into a Japanese-American industry. Often distributed along with the press releases on the MTI is a pretty brochure entitled "Japanese Steel in the '90s," subtitled "Partnering with American Producers." The section on partnering makes the needs behind a new rhetoric of cooperation clear:

> In the late 1970s, the American steel industry began a sharp decline, and lost its competitiveness in world steel markets, because its facilities had become obsolete due to very limited capital investment. . . . Since the early 1980s, the Japanese steel industry has helped foster American steel's revitalization through technological cooperation and joint ventures. These efforts have been well appreciated by U.S. steelmakers, since the availability of capital and technology from Japan contributed to their modernization programs. . . . Today, almost one out of four people employed by a U.S. steel company works at plants jointly owned by a Japanese steelmaker.

Nevertheless, uncannily reflecting *Iron Maze*'s image of mills turned into amusement parks (of goods production giving way to service production), the last page of "Japanese Steel in the '90s" serves as a reminder of the new modes by which revitalization will occur also as a transformation: this section, entitled "Diversifying for Corporate Strength," tells us,

> over the past two decades . . . the [steel] industry has been confronted by various structural and foreign exchange crises which have had a negative impact on demand. . . . To maintain a strong corporate financial position over the long-term, producers needed to develop steel recession proof alternative activities. . . . The industry's initial diversification efforts concentrated on areas of familiarity, including electronics and information systems. . . . Eventually, several producers moved into software, peripheral equipment, and other electronic areas. . . . Steel producers are also taking advantage of their valuable real estate holdings and engineering know-how to develop industrial parks, entertainment centers, and urban projects.

Thus, to go back to my opening comments on binary oppositions like that in Anderson between physically bodied local relations and immaterially disembodied and discursive national (and by extension transnational) relations, it seems to me we can make no blanket arguments about the local and the global. Quite the contrary, we need to understand that there are myriad ways in which they interact, in which one can be the residual or emergent expression of the other. For example, in the era of what Klaus Offe or Lash and Urry term "disorganized capitalism" (the capitalism of post-Fordism), many of the discursive strategies that culturalist theory values as subversive—alterity, freefloatingness, decenteredness—turn out to be usable strategies of a capitalism that itself operates as local intervention: hence, for instance, the rise of small shops (able to change easily the object of production, able to modify in scale and service, able to themselves be floated elsewhere at a moment's notice). For example, as John Hoerr argues in *And the Wolf Finally Came*, it was to a very large degree the very fact of vertical integration that spelled problems for the U.S. steel industry. According to Hoerr, discussing the decline of large-scale steel production in the Northeast of the United States,

> The steep hills and valleys that separated the towns also helped Carnegie and U.S. Steel keep the working populations segregated in the various communities and thus relatively ignorant of each other's problems. By an accident of geography, they conformed to what has become today's conventional wisdom among manufacturing managers. The smaller the plant, the easier it is for management to foster a family-like atmosphere and maintain control of the work force. This is a large reason why manufacturing companies, starting in the 1960s, have built new, small plants in the South and Southwest rather than expand their old plants in the Northeast. A rule of thumb is that management's "span of effective control" limits the worker population to about five hundred. In larger plants, management bureaucracies bear down on the workers, forcing them to define their own interests separate from management's. The individual psyche is less penetrable, less open to management influence, and worker solidarity grows correspondingly. The Mon Valley plants thus far exceeded the modern rule-of-thumb limit, each employing from three thousand to nearly ten thousand workers.[20]

But even as these works project the possibility for new social formations based on emergent corporations, it is necessary to note limitations as to the extent to which such in-corporation of elements in the global economy is really collective in nature. We need, for instance, to take to heart the admonitions against globalizing theory that are expressed by Neil Lazarus in his important article, "Doubting the World Order: Marxism, Realism, and the Claims of Postmodernist Social Theory."[21] Lazarus reminds us that most discussions of a contemporary global condition (whether it be called postmodernist or consumerist or post-Fordist or whatever) are projections from one pole in today's mode of production—a mode which is itself a complex overlay of particularized modes—more particularized spatiality, for example (to take just one case, in many countries, goods production is far from post-Fordist). The celebration of movement, of economically advantageous decenterings of subjectivity, the ability to mediate human contact through cybernetic chains of globalized that we find in new global cinema are all forms of privilege available only to certain sectors of the modern world-system.

Not surprisingly, this emergent cinema itself emphasizes the privilege. We are often in a world of special individuals whose global story takes place against a backdrop peopled with, precisely, the people. The heroes engage in adventures for which everyone else are, at best, passive bystanders or, at worst, victims of the high-level machinations of the traveling hero. (The contrast of specialized globalist foreground and anonymous background becomes an explicit theme of cyberpunk fiction. In William Gibson's *Count Zero,* for example, one of the primary figures, a computer hacker, becomes a jacked-in, on-line guru by manipulating data that makes him a financial "killing" that translates into a real killing of the population of several African countries.)

If I pinpoint one trend in new American global cinema, we also need to keep in mind other trends (which are not necessarily subversive or progressive or whatever—as we'll see in the case of terrorist and hostage films). Take, for instance, Jarmusch's *Night on Earth* which shares some with globalist American cinema: an emphasis on movement (planes, taxis), on communication (the first section is organized around phone calls, some from within taxis), on services (the taxi-drivers themselves, the Hollywood producer of the first sequence), on interaction that is less corporeal than information (the only sex here is sex talked about). One might even argue that the film is an allegory itself: just as each segment lifts itself up out of isolation to hint at a larger globality, the relatively avant-gardist Jarmusch gets a chance with this film to become more mainstream through the choice of known, big actors from a number of national cinemas. At the same time, *Night on Earth* is only incompletely a global film. On the one hand, we might note that the film's globalism is resolutely American and European (getting no farther from the First World than the soulless bleakness of Finland). On the other hand, for all the film's hints at a unity among sequences (all take place in taxis at the same moment in various parts of the [Western] world), there is a relative disunity in the film. Unlike *Mystery Train* where the three seemingly separate stories slowly revealed themselves to have all sorts of intriguing overlaps, *Night on Earth* holds out no mediations, few possibilities for lasting in-corporation (here, the motif of the taxi can suggest the fleetingness of new human contact as much as its solidification: where *Iron Maze* or *Mr. Baseball* can hint at new communities, each segment of *Night on Earth* hints only at evanescence, the transitoriness of connection). And just as the space between segments remains unmediable, so does Jarmusch seem, more generally, a director of spaces in between.

Mainstream globalist cinema has little interest in the space in between: in the era of global informatics, all spaces are supposed to be bridgeable and whatever cannot enter into the "net" (Bruce Sterling's word for the dominant structure of links) is consigned to forgetfulness, only returning as vague images of an unassimilated background (for example, the shantytown and the vast and empty deserts alike in Sterling's *Islands in the Net*). Against this, we might then notice how a number of films emphasize precisely that which is left out or left over from globalism: for example, in that genre of films that has come to be called the NBF (Near Bad Future or New Bad Future), inner cities are portrayed as wastelands, as wrecked battlefields; countrysides are dismal voids—hellholes in which one waits in deadness for the force of events (see, for example, films of rural emptiness like *The Hot Spot* or *Gas Food Lodging*). Jarmusch, too, is a director of detritus, of the space in between as wasteland (and of the non-mainstream figures who wander through such sites, their errancy being a perfect way of living out marginality—see, for instance, the Winona Ryder character in *Night on Earth,* preferring to remain a grubby cabbie rather than become a Hollywood star). Whether the image is that of an urban professional speeding through a space she treats as void (Gena Rowlands in the first segment of *Night on Earth* looking out of the taxi window at an L. A. that to her can only appear low-life) or of Brooklyn as a deterritorialized contrast to First World Manhattan (as in the second segment of the film) or of Finland itself as one vast wasteland writ large, *Night on Earth* insists on an experience that cannot be assimilated to a globalist project of economic amelioration. But one would not want thereby to insist on a supposed progressiveness of the NBF films. On the one hand, as we've already noted, Jarmusch's film can do little but *describe* the space in between which, rendered as passive, can have no productivity (the film's last image is of drunks immobile on the sidewalk): Jarmusch's cinema sinks characters down into a weighty situation of ineffectuality. As in cyberpunk, there is a recognition of disenfranchised masses, but the representation can never get beyond portraying them as literally a mass without agency. On the other hand, some films will easily turn from a recognition of the spaces left behind by global capitalism to a suggestion that these spaces need to be colonized or pauperized even more within the limits of a policed state (see Jonathan L. Beller's essay on the ambiguities of *Robocop 2*). In their image of a fundamental incompatibility of informational-professional-managerial space with other spaces, the NBF films are potentially little different than mainstream that concentrate on the postmodern condition and fade all other experiences into vague background.

Take, for instance, another film of international mediation, *Green Card*. The film is vaguely a remake of a Hollywood 1930s screwball comedy: in the frantic and frenetic space of the big city, two people from different walks of life engage in a bickering that is really a form of amorous conquest and the more earthy of the two takes the other away from a boring, artificial life (incarnated in an inappropriate, deadly dull fiancé). In this respect, the "greenness" in the title might be a reference not only to the bureaucratic activities that allow international mediations, but also the "green place" necessary to the formation of the couple in the screwball comedy. Borrowing from Northrop Frye's reading of Shakespearean comedy, Stanley Cavell has argued that screwballs need a narrative movement from the crush of the big city life (where the blossoming love itself is crushed by urban pressures—especially the suspicion of the Other which each member of the amorous couple internalizes) to an ostensibly less artificial, more immediate, more natural space where pretenses can fall and love can find true expression. But *Green Card* offers several significant modifications of the tradition. First, the special "green" place here is not outside the city but within it—for instance, in the wonderful tropical garden growing in the middle of the apartment or the rooftop where the American and the Frenchman can flee street-level problems for a bit of ludic fantasy. And this suggestion that the city itself offers sites of respite fits both with the emergent globalist discourse of postindustrial urbanistics (the world is a series of linked metropolises with nothing in between—an image offered its negative image in cyberpunk where the in between is the space of wasteland ruin) and allows the film to participate, as do many of the new films on urban professionals, in sixties bashing: against the real promise of yuppie apartment gardens and rooftop idylls is contrasted the liberalist ridiculousness of the heroine's efforts in ecology and in urban renewal through inner-city landscaping programs.

Most of all, *Green Card* takes one of the central distinctions in the modern world-system—the difference between core and periphery economies—and renders it not as contradiction but as admirable hierarchy. The green place that offers the context in which the couple can form is quite simply "Third Worldism" itself, here rendered as exotic backdrop, as inspiring ambience. From the opening to the closing narrative scenes in the diner "Africa" where the two white people come to measure the progress of their relationship and from the opening music in which the woman watches African Americans playing ethnicized music in the subway to the end-credit music where the liberationist song, "Keep Your Eye on the Prize," is transformed into a consecration of the couple's love, *Green Card* takes Africa as a periphery ready and willing for mainstream acts of textual poaching. The seemingly appreciative representation of local musical forms slides easily into exploitation; in this respect, *Green Card* is in line with other new urban professionalist films such as *Something Wild* which, despite its title, is actually about the putting at bay of wildness (dark-haired Lulu becoming an obedient blonde housewife) and also uses African American music and motifs at the beginning and end as markers against which we measure the progress of white love. (In spite of his petition-signing and music-video production that insist on the problems the U.S. core causes for its peripheries, director Jonathan Demme seems to participate in the privileged, globalist, and systemic reappropriation of localist, antisystemic resistances. Not for nothing was his lauded last film, *The Silence of the Lambs,* a celebration of the FBI as a site in which feminism can bloom, in which multiracialism can flourish [Clarice's black roommate], in which men and women can find allegiances beyond the bothers of sexual desire [Jack Crawford's professional relationship with Clarice, encapsulated in the extreme close-up of their handshake at the end and contrasted with Lecter's and Buffalo Bill's perverse sexualizing of all male-female encounters].) Such imperial reappropriations of localist motifs remind us that multiculturalism has to be more than just the insertion of elements of one culture into another; we have to examine how this insertion occurs, in what forms (for example, its narrativization here as inspiration for the whites), and to what ends. The distance is not far from *Green Card* or *Something Wild* to that ultimate yuppie film, *Ghost,* where an (in)famous scene has Ota Mae (Whoopi Goldberg) lend her body to the ghostly Sam (Patrick Swayze) so he can kiss Molly (Demi Moore) one last time but where the film's momentary flirtation with the figuration of interracial, homosexual love is suddenly elided as the visuals substitute Sam for Ota Mae.

In both *Iron Maze* and *Mr. Baseball,* macho Americans discover it is better to work with the Japanese than to engage in Japan-bashing. In fact, as much as our media give attention to such bashing and make it one of the common tropes of the day, the new global films suggest that it is more necessary to form advantageous alliances than to constitute the other as Other (which is not to say that the films are not still caught up in projections of superiority: Americans need the rest of the world, but they still assume the partnership is one of unequal degrees of power and value—as Michael Douglas's police detective character in *Black Rain* says to the Japanese cops whose bureaucracies block them from chasing down a known criminal, "I am the answer to your problems"). Japan-bashing, I would argue, is a localist response that is exceeded by global economies; primarily an ideology of petit bourgeois entrepreneurism and of white working-class ressentiment, Japan-bashing is, like the French anti-Semitism analyzed by Jean-Paul Sartre, an economic ideology rather than an ontology (of same and Other). For all its terrible ugliness and real danger, racism expresses a discontent (however displaced) with the operations of the economic system, a discontent often absent in the new globalism where any disquiet turns at most into a more passive (and often opportunist) cynicism. As Chris Connery argues in his symposium paper,

> Pacific Rim discourse is a *non*-othering discourse. Unlike Orientalism, which [Edward] Said delineates genealogically as a discursive formation centered on a fundamental othering—an othering grounded in the specific histories of colonialism and imperialism—Pacific Rim discourse presumed a kind of metonymic equivalence. Its world is an interpenetrating complex of inter-relationships with no center: neither the center of a hegemonic power nor the imagined fulcrum of a "balance of power." . . . While Cold Warriors had wanted a strong, economically vibrant Japan, they had imagined Japan as a strictly *regional* hegemon. Japan as global power necessitated a reimagining of global categories.[22]

Racism, Benedict Anderson provocatively argues in *Imagined Communities*, sits uncomfortably with nationalism and, we might argue by extension, with globalism: by assuming a biological basis for exclusion (or inclusion), racism cannot easily adapt to changing market conditions and needs. In Anderson's words,

> If nationalism has about it an aura of fatality, it is nonetheless a fatality embedded in history. Here San Martin's edict baptizing Quecha-speaking Indians as "Peruvians" . . . is exemplary. For it shows from the start the nation was conceived in language, not in book, and that one could be "invited into" the imagined community. . . . [Racism] erases nation-ness by reducing the adversary to his biological physiognomy. . . . The fact of the matter is that nationalism thinks in terms of historical destinies, while racism dreams of eternal contaminations.[23]

In this respect, Japan-bashing may not only be a reactionary ideology (which as we see, nonetheless, has undeniable effects even in a global culture that wants to dispense with it) but a residual one, increasingly under assault by a new, economically pragmatic, emergent ideology that needs the Other.

But I think Fredric Jameson may be oversimplifying the asynchronous historicity of the global present when in *The Geopolitical Aesthetic* he posits the full opposition of racism and globalism:

> In the absence of general categories [such as the global or the multinational] under which to subsume such particulars [as "a multiplicity of nation states (and fantasmatic nationalisms)"], the lapse back into features of the pre–World War I system is inevitable and convenient (it includes all the national stereotypes which, inevitably racist whether positive or negative, organize our possibility of viewing and confronting the collective Other). It is also important to stress the fact that these archaic categories will not work for the new world-system: it is enough, for example, to reflect on the disappearance of specifically national cultures and their replacement, either by a centralized commercial production for world export or by their own mass-produced neotraditional images, for the lack of fit between the categories of the nineteenth century and the realities of the twenty-first to become apparent.[24]

We need first of all to recognize that the new post-Fordism can easily fall back into older and aggressive, rather than cooperative or accommodationist, modes in tense situations. If some recent American films represent mediations and incorporations with the global Other, we might note how another American genre of internationalism—the-terrorists-who-take-hostages-in-an-enclosed-space-but-are-then-defeated-by-a-new-remasculinized-hero genre (*Die Hard, Die Hard 2, Under Siege, Passenger 57*)—refuses mediation and reasserts the irreducible integrity of the local. On the one hand are the international terrorists, often a pluralist assemblage of different races and ethnicities. On the other hand is the local hero, often very rooted in a local culture (in the *Die Hard* films, the hero is a New York cop out of place in Los Angeles and Washington—alternate centers of global finance and global politics; in *Under Siege,* the hero refuses political ceremony to stay down in the ship's marginalized kitchen; in *Passenger 57,* the hero admits his antiglobalist resistance to flying). The hero is always a figure who has suffered, who has been de-masculinized (in *Under Siege,* he's been demoted; in *Passenger 57,* he suffers the trauma of his wife's death; in *Die Hard,* he is a victim of the feminism that has caused his wife to leave him and reassume her maiden name). Fighting the internationalist threat will grant the hero a return to the real man he once was (and all the films reward the hero by turning into available and pliant girlfriends or playmates or wives women who had only hours or minutes before been antagonistic to the hero).

But even as they engage in regressive fantasies of remasculinized local heroes, the films also contain hints of globalist attitudes. First of all, they generally see the international terrorists not as honest participants in global culture but as deviates from the true course: they pretend to be terrorists but they are really nothing but thieves (*Die Hard*) or they work for revolutionaries but without real commitment for their own (*Die Hard 2; Passenger 57*) or (worst of all) they become terrorists as a way of replaying the evils of sixties counterculturalism (*Under Siege*). Like several recent new professional-managerial-class films which locate the villain as the embodiment of the post-modern condition (*Ghost; Pacific Heights*—although both of these also give the evil yuppie a working-class or low-class ethnic partner to reinvest in older myths of the dangerous masses), the terrorist films engage in an inoculation by which it is assumed that some professional globalists can be aberrant all the better to argue that the system of globalization itself is not bad. Second of all, even as these films represent the integrity of the local, they still individualize localism in the form of the hero, relegating the rest of the local world to background (the anonymous hostages, the passive witnesses, the masses of victims [as in *Die Hard 2* which has a whole 747 crash but then shows no major reaction to the fact, the film registering the deaths but then gliding over them]). All of this—the indifference toward the masses, the remasculinization of the loner individualist, the representation of the terrorist or revolutionary as pervert or psychopath—goes hand in hand with another representation or, rather, nonrepresentation: the image of those at the top of multinational global power. The films offer a relative indifference toward global managers, and in this way they are curiously complementary with the NBF films which frequently end with loads of destruction from which economic leaders emerge invulnerable and exempt (see, for example, the ending of *Robocop 2* where the corporate bad guy drives off in safety).

Just as Althusser's emphasis in ideological state apparatuses should not lead us to ignore the operations of what he calls repressive state apparatuses (although gives less attention to), we should note those cases where global negotiations fall back into acts of policing. This case is explored, to take a local example, in Rob Wilson's little reflection on myths of American power, "Sublime Patriot." Although he is not using the same terms, Wilson's analysis is in some degree about the residual nature of American nationhood and the ways residual ideology can easily get retooled in crisis moments. Wilson notes how, against all actual evidence as to the global background in the production of Patriot missiles , George Bush's rhetoric reappropriates and re-Americanizes the missile as local product, local joy. Wilson asks, "How can spectacles of natural/technological sublimity (powers), or discourses of republican principle (rights), resonate in the unstable zones of Multinational Capital?"[25] (Note how even the language is one of asynchronous levels: there is a geopolitical economic "zone" of Capital; this gets cultural representation in the form of "spectacles"; and these are only effective if they can find "resonance"—in other words, the phrase offers a theory of politics, of culture's relation to politics, and of the inscriptions of subjects in culture and in politics.)

The problem with Jameson's formulation comes in large degree, I think, from his conception of "the new world system" as described in his last sentence. For the Adorno-inspired Jameson, there is a sameness spread throughout the world system—an administered rationality in which to the overall process of global commercialization local cultures respond primarily by mimesis, by turning their own "neotraditional images" into explorable objects of mass production. No doubt this is one tendency in the world system, but as Wallerstein argues in *Historical Capitalism,* the system works also by differentiation as much as by leveling. For example (in an argument that can also risk closing off resistance as much as Jameson's argument does), Wallerstein argues that global culture needs to produce local conditions that are not fully capitalized or modernized or equalized. For Wallerstein, the system can produce its own differences: "Indeed, so much were the employers of wage-labor unenthusiastic about proletarianization that, in addition to fostering the gender/age division of labour, they also encouraged, in their employment patterns and through their influence in the political arena, recognition of defined ethnic groups, seeking to link them to specific allocated roles in the labour-force, with different levels of real remuneration for work."[26]

But if we would want to understand racism as reactionary, residual, and regressive, we need not automatically take the newly emergent globalism to be automatically progressive. I have already noted that it is a globalism with class limits—limits about professionalism, around the myths of core superiority, and so on. Looking, in particular, at the role of the concept of culture in the new geopolitical space, Wallerstein argues that there are in fact two potentially divergent notions whose convergence it is the role of the dominant ideology to engineer: on the one hand, culture is an expansive and even universalizing concept, suggesting a community to which people can adhere; on the other hand, culture is a restrictive and even particularizing concept, suggesting a hierarchy that excludes those who are not deemed to be cultured. Films like *Iron Maze* and *Mr. Baseball* thus operate not only by processes of incorporation but also restriction: only some people are given the privilege of participating in the crossing of frontiers (thus, *Iron Maze* can suggest a new worker-owner alliance, but it also has to imply that women, governed more by carnal desire than by the necessities of business unity, have no place). The extreme flipside of such privilege, as I have noted, is a rendering of the people as anonymous masses or mobs or even brute materiality to be callously destroyed (by characters in the films, but also by the films themselves).

Take, for instance, another new alliance film, the vampire film *Innocent Blood* in which all-American cop and French vampire join forces to destroy power-hungry Mafiosi very strongly coded in Italian stereotypes. Filmed in Pittsburgh, *Innocent Blood* has a universalizing tendency even in the nature of its production history: where a local filmmaker like George Romero made site-specific horror films that implied a connection of monstrosity to the breakdowns of everyday life in the de-industrialized rust belt (see, especially, Romero's vampire film, *Martin*), the new corporatist big-budget horror film downplays localism. The film is produced in Pittsburgh not to make use of the semantic particularity of the city but to take advantage of local financial benefits (especially, low or no union rates). Or, rather, the film sets out to effect a new emergent semantics of this city—namely, in the age of hi-tech corporatism, all big cities come to look alike, the little postmodern flourishes that were tacked onto company buildings in the eighties working less to inscribe difference onto the buildings (their possible difference from the sixties and seventies International Style) than to make them all appear strikingly the same. Like another Pittsburgh film, *The Silence of the Lambs* (in which all scenes except for those at FBI headquarters were filmed in Pittsburgh although none of the scenes are supposed to take place there), *Innocent Blood* figures a universalizing of local conditions.

For locals, the opening image of *Innocent Blood* has the immediate value of an essential icon: sweeping forward, the camera moves over the center point of Pittsburgh, a triangular piece of land formed by the perfect confluence of three rivers and ringed by the gleaming steel and glass of corporate headquarters and corporate-like hotels. The triangle is probably the city's most stock image, reproduced on T-shirts and postcards, flashed at the beginning of new shows, signaled to passengers on flights into and out of the region. And it may have a currency beyond the local: the modernization of the triangle figures as the opening of Cecil B. DeMille's 1947 national(ist) epic, *Unconquered*.

It is not accidental that second-string cities like Pittsburgh have become recurrent hosts to horror films especially (in this case, the Romero films, Argento and Romero's *Two Evil Eyes,* Demme's *The Silence of the Lambs;* and in Cronenberg's *Videodrome,* it's from Pittsburgh that the evil plot to change the world televisually originates). Beyond the local dealings that make genre filming cheaper in the smaller city than in, say, Los Angeles or New York, locales like Pittsburgh that seem to have borne the worst of the brunt of deindustrialization serve easily in the production of horror as political and economic allegory. As capitalist perfection and expansion mean increasingly that that which cannot be capitalized becomes pushed to the periphery, local spaces become apt sites for narratives in which the system represses its monster and then has to battle their fiendish return. From the ghettoes (*Wolfen, Assault on Precinct 13, Candyman*), from the industrial wastelands (*Alligator, The Hills Have Eyes*), from deindustrialized rust belts (*Texas Chainsaw Massacre*) come the monsters to enter violently into a seemingly squeaky-clean, hi-tech, gleamy world of rationalized perfection (the corporate tower of *Gremlins 2*).

Capitalism, of course, is nothing if not resilient. An industrial nightmare up to the 1940s, a deindustrialized horror of unemployment even now (see the documentaries of Tony Buba on the down-and-out neighborhoods), Pittsburgh yuppifies in the seventies and eighties and, for its professional-managerial class, transforms de-industrialization into postindustrial informatics: de-emphasizing heavy industry, the city becomes one of the country's very largest sites of corporate headquarters.

In *Innocent Blood,* this postindustrial corporatism shows up as the dark, anonymous styleless skyscrapers of the opening shot before the film leaves this large view to move in quickly to street-level (and below street-level) drama. Thereafter, the large corporations exist in *Innocent Blood* only as evanescent images glimpsed vaguely in the background of a few shots. But the film's vagueness about the sites of power (of the sighting of power) has as its correlate a fuzziness about the local (for Pittsburghers, indeed, there is something comical about *Innocent Blood*'s "creative geography" in which real neighborhoods are mentioned but out-of-place). The interweavings of power between the global and the local are displaced into a series of anecdotes or clichés about the Italian Mafiosi who are presented as the real forces of power here. There is a Mafia so represented through comical stereotypes (Italians as the supreme stylists of bad taste) that the film's allegory of power seems to undergo a derealization (one complemented by the film's relative disinterest in the life of locals—we see few ordinary people in background shots; in the film's finale, the

Mafia vampire and the French vampire battle out in a city street from which all citizens, including those in an exploded bus, have been absented and ignored).

But even as it de-realizes manager and worker alike (rendering both the corporate building and the street as de-peopled universe) and even as it assigns the means of power to a group of people presented as ridiculous (not for nothing is the lawyer of the bad-taste Mafiosi played by the derisory comic Don Rickles), *Innocent Blood* suggests new, more rationalist, more young professionalist corporate power in the alliance of the young French vampire, Marie, and the street cop. Unlike *Iron Maze* or *Mr. Baseball, Innocent Blood* certainly represents their alliance as sexualized, but their romantic interlude is still portrayed as a step in a larger, rational goal of cleaning off the streets a vulgar power turned aberrant. *Innocent Blood* offers a deliberate banalization of the vampire myth: if the stereotyped Mafiosi form a (doomed) vampirism, the alternative will be the new accommodationist vampirism of Marie. Where the classic Dracula vampire brings the baggage of a decadent aristocracy (no matter how much it revitalizes itself in the New World), Marie is simply an ordinary girl, her Frenchness indicating not so much aristocratic otherworldliness as simple difference that can be mediated by corporatist alliance (at the end, she and the hero will be a team; as in *The Howling,* with its werewolves trying to learn to live among ordinary people, *Innocent Blood* imagines an accommodation within the space of modernity between worlds of difference).

But even the classic vampire story has its bearing on the case of new cinema. In his already classic essay from 1983, "The Dialectic of Fear," Italian Marxist Franco Moretti has suggested the appropriateness of the vampire as allegory of capital.[27] Where an easy interpretation would see Dracula simply as a residual figure doomed to disappear under the force of nascent reason, Moretti complicates the reading by noting that Dracula has many of the elements of the emergent system: the perfect capitalist, Dracula desires for expansion, the cannibaization of new markets. Moretti suggests ingeniously that the capitalist is split in the Dracula story in its two figures: the vampire and the American Morris (whose blandness hints at the reality of a cold rationality of expansionism that is unrecognized and occluded by being cast into the more flamboyant old-country). Coppola's *Bram Stoker's Dracula* captures the ambivalences. Dracula here is, on the one hand, the figure bound to a past, condemned to repeat it. On the other hand, he is perfectly modern, a mutating self who can pragmatically readapt to each new situation. Like the nascent art of cinema, with which he is associated, Dracula is modernity that knows no barriers of space or time. In his ability to be anything, go anywhere, he is more the figure of a service economy than the film's ostensible hero, the real-estate agent (Keanu Reeves) unable to negotiate any space at all.

There is another way in which Dracula seems to me to fit with the new projections and fantasies of global economy, and I want to conclude with some initial thoughts about this. For all its figuration of a new, de-corporealized, incorporated, multiply allied trans-subject, new culture also seems to me concerned to reassert intense subjectivity in the form of the virtuoso. Insofar as the new globalist culture is about movement, about the ease of transition, about the mastery of the flows of information, about privilege, there will be a celebration of special figures who move easily through the networks of knowledge and service.

Coppola's *Dracula* is about such a figure, but the film is in this respect also an allegory of itself. In fact, many of Coppola's films are about overachievers trying to buck a system that they would also like to succeed in (for example, *Tucker* or the later *Godfather* films). What after all is Coppola himself but a sort of vampire in the studio system—a remnant of an auteurist past trying to expansively move in on the present? His films themselves become flamboyant demonstrations of virtuosity in which all of existence is transcoded to the demands of an insistent ego, in which all of reality is put under the pragmatic gaze of an emphatic reason (Coppola's studio filming as a sort of controlled laboratory experiment). But in this respect, the new film director as superstar is only one of the virtuosos projected up by global privileges.

In academia, for example, not merely do we have the rise of the superstar but the rise of the jet-setting superstar (a celebrification of what Edward Said calls "traveling theory"). Said's *Musical Elaborations*, in fact, seems symptomatic with its increasing recognition of the potentially political powers of the virtuoso (how not to see Said himself in his description of prodigy Glenn Gould's "way of being able to quote both musically and intellectually more or less anything at any time"?). For all of his attention elsewhere to communalized forms of antisystemic activity, Said here valorizes the performing self as the especial means by which the dominant narrative of the West is reworked, refused, re-elaborated.[28]

Jameson's recent work, too, seems in the face of late capitalism's systematic regularity to assume that antisystemic forces can come only from the aggressively performative thrusting forward of the virtuoso (and his own critical performances are nothing if not virtuoso). When the book comes closest to engagement with "Third World" cinema, it does so to dent the effectivity of this cinema: "Third-World cinema itself is rarely today defended as a space in which models for alternate cinema are to be sought. Indeed the term Third World seems to have become an embarrassment in a period in which the realities of the economic have seemed to supplant the possibilities of collective struggle, in which human agency and politics seem to have been dissolved by the global corporate institutions we call late capitalism." (This seems to me to get things wrong: the term "Third World" has been called into question not because the space of struggle has disappeared or been absorbed, but because the idea of Thirdness implies a hierarchy that precisely encourages disappearance or absorption—the "Third World" as primitive or savagely marginal.) On the other hand, then, Jameson will argue for an especial privilege of the artist qua artist in resisting absorption: Jameson's one discussion of "Third World" filmmaking follows a chapter on, among other things, high art in Godard—a chapter in which we are enjoined to "do Godard the justice of rising to the occasion of the sublime itself, which he is one of the very rare artists in our time to attain for fleeting instants."[29] In the last chapter—on the Philippine filmmaker Kidlat Tahimik—there will be a revealing mimesis between the virtuoso creative artist and the virtuoso critic, each presented as performing trenchant acts of clairvoyance:

> The conception of cognitive mapping I have proposed elsewhere was intended to include that possibility as well, and to be prescriptive as well as descriptive. . . . But since it has been affirmed as an activity of individual and collective subjects in general, . . . it is obviously encouraging to find the concept of mapping validated by conscious artistic production, and to come upon this or that new work, which, like a straw in the wind, independently seems to have conceived of the vocation of art itself as that of inventing new geotropical cartographies.[30]

I do not want to overstate my reservations about these points in Jameson (one of the most decisive critics for my own thinking as my reading of the American films as political allegories bears out). But moments like these surprise me in their invocations of the special instances in which, in the bland anonymity of the administered society, a few privileged figures are thrown up to grasp the sublimities that others miss in the blandness of the quotidian. The glimpses of the virtuoso individuality that we see here or in *Musical Elaborations* seem to me easily of the same moment as the new consumerist cultural studies (i.e, Henry Jenkins or John Fiske), with resistance figured as creative shopping, or as the new globalist virtuoso performers in popular culture.

What else does Michael Jackson's video "Black or White" do but offer a virtuoso vocation of art as that of "inventing new geotropical cartographies"? Neither black nor white himself (surgery having weirdly turned him a curious pink), Jackson travels boldly through multiple worlds—through ethnicities rendered as backdrops and robbed of identity through mixture (India dancing against the backdrop of a rust-belt factory; African tribesmen in a recording studio)—and through multiple spaces (from white suburbia to the empty detritus of the inner city rendered as spectacle for the virtuoso dancer—Jackson treating the slum street as studio set straight out of *Singin' in the Rain*). This is the cartography of the new globalist trans-subject—faces blurring into each other—but with one subject (the elusive Jackson) also maintaining his prodigious privilege. Here, the new professional globalism achieves perfection: no frontiers, no limits, anything becomes anything else, everyone and everything linked but, at the same time, so many frontiers (art and ordinary life, privilege and anonymity, wealth and deprivation).

In an article on "Cosmopolitan and Locals in World Culture," Ulf Hannerz gives especial privilege to intellectuals in the various landscapes of border-crossing: "Generally expansionist in its management of meaning, it [the cosmopolitan orientation] pushes relentlessly in its analysis of the order of ideas, strives toward explicitness where common sense, as a contrasting mode of meaning management, might come to rest comfortably with the tacit, the ambiguous, and the contradictory. In the end it strives for mastery."[31] With Hannerz, with Said on traveling theory, I too believe that intellectuals have unique relations to knowledge. But I think these relations are material in origin (intellectuals have the research time, the research tools and opportunities, and so on, to make meaning connections) rather than ontological (as in Jameson's invocation of the artists or in Hannerz's tendency to assume an explicitness of analytic intellect over against the murky but comfortable sinking into contradiction and common sense of the noncosmopolitan masses with their localized semi-knowledge). The mastery that Hannerz sees intellectuals striving for is an ambivalent one, and one modest ambition of collections like this might be to render ambiguous and contradictory any virtuoso or especial intellectual position through a qualifying multiplication of knowledge sites.

Notes

1 Benedict Anderson, *Imagined Communities: Reflections on the Origin and Spread of Nationalism*, 2d ed. (New York: Verso, 1991), pp. 76–77.

2 Ibid., p. 77.

3 Eve Kosofsky Sedgwick, "Nationalities and Sexualities in the Age of Wilde," in *Nationalities and Sexualities*, ed. Andrew Partker et al. (New York: Routledge, 1992).

4 Anderson, *Imagined Communities*, p. 14.

5 Ibid.

6 Jean-François Lyotard, *The Postmodern Condition: A Report on Knowledge*, trans. Brian Massumi (Minneapolis: University of Minnesota Press, 1984).

7 Ibid., p. 53.

8 John Hoerr, *And the Wolf Finally Came: The Decline of the American Steel Industry* (Pittsburgh: University of Pittsburgh Press, 1988).

9 Mitsuhiro Yoshimoto, "The Difficulty of Being Radical: The Discipline of Film Studies and the Postcolonial World Order," *boundary 2* 18, no. 3 (Fall 1991): 242–257.

10 Richard Rorty, "Solidarity or Objectivity?" in *Post-Analytic Philosophy*, ed. John Rajchman and Cornel West (New York: Columbia University Press, 1985), pp. 3–20.

11 Immanuel Wallerstein, *Geopolitics and Geoculture* (New York: Cambridge University Press, 1991).

12 Mike Featherstone, "Introduction," *Theory, Culture, Society* 7, nos. 2–3 (1990): 2.

13 Mitsuhiro Yoshimoto, "Real Virtuality," in this volume.

14 Arjun Appadurai, "Disjunction and Difference in the Global Cultural Economy," *Theory, Culture, Society* 7, nos. 2–3 (1990): 295–310.

15 Hoerr, *And the Wolf Finally Came*.

16 Richard Preston, *American Steel: Hot Metal Men and the Resurrection of the Rust Belt* (New York: Prentice-Hall, 1992).

17 Ibid.

18 Ibid.

19 Ibid.

20 Hoerr, *And the Wolf Finally Came*, p. 91.

21 Neil Lazarus, "Doubting the World Order: Marxism, Realism, and the Claims of Postmodernist Social Theory," *differences* 5, no. 5 (1991): 94–137.

22 See Christopher L. Connery, "The Oceanic Feeling and the Regional Imaginary," in this volume.

23 Anderson, *Imagined Communities*, pp. 145–149.

24 Fredric Jameson, *The Geopolitical Aesthetic: Cinema and Space in the World System* (London: British Film Institute, 1992).

25 Rob Wilson, "Sublime Patriot," *Polygraph* 5 (1992): 67–77.

26 Immanuel Wallerstein, *Historical Capitalism* (London: Verso, 1983), p. 28.

27 Franco Moretti, *Signs Taken for Wonders: Essays in the Sociology of Literary Forms* (London: Verso, 1983), pp. 83–108.

28 Edward Said, *Musical Elaborations* (New York: Columbia University Press, 1991).

29 Jameson, *The Geopolitical Aesthetic*.

30 Ibid.

31 Ulf Hannerz, "Cosmopolitan and Locals in World Culture," *Theory, Culture, Society* 7, nos. 2–3 (1990).

THE OCEANIC FEELING AND
THE REGIONAL IMAGINARY
Christopher L. Connery

●

The "spatial turn" has been increasingly evident in a variety of disciplines, political positions, and analytical frameworks during the last twenty years. The critique of historicism, the disappearance of depth, the general flattening out, and other intimations of the spatial are indeed defining features of our putative new era. New geographies and new cartographies have arisen to map it; the Pacific Rim is one newly imagined space. I have argued elsewhere[1] that during the late cold war years, roughly 1975–1989, the mythology of the Pacific Rim was symptomatic of the particular crisis of self-imagining faced by the United States in that era. This was an era when the cold war binary had fundamentally lost its meaning, when the great postwar U.S. expansion had met its first significant downturn, and when capitalism's success in one area of the Other (Japan and the East Asian NICs) had problematized the once easy identification of success-ful capitalism with the West.[2]

The Pacific Rim served the needs of its period in a particular way. Consider the rim. Its circularity conveyed at once the universality of the last horizon and the final Emersonian Circle, yet its linearity served less to contain than to exclude: the Third World, the U.S. "rust belt," and even Europe—front line of the old, tired, cold war binary and still only groping toward Maastricht—were all, like the moribund socialist world in the post-Vietnam era, off the rim. The Pacific Rim was the geo-imaginary of the postoriginary, where source or desti-nation of commodity or capital counted less than circulation, pure flow. The challenges to the concepts of both "the West" and "the nation" created a need for new spaces within which history could take place. The Pacific Rim was the "spatial fix" (David Harvey's coinage in *The Limits to Capital*) for the perceived despatializing tendency of multi- or transnational capitalism.

James O'Connor, one of the first Marxist theorists of the mid-seventies' crisis, points toward one facet of the national problematic in his notion of the roles of legitimation and accumulation in the capitalist state.[3] Certain aspects of the way the state legitimates the system of capital (education and welfare, accommodation to labor, etc.) will come into conflict with the state's function in supporting capital accumulation, and this conflict is one source of fiscal crisis. The emerging dominance of transnational corporations problematizes the spatiality of legitimation. Accumulation occurs more and more beyond the parameters of the state, but ideological apparatuses and other organs of the legitimation function cannot be so easily deracinated.[4] The imagination of the Pacific Rim can be read as one attempt to conceptualize—and it is important to note that this conceptualization is primarily for U.S. consumers—an arena for a hoped-for legitimation through the false promise of spectacularity provided by common Pacific Rim tropes of the dynamic, the new, the revivified, and the miraculous. As Bruce Cumings mocks "Rimspeak," "[t]ropes of dynamism and miracles also say this: Capitalist universalism is the only thing I can see; thus I discover the Pacific Rim."[5]

The myth of free-market capitalism has always implied a teleology of equilibrium. The Pacific Rim's putative dynamic yet equalizing flows, wherein everyone on the Rim benefits, is in one respect the imagining of postnational equilibrium (Pacific Rim discourse was always antiprotectionist; President Clinton's trip to Asia in the autumn of 1994 reactivated many of the discourse's tropes and concluded with plans for a Pacific free-trade zone similar to that provided for by NAFTA). Yet a fundamental character of the Pacific Rim as spatial image—its exclusivity—reveals the disequilibrium and differentiation that Marxist and non-Marxist geographers recognize as fundamental to the spatiality of capitalism. The Pacific Rim as "growth region" within a global disequilibrium thus partakes of the character of regions as they have come to be understood since the onset of capital's postwar "restructuring" (variously termed post-Fordist, postmodernist, etc). For the Pacific Rim to exist, there must be differentiated regions that are off the rim, in stagnation or decline.

The region (the term as commonly used in this period refers primarily to the subnational region) has emerged as a primary category in postmodern geography and political economy. The promise and contemporaneity of regionalism is stated most forcefully by Edward Soja:

At present, the relatively new field of regional political economy and a reinvigorated and reoriented regional industrial geography seem to be the most insightful and innovative areas for analyzing the macro-, meso-, and micro-political economies of restructuring. Both can be called flexible specializations, for they are less concerned with old boundaries and disciplinary constraints and are thus more open to timely adaptation to meet new demands and challenges. The regional perspective facilitates the synthesis of the urban and the global while remaining cognizant of the powerful mediating role of the national state even as this role dwindles somewhat in the current era. The mutually responsive interplay of regionalization and regionalism provides a particularly insightful window on to the dynamics of spatialization and geographically uneven development, gives greater depth and political meaning to the notion of spatial divisions of labor, and abounds with useful connections to the revamped social ontologies discussed earlier. Just as important, its openness and flexibility, its inclination to try new combinations of ideas rather than fall back to old categorical dualities, makes *critical regional studies* [emphasis in original] the most likely point of confluence for the three streams of contemporary restructuring. Here is where our understanding of post-fordism, postmodernism, and a post-historicist critical social theory may most bountifully take place.[6]

The critical turn toward regionalism began in the mid-seventies. The *International Journal of Urban and Regional Research,* where much of the important theorization and conceptualization of regionalism has taken place, began publication in 1977. Although this coincides roughly with the onset of Pacific Rim discourse, the Pacific Rim is articulated as region only in journalism and in late capitalist boosterism for popular audiences, such as in the work of Alvin Toffler, Kenichi Ohmae, and others.[7] Though it must be emphasized that scholars in the field of "critical regionalism" would never take seriously the idea of the Pacific Rim as an area of analysis,[8] I believe that Pacific Rim discourse is a displaced version of a similar problematic. One of the factors that stimulated the growth of critical regional studies was the emergence of new regions of economic growth, such as the U.S. Sun Belt, southern Germany, the "Third Italy," or Silicon Valley, and the decline of other regions, particularly ones that one would associate with an earlier industrial era. This process made it impossible to ignore the materiality of capitalist space. But critical regionalism's origination in the binarisms of developed/underdeveloped, expansion/contraction, or growth/stagnation is significant. The concept of region, arising as it does within a binary logic of difference, is a semiotic utopia, a "spatial fix" for those faced with analyzing the always differentiating but always concealing logic of capital. The region, less encumbered by the various ideological or mythical mystifications that pervade the state, will be where history and analysis take place. Regions, saturated as they are with the always signifying real, are models of flexible semiogenesis. Soja's enthusiasm for the field of critical regional studies, as noted in the passage quoted above, is one indication of a general hunger for the spatial fix during the period under discussion.

Most of the important critical regional studies incorporate a logic of disequilibrium and take seriously the disjunctive and contingent character of regional differentiation. The restiveness of the category of region and the recognized dangers of its reification are evident in the following passage by Storper and Walker:

> We prefer the term "territory" to "region." Territory is less theory-laden and more open to fresh connotation; it can refer to any geographical scale, as it denotes functional interaction rather than bounded spaces; a fabric of related places with some coherent linkages may constitute the territory of an industry, or a "territorial complex." The concept of region suffers from being unduly identified with sub-national regions, whereas the developmental processes we are concerned with take place at the sub-national, national, and international scales at once. The concept is further handicapped by a long tradition of treating areas as self-evident units, such as the Mississippi River basin, the state of Georgia, or the northeastern manufacturing belt. It is, moreover, often taken to be a natural rather than a socially constructed and reconstructed fabric.[9]

Storper and Walker prefer the "territorial industrial complex" as their unit of analysis. Built into the notion of the territorial industrial complex, though, is flexibility, instability, and the certainty of eventual change. It is the geography of a more fluid, post-Fordist capitalism.

By decentering a particular industry or corporation from the position as sole defining element of a region, the dynamism and disequilibrium that account for regional change are spatialized and made an essential character of the unit of analysis. Recent work in critical regionalism and industrial geography has clearly had great value in allowing a more complete analysis of the workings of industrial capitalism, though we have seen that even radical geographers like Storper and Walker are not immune to the Rim's signifying seduction. Contingent spatialities, dynamic space, or spatialities with built-in resistance to reification have also become commonplace in cultural theory, wherein every

field of analysis is now a "site of contestation," where the putatively false teleologies of market equilibrium or world socialism are suspended in the pure
dynamism of the present resistance-saturated moment.

Both critical cultural theory and critical regionalism can survive with the
always continuing spatial fix of flexibility, contingency, or self-negation. Pacific
Rim discourse functioned in a different way. It was an attempt to supply a
restructuring global capitalism with its spatial fix, but by being a trope for
capitalist universalism, it had to incorporate into its mode of discursive existence the related tropes of teleological equilibrium and end of history. As such it
could never be truly localized or regionalized and still retain its mythological
promise. The Pacific Rim, like the ever-expanding Emersonian Circle, had to
transcend itself and enclose the entire developed world—thence Pacific Rim
booster Alexander Besher's use of the term "global rim"[10] or "management
guru" Kenichi Ohmae's notion of the ILE (Interlinked Economy), which he
elaborates in his recent book *The Borderless World* (1990):

> An isle is emerging that is bigger than a continent—the Interlinked Econ-
> omy of the Triad (the United States, Europe, and Japan), joined by aggres-
> sive economies such as Taiwan, Hong Kong, and Singapore. . . . It is
> becoming so powerful that it has swallowed most consumers and corpora-
> tions, made traditional national borders almost disappear, and pushed
> bureaucrats, politicians, and the military toward the status of declining
> industries.[11]

Ohmae's swallowing image is significant, because only on the scale of the whole
world can "localizable" ideological elements be disappeared; only in the final
circle can capital operate with total transparency.

The Pacific Rim is a mythological region, but as I have argued above, its
creation and historical logic partake of certain elements of the regional imperative. This is particularly evident in the binarism implied in the Rim's very
precariousness. It was never merely the Rim, though, but rather the Pacific—
the Last Ocean—that allowed this pseudo-region to function as a space for revel
at the shore of the economic sublime. A rim encircles, and its interior, in
rimspeak, is the void that gives substance to what surrounds it. Within the Rim,
the Pacific, rather than being simply the largest expanse of the world ocean,
becomes subordinate to the Rim's dynamic, though still fundamentally insub-
stantial, terrestriality.

In addition to functioning as U.S. capital's spatial fix, a critical regionalism for uncritical universalists, the Pacific Rim was the culmination of capitalist Western European and U.S. mythological orientation toward the ocean, which, as we will see below, floated binarisms, ambiguities, and sublimities of its own kind. Modernity arose out of the world ocean, first made appropriately spatial in Magellan's westward journey across the Pacific. Ocean as source and ocean as destiny figure in the ocean's mythological temporality; it is both life-giving mother and final frontier. The conquest of the world ocean being coterminous with the rise of Western capitalism, it is natural that the ocean has long functioned as capital's myth element, down to the postfrontier of Pacific Rim discourse. Tropes of oceanic sublimity, as in the "oceanic feeling" discussed below, need to be read against ocean as created,[12] mythological space, and it must always be borne in mind whose and what interests are served by that mythology. It is to Ocean as myth element and telos that I will devote the rest of this paper.[13]

The Oceanic Feeling

The "oceanic feeling" is invoked by Romain Rolland, novelist, biographer of Ramakrishna and Vivekananda, and Indophile devotee of the *Baghavad Gita* in a letter to Freud following a reading of Freud's *The Future of an Illusion*. Freud reports that for Rolland, the oceanic feeling was "a sensation of 'eternity,' a feeling as of something limitless, unbounded—as it were, 'oceanic.' . . . One may, he thinks, rightly call oneself religious on the ground of this oceanic feeling alone, even if one rejects every belief and every illusion."[14] Freud could not feel it. He could see in the oceanic feeling only a survival of an infantile stage of ego development. For Freud, this childlike "oceanic feeling" of limitlessness and boundlessness becomes sublimated in the adult ego's adaptation to the neurosis of "civilization,"[15] although the Kantian and Romantic claims for an aesthetic sublime provide an always renewable source for a "fictive experience of self-empowerment."[16]

The ocean is a prime activator of the trope of the sublime: limitless, unfathomably deep, indefinite. As Melville writes in *Moby Dick*, "[i]n landlessness alone resides the highest truth, shoreless, indefinite as God."[17] In the language of Western expansionism, whether of empire or of consciousness, whose oceanic moves I will discuss further below, this oceanic sublime is an oft-invoked source of inspiration. Emerson, in "Circles," writes that "the only sea is limitation," whose shores will always disappoint and deject, but goes on to invoke a universal ocean, "fluid and volatile," the "flying Perfect." Rob Wilson has cogently analyzed the *pragmatic* character of the sublime in the context of U.S. expansionism, in terms which apply easily to its oceanic version:

> This trope of the sublime proved habitually pragmatic: immensity implied an (imagined) vacancy, and emptiness the possibility of strong and various deeds (great poems) to be outdone. Converting fullness into emptiness and vacancy into possibility, the American sublime helped generate its own sublime consequences and works—transport, aggrandizement, achievement on a Euro-competitive scale. Circularity was not so much a logical problem (tautology) or way of over-imagining (hyperbole) to be avoided, but an identity-consolidating tactic to circulate fresh transport, surplus, and self-empowerment.[18]

Perhaps, though, the ocean is *too* external: its assimilability, even to the flexible and contingent pragmatism of American sublimity, is always in doubt. The solidity of even the vastest American prairie or deepest Adirondack mountains allows conversion into images of sublimity that the ocean does not. Even for mythographer Roland Barthes, the ocean resists signification: "Here I am before the sea; it is true that it bears no message."[19] Yet signify it does, although in a manner beyond resolve. Is it the void beyond and outside of the terrestrial real? a blank interstitial element? Is it a pure void that activates the terrestrial symbolic system? Is it the real beneath the floating discontinuousness of land; the universal syntax? The ambiguity that inheres in the ocean's very liquid element renders it uncertain whether it is "another vast metaphor or an indifferent energy flatly separated from human discourse."[20]

The Element

Liquid is always the problem element—shapeless but not abstract; temporal; changeable. Bachelard writes: "Water is truly the transitory element. It is the essential ontological metamorphosis between heaven and earth. A being dedicated to water is a being in flux."[21] Bachelard's meditation on water, "a substantial nothingness," is on its surface antisublime. Only fresh water—living water, as in the magical springs and rivers of Homeric Greece—functions as a real mythological element. For Bachelard, the sea is "inhuman water, in that it fails in the first duty of every revered element, which is to serve man directly."[22] Beyond the human, beyond daily life and thus beyond dreams—apprehensible only to the iterable, narrative faculty, rather than to the oneiric, poetic power of the psyche—Bachelard finds that sea water is beyond theory and unworthy of analysis. "Natural dreams create a fable about what has been seen, touched, and eaten by the dreamer. . . . The sea-oriented unconscious is . . . a spoken unconscious, an unconscious too dispersed in adventure tales, an unconscious that never sleeps. . . . It is less profound than that unconscious which dreams about common experiences."[23]

Bachelard's ocean is the inhuman sea of the "Book of Revelation," also invoked by W. H. Auden: "The sea, in fact, is that state of barbaric vagueness and disorder out of which civilization has emerged and into which, unless saved by the efforts of gods and men, it is always liable to relapse. It is so little of a friendly symbol that the first thing which the author of the Book of Revelation notices in his vision of the new heaven and earth at the end of time is that 'there was no more sea.' "[24]

The categorical difficulty and ontological uncertainty that we find in Bachelard's ocean resurfaces in a recent article on the sublime and slime, "Philosophy (and Sociology) in the Wetlands: The S(ub)lime and the Uncanny." In slime—the dark ooze of swamps, wetlands, female genitalia, and all else that belongs to the uncanny obverse of the sublime—author Rod Giblett has found a figure that tropes the capitalist/masculinist will to fill in, "[a]nd so attain to the sublime heights of capitalism, theory, and the super-ego in which men (I don't exclude myself) can calculate themselves as independent of nature and repudiate their connections with their mothers, their own bodies, and with mother earth . . . and can continue to exploit the natural environment with impunity a highly dubious, masculinist, and (self) destructive enterprise—through the triumph of capitalist modernization and of modernity."[25] Giblett needs slime as the fecund, intermediate element, much as Bachelard locates paste, the combination of water and a solid, as the basic component of materiality itself. Part of Giblett's article is a criticism of Sartre's antislime, pro-river excesses in *Being and Nothingness,* whose unreflective masculinism Giblett exposes to notable effect. But where, and what, is the ocean? Even in Giblett's brilliant chart, his inclusive "geocorpography of modernity," ocean does not appear, although sun, fire, earth, city, land, and mass all do. The bottom of the chart groups in one category primeval slime, wetland, abjection, soft, writing, trace, feminine, unconscious, id, Hell, infinite temporality, eternity, and cloaca, and, in another, liquid, water, river, depth, flow, masculine, conscious(ness), and temporarity.[26] Slime must function, in the logic of this system, as the crucial middle element because it can be filled in and thereby function as the object of the masculinist, capitalist subject. But it is uncanny, it must be stressed, and thus only a temporary return of the repressed. The ocean, though, can never be filled in. Like a mother, it can never be forgotten; it is as primary and extensive an element as sky.

The identification of the ocean with a strictly maternal femininity, and there is scarcely a single piece of Western writing on the ocean that does not make this identification, is certainly one source of the ocean's unassimilability for Giblett and other theorists of slime (he cites Zoe Sofoulis and Jane Gallop). But in order for ocean to function as maternal presence on the elemental level, it cannot be the "substantial nothingness" which nonetheless nourishes, as do Bachelard's *eaux vivantes*. To de-aquify sea water, Bachelard invokes Jules Michelet, for whom ocean water was not water per se, but more than water. Michelet's chapter on the character of water is called "The Sea of Milk" ("La mer de lait"). His sea water is mucus: slimy and teeming with life. The ocean is sublime slime, uncanny and sublime at once.

Jules Michelet's *La Mer* was published shortly after Melville's *Moby Dick*, and the two works have much in common. Both ascribe critical significance to the whaling industry in stimulating the earliest voyages into the far reaches of the ocean; both reflect the rapid mid-nineteenth-century advances in marine biology and oceanography, the product of those voyages of scientific exploration which followed upon Western expansionism and world conquest; both find common to Western humanity a kind of "oceanic feeling," as seen in Melville's silent ocean-gazing crowds at the Battery and in Michelet's descriptions of beachgoers. Both books are filled with the materiality of ocean water. Melville's ocean varies in shape and color, has local characteristics, and shows the tracks of surface-swimming whales. Although Michelet begins his book with an evocation of the ocean's primitive fearsomeness, its nonbreathable, alienating difference, this is merely to prepare the reader for the rhetorical reversal to come in his eulogy for the sea of milk. The mucus, the viscosity which one feels on one's hands as sea water courses through them, the slipperiness that makes fish shine, is "l'élément universel de la vie."[27] And this element is not simply a nutritive Outside, but a reorganized, chaotic version of the body itself, where bones, blood, marrow, and human energy are simply divided up and redistributed among the various life elements of the sea.[28] Michelet's ocean is far from the dead inhumanity ascribed to the oceans of the New Testament or Douglas MacArthur. This living, always nourishing ocean is "la grande femelle du globe, dont l'infatigable désir, la conception permanente, l'enfantement, ne finit jamais" [the globe's great female, whose tireless desire, ceaseless procreation, and childbirthing never end].[29] Could the ocean, then, be a kind of maternal sublime, a horizon that is also a source?

Michelet condemns ocean voyages of conquest and violence, and ends his book with a chapter called "*Vita Nuova* des nations," containing pleas for aquaculture and seaside sanatoria. Just as he ends *La Peuple* with a plea for universal love as the answer to class conflict, so does he in the final section of *La Mer* prescribe partaking of the oceanic universal life energy as a cure for the ills of nations. Michelet is a man of the shores, a bather, a breather of ocean air. He prefers tide pools to the wild and endless open sea. Here he shares ground with Bachelard, who goes beyond Michelet in seeing all movement far into the sea as will to power. Identifying the sea as in no way a body, as an always beyond, a realm of pure struggle, Bachelard's ocean is "a dynamic environment that responds to the dynamic quality of our assaults,"[30] Bachelard identifies the Swinburne complex as an activation of the ambivalent dualities of human and ocean. "More than anyone else, the swimmer can say: the world is my will; the world is my provocation. It is I who stir up the sea."[31] Bachelard wrote *Water and Dreams* during the Nazi era. Perhaps he had made a connection between the Swinburne complex and the horrors that arose from late Weimar and post-Weimar Germany, which, as was documented in the photography of Kurt Reichert and the films of Leni Riefenstahl, was obsessed with swimming and diving. "[H]e who would be a superhuman very naturally rediscovers the same dreams entertained by the child who would be a man. To govern the sea is a superhuman dream. It is both an inspired and a childlike will."[32] Bachelard was not an ocean swimmer; Michelet was, as one would expect of an historian of his kind. Michelet had greater company among the swimmers, whalers, traders, conquerors, regressives, and other activators of history who went into the ocean.

Ariston Men Hydōr[33]

The popularity of Western naturalism's commonplace hypothesis of an aquatic origin for all life added a new mythic dimension to oceangoing. It becomes not just a journey into the beyond, into a future—an exploration[34]—but a journey back to the source. Ocean as origin serves many purposes: it stakes a claim; it universalizes, by humanizing the inhuman element and thus overcoming that Emersonian dread of limits, wherein earth's ocean could function as an absolute horizon rather than a "flying Perfect." The watery way to origins gets read in nearly all registers of human temporality: in phylogenesis, in ego development, and in the political, social, and economic history of the West.

Sir Alister Clavering Hardy, a twentieth-century marine biologist who wrote on plankton, evolution, and the connections between natural science and religion, is the best known of those evolutionary biologists who suggested that human anatomy itself was shaped by amphibious living; that erectness, symmetry, hairlessness, the streamlinedness of remaining hair tracks, the proportions of limbs to trunk and arm to legs, and the layer of subcutaneous fat so conducive to buoyancy were all adaptations to a life of swimming.[35] Carl Sauer, a distinguished twentieth-century U.S. geographer, went even further than Hardy, hypothesizing that Stone Age beach culture was the origin of social life and that not only physical, but social features of "humanity" originated in the nature of amphibian life on the beach:

> In swimming and diving there is no significant advantage of sex and least of age. When European discoverers got overseas they were amazed to see the aquatic skill and enjoyment of the inhabitants of warm and temperate coasts. Whether very primitive like the Tasmanians and natives of the gulf of California or of advanced cultures like those of the South Seas and the Caribbean, both sexes were adept swimmers and divers. They swam for a purpose, and for the pleasure it gave. Everyone, young and old, went into the water. Such joint activity, referred back to primeval times, would provide for the participation of the males in getting food and in sharing responsibilities.

> Settling inland—whether in savanna, forest, or desert—required other skills and offered reduced satisfaction.[36]

The physical and intellectual satisfactions offered by swimming and diving were (re)acquired fairly recently by Westerners. The first major swimming treatise of the modern era—Everard Digby's *De Arte Natandi* of 1587 (translated from Latin into English a few years later)—argues that swimming ("art" and "science") is "natural" to humankind. Yet the strangeness of its suggested means for entering the water indicate that the conceptual boundary between terrestrial and aquatic activity is still somewhat mysterious: "laying his hands on his neck and forcibly running to [the] bank, where declining his head downwards and turning round over with his heels, he may light into the water upon his back."[37] Swimming as transcendental experience—a spiritual, originary, mystical, or purifying exercise—is a later development, corresponding in the West nearly exactly to the high period of industrial capitalism—romanticism and modernism. Before the nineteenth century, swimming was comparatively rare; many of the best-known ocean explorers were in fact nonswimmers. The connection between early-nineteenth-century Byronic swimming, Michelet's ocean bathing, Swinburne's S and M by the sea, Goethe's cold baths (which "transformed bourgeois sensual exhaustion into a fresh and vigorous existence"[38]), and the triumph of the will captured on film in the swimming and diving sections of Leni Riefenstahl's "Olympia" (1937) all mark an era when swimming provided a primary avenue to self-fulfillment or self-transcendence.

England, first in empire and industry in the nineteenth century, was also first in swimming. Swimming was intimately connected to the classicism that also served the imperial mission so well. The ancient Greeks were not prolific pool builders, but British romantics, so fond of evoking Greek nymphs and water deities, often used Greek sources for their natant lyricism. Imperial Rome, however, was one of the great ages of swimming and pool construction. So central was swimming to Roman life that Rome was unequaled in pool construction until the industrial revolution. The perceived shared passion for swimming was not a negligible factor in the metaphoric equivalence of imperial Rome and imperial Great Britain as viewed by several generations of scholars, civil servants, and swimmers.

While England dominated swimming in the nineteenth-century, the breast stroke was most common, and all swimming tended toward maximum immersion, which maximized the amphibian or ichthyal connection. The rare Elizabethan swimmers used dogs for models for strokes, but by the nineteenth century, under the influence of the naturalists, frogs were often kept in pool-side basins as models for proper kicking technique and for the correct posture of the chest.[39] Overarm strokes, inspired by techniques observed by South Sea Island and Caribbean swimmers, became fashionable at the end of the century, but were first thought too crude because they were noisy and because much of the body was outside the water.[40] In the overarm stroke, swimming had left the Romantic era and entered a more fully human-centered, but still imperial[41] modernism. German idealism also inspired a great love for swimming, and particularly for diving. Germans and Scandinavians dominated diving in the late nineteenth and early twentieth centuries, when the swallow dive was the dive of choice from the high board. The German diver bears the same relation to the English long-distance swimmer as does German orientalism to its more practically imperialist English version.

Western romantic swimming, from Byron to Swinburne and Valéry, who extolled "fornication avec l'onde," partook of a masculinst sexual character that retained phallic penetration while maintaining a power-conferring outside that was at once the realm of origin, extratemporality, and maternality. The male coital return to maternal water, sex as swimming, is traced, with all the excesses of phylogenetic parallelism, in Sandor Ferenczi's *Thalassa: A Theory of Genitality.* Ferenczi follows Freud's work on eros and the death instinct,[42] holding that every act of (male) intercourse is an attempted return to the intrauterine situation, whose waters are phylogenetic holdovers of Michelet's mucus, the ocean. The phylogenetic parallel is due to the fact that reproduction through sexual union is a consequence of the move out of the water:

> the penis in coitus enacts not only the natal and antenatal mode of existence of the human species, but likewise the struggles of that primal creature among its ancestors which suffered the great catastrophe of the drying up of the sea.

> The possession of an organ of copulation, the development within the maternal womb, and the circumvention of the great danger of dessication—these three thus form an indestructible biological unity which must constitute the ultimate basis of the symbolic identity of the womb with the sea and the earth on the one hand, and of the male member with the child and the fish on the other.[43]

The memory of an initial liquid state, a watery oneness with nature that is precisely the oceanic feeling, is conceptually well beyond Emerson's liquid imagery in "Nature." Ferenczi also goes beyond Freud in making phylogenetic claims for a kind of "oceanic feeling." In that swim which is the return of the intrauterine,[44] homeostasis/death and life/eros are united.

Just as this union happens as man enters the ocean, so does Western history itself. Norman O. Brown, combining Hegel and Freud, has shown the connection, in Hegel, between history and the death instinct. Freud's theory of aggression, the result of an extroversion of the death instinct that drives humans to seek mastery over nature and their fellow humans, is related to Hegel's master-slave dialectic, "a transformation of the consciousness of death into a struggle to appropriate the life of another human being at the risk of one's own life: history as class struggle."[45] This fundamental dialectic with externalized death is what makes time, and thus history. The dynamic relationship between humans and the ocean—the assault on the sea, the risks taken in all ocean voyages—activates history according to a similar logic of master-slave. Oceangoing activates Western history, and proximity to the sea is one of several primary "natural" factors separating those regions that entered world history from those that did not:

> The sea gives us the idea of the indefinite, the unlimited, and the infinite; and in feeling his own infinite in that Infinite, man is stimulated and emboldened to stretch beyond the limited: the sea invites man to conquest, and to piratical plunder, but also to honest gain and to commerce. The land, the mere Valley-plain attaches him to the soil; it involves him in an infinite multitude of dependencies, but the sea carries him out beyond these limited circles of thought and action.[46]

The oceangoing trader is a gambler. He risks all in an element that, like a slave, is "treacherous, unreliable, and deceitful," though the ocean often looks "boundlessly innocent, submissive, friendly, and insinuating." All of Hegel's historical actors, Greeks and Western Europeans foremost, were people who took to the sea in a move beyond human limitations. For Schumpeter, the high capitalist embodies the heroism of "navigare necesse est, vivere no necesse est" [seafaring is necessary, living is not necessary].[47]

The identification of Western civilization as an oceanic civilization was strong in Hegel and continued to be made as the idea of "Western" civilization was constructed and canonized. Hegel, Michelet, and nineteenth- and twentieth-century British classicists made much of the identification between Greeks and the sea. The word θάλασσα (thalassa) conjured up for generations of classicists the passage in Xenophon's *Anabasis* where the army of 10,000, retreating from Persia, reached the Black Sea and made that cry of return to their safe passage home;[48] the affinity for the sea became one of the markers of Greek civilization. The swimming career of Lord Byron, and the motto of the Eton swimming society, which is the title of this section of the present article, are evidence of the nineteenth-century classical urge that drove so many young men into the water to swim. Classics and empire-building were water sports. Michelet had condemned the Middle Ages for the pervasive horror of ocean water, a horror that would be relieved only with the rise of ocean trade and the revival of the Roman tradition of swimming.

George Kennan, the primary liberal Hegelian of the twentieth-century, was a thalassophile who distrusted all landed interiors. He was one of the last diplomats to have, like Hegel, a geographically distinct concept of Western civilization: Western Europe was the source and origin. Kennan wrote often of the Soviet national character as having been determined less by Marxism than by its vast open plains—its terrestriality. American isolationism had always found its greatest support in the U.S. interior, and it was indeed the interior that was last integrated into the world capitalist system. Kennan feared the insular tendencies that periodically surfaced in the United States almost as much as that landlocked tyrannical illiberality spawned on the Russian steppe.[49] Kennan's containment was containment of the awesome landedness of the Eurasian continent. We can read the cold war on one level, as Orwell did in *1984* with the names of his world powers, as Ocean vs. Land.

The idea of the West as trade-borne land of the free has a long history. Long before the world actually became unified through the operation of multi- and transnational capital, capital adopted a myth of a world unified through oceangoing trade, whose unity was presenced in the liberality and putative limitlessness of the free market. The market, according to this mythology, not only promised a telos of utopian equilibrium, but made *visible,* through its abundance of merchandise, a market form of global unity. A claim was made very early in the history of capital that the sea-trade emporium was synecdochic for the entire world and that the market was subject to a preexisting and natural global logic. Joseph Addison, in a 1711 essay extolling the Royal Exchange in London entitled "Trade as a Civilizing Force" writes: "Nature seems to have taken a particular Care to disseminate her Blessings among the different Regions of the World with an Eye to this mutual Intercourse and Traffick among Mankind, that the Natives of several Parts of the Globe might have a Dependance upon one another, and be united together by their common Interest."[50] Trade as a means toward a kind of original unity in the Ferenczian sense is described by psychoanalytic anthropologist Géza Róheim, in *The Origin and Function of Culture.* The original traders were medicine men, skilled wooers of the Other, and "the phantasy of an exchange of body contents, a mutual mother-child situation, underlies trade."[51] Original ocean trade is then a purely fluid trade. The thalassal regressive trend is enacted in both sexual intercourse and ocean commerce.

Both Michelet and Melville saw whaling as an oceanic activity of a particular kind and located in both its global scope and its violence a marker of a new phase in the relationship between humans and the ocean. (That the whale was originally a land mammal, which shed its limbs and returned to the ocean in what could be read as a successful Ferenczian gesture of phylogenetic regression, may or may not add to the whale's mythological importance.) Michelet's chapter on the whale is the central chapter of his book; whales are the ocean's finest denizens. He opens his section on the conquest of the sea with whaling, and matter-of-factly describes the whale hunt as the source of European man's first venture into the far seas.[52] Melville writes of the whaling ship as the first U.S. factory, with a division of labor and a proletarianized crew that prefigured later nineteenth-century factories: the Pacific as Ur sweat shop. That whales were hunted for their oil, which was used in industry, is another reason to link whaling to the industrial, rather than to the agricultural economy with which one would normally associate fishing.[53] Whaling was also the U.S.'s first truly global trade. U.S. whalers were the first Westerners to hunt the sperm whale, which took them all over the Pacific. Melville's Pacific Ocean—the industrialized ocean of U.S. whalers—is the first evocation of the American Pacific, from which it is only a short conceptual distance to the Pacific Rim.

The Last Ocean

The Pacific Ocean as temporal destiny is an American idea; Western history as constant westward motion would of course not appeal to any countries east of the Atlantic. The temporality of the westward telos replaces, in the United States, the language of the world ocean that accompanied earlier Western European oceangoing trade, which arose coterminously in all oceans. Repressed in early U.S. Pacific discourse, of course, is the role of Western Europe's Pacific trade in the world system prior to 1800. Spain's trans-Pacific silver trade, which linked several major economies, is one notable example. America's Pacific[54] is an extension, temporally and geographically, of the "American West," but nineteenth-century U.S. expansionists and imperialists spoke not solely in the language of expansion outward and beyond into the new. The globe's finite circularity made the expansion into the final frontier also a return to putative origins. William Seward, Lincoln's secretary of state, saw in the geographical position of the United States, between the Atlantic and the Pacific and thus in a sense "between" Western Europe and East Asia, in Hegelian terms: as originally an impediment to, but finally a catalyst for a life-renewing completion of a temporalized circle. The putatively millennia-old logic of pure expansionism posited an eternal westward movement, "until the tides of the renewed and the decaying civilizations of the world meet on the shores of the Pacific Ocean"[55] or, as John Hay would write later in the century, "where the Far West becomes the Far East."[56] The physical presence of North America, found unexpectedly in Western Europe's great oceanic gamble, becomes installed into a crucial position in the dialectic which pushes history to completion. Fused in the overflow of the land of the new, the two old continents are regenerated.

But for the United States to function as pure synthesis, various old binaries had to end. The Pacific, as extension of the U.S. western frontier, had to become something less than, or unlike, an ocean. Mid-century writers such as Melville or Fenimore Cooper made much of the connection between the inland prairie and the ocean (as did Carl O. Sauer a century later). This move is both a projection of the interior into the exterior and a claim for U.S. capacity to absorb its newly prairied outside, just as the terrestrial prairies had been conquered, graded, and apportioned. The rhetoric of late-nineteenth- and early-twentieth-century U.S. expansionists is full of efforts to make the Pacific less than an ocean, as in Whitelaw Reid's use of the term "American Lake," or less than water, as in Admiral Alfred Mahan's terrestrializing logic in his enormously influential advocacy of increased U.S. naval power at the end of the nineteenth century.

Mahan's ocean was an ocean over which land powers communicated. Throughout *The Influence of Sea Power upon History 1660–1783*, first published in 1890, he uses a language that suggests, according to a particularly U.S. logic, many fundamental equivalences between sea and land. For example:

> The first and most obvious light in which the sea presents itself from the political and social point of view is that of a great highway; or better, perhaps, of a wide common, over which men may pass in all directions, but on which some well-worn paths show that controlling reasons have led them to choose certain lines of travel rather than others. These lines of travel are called trade routes; and the reasons which have determined them are to be sought in the history of the world.[57]

Mahan's notion of sea-lanes, and the importance of their control, influenced U.S. strategy in Asia and the Pacific through the cold war, long after long-range weapons had made such strategic considerations totally irrelevant. It was the strength of Mahan's terrestrializing vision, his notion of an ocean crisscrossed by highways and bridges, that ensured his continued influence on U.S. Pacific strategy.

Douglas MacArthur recalled his expansionist predecessor Whitelaw Reid in referring to the Pacific as an "Anglo-Saxon lake." MacArthur's Pacific is totally terrestrialized: MacArthur the cold war warrior saw the chain of islands from Japan, through Taiwan, and down to the Philippines as the forward line of the cold war frontier; MacArthur the World War II strategist saw the chain of U.S. possessions from the Philippines, through Midway and Hawaii not simply as a projection or extension of U.S. power, but also as a line of vulnerability leading back into the heartland. Colonies conceived as liabilities to the colonial power is an old imperialist trope, of course, but MacArthur's early ambivalence about just what was happening on the "Anglo-Saxon lake" is symptomatic of a particularly American form of imperialism, which never sees itself as a colonial power. Rather, the U.S. colonial mission is always limited in time and merely an agent in the greater logic of commerce and development. This was an imperialism that adopted some of the logic of transparency that we have seen in the language of ocean trade. That the U.S. imperial project in the Pacific would center on commercialism, rather than overt pursuit of possession, was recognized frankly by William Seward. U.S. expansionist policy in the Pacific and in East Asia was justified by its liberal defenders as not an extension of the U.S. as political power, but of the extension of the idea of open access and free trade as embodied in the United States as a political and ideological unit. The terrestrializing of the Pacific thus had as its obverse a Pacification of Asia and the Pacific islands: a borderless proto-rim where free access reigned.

The American completion of the circle and the ushering in of the age of deliverance was a myth that served imperial and expansionist interests well. It also served anti-imperialist, antinationalist, and antifascist internationalist tendencies. Late-nineteenth-century anti-imperialists in the United States saw clearly the connection between the U.S. moves in Hawaii and the Philippines and the oppression of African Americans at home, and saw both as atavistic holdovers.[58] During the first half of the twentieth century, there was a belief among socialists and left liberals that a democratic U.S. tradition could be strengthened and fulfilled by the right kind of international behavior. The Asia scholars associated with the Institute for Pacific Relations and the journal *Amerasia,* represent a tradition that is *pre*–cold war—antifascist, left-wing humanist. As E. H. Norman, Canadian founding editor, wrote in 1937, in the first issue of *Amerasia:*

> We are also united in striving to attain the ultimate objective of promoting among all peoples inhabiting the periphery of the Pacific Ocean a harmony of relationships which transcend the merely legalistic concepts of justice with its emphasis on property over human rights or upon specious national honor or sovereignty over the economic welfare and the spiritual needs of the 700 million people who live on the islands or in the countries bordering the Pacific.[59]

The Golden Gate International Exposition in San Francisco, held on Treasure Island (especially constructed for that purpose) in 1939–1940, also partook of this liberal internationalist spirit. The exposition has been condemned by exposition connoisseurs for its crass commercialism, but this might be in part because its aesthetic instincts were more populist. Structures such as the exhibition's Elephant Towers, a cubist vision of a Mayan-Cambodian hybrid, were far less monumental and imposing than the Beaux Arts aesthetic that dominated the more consciously imperial Panama Pacific International Exposition of 1915, though the same architects were in charge of both projects. This 1939 vision of the Pacific, a cross between WPA populist aesthetics and Trader Vic's, prefigured the postwar boom of the South Pacific style which swept Los Angeles, particularly the white suburbs of the San Fernando Valley, in the 1950s and 1960s. This was a time of tikis and tiki torches, and of barbecues in orchidean backyard lanais, where, to the "exotic" sounds of Martin Denny's Hawaiian combo, newly arrived southern Californians could imagine themselves part of a transpacific postwar paradise of pure relaxation, where the Polynesian bliss of "interchangeable days" extolled in Melville's *Typee* could be enjoyed at least on weekends.[60]

The last major U.S. prophet of an oceanic vision is Charles Olson, who published his study of Melville, *Call Me Ishmael,* in 1947.[61] Many of the various strands of oceanic thinking I have been exploring thus far come together in this book, as well as in *The Mayan Letters* and certain of the *Maximus Poems.* Much of Olson's creative life was devoted to a search for origins: he studied Mayan, Sumerian, Egyptian, and Babylonian myths and just prior to writing *Call Me Ishmael* had begun to read Freud, whom he claimed as a major influence. Olson's search for origins was a search for deliverance, as in political Freudianism. For Olson, that deliverance was found on the Pacific.

Olson read Freud and worked on *Call Me Ishmael* while serving during the war at the Office of War Information, in its early years a bastion of liberal antifascist idealism that was a direct descendant of the federally supported writers projects of the New Deal.[62] Olson had become an admirer of Mao Tsetung (who later would emerge as the twentieth century's foremost heroic swimmer; his river swims were emblematic to many Chinese of the power of the revolutionary will). *The Mayan Letters* and poems from the 1950s such as "The Kingfisher" quote Mao with approval and partake of a sense of a trans-Pacific deliverance for Mexico and the West in general. Mao was an appropriate icon for Olson's posthumanist, postsubjective projectivist aesthetic, and Olson seems to have thought at one time that there was a real chance that the United States' China policy, swept up in an antifascist tide, could be oriented toward Mao, reflecting a Henry Wallace-ite social democratic triumph internally. The right-wing U.S. China lobby triumphed in its efforts to turn U.S. policy against Mao Tse-tung and the CCP, though, specifically by the cancellation of Vice President Henry Wallace's planned visit with Mao in 1944.[63] The cold war was beginning to emerge from World War II. For Olson and like-minded antifascists, the U.S. wrong turn became more clear with the dumping of Henry Wallace in favor of Harry Truman for vice president at the 1944 convention and the gradual ascent of anticommunism over antifascism.

Olson, like many U.S. leftists, had eschewed the search for an electoral political cure for Western culture's sickness as the national security state consolidated at the end of World War II. He chose poetry and vision, and an early version of the spatial fix that would resurface later, as we have seen, in various forms. Olson subscribed to a westward-moving teleology of Pacific circle-completion that was purely American but gave it a projectivist twist that promised to leave its place-boundedness behind, while retaining the spatiality that was so essential to his projectivist poetics. "Space has a stubborn way of sticking to Americans, penetrating all the way in, accompanying them. It is the exterior fact. The basic exterior act is a BRIDGE. Take them in order as they came: caravel, prairie schooner, national road, railway, plane. Now in the Pacific THE CARRIER. Trajectory. We must go over space, or we wither."[64] The progress is from bridge to carrier; from a journey that begins and ends in terrestriality to a pure trajectory, a pure oceanic deliverance.[65] In the final Pacific trajectory, of which Olson's Melville was a prophet, Western exploration, and the humanist-individualism that it both depended upon and engendered, is over, and the posthumanist, postindividualist imaginary that had been temporarily corrupted by fascism can finally be lived authentically. Olson's mythology of the Pacific as site of trajectory depended, however (and here he shared ground with U.S. imperialists and expansionists), on the Pacific as empty space, a void whose conscious crossing would de-terrestrialize and render void the finished inland expanses. U.S. citizens could live the collectivity that was their destiny: "The Pacific is the end of the UNKNOWN which Homer's and Dante's Ulysses opened men's eyes to. END of individual's responsibility only to himself. Ahab is full stop."[66] The last section of *Call Me Ishmael*, from which both of the above passages are quoted, is called "Conclusion: Pacific Man."

The Body of Pacific Man

Ferenczi's thalassal regressive trend is dependent on a logic of autotomy, the reflexive dropping off of an irritating, painful, or traumatized organ, such as the commonly observed phenomenon of the lizard dropping its tail. This antecedent stage of repression in reptiles and lower organisms surfaces in the male erection, which for Ferenczi represents the male desire to detach the penis from the rest of the body. Ferenczi's phallus, a miniaturized version of the ego itself, is striving to be a fish swimming in the intrauterine sea.[67] Pacific man, egoless, posthumanist, collective, constantly nourished by the sea of milk, filled with the oceanic feeling, is a fish. The phylogenetic journey from land to sea was made before, by whales, whose autotomy was nearly complete. Ahab's hunt was after devolution.

Many of the swimmers in Sprawson's book speak of the "feel for water" necessary in successful competitive swimming. Early English swimmers, until Victorian times, resisted wearing clothes; pre-Victorian, like most Weimar swimmers, were mostly nude, presumably to avoid interference with the feeling. The practice of body shaving began with Australian swimmers in the 1950s and spread to the United States in the 1960s. The better times made by shaved swimmers were not due to decreased resistance—the tiny air bubbles that formed around body hair counted for nothing—but to what Olympic swimmer Murray Rose described as "the immediate sensual awareness of the water as he dived in, the feeling that he was suspended, united with the element."[68] Shaving was the first stage of the swimmer's autotomy.

Traces of regionally specific bodily modification remain in popular versions of Pacific Rim discourse. The Pacific Rim denizen par excellence, the free-floating de-corporealized "symbolic analyst" in Robert Reich's *The Work of Nations,* is the latest indication of the effort of transnational capital to appropriate a postindividual fish/cyborg to its own ends. The Pacific Rim body is most visible, naturally, in film and theater, and body modification is rarely absent in U.S. productions on trans-Pacific themes. David Hwang's *M. Butterfly* is analyzable in terms of orientalist fantasy and cross-gender politics, but also as an instancing of a new Pacific body.

The "opening of China" film and television documentaries in the 1970s devoted an inordinate amount of time to shots of large crowds of young and old practicing the fluid movements of *taijiquan* (tai chi). Pacific men like the Nick Nolte character in *Who'll Stop the Rain* (Karel Reisz, 1978) and various western kung-fu fighters show in their practice of *taijiquan* evidence of an inner, spiritual development that complements their physical power: East meets West. Peter Wang's *A Great Wall* is a trans-Pacific roots-search cum Pacific family formation film, and Leo Fang, the Chinese-American father played by the director, becomes a convert to *taijiquan* in his suburban Bay Area patio by the film's end. The San Francisco Mime Troupe's 1993 production, "Offshore," is a critique of transnational capital's operations and a satire of Pacific Rim booster-ism. One of the characters, Carlton Lee, is a Chinese-American entrepreneur who wants to help a Sacramento valley electronics firm relocate production to southeast China. His first song, "My Time," reads:

> I'm the new man, of the future
> On the brink, no illusion
> Brand new link, East West fusion
> It's my turn, it's my time
>
> Got the soul of Confucius and the balls of Donald Trump
> I do my Tai Chi work out with barbells to pump
> I like my Chinese folksongs with a country western beat
> Got a laser graphic abacus to add my balance sheet
>
> Europe's lost its luster
> America's over the hill
> The future's the Pacific
> Golden Boy's Gonna Kill.[69]

The American workers in *Gung Ho* (Ron Howard, 1985), a film about Japanese-American cooperation to revive a decaying U.S. steel-belt town, initially ridi-cule their new Japanese boss's insistence on Japanese-style group exercises at the beginning of each working day. At the film's end, though, with the achievement of a new and successful production style forged of Japanese cooperativeness and seriousness purged of its rigidity though an American "go for it" enthusi-asm, the American workers do enthusiastic group jumping jacks, producing trans-Pacific bodies on and off the shop floor.

Autotomic loss of limbs and extremities—the Pacific Rim body as a body without extremities—figured prominently in two U.S. yakuza films that ap-peared at the beginning and end points of Pacific Rim discourse, *Yakuza* (Syd-ney Pollack, 1975) and *Black Rain* (Ridley Scott, 1989).[70] Pacific Man is formed primarily through finger loss (in both films, the yakuza custom of autodigitec-tomy as a sign of loyalty is given major play); the character of Charlie (played by Andy Garcia) in *Black Rain* achieves his greatest transpacific signifying power after his decapitation.

Pacific Rim body formation has been a rare filmic trope since Pacific Rim discourse began to attenuate in 1989. The iron-pumping body for men and women, revived in action films like *Terminator 2* and in music videos by Marky

Mark and Madonna, is not a body for tai chi or swimming, but for aggression or self-defense during a period whose mythology makes few appeals to the transnational or global imaginary. In the United States in the early 1990s, all regions are local, and they aren't on rims.

U.S. capital's mobilization of the Pacific Rim myth in the late cold war years, with its regional utopianism and its accretions of the self-transcendence, transformation, and interconnection promised in various versions of the oceanic feeling, was a discursive strategy that allowed the channeling of even the most liberatory Western visions into a naturalized capitalist logic. The inconsistent life of the discourse—it fades in and out—shows that capital, even as it becomes daily more invisible in its operation, is still incapable of generating a sustained and convincing global mythos. Since there is clearly some kind of need for globalist thinking, it is important that socialism not abandon the global sphere. In a similar vein, by de-nationalizing and globalizing questions of race and ethnicity in *The Black Atlantic,* Paul Gilroy rescues these critical categories from localized essentialisms. As for the Pacific, people like the King of Tonga, the Bamboo Ridge writers, Epeli Hau'ofa,[71] Rob Wilson, and some of the other authors in this volume are mounting a claim for it as a local, rather than as a universal or millenarian, ocean. This new spatialization does not merely serve to generate another "site of contestation," a new academic currency. The Pacific as Last Ocean was the final link, the totalizing telic symbol of the global saturation of capital. The Pacific as locality pulls a large part of the globe back out of the end of history, and might make it imaginable as a place where capital's hegemony could be *un*-imagined, rather than totalized.

Notes

1   See my "Pacific Rim Discourse: The U.S. Global Imaginary in the Late Cold War Years," *boundary 2* 21, no. 1 (Spring 1994): 30–56. Important critiques of the Pacific Rim idea and other late capitalist myths of the Pacific/Asia region are found in Bruce Cumings, "The Political Economy of the Pacific Rim," in *Pacific Asia and the Future of the World System,* ed. Ravi Palat (Westport: Greenwood Press, 1993); Arif Dirlik, "The Asia-Pacific Idea: Reality and Representation in the Invention of a Regional Structure," *Journal of World History* 3 (Spring 1992); Masao Miyoshi, *Off Center: Power and Cultural Relations between Japan and the United States* (Cambridge: Harvard University Press, 1991) and "A Borderless World? From Colonialism to Transnationalism and the Decline of the Nation-State" in this volume; Rob Wilson's essays in this volume, his book, *Reimagining the American Pacific: From* South Pacific *to Bamboo Ridge* (forthcoming, Duke University Press), and Rob Wilson and Arif Dirlik, "Introduction: Asia/Pacific as Space of

Cultural Production," in Wilson and Dirlik, eds., *Asia/Pacific as Space of Cultural Production*. I would like to acknowledge here the help and encouragement I received from Jim Clifford, Arif Dirlik, Carla Freccero, Susan Gilman, Sharon Kinoshita, Masao Miyoshi, Mary Scott, Carter Wilson, and Rob Wilson.

2   The Pacific Rim never had a totalizing claim on the geo-imaginary, nor did it come to a definitive end in 1989. It coexisted with racist and jingoist Japan-bashing, and versions of Pacific Rim discourse continue to surface today.

3   James O'Connor, *The Fiscal Crisis of the State* (New York: St. Martin's Press, 1973).

4   R. J. Johnston, "The State, the Region, and the Division of Labor," in *Production, Work, Territory: The Geographical Anatomy of Industrial Capitalism*, ed. Allen Scott and Michael Storper (Boston: Allen and Unwin, 1986), p. 272.

5   Bruce Cumings, "Political Economy," p. 23.

6   Edward Soja, *Postmodern Geographies: The Reassertion of Space in Critical Social Theory* (London: Verso, 1989), p. 189.

7   See Christopher Connery, "Pacific Rim Discourse," for a more complete list.

8   However, one of the major texts of critical regionalism contains within its preface (both the passage's location in the preface and its tone indicate the extraneous character of the argument) the following instancing of what can only be read as barely repressed Rimspeak:

> This book, like all human projects, grew from a particular material base set in time and place. Our good fortune has been to live and work in California. This amazing state is now to be numbered among the mightiest industrial economies on earth, and serves as the core territory for the aerospace, micro-electronics, and film industries, a troika of powers for good and ill like none other in today's world. Those living in the eastern United States and in Europe are, it must be said, often disinclined to take Californians seriously; the latter reciprocate by exporting the personal computer, Star Wars, and Ronald Reagan. Our perspective has been skewed in important ways by the view from California, on the edge of the booming northern Pacific Rim; hence the overriding emphasis given here to economic growth and geographic expansion in modern industrialization. To the observer looking out from the brutal terrain of Liverpool's docklands, south Chicago, or the slums of Kingston, this emphasis will doubtless appear to give a rosy tint to capitalism's forward march, painting a picture that does little justice to those left behind, left out, or ground beneath the juggernaut. Nevertheless, others are better positioned to depict the devastation of unemployment in the First World or underdevelopment and imperialism in the Third.

Michael Storper and Richard Walker, *The Capitalist Imperative: Territory, Technology, and Industrial Growth* (New York: Basil Blackwell 1989), p. ix. A version of Pacific Rim discourse could also be operative in Edward Soja's book, which ends with a case study of Los Angeles, illustrative of the new critical regionalism. The title of his penultimate chapter "It All Comes Together in Los Angeles," is both a celebration of critical regionalism's promise and an ironic commentary on Pacific Rim boosterism, wherein L.A. is the capital of the Rim. One must ask, though, whether irony is sufficient armor against the interpellative power of Rimspeak?

9   Storper and Walker, *Capitalist Imperative*, p. 183.

10   Alexander Besher, *The Pacific Rim Almanac* (New York: Harper Perennial, 1990), p. xxi–xxii.

11   Kenichi Ohmae, *The Borderless World* (New York: Harper Business, 1990), p. x–xi.

12   For the idea of the "created Pacific," see O. H. K. Spate, *The Spanish Lake* (Minneapolis: University of Minnesota Press, 1979), p. 1, and all of chap. 1, "The World Without the Pacific."

13   For other trajectories of the Western imagination of the ocean see: Alain Corbin, *The Lure of the Sea: The Discovery of the Seaside in the Western World 1750–1849*, trans. Jocelyn Phelps (Berkeley and Los Angeles: U.C. Press 1994); and Jean-Didier Urbain, *Sur la plage: Mœurs et coutumes balnéaires* (Paris: Editions Payot), 1994.

14   Sigmund Freud, *Civilization and Its Discontents*, trans. James Strachey (New York: W.W. Norton, 1962), p. 11.

15   The vagueness of Freud's notion of sublimation results, according to Norman O. Brown, in Freud's lack of sufficient analysis of the antagonism between "man and culture." What was needed was attention to social transformation. Norman O. Brown, *Life Against Death: The Psychoanalytical Meaning of History* (Middletown: Wesleyan University Press, 1959), pp. 139 ff. See also Norman O. Brown, *Love's Body* (New York: Vintage, 1966), chap. 8: "Boundary."

16   Rob Wilson, *American Sublime: The Genealogy of a Poetic Genre* (Madison: University of Wisconsin Press, 1991), p. 211.

17   Herman Melville, *Moby Dick*, chap. 23, "The Lee Shore" (Berkeley: University of California Press, 1979), p. 111.

18   Rob Wilson, *American Sublime*, p. 12.

19   Roland Barthes, *Mythologies*, trans. Annette Lavers (New York: Farrar, Straus, and Giroux, 1991), p. 112.

20   Rob Wilson, *American Sublime*, p. 56.

21   Gaston Bachelard, *Water and Dreams: An Essay on the Imagination of Matter*, trans. Edith R. Farrell (Dallas: Pegasus Foundation, 1983), p. 6.

22   Gaston Bachelard, *Water and Dreams*, p. 152.

23   Ibid., p. 153.

24   W. H. Auden. *The Enchafèd Flood; or The Romantic Iconography of the Sea* (New York: Random House, 1950), pp. 6–7.

25   Rod Giblett, "Philosophy (and Sociology) in the Wetlands: The S(ub)lime and the Uncanny," *New Formations*, no. 18 (Winter 1992): 159.

26   Ibid., p. 147. This is a chart.

27   Jules Michelet, *La Mer*, ed. Marie-Claude Chemin and Paul Viallaneix (Lausanne: L'Age d'Homme, 1980), p. 76. For analysis of the rhetorical strategies in *La Mer*, see Linda Orr, *Jules Michelet: Nature, History and Language* (Ithaca: Cornell University Press, 1976), pp. 152–174.

28 Jules Michelet, *La Mer*, pp. 193–194.

29 Ibid., p. 74.

30 Gaston Bachelard, *Water and Dreams*, p. 167.

31 Ibid., p. 168.

32 Ibid., p. 179.

33 "Water is best," first line of Pindar's *Olympian Odes* and adopted in 1828 as the motto for the Old Etonian swimming society. From Charles Sprawson, *Haunts of the Black Masseur: The Swimmer as Hero* (New York: Random House, 1992), p. 83.

34 The etymology of the word "explore"—to cry out at the sight of land—suggests that all explorations are ocean voyages whose goal is a return to land.

35 Alister Clavering Hardy, *Darwin and the Spirit of Man* (London: Collins, 1984). Also Alister Clavering Hardy, *The Living Stream: A Restatement of Evolution Theory and Its Relation to the Spirit of Man* (London: Collins, 1965). See also Carl O. Sauer, "Concerning Primeval Habitat and Habit," in Carl O. Sauer, *Selected Essays 1963–1975* (Berkeley: Turtle Island, 1981), pp. 109–110.

36 Carl O. Sauer, "Concerning Primeval," p. 111.

37 Digby's entire text, with woodblock illustrations, is reprinted in Nicholas Orme, *Early British Swimming: 55 B.C.–A.D. 1719* (Exeter: University of Exeter, 1983). This passage is from page 126.

38 Quoted in Charles Sprawson, *Haunts*, p. 207.

39 Ibid., p. 23.

40 Ibid., p. 22.

41 As evidenced partly in the unacknowledged appropriation of Third World technical resources. The stroke became popularly known as the "Australian" crawl rather than by a name that reflected its true origins.

42 The most useful work on eros and the death instinct remains Norman O. Brown, *Life Against Death: The Psychoanalytic Meaning of History*. See especially chap. 8, "Death, Time, and Eternity," and chap. 9, "Death and Childhood."

43 Sandor Ferenczi, *Thalassa: A Theory of Genitality*, trans. Henry Alden Bunker (New York: Psychoanalytic Quarterly, 1938), pp. 49–50.

44 Sprawson mentions that all of the famous male swimmers in his book were reported to have had strong attachments to their mothers and alienation from their fathers. This is of course the claim made about nearly all marginalized groups in contemporary western society. Sprawson, *Haunts*, p. 145.

45 Norman O. Brown, *Life Against Death*, p. 102.

46 G. W. F. Hegel, *The Philosophy of History*, trans. J. Sibree (New York: Dover, 1956), p. 90.

47 Joseph Schumpeter, *Capitalism, Socialism, and Democracy* (New York: Harper, 1950), p. 160.

48 The significant identification of Greeks with ocean trade is made everywhere, and the passage in the *Anabasis* was such a common school text in England that it remained in the memory of nearly every English bourgeois who had received a classical education. For a representative text on the oceanic character of the ancient Greeks, see Alfred

Zimmern, *The Greek Commonwealth: Politics and Economics in Fifth Century Athens* (Oxford: Clarendon, 1931), p. 318 and pp. 24–35, 314 ff.

49 Anders Stephanson, *Kennan and the Art of Foreign Policy* (Cambridge: Harvard University Press, 1989), pp. 203–204.

50 Quoted in Mary Layoun, *Travels of a Genre: The Modern Novel and Ideology* (Princeton: Princeton University Press, 1990), p. 252.

51 Géza Róheim, *The Origin and Function of Culture* (New York: Nervous and Mental Disease Monographs, 1943), p. 52.

52 Herring and cod, however, were probably more important than whales in voyages to Greenland and northeastern North America before 1600.

53 This is one of the points in A. R. Michell's article "The European Fisheries in Early Modern History," quoted in Immanuel Wallerstein, *The Modern World System,* vol. 2. (New York: Academic Press, 1980), p. 39.

54 This is Rob Wilson's usage.

55 William Seward, quoted in Richard Drinnon, *Facing West: The Metaphysics of Indian-hating and Empire-building* (Minneapolis: University of Minnesota Press, 1980), p. 271.

56 Quoted in Bruce Cumings, *The Origins of the Korean War,* vol. 2 (Princeton: Princeton University Press, 1990), p. 24.

57 Alfred T. Mahan, *The Influence of Sea Power upon History 1660–1783* (Boston: Little, Brown, 1918), p. 25.

58 See Philip S. Foner and Richard C. Winchester, eds., *The Anti-Imperialist Reader: A Documentary History of Anti-Imperialism in the United States, vol. 1: From the Mexican War to the Election of 1900* (New York: Holmes and Meier, 1984), particularly the chapters on the Philippine war and the annexation of Hawaii.

59 Quoted in John W. Dower, ed., *Origins of the Modern Japanese State: Selected Writings of E. H. Norman* (New York: Pantheon, 1975), 38–39.

60 For an earlier playing out of Pacific identities, see Beth Bailey and David Farber, *The First Strange Place: The Alchemy of Race and Sex in World War II Hawaii* (New York: Free Press, 1992).

61 Although Robinson Jeffers could lay claim to being the United States' most important twentieth-century poet of the Pacific, Jeffers's sublime Pacific was a call to the final inhuman; it was the Pacific from which the early Robert Frost fled, as evidenced in Frost's "Once By the Pacific."

62 Allan M. Winkler, *The Politics of Propaganda: The Office of War Information 1942–1945* (New Haven: Yale University Press, 1978), p. 21. Tom Clark, *Charles Olson: The Allegory of a Poet's Life* (New York: Norton, 1991), pp. 84–107.

63 Tom Clark, *Charles Olson,* p. 85.

64 Charles Olson, *Call Me Ishmael* (New York: Reynal and Hitchcock, 1947), p. 114.

65 Recalling also the Walt Whitman of "Crossing Brooklyn Ferry," "O Pioneers," and "Out of the Cradle, Endlessly Rocking."

66 Charles Olson, *Call Me Ishmael,* p. 119.

67 John Cowper Powys, in *A Philosophy of Solitude* (New York: Simon and Schuster, 1933),

writes at length of the ichthyosaurus ego, a devolutionary retreat from the vulgarity and horror of contemporary life. Needless to say, the ichthyosaurus ego lived aquatically.

68   Charles Sprawson, *Haunts,* p. 14.

69   San Francisco Mime Troupe, "Offshore," 1993. Lyrics by Joan Holden, with Chung Chiao, Patrick Lee, Keiko Shimosato, and Michael Gene Sullivan.

70   See my "Pacific Rim Discourse: The U.S. Global Imaginary in the Late Cold War Years" for additional material on these films.

71   See, for example, his paper "Our Sea of Islands," in *A New Oceania: Rediscovering Our Sea of Islands,* ed. Eric Waddell (Suva: School of Social and Economic Development at the University of the South Pacific, 1993), pp. 2–16.

GOODBYE PARADISE:

GLOBAL/LOCALISM IN THE

AMERICAN PACIFIC

Rob Wilson

●

A frightening type of *papalagi* architecture is invading Oceania: the super-stainless, super-plastic, super-hygenic, super-soulless structure very similar to modern hospitals; and its most nightmarish form is the new-type tourist hotel—a multi-story edifice of concrete, steel, chromium and air-conditioning.—Albert Wendt, "Towards a New Oceania"

Ever wonder why there is a McKinley Street and a McKinley High School, but no Cleveland *anything* in Hawai'i?—H. K. Bruss Keppeler, "Native Hawaiian Claims"

Our visitors [tourists] come here with a perception of what Hawaii is to them—Paradise. —Visitors Experience Task Force, 1993 Tourism Congress[1]

Cyborgs Across the Asian/Pacific

Recent figurings of capitalism as a global system, associated with the rise of postmodernism into First World cultural dominance and the heteroglossia of postcolonial contentions, have been driven by various material forces. These forces, at a macrolevel of analysis, would include: a telecommunications revolution in media, transnationalization of production and the rise of the transnational corporation as the locus of economic activity, and the change of the modernist nation-state from manipulator of internal conflict and territorial paranoia over NATO and the Pacific to just-in-time manager of what Kenichi Ohmae pronounces as the new "borderless interlinked economy."[2] Accelerated during the creative-destruction dynamic of the 1980s, cybernetic technologies and more global modes of production/representation have generated what cultural critics and management gurus alike now recognize as "the globalization of capitalism" on a sweeping scale of global/local interaction that is the source "at once of unprecedented unity globally and of unprecedented fragmentation," as Arif Dirlik has outlined.[3] We are only just beginning to come to terms with the post-national geopolitics and cultural implications of this new global/local interface, entrenchments of community and power into forms of place-bound identity, and what Arjun Appadurai has called "the global production of locality."

In Asian/Pacific interzones of heightened globalization and localization, "global cities" like Taipei, Hong Kong, and Singapore have sprung up—cities that unevenly fuse transnational technologies to local customs. Thus can be seen the re-articulation of Confucian spiritualism to the labor of microchip production and fashion semiotics. Masahiro Mori, lauding such developments, has even made the technoeuphoric claim that cyborgs of transnational construction "have the buddha-nature within them."[4] In effect, the Pacific Rim is being transformed into a region of *dematerialized cyberspace* linking the Pacific coast of California to Hong Kong and Japan (as foreshadowed in spectacles like *Blade Runner*). Pacific Rim sites are said to play a vanguard role in this global/local restructuring and, in effect, are helping to decenter settler countries like the United States, Canada, and Australia from narratives of national identity that would look back to the Western Europe-as-old-world capitalism model. *Globloc* is the new coinage in postmodern Japan, I have heard: the intensified permeability of any locale in the age of our global economy makes for the world shopping-mall culture of a consumption-oriented novel rooted in brand-glutted subjectivity like Banana Yoshimoto's *Kitchen* or Douglas Coupland's North American world drifters and global "mcjob" hunters in *Generation X*.

The United States is a refiguring cold war nation-state facing the last phases of military hegemony in the Pacific region: it spreads across the Asia/Pacific ocean like some clunky old-world (nuclearized, Fordist, military-industrialized) First World godzilla. By diverse accounts, the local as ground and space of cultural identity is increasingly being integrated into—if resistant of—global agents and transcultural forces across this new Pacific in ways, I will claim, that challenge and undermine the imagined community of the settler nation-state.

As one cultural premonition, consider Philip K. Dick's geoimaginary vision of San Francisco in the year 2018 in *Do Androids Dream of Electric Sheep?* (1968). The Rosen Association, which engineers and produces the "Nexus-6" android, has already spread across the Pacific coast of the United States to a passive Russia, as well as to an offworld colony of "New America" on Mars. This transglobal corporation is so flexible and mobile in its high-tech feats of generating temporary-contract cyborgian labor that the transnational police forces of these nation- and city-states cannot prohibit (or even locate) them. If agency of production has been globally mystified, as in *Blade Runner*, the colonial dynamics of global capital remain intact and rising: "Legally, the manufacturers of the Nexus-6 brain unit operated under colonial law, their parent autofactory being on Mars."[5]

In Dick's novel the romance-quest of Rick Deckard to find and police the very boundary between the human and the high technological depends on his prior film-noir-like search to locate the agents, corporations, and instruments of global capital in its latest transnational and supralegal mode. These biocustom-engineered cyborgs of the Asia/Pacific that Deckard searches for within the neocolonizing heart of late-capitalist desire would serve, as the TV ads for the Rosen Association announce, to duplicate those "halcyon days of the pre–Civil War Southern states" as "body servants or tireless field hands." Short of this racial humiliation, feminized cyborgs can be turned (like the "Rachel Rosen" prototype) into pleasure machines for scopophilic desire like so many postpastoral electric sheep chewing on the grasses in a transnational limbo.[6]

As John Naisbitt and Patricia Aburdene hector the case for transnational prosperity in *Megatrends 2000*, if belatedly preparing the U.S. cold war imaginary for "the rise of the Pacific Rim" and new strategies of compulsory globalization, "In the fast-paced Pacific Rim, the economic advantages belong to the swift."[7] Given global capitalization of the Asian/Pacific local, power/knowledge still belongs to the conquest of space by time: that is, to the dematerialized movements of hypercapital and information highways across the Pacific as commodity chains diffuse across regions and reconfigure nation and globe into a cybernetic matrix of speed and profit.

Given this global restructuring of local spaces of identity and prior community, multiplex Pacific Basin cultures inside the Pacific Rim do not factor in as agents or locations of resistance so much as sites of tourist simulacrum and rest (or vacant spaces for weapons disposal) for Pacific Rim profit, tropological production, and pleasure. As postnational subject, in *Electric Sheep* Deckard moves from the servomechanism of the American nation-state to become that lovable lackey, a Pacific Rim megatrend agent.

Later, down the highway toward *transnational postmodernity* and "jacking" into the disembodied rush of space-become-information-matrix, Rick Deckard is superseded by the cyborg cowboy, Case, in William Gibson's *Neuromancer*, for whom the whole world has become a "Chiba City" of global instantaneity. Turning the Pacific into sublime cyberspace, Gibson's heroes of transnational euphoria can leap across the orientalist dangers of cybernetic infinitude, forever in the hire of an evermore dematerializing corporation: "With his deck, he [Case] could reach the Freeside decks as easily as he could reach Atlanta. Travel was a meat thing."[8] Labor is a meat thing too, as feminist critics have shown of the transnational exploitation that now goes on in "peasant Asia" and the *maquiladoras* of Mexico. From Tokyo to the trans-American sprawl, the dynamics of the Pacific Rim (from one view in Vancouver) have all but dissolved into what William Gibson has lyricized "the bodiless exultation of cyberspace,"[9] as the doped-up cyborg promises to redeem the local Pacific from global isolation, if not the race and class contradictions of material history, in a new *transnational sublime.*

The neo-eclecticism of postmodern philosophies and tastes to consume, create, and mimic cultural difference and nomadic flux—what James Clifford et al. would now theorize and embrace as so many "discrepant cosmopolitanisms" routing and rerooting across spaces of local globality[10]—cannot be dissociated from the mode of postindustrial production. An "eclecticism in labor practices" and an international redivisioning of labor is taking place such that sweat shops and family labor systems can coexist in the same urban space with spectacular telecommunication networks that would dematerialize local earth and sweatshop into the capitalogic of time-as-money.[11] Clifford's invocation of a "hybridity" discourse, which has all but achieved normative status in postcolonial studies, aims to articulate a third or *in-between* space of "borders/ diasporas." This aim is such that modernist binary oppositions of global capital posed against local culture are resisted and textualized even as to-and-fro transcultural flows (as in the scholarship of *Public Culture*) are foregrounded: "Too often we are left with an awkward gap between levels of analysis: generic global forces/specific local responses," as Clifford stages the opposition.

Riding the *diasporic* global/local interface of an ever-creolizing transnational cum local poetics emanating from the "black Atlantic" to the U.S./ Mexican border, Clifford would resist both a totalizing "globalism" that is self-defined as progressive and historically dynamic and any "localism" that remains too " 'rooted' (not routed) in place, tradition, culture, or ethnicity conceived in an absolutist mode." This warning against local entrenchment and praise of global hybridity should give us regional pause, however, especially in the Pacific Basin region where micropolitics and not just megatrends would trouble the postcolonial horizon with alternative spaces and claims. Aboriginal claims at the local level (resurgent in Hawaii, Australia, Taiwan, and New Zealand to be sure) can become subordinated, in such a "transcultural" euphoria analysis of the by-now-transnationalized *ethnoscape,* to more flexible/impure/creolized articulations of syncretic transformation at the border. The local needs to be worried into existence as the site of critical regionalism and what Raymond Williams called "the bond to place" as ground of resistance to transnational capitalism.[12]

The dynamism of capitalism as a global system has been tied to the *telos* of a technoeuphoric poetics of what David Harvey has called "creative destruction." In this poetics, as Karl Marx noted at the outset of technological modernity, "all that is solid melts into air" and those Chinese walls of tradition, region, and local identity are relentlessly battered down by commodity exchange, cultural interchange, and forces of technological innovation.[13] This bashing of the "Asiatic mode of production" has reached such an advanced state of Deleuzian sublimity, within cultures of Pacific Rim postmodernity, that Takayuki Tatsumi, reflecting on the spread of cyberpunk culture across the region during the hypercapitalist 1980s, can claim that, in science fiction visions of globalized space in *Neuromancer* (1984) and *Mona Lisa Overdrive* (1988), William Gibson had circulated "the signifier of Japanese language—like 'Chiba City' or 'Gomi no Sensei'—as its 'semiotic ghost'" without ever having visited Japan itself.[14] Gibson's "semio-tech" misperception of an overtechnologized matrix of cybernetic sublimity from a trans-Pacific Apple PC in Vancouver, Canada, feeds back into formations of "Japanese postmodernism" to refashion local style, techno-identity, and to prefigure everyday Japanese custom. (Japan's Ainu, needless to say, do not figure in technoeuphoric visions of Japanese postmodern identity as cyborgian "technoscape," as the feminist fiction of Tsushima Yuko has suggested in works like *Woman Running in the Mountains*.)

Pacific Rim visions of "flexible labor production" and the global mishmash of styles spreading across the Asia/Pacific reaches an epiphanic level of new-world intensity and global spectacle in Ridley Scott's *Blade Runner*. There, the Babel-like Tyrell Corporation pyramid rises up out of the filthy Third World heteroglossia of Los Angeles streets to dominate all prior modes of production ("I just make eyes" says old Chun in his refrigerated sweat shop in late capitalist Chinatown) and to intimidate urban subaltern agents ("He knows everything. He big genius"). Like some postmodern version of Blake's anti-God, Urizen, Tyrell seemingly reigns over space, time, capital, and body and panoptically enchains worker-subjects from a Tower of Babel ziggurat over the cityspeak. Although as Roy Baty, the Blakean-liberation cyborg, confesses to Tyrell before bashing out the corporate head's eyes with de-oedipalizing glee, "*You're a hard man to see.*" Today's grimy-chic "blade runner look" of postindustrial ruin and multicultural sublimity now rises, as in Los Angeles and

Vancouver—fusing with Tokyo and Hong Kong into "the 'capital of capital' in the Pacific Rim"—and threatens to turn into the cultural dominant of contemporary urban design. The look resurfaces in Ridley Scott's *Black Rain* (1989) as the trademark postindustrial skies hovering over Osaka.[15] Given global technologies of representation and image-exchange, Hollywood can in such blockbusters generate and control the emerging spaces and subjects of this Asian/ Pacific transnational sublime as a space of sheer cultural immensity (the multicultural city gone offshore if not "offworld") and of labor domination (the cyborg-human now starring as transnational subject).

Given brave new worlds and emergent regimes of global production flowing into older spaces of local culture, as well as more hybrid fusions of technology and organic agent into "buddha-nature," the difficulty facing postmodern cultural production at present is the contemporary problematic of "Time-Space" *unrepresentability*. By this I mean, the inability to map, cognize, or aesthetically represent at a local level what Fredric Jameson clunkily calls our "whole world system of present-day multinational capitalism" since this everyday totality impinges on disparate locales.[16]

Because the local, as refigured in various disciplines from cultural geography to ethnography to urban studies as some innovative and mobile global/ local interface, has to think and feel the power of global capitalism in its full spatiality, the aesthetics of region, place, and location are very much back on the postmodern agenda: "In clinging, often of necessity, to a place-bound identity, however," as David Harvey warns within contexts of global-local marketing propagated by Kenichi Ohmae, Robert Reich, and others, "such oppositional movements become a part of the very fragmentation which a mobile capitalism and flexible accumulation can feed upon."[17] The reassertion and coalitional construction of "place-bound identity," as I will detail through a focus on the Bamboo Ridge culture in Hawaii, nonetheless has become crucial to the preservation of cultural difference for many locals, given the spread of cyborgs across the Asia-Pacific zone. In the case of indigenous Hawaiians, this transnationalization of local space and identity threatens cultural survival itself.

"Paradise" in the Pacific

Confronting the power of transnational technologies of late-capitalist spectacle, localistic orientations have reasserted themselves in the face of overwhelming modernization in Hawaii, despite the fact (as Noel Kent has observed) that any " 'localism' is all too easily equated with parochialism in this metropolitan age."[18] Paradoxically, the most local works of postmodern cultural production in Hawaii are already affected if not *invaded*[19] by this geoimaginary problematic, such that the global/local interface is for Pacific authors a predicament they must work through in order to affirm and defend some enclave of "local culture."

This has been the case with the emergence of the "local literature" movement at *Bamboo Ridge* journal and press which, since its founding in Honolulu in 1978, has resisted the metropolitan assumption that writers in Hawaii "are subordinate to the mainland" or, as the local poet Eric Chock remarked, the belief that "we [in Hawaii] are really no different here and can even be *like* the mainland if we try hard enough."[20] It is within the context of "global localism" that I will discuss the localistic culture articulated in the movie *Goodbye Paradise* (1991), which, given Hawaii's *peripheralization* to the Pacific Rim economy of California, is the first feature-length movie ever to be produced entirely in Hawaii.[21] Kayo Hada's *Picture Bride* (1995) set in the ethnic plantation culture of Waialua Sugar Company in 1915, is only the second locally produced independent feature film to be made in Hawaii. Combining the work of Asian-American artists with transnational superstars like Toshiro Mifune from *Black Rain*, *Picture Bride* explores the ethnic makings, discrepancies, and tensions of plantation culture in Hawaii.

Goodbye Paradise, even in its tropologically overdetermined title, recalls earlier tropes and Edenic master-narratives of Hawaii as a lingering Asian/Pacific paradise in the South Seas. These tropes of gardenlike embodiment in the out-of-history (actually North) Pacific retain some material legitimacy in the postmodern American imagination, even while prior master-narratives of the United States as "utopia achieved" bite the deregulated dust of late capitalist Reaganomics.[22] Paul Theroux, wandering as voraciously as Malinowski or Henry Adams across the vast Pacific (his "happy isles of Oceania") in an inflatable kayak with a stack of Euro-American intertexts, a broken male heart, and a dog-eared copy of the *Sexual Life of Savages,* does not really find "the happy isles of Oceania" he craves until he is back in his multicultural Asian/Pacific home in Honolulu. "It often seemed to me that calling the Hawaiian Islands 'paradise' was not an exaggeration, though saying it out loud, advertising it, seemed to be tempting fate," Theroux confesses, just before ending his transnational tourist romance-quest for Pacific paradise in the $2,500-a-night Orchid Bungalow at the Mauna Lani.[23] Perhaps Armine von Tempski, in her 1940 autobiography *Born in Paradise,* put this claim for paradise in the American Pacific most ostentatiously (as befits the granddaughter of Polish nobility and heir to the sixty-thousand-acre Haleakala Ranch on Maui): "Attaining Paradise in the hereafter does not concern me greatly. I was born in Paradise."[24]

Not to be outdone by Armine von Tempski's Nietzschean literalization of the literary-Biblical trope of paradise as the Americanized Pacific, the team of legal, social, and economic policy theorists charting the materials costs of inhabiting the contemporary state of Hawaii in the cost-benefit collective analysis, *The Price of Paradise: Lucky We Live Hawaii?*, answer a qualified "yes" to affirming life in this tax-ridden Eden. Sumner J. La Croix, a professor of economics at the University of Hawaii at Manoa in Honolulu, assesses in chapter 21, "Cost of Housing," that, despite the highest housing and cost of living expenses in the United States, Honolulu has clean air, clean water, warm winters, moderate summers, beautiful forests and mountains, spectacular views, a culturally diverse ethnic population tied into Asian and Pacific culture, good food, a varied night life, and, he proudly concludes: "No place is right for everyone but, aside from the high cost of living, Hawaii is most people's idea of paradise."[25] *Most people's idea of paradise,* unless, for example, you are a native Hawaiian whose culture is being transformed into tourist simulacra or whose land has been alienated into military and state profit and for whom the struggle for national sovereignty is gathering juro-political force.

Can "paradise" be consensually recuperated and natives pacified in the ecotourism of the American Pacific, even within a cost-benefit analysis? Yes, claims the tourist-knowledge apparatus of *The Price of Paradise,* "as long as Honolulu retains its unique beauty, environment and cultural attractions"[26] and local citizens can endure a tourist-driven economy in which "we get less for more," as runs the volume's general refrain.[27] "Paradise," despite threats of overgovernment and international flux and tourist stagnation, is here—if only as a hegemonic regional trope—to stay.

The title of Eric Chock's Bamboo Ridge Press collection *Last Days Here* is meant to suggest the imminent phasing out of local Hawaiian culture, language, and customary difference in and around Honolulu's Chinatown. Chock's cultural ties to place-bound identity and community are strong, as shown in mixed-ethnic poems like "Tutu on Da Curb" ("Her hair all pin up in one bun, / one huge red hibiscus hanging out / over her right ear") or "Chinese Fireworks Banned in Hawaii" ("cousins eat jook from the huge vat / in the kitchen"). However, the title poem to his Pacific-local-oriented collection is more ominous. It shows a fished-out and polluted river near Honolulu Chinatown, where an old Chinese man fishes if only to keep his old customs and preserve his ghostly memories of place and keep local identity intact:

The empty bucket stares a moment
toward his brain, so he closes
the closet door, hums
the ashes off his cigar,
and goes in to dinner.
He will never forget his days here
In the dirt under the mango tree
prints of chicken feet
go every which way[28]

Given the costs of displacement and deskilling, "Paradise" (minus the chicken prints, ethnic smells, rotting tilapia, and sulking Hawaiian natives, to be sure) remains a white-mythological trope through which to structure and integrate Hawaii into the mainland and transnational tourist flow. Paradise tropes project a vacation space of Pacific culture that, despite much evidence to the contrary (such as the American-backed overthrow of the Hawaiian monarchy in 1893), remains outside the workaday labors of Euro-American history. Can "paradise" ever write back to challenge the Edenic fantasies of the American empire? One of cultural critic Stephen Sumida's strongest claims about the local literature movement in Hawaii that has flourished since the late Talk Story conferences of 1978 and 1979 is that, by resisting the sway of hegemonic national culture, "the facile image of Hawai'i as paradise, everywhere associated with pop literature, music, film, and travel poster-graphics of Hawai'i, is contradicted by nonfictional and fictional works [of local literature such as Milton Murayama's *All I Asking for Is My Body* (1975)] that may serve as prototypes in the development of Hawaii's literature beyond the simple pastoral."[29] Circulated through the pastoral discourse of authors like Mark Twain, Robert Louis Stevenson, and James Michener, and rehashed as the "Blue Hawaii" fantasy of American popular culture, "the facile image of Hawaii as paradise" has been challenged as the de-historicizing fantasy of a dominant culture expanding its terrain and *telos* of development-driven material prosperity—at whatever cost to indigenous or local culture—into the Asian-Pacific.

During this transnationalization, the outer island of Maui risks becoming a suburb for Hollywood scriptwriters. Posthurricane Kauai is doing everything it can to attract more Stephen Spielbergs to come over from the Rim, film more *Jurassic Parks*, and turn the wilderness and eco-history of Hawaii into a theme park. Even the backside of Diamond Head on Oahu was reconstructed by the former Waihee administration into a state-funded film studio. In short, this production of Hawaii into a "paradise of the Pacific" needs to be placed in politicized italics and undermined as a trope of the dominant discourse helping to naturalize the American idea of the Pacific as a dreamy space both within and outside (exotic oriental other) the dynamic workings of national/transnational capital in its global reach.

Crucial to the entry of California, if not the Pacific Northwest, into the dynamism of the world system as recentered in the Pacific Rim in 1848 was communication with, labor from, and representation of Hawaii. In brief, Hawaii served as the intermediating space in the creation of an "American Pacific," transmitting the cheap labor and abundant resources of the Asia-Pacific region to mainland America via the West Coast. As mediating link to the markets of Canton and the whaling waters off Japan and furs of Alaska, Hawaii was linked and appropriated within seventy years (from the arrival of New England Calvinist missionaries in 1820 to the overthrow of the Hawaiian monarchy in 1893) to American national self-interests. Twin strategies (apparent in the Sacramento journalism of Mark Twain, for example) of discourse developed during the course of the nineteenth-century process of modernization on the American capitalist-democracy model: first, *commercialization* via the imposition of the plantation economy and all but total alienation of native lands by 1848; and, second, *pastoralization* into a Pacific "paradise" forever outside of Euro-American time and space—that is, outside the dynamism of Hegelian history.

The space of Hawaii could lead American patriots and citizens, in James Jones's novelistic metaphor, *from here* (plantations, racial troubles, military battles) *to eternity* (paradise rephrased as a multicultural fusion in the Asian/Pacific little bars and dance clubs of River Street).[30] As the key American outpost into the Asia-Pacific at Pearl Harbor (what the Hawaiians knew as "Pearl Lake") since the early 1880s, the space of Hawaii could be irrevocably linked to economic domination and military surveillance and yet paradoxically preserved, by sublimating body tropes of heaven-on-oceanic-earth as a region of oceanic fantasy—at the Royal Hawaiian—forever immune to capitalist destruction and ecological damage, as what Twain rhetorically boasted (in a key line for the tourist industry) were "the loveliest fleet of islands that lies anchored in any ocean."[31]

Goodbye Paradise *As Global/Local Community*

Goodbye Paradise, the movie produced and directed by Dennis Christianson and Tim Swage (released by Pacific Focus Inc./Axelia Pictures International,

1991), made its world premiere at the International Film Festival at the East-West Center in Hawaii, which features Asian/Pacific films. This movie portrays the upscale gentrification of Honolulu's Chinatown through the closing of an old bar, called the Paradise Inn, and its abrupt transformation by Pacific Rim management into "Katrina's in Chinatown." Focusing on the last Saturday in the business life of this multiethnic bar and a small upstairs business complex operating since the 1930s, the film traces the commodified conversion into a site for the consumption of "California cuisine" and an upscale art gallery. The half-million dollar movie thus traces, on a small and contradictory scale of place-bound sentimentality to be sure, the threatened fate of Hawaii's local culture/literature/film within a global context of cultural reinvention and economic displacement.

As *Goodbye Paradise* problematizes through the cynical yuppie gaze of the Chinese-American owner of the Paradise Inn bar, John Young, for whom "public opinion is a commodity you buy and sell like anything else," the Hawaiian local must put itself on the pathways of transnational capital to prosper, as is painfully clear in a tourist-driven economy where more visitors mean surplus value for everybody from university professors to hotel busboys: since the "jumbo jet age and mass tourism" came to Hawaii in 1970 and boomed into a global/local necessity the poetics of place began to be reconstituted into an "ex-primitive" or user-friendly tourist landscape.[32]

This process of global modernization has, in many respects, already become a recognizably postmodern process of mimicking, simulating, and, in effect, imagistically displacing local style and indigenous customs, as in the commercially recontextualized hula of the Kodak Hula Show or the Mormon-sponsored performance of South Pacific cultures as Hawaiian at the Polynesian Cultural Center: "See all of Polynesia! All in one place!" proclaims one of their 1993 ecotourist center advertisements. Inputs from global culture, technologies of the video image from Betamax to IMAX and commodity forms, would thus disrupt the ethnically mixed community of locals who once took care of one another during the postwar era (oversentimentalized in the film through the pidgin-speaking pathos of Pat Morita, playing Ben, a former pineapple cannery worker turned street person and drunk).

Locals and locales, in and around Honolulu's Chinatown (or in more staunchly Hawaiian communities like Waianae on the leeward coast of Oahu) are confronting the transformation of the American Pacific region into the site of a highly simulated transnational ethnicity that goes under the user-friendly rubrics "ecotourism" or "cultural tourism." Haunani-Kay Trask argues this postcolonial scenario, while defending the resurgent claims of the Hawaiian sovereignty struggle one hundred years after the McKinley-endorsed American annexation of the native kingdom and land, in saying "Burdened with commodification of their culture and exploitation of their people, Hawaiians exist in an occupied country where hostage people are forced to witness (and, for many, to participate in) their own collective humiliation as tourist artifacts for the First World."[33]

Indigenous Hawaiians (20 percent of Hawaii's population by the most expansive count of mixed-blood quantum) do not necessarily want to be absorbed into the great American multiculture, as Trask has relentlessly argued of the *kanaka maoli,* and in fact are forging a Pacific version of culturalism-nationalism tied to the preserving of language, custom, and land. But Big Sharon, the big-hearted Hawaiian waitress in *Goodbye Paradise,* nostalgically dances with Joe and Tiny to the awesome Gabby Pahanui's slack-key "Moonlight Lady" to signify the threat of global foreclosure, from the Pacific Rim to the multiethnic proletarian culture in Hawaii of those "who work in the fields by day" and would still party at the Paradise Inn at night.

Goodbye Paradise warns that the ethos of contemporary tourist-driven Hawaii has seemingly become one (as the hospital warns Joe, who gets behind on his payments for Ben) of "just doing business" and following the economistic mandates of turning place into space and both into accumulated powers of time and money. (As Hawaii property-law expert David Callies rather preposterously claims of the resort takeover of local landscapes, "Golf courses tend to be good neighbors," whatever the shape or size of the neighborhood that is left.)[34] As the movie quite *unphotogenically* intimates—the constrained image-scheme recalling in a lesser key Nagisa Oshima's refusal of the color green and "characters sitting and talking on *tatami*"—"paradise" seen as a distinctive Pacific space and unique location of Hawaiian culture may be phased out piece-by-piece and neighborhood-by-neighborhood in the name of California cuisine and the rise of trans-Pacific profits.

In the movie's one contentious narrative twist, the agent of the cultural change in *Goodbye Paradise* is no global outsider from Japan or Hong Kong, however (as in the reiterative orientalism of TV's recent *Raven* series, with its endless supply of inscrutable yakuza, Samoan bouncers, and slimy Japanese businessmen invading a calmly photogenic Hawaii), but the yuppie architect son of the original owner, Mr. Waichee Young, who as a second-generation Chinese had worked his way up from his father's plantation on Maui to owning business and real estate in Honolulu. This older Mr. Young hovers over the movie like a *genius loci,* his calming voice-over of decency and paternalistic good cheer recalling the *haole* bar manager, Joe Martin, to an ethic of care, compassion, and humor that his architect son is helping to phase out. Transnational capitalism of the "Pacific Rim cuisine" variety still demands proponents and agents expressing the "TNC"-class interests, and here a local Chinese arises to fill the roll.

This Asian-American MBA-wielding son, John Young, has married a vulgar capitalist haole from California (who, in true postmodern intertextual fashion, looks and acts like the Ivana Trump of Chinatown). She embodies a cool blonde style of selfishness and profit, local indifference, and feels no ties to the old compassionate ethic and community loyalty to the locale that Young's father kept toward his workers and his tenants: a local multiculture comprised of Cook, the thrifty and scurrilous Chinese who plans to open his own Thai restaurant ("it's just Chinese food with peanut sauce and curry"), Tiny, the huge Hawaiian with a heart of gold and scraps of Hawaiian wisdom about *mahus* and the moon, Big Sharon, Little Sharon, Billy, and even Lieutenant Nomura and Evelyn and Elmira Lymon—the old Catholic sisters who are coldly being evicted.

The Chinatown neighborhood around the Paradise Inn bar, personifying the mix and scrappy endurance of local identity, "has survived disease, fire, war, and even tourism," as old Mr. Young quips, but the attack of California cuisine on local favorites like Spam musubi seems ever more dangerous to the fate of Hawaiian hybrid/indigenous identity. The movie is thus riddled with a recognizably postmodern nostalgia for what David Harvey calls (after the affirmative rearguard "critical regionality" theorized by British architect Kenneth Frampton) cultivating and amassing the oppositional force or a "place-bound identity."[35] For example, Tiny's unironic affirmation of Hawaiian local identity as the upbeat (essentialist) claim that "Chinatown is always going to be Chinatown, Joe" does not match the global/local circumstances, nor does Joe's one-man charity organization to expend a thousand points of socialist-Christian light on Hotel Street. Even nostalgia must have some critical edge to it, becoming grounded and politicized as a mobilizing vision of place.

Given Hawaii's state economy, where it costs 34 percent more to live than it does on the mainland[36] and where state and local government collect 30 percent more taxes per person than the U.S. national average,[37] the movie is correct to suggest that one tends by economic necessity (as much as by local tradition) to build an *ohana* (extended family) of mothers, fathers, uncles, aunts, grandparents, friends, "or other reluctant but cooperative souls" in order to survive.[38] This results in a watered-down parody of residual Hawaiian values in *Goodbye*

Paradise, here captured through the hearts of gold in Tiny (the huge Hawaiian bouncer) and Billy (the half-Hawaiian, half-Chinese bartender) who finally, with saintly Joe, decide to "stay in the neighborhood" for food and bonds of local affection after the bar is closed.

Transnational tourism has already become the "primary export" of Hawaii (like the casino economy of Nevada)[39] and, in this process of consensual displacement, the state's natural beauty and landscape sublimity has been seemingly instrumentalized into its primary "asset."[40] The language of Pacific Rim economism can always conclude that supply-and-demand dynamics will keep the cost of living in Hawaii very high but the standard of living "admirable." Still, the claustrophobic and residually impoverished spaces of Honolulu's Chinatown cannot compete with the scenic and sensual allure of hotel-heaven Waikiki or the "fearful beauty" of the wilderness in Hawaii Volcanoes National Park. To invoke the pan-judgmental "tourist gaze" of Paul Theroux, in its full orientalist and exotic splendor, "The two most obvious facts of Hawaii are the huge sluttish pleasures of its Nipponized beachfront hotels and, in great contrast, its rugged landscape of craggy volcanoes and its coastal headlands."[41] Hawaiian nationalism, in such a calculus, is never even mentioned as a real or emergent threat to tourist pipe dreams of a native-emptied resort or volcano. Cultural nationalism in the new Pacific cannot be marketed as ex-primitive tourist delight—at least not yet.

In a theme that resonates with the complex social dynamics driving the contemporary "local literature" movement in Hawaii, *Goodbye Paradise* helps to show (through the synecdochic allegory of the bar as space of local culture) that a once-pastoral ethic of mutual care and multicultural unity in Hawaii is fast giving way in contemporary Honolulu to an ethic of profiteering and a fluidly delocalizing style of image- and self-promotion. In the imaginary polity of *Goodbye Paradise,* this restructuring most hurts the old residents and scrappy citizens like old Ben and the white Christian ladies who live over the bar, although the costs to indigenous Hawaiians are barely even measured.

Local KHON TV news celebrity, Joe Moore, plays (and, saintlike, overplays) bar manager Joe Martin, who in feeding stray cats, putting drunks in taxicabs home, caring for street people and the elderly holds on to a virtually Christian socialist ethic of neighborhood care and concern (*aloha* spirit affirmed as local core), like that of the old Mr. Young who had years ago taken him in as a stepson after his dog soldier days in Vietnam had landed him across the Pacific in Hawaii. While *Goodbye Paradise* gets excessively sentimental through Moore's unselfish unconcern for money, and waxes nostalgic for the multiethnic *all-in-*

the-ohana Hawaiian way of life in old Honolulu that is now being phased out from the inside by transnational capitalist transformations of the inner city into upscale real estate, it does show the process and cost of cultural displacement at work in downtown Honolulu.

Goodbye Paradise reveals, humorously and tenderly by turn, the creolized multicultural community that came about and was forged over years of coexisting on the plantation as in the bar, mixing Chinese cook, Hawaiian bouncer, Chinese owner, Japanese cop, white manager, and half-Chinese, half-Hawaiian bar hostess with newcomer haole waitress from the American south, even as this local community is now being disrupted, phased out, molested from local space. Threatened is that very complex of Hawaiian values, still much touted at the core of local culture, called *aloha 'aina* (love of the land) which, even transformed from its agricultural origins in taro farming, implies (in Sumida's multicultural rephrasing) "symbols and metaphors integral to the Hawaiian language [which] bind love of the land (i.e., if you love and cultivate the land, the land will return by feeding you), family, sustenance, and culture itself into a rich complex of values—values involving reciprocity among people and between people and nature."[42]

Like the starry-eyed localist hero, Ben Knox, who squats on the Scottish beach in Bill Forsyth's *Local Hero* (1983) to resist the transnational encroachment of an oil refinery from Texas and Aberdeen on the pastoral community at Furness Bay, Joe Moore, local news anchor, plays a *local hero* of the scrappy resistant multiculture and agent of this uncanny *aloha* spirit of "reciprocity among people." Martin labors to up-build and preserve local charms and local mores from the damages of historical molestation and that American commonsense master-narrative called "progress." That this localized and working-class *haole* who came to Hawaii by way of Vietnam, across Asian/Pacific space, loses spatially and politically but gains a moral-sentimental victory of love over time and money offers little consolation. Two capitalist ethics here compete, one residually paternal and the other more brutally transnational. The former wins only at the symbolic level as the bar gets closed and redone into California cuisine art. Both ethics all too easily repress the presence of the Hawaiian sovereignty movement, which is presently refusing such accommodations to state-driven future planners and economistic knowledge-workers from the University of Hawaii calculating their own "price of paradise."

At least since 1988 it has become apparent that the majority of Hawaii's multicultural citizens have opposed the influx of overblown foreign investment in general, and Japanese investment in particular.[43] Almost two-thirds of the hotel rooms in the state are owned by foreign investors, especially Japanese, so this retrenchment in the local economy and place can be read as a defensive reaction to the makings of a borderless transnational economy that peaked across the decade of the 1980s and is dismantling place and culture of the very distinctiveness that makes Hawaii attractive. This new Pacific of hotel resorts and microchip factories is the dream of the Pacific Rim, the paradise of APEC. But the loss of land and property imparts a sense of lost control, and cultural displacement, from Honolulu to Vancouver, works to dismantle dreams of individual homeownership. Yet the postmodern context of hyper-capital mobility is such that the local is increasingly affected by the invasion and retreat of global capital, in this instance the very mobility of the Japanese yen in foreign real-estate markets like upscale Kahala in Honolulu, or Indonesian capital from the notorious transnational big spender Sukarman Sukamto developing place into capitalized space at "Landmark Waikiki."[44] The local is driven up, down, and out by fluctuations in the global financial system, as neighborhoods like Kahala experience the influx and outflight of Tokyo yen given the dynamics of repatriated capital that burst in 1991.

"Local assets," given the makings of a deregulated global economy reorganized and dynamized around the Pacific Rim from NAFTA to APEC, are palpably threatened by capital from Japan, Australia, Taiwan, Canada, or California. Furthermore, much like a country or a company the local economy of Hawaii is instantly affected by global events (in economics and politics) such as the 1985 United Airlines strike, Operation Desert Storm in 1991, and the national recession, as those events affect the tourist flow from Pacific Coast states like California.

As what some would call a *tourist microeconomy,* the state of Hawaii must compete with countries and city-states like Bermuda, Fiji, Hong Kong, Las Vegas, and the Bahamas for tourist capital, and market its local soul as the stuff of global fascination and redemption. Also, given the global and transnational dynamics of knowledge flow and productive employment, "Hawaii may very well have a brain drain problem [of out-migration] like that commonly found in third-world countries."[45] This is especially so, in postindustrial terms, given the global shift toward developing a tourist-driven local economy that is riddled by low-wage and low-skill service industries. In Hawaii this means that pineapple production and sugar plantations are being phased out and tourist resorts and golf courses are phased in as is happening with Hamakua Sugar on the Big Island, or, on a near-total scale, to the Dole-run island of Lanai. Given the rise and spread of tourism into the major global industry, cultural criticism must now stand and measure the costs and claims of this transcultural flow on local place-bound identity, in Hawaii as in England.

According to David McClain, Walker Distinguished Professor of Business Enterprise and Financial Economics and Institutions at the University of Hawaii at Manoa and advocate for transnational restructuring of the local, Hawaii's market of 1.1 million people is quite "unsophisticated" compared to Asian citizens and those of the West, since "related and supporting industries for anything but travel and tourism are not world class" and cannot compete with Pacific Rim countries that manage and evaporate the interior Pacific with their APEC-like gaze from Hong Kong to Los Angeles.[46] In social science ways, this economistic discourse establishes that, with an entrenched elite who benefit from restricted competition, the state of Hawaii resembles a "one-export-commodity developing country model, with an overdeveloped public sector that adversely affects entrepreneurial activity and an entrenched elite trying to maintain its privileges": such factors prevent Hawaii's long-delayed emergence into the "Capital of the Pacific."[47]

The "Pacific Basin" is already being bypassed, if not ignored, in most Pacific Rim mapping of capital's megatrends. This Pacific "finanscape" center can better be located in Hong Kong, Tokyo, Los Angeles, Vancouver, or Sydney.[48] With an acute sense of Pacific Rim decentering, Meaghan Morris has described the metamorphosis of the Sydney Tower in Australia into a technological icon of Pacific Rim domination from down under, as if for once undoing the tyranny of northern space and Atlantic time: "Inside the Tower, electronic communications were repeatedly invoked as enabling Australia's integration into the age of global simultaneity: no more time lag, no more 'isolation' by vast space from the rest of the world and from each other."[49] With canny cultural politics, Morris is again thinking through the sway of Euro-American cultural technologies over Pacific cultures and remote spaces in her uncanny reading of the Australian film *Crocodile Dundee* (1986) as an "*export-drive* allegory" in which a Pacific wilderness space and alien culture on the outback "manages to export its crocodile-poacher and, with a little help from the American media, market him brilliantly in New York."[50]

The transnational "cyborg of Buddha-nature" promises to redeem the ancient Pacific of sleepy Edens and Asian locales of feudal patriarchy from any lingering sense of global isolation. Meanwhile, local Pacific space is being reconstituted (in Sydney or Honolulu) into a tourist landscape (as outback/as Eden) on the transcultural flow from Tokyo and Indonesia. An *aloha* to local culture, *Goodbye Paradise* was barely shown in Honolulu, never mind Sydney or Los Angeles: pastoral politics do not circulate in cyberspace. But a micropolitics of place and identity, from Bamboo Ridge to Suva to Papua New Guinea, surges up elsewhere and otherwise to challenge the global flow of representations and the glut of cargo-cult culture.

According to the multicultural politics and affirmative idealism that drive the plot of *Goodbye Paradise,* then, to return to that ill-fated local bar and small-scale movie circulating in its praises, racial and ethnic jokes can abound in an economy of mutual exchange in which "the rules down here" specify that you "make one joke and take one joke." Despite the multicultural mix and mixed-blood match (Joe quits as Young's manager and goes off with the Asian local, Billy), the movie does, like *Hawaii Five-O,* preserve a racial hierarchy, with Hawaiians kept in lowly physical service positions (Big Sharon, Tiny), Japanese in middle management positions (Lieutenant Nomura), the charitable white as paternal *luna* managing the plantation (Joe Martin), and the Chinese scrapping to rise from farmer rags and stigmatized pidgin (like Ben's) to yuppie riches (like John "Junior" Young's) in two generations.

Despite the contradiction-ridden nature of local culture, ethnic customs and ways of life do linger on and would collage and endure across time and memory. Of each local Hawaiian character in *Goodbye Paradise,* with the crucial exception of the transnational operator, John Young, it could be said, as Juliet Kono Lee claims in "Yonsei" of her American-pop fourth-generation son moved so far from prior generations of Japanese who worked the sugar plantations on the Big Island,

> Your blood runs free
> From the redness of soil.
> But you are mired
> Into this locality.[51]

Rodney Morales voices this Pacific-local claim for place-bound identity in a short story about a surfer with a mystical attachment to the Pacific Ocean and Hawaiian/local culture, "*Me and the Pacific have this thing, see?*"[52] And Joseph P. Balaz also invokes the localist claim, enunciated in his beloved Hawaiian creole English (pidgin), "Eh, like I told you, / dats da continent— / Hawai'i / is da mainland to me."[53]

Digging Down into "Paradise"

During a recent excavation in Honolulu's downtown Chinatown, where the old Wong building was being demolished to make way for a new housing project, material archaeologists for the city were again astonished to find layers of local and Hawaiian culture reaching back to a seventeenth-century Hawaiian settlement. Just ten feet of soil provided a chronological history of Honolulu Chinatown from the mid-1600s through the eighteenth and nineteenth centuries. The eighty-seven-year-old Wong building was the last wooden structure in Hawaii and had housed the old Cebu Pool Hall, a local Filipino hangout fallen into decrepitude in the 1970s.

Like some deeper cultural unconsciousness rooted to place and memory, beneath the Wong building were three burn layers pointing to three separate Chinatown fires. Radiocarbon dating further suggested a precontact Hawaiian settlement called Kikihale (supposedly named after a daughter of Kou, a former chief on Oahu) where Kamehameha the Great had later quartered his lieutenants and retainers after the conquest of Honolulu on his way to uniting Hawaii into a new nation comparable to the states of Cook, Vancouver, and the missionaries from Boston. Other findings included objects of indigenous Hawaiian material culture that ranged from a drilled shark's teeth to bits of shell necklaces, Chinese porcelain from the 1700s, ale bottles from Glasgow, champagne bottles from Paris, and samples of English creamware.[54] Globalized into American space, Honolulu covers up, just barely, another history of local spaces and cherished modes. "Honolulu," as Samuel Kamakau records, "was originally a small place at Niukukahi [at the junction of Liliha and School streets] which some man turned into a small taro patch. Because of their aloha for him, his descendants gave this name to the whole *ahupua'a* [a land section extending from the mountains to offshore reefs]."[55]

By the international traffic of Honolulu Harbor, buried beneath the ethnic community of the Paradise Inn, *local* culture was *global* in a complex Asian/Pacific/European mix that expresses the vernacular history of Hawaii as a place amalgamating the debris of an Asian/Pacific future. No android's limb was found.[56]

Notes

1   My first epigraph, by the Samoan novelist Albert Wendt, is taken from what is considered the most powerful reassertion of Pacific regional identity against hegemonic mo-

dernity, "Towards a New Oceania" (reprinted in *Writers in East-West Encounter: New Cultural Bearings,* ed. Guy Amirthanayagam [London: Macmillan, 1982], p. 210). The second, which depends on knowledge that President Grover Cleveland and his Blount commission *opposed* and considered illegal the overthrow of Queen Lili'uokalani by an oligarchy of American businessmen in 1892, is taken from the only article on cultural politics in *The Price of Paradise: Lucky We Live Hawaii?* (ed. Randall W. Roth [Honolulu: Mutual Publishing, 1992], p. 198), which I will use to access the dominant discourse of Hawaii-as-American-Pacific paradise. The final epigraph expresses the position of the third tourism congress sponsored by the Hawaii Department of Business, Economic Development, and Tourism: quoted in Stu Glauberman, "Tourism Congress to Seek Solutions," *Honolulu Advertiser,* December 13, 1993, p. C1.

2 See Kenichi Ohmae, *The Borderless World: Power and Strategy in the Interlinked Economy* (New York: Harper, 1990).

3 Throughout my reading of this global/local interface, I draw on speculations of Arif Dirlik who argues that "the transnationalization of production" has given us a capitalist postmodernity at once "of unprecedented unity globally, and of unprecedented fragmentation." See Arif Dirlik, *After the Revolution: Waking to Global Capitalism* (Middletown, Conn.: Wesleyan University Press, 1994). On transcultural configurations in this intensified global/local world-system, see Arjun Appadurai, "Disjuncture and Difference in the Global Cultural Economy," *Public Culture* 2 (1990): 1–24, and "The Globalized Production of Locality," a presentation given at East-West Center in Honolulu, February 17, 1994.

4 Masahiro Mori, *The Buddha in the Robot: A Robot Engineer's Thoughts on Science and Religion* (Tokyo: Kosei, 1981), p. 13.

5 Philip K. Dick, *Blade Runner* [*Do Androids Dream of Electric Sheep?*] (New York: Ballantine, 1991), p. 24.

6 Ibid., p. 14.

7 John Naisbitt and Patricia Aburdene, *Megatrends 2000: Ten New Directions for the 1990s* (New York: Avon, 1990), p. 198.

8 William Gibson, *Neuromancer* (New York: Ace, 1984), p. 77. On Japan as panic site of reconfigured subjectivity (the sublime cyborg), exotic othering, and Western dismantlement in the New Pacific, see David Morley and Keven Robins, "Techo-Orientalism: Futures, Foreigners, and Phobias," *New Formations* 16 (1992): 136–156.

9 Gibson, *Neuromancer,* p. 6.

10 James Clifford, "Borders and Diasporas," unpublished lecture for "Borders/Diasporas" Conference, Center for Cultural Studies, U.C. Santa Cruz, April 3–4, 1992. Subsequent references to Clifford will be to this analysis, but see also "Traveling Cultures" in *Cultural Studies,* ed. Lawrence Grossberg, Cary Nelson, and Paula Treichler (New York and London: Routledge, 1992) where Clifford warns against a "local/global dialectic [that may tip] a little too strongly towards 'external' (global) determinations" (p. 100). For a canny mixed-blood poetics of "critical creolism" as a global/local phenomenon of emergent "counter-nations" like the Hopi nation and the Chicano southwest, see Kei-

jiro Suga, "Critical Creolism Stands by Chicanos in Their Endless Journey from/to Aztlan," *Meli-Melo* 9 (1992): 98–108.

11   David Harvey, *The Condition of Postmodernity: An Inquiry into the Origins of Cultural Change* (Cambridge, Mass.: Blackwell, 1990), p. 187. Also see David Harvey, "From Space to Place and Back Again: Reflections on the Condition of Postmodernity," and Mike Featherstone, "Global and Local Cultures," in Jon Bird, Barry Curtis, Tim Putnam, George Robertson, and Lisa Tickner, eds., *Mapping the Futures: Local Cultures, Global Change* (London and New York: Routledge, 1993).

12   Rob Wilson, "Blue Hawaii: Bamboo Ridge and 'Critical Regionalism,'" in *What's in a Rim? Critical Perspectives on the Pacific Region Idea,* ed. Arif Dirlik (Boulder, Colo.: Westview, 1993), pp. 281–304.

13   See Karl Marx and Friedrich Engels, *The Communist Manifesto* (London: Penguin, 1967), pp. 83–84: "In place of local and national seclusion and self-sufficiency, we have intercourse in every direction, universal interdependence of nations. And as in material, so in intellectual productions."

14   Takayuki Tatsumi, "The Japanese Reflection of Mirrorshades," in *Storming the Reality Studio: A Casebook of Cyberpunk and Postmodern Fiction,* ed. Larry McCaffery (Durham, N.C.: Duke University Press, 1991), pp. 367–372.

15   Edward Soja, *Postmodern Geographies: The Reassertion of Space in Critical Social Theory* (London and New York: Verso, 1989), p. 192. On the "blade runner look," see Norman M. Klein, "Building Blade Runner," *Social Text* 28 (1991): 147–152: "The film *Blade Runner* has achieved something rare in the history of cinema. It has become a paradigm for the future of cities, for artists across the disciplines."

16   On this *sublime* problematic confronting the postmodern subject as the inability to grasp the "whole world system of present-day multinational capitalism," articulated through Jameson's "cognitive mapping" of cultural objects and the matrix-quests of cyberpunk science fiction, see Peter Fitting, "The Lessons of Cyberpunk," *Technoculture,* ed. Constance Penley and Andrew Ross (Minneapolis: University of Minnesota Press, 1991), pp. 310–311.

17   David Harvey, *The Condition of Postmodernity,* p. 303.

18   Noel Kent, "To Challenge Colonial Structures and Preserve the Integrity of Place: The Unique Potential Role of the University," in *Restructuring for Ethnic Peace: A Public Debate at the University of Hawai'i,* ed. Majid Tehranian (Honolulu: Spark M. Matsunaga Institute for Peace, 1991), p. 119. For a related analysis, see Eric Yamamoto, "The Significance of Local," *Social Process in Hawai'i* 27 (1990): 12–19.

19   This is the polemicizing verb used by Albert Wendt in "Towards a New Oceania" to resist the culturally disruptive effect of modern architecture on the "faa Samoa" in Western Samoa.

20   Eric Chock, "On Local Literature," *The Best of Bamboo Ridge,* ed. Eric Chock and Darrell H. Y. Lum (Honolulu: Bamboo Ridge Press, 1986), p. 8. For a grounded and affiliated analysis of Hawaii's "local literature" movement as place-bound identity and discrepant community, see Rob Wilson, "Blue Hawaii: Bamboo Ridge as 'Critical

Regionalism,' " in *What's in a Rim? Critical Perspectives on the Pacific Region Idea*, ed. Arif Dirlik (Boulder, Colo.: Westview, 1993), pp. 281–304.

21 See Philip Damon's review, "Appealing 'Paradise' Goes Far Beyond Its Island Home," *Honolulu Advertiser*, May 29, 1992, p. C2. "Peripherilization" implies the ongoing global process of uneven geographical development: see Gareth Evans and Tara McPherson, "Watch This Space: An Interview with Edward Soja," Working Paper, no. 9, 1990–1991, Center for Twentieth Century Studies, University of Wisconsin at Milwaukee.

22 Jean Baudrillard traverses the freeways, empty deserts, and Disneyesque simulacra of American-sublime space as some neoprimitive "utopia achieved" in *America*, trans. Chris Turner (London and New York: Verso, 1988). For postnational movements in the United States that would "expose national identity as an artifact rather than a tacit assumption" of homogeneity within the American imaginary, see "New Americanists 2: National Identities and Postnational Narratives," *boundary 2* 19 (1992), edited by Donald Pease; and Amy Kaplan and Donald Pease, eds., *The Cultures of U.S. Imperialism* (Durham, N.C.: Duke University Press, 1994).

23 Paul Theroux, *The Happy Isles of Oceania: Paddling the Pacific* (New York: G. P. Putnam, 1992), p. 482. For a polemic against Theroux's neo-imperial attitudes toward Pacific peoples, see Rob Wilson, "Paul Theroux's Venemous Views," *Honolulu Advertiser*, Jan. 8, 1994, which resulted in a storm of controversy and several defenses from tourist-industry employees (including the Hawaii coffee-table-book writer, Jocelyn Fujii) of Theroux's Pacific writings in *Happy Isles of Oceania* as "honest," "truthful," and "accurate."

24 Quoted in Stephen H. Sumida, *And the View from the Shore: Literary Traditions of Hawai'i* (Seattle: University of Washington Press, 1991), p. 91.

25 Sumner J. La Croix, "Cost of Housing," *The Price of Paradise*, p. 136.

26 Ibid., p. 138.

27 Michael A. Sklarz, "High Rents," *The Price of Paradise*, p. 144.

28 Eric Chock, "Last Days Here," *Last Days Here* (Honolulu: Bamboo Ridge Press, 1989), p. 71. On Chock's Pacific localism and innovative use of pidgin (Hawaii creole English) in his poetry, see Gayle K. Fujita Sato, "The Island Influence on Chinese American Authors: Wing Tek Lum, Darrell H. Y. Lum, and Eric Chock," *Amerasia* 6 (1990): 17–35.

29 Stephen H. Sumida, *And the View from the Shore*, p. 38. On the complex plantation vision in Murayama's novel, see Rob Wilson, "The Languages of Confinement and Liberation in Milton Murayama's *All I Asking for Is My Body*," in *Writers of Hawaii: A Focus on Our Literary Heritage*, ed. Eric Chock and Jody Manabe (Honolulu: Bamboo Ridge Press, 1981), pp. 62–65.

30 James Jones's World War II novel, *From Here to Eternity*, became an Academy Award winning movie in 1953, with outdoor shots of Schofield Barracks, Kuhio Beach, Halona Cave, and Waialae Golf Course, though the multiculturalism of Hotel and River streets was filmed in Hollywood and "faked": see Robert C. Schmitt, *Hawaii in the Movies, 1898–1959* (Honolulu: Hawaiian Historical Society, 1988), pp. 60–62.

31 Mark Twain, *Letters from Hawaii*, ed. A. Grove Day (Honolulu: University of Hawaii

Press, 1975), p. vi. See Sumida, *And the View from the Shore*, pp. 38–56, on Twain's vision of a race- and class-divided "Pacific paradise."

32   James Mak and Marcia Sakai, "Tourism in Hawai'i: Economic Issues for the 1990s and Beyond," in *Politics and Public Policy in Hawai'i*, ed. Zachary A. Smith and Richard C. Pratt (Albany: State University of New York Press, 1992), p. 187. On any day, there are some 170,000 tourists in Hawaii: "In 1989, nearly 6.6 million tourists visited" (p. 193), a figure subject to fluctuations in the economies of the United States, Japan, and Europe. Given intensified global flows, the authors accurately note that "in recent years, there is a growing local resentment against nonresident ownership of hotels, golf courses, residential real estate, and other real assets" (p. 193).

On this complex social issue of global tourist culture and Pacific accommodations and indigenous resistances expressed in the complexly situated languages of cultural nationalism, see Andrew Ross, "Cultural Preservation in the Polynesia of the Latter-Day Saints," *The Chicago Gangster Theory of Life: Nature's Debt to Society* (London and New York: Verso, 1994), pp. 21–98. For a native Hawaiian view tied to Polynesian models of space, time, and identity, and yet sympathetic to cultural tourism in the globalizing Pacific, see George Kanahele, "Tourism: Keeper of the Culture," in *Ecotourism: Business in the Pacific Promotes a Sustainable Experience*, ed. John E. Hay (Conference Proceedings, University of Auckland and East-West Center, Honolulu, 1992), pp. 30–34; and George Kanahele, *Ku Kanaka, Stand Tall: A Search for Hawaiian Values* (Honolulu: University of Hawaii Press, 1986).

33   Haunani-Kay Trask, "*Kupa'a 'Aina* [Hold Fast to the Land]: Native Hawaiian Nationalism in Hawai'i," in *Politics and Public Policy in Hawai'i*, p. 246.

34   David L. Callies, "Development Fees," *The Price of Paradise*, p. 170.

35   See Kenneth Frampton, "Towards a Critical Regionalism: Six Points for an Architecture of Resistance," in *The Anti-Aesthetic*, ed. Hal Foster (Port Townsend, Wash.: Bay Press, 1983), pp. 16–30; and Kenneth Frampton, "Place-Form and Cultural Identity," in *Design After Modernism: Beyond the Object*, ed. John Thackara (London: Thames and Hudson, 1988), pp. 51–66.

36   Leroy O. Laney, "Cost of Living," *The Price of Paradise*, p. 29.

37   Jack P. Suyderhoud, "Government Size," *The Price of Paradise*, p. 53.

38   Leroy O. Laney, "Cost of Living," *The Price of Paradise*, p. 27. It is worth recalling here the argument of Raymond Williams, who saw "bonds to place" increasingly serving as a local strategy of transnational resistance, given the new international division of labor and production: "But *place* has been shown to be a crucial element in the bonding process—more so perhaps for the working class than the capital-owning classes—by the explosion of the international economy and the destructive effects of deindustrialization upon old communities. When capital has moved on, the importance of place is more clearly revealed." See "Decentralism and the Politics of Place," *Resources of Hope: Culture, Democracy, Socialism*, ed. Robin Glade (London: Verso, 1989), p. 242.

39   James Mak, "Tourist Taxes," *The Price of Paradise*, p. 97.

40   David McClain, "Hawaii's Competitiveness," *The Price of Paradise*, p. 10.

41 Paul Theroux, *The Happy Isles of Oceania*, p. 473. On the British lineage of Theroux's "tourist gaze" that prefers wilderness scenery to the turmoil of history, see John Urry, *The Tourist Gaze: Leisure and Travel in Contemporary Societies* (London: Sage, 1990): "travel [remains] the marker of status" (p. 5) and *disgust* toward Pacific natives (especially Melanesian peoples and Samoans) functions as a sign of a globally threatened late-imperial superiority.

42 Stephen H. Sumida, *And the View from the Shore*, p. 108. For a more place-bound treatment of Asian-Pacific American identity in Hawaii, see Stephen H. Sumida, "Sense of Place, History, and the Concept of the 'Local' in Hawaii's Asian/Pacific Literatures," in *Reading the Literatures of Asian America*, ed. Shirley Geok-lin Lim and Amy Ling (Philadelphia: Temple University Press, 1992), pp. 215–237.

43 James Mak and Marcia Y. Sakai, "Foreign Investment," *The Price of Paradise*, p. 33.

44 Ibid., p. 36. Throughout 1993, the Indonesian national, Sukarman Sukamto, became the focus of local controversy concerning the site, form, and funding of a Hawaiian Convention Center which he wanted to place on the Aloha Motors site along with an array of resort hotels and shops to be owned and run by his Indonesian conglomerate. Other "local" holdings of Sukamto in Hawaii include the Waikiki Landmark luxury condominium adjacent to the convention center property (which he sold to the state for $136 million in 1993) and the Bank of Honolulu.

45 Walter Miklius, "Out Migration," *The Price of Paradise*, p. 243.

46 David McClain, "Hawaii's Competitiveness," p. 10. All of APEC's (Asian Pacific Economic Convention) fourteen countries are located on the Pacific Rim from South Korea to New Zealand to Canada to Indonesia. "Pacific Basin" island states, sites, and countries are viewed only as tourist sites, not as global agents. For Hawaii's pretensions to being a Pacific Rim player, see Noel Jacob Kent, "The Pacific Rim Strategy," *Hawaii: Islands under the Influence* (New York: Monthly Review Press, 1983), pp. 95–103.

47 Ibid.

48 See Arjun Appadurai, "Disjuncture and Difference in the Global Economy" on "the five dimensions of global cultural flows," which he terms (a) ethnoscapes, (b) mediascapes, (c) technoscapes, (d) finanscapes, and (e) ideoscapes. Hawaii, like Vancouver B.C. in the Pacific Northwest, is as much *ethnoscape* as *finanscape* for the inrush of Asian capital and trans-Pacific tourist flow: on the global/local interface, see Katharyne Mitchell's superb study of transnational disruptions via Hong Kong capital of place-bound identity in Vancouver on the Pacific coast of Canada, "Multiculturalism, Or the United Colors of Capitalism," *Antipode* 23 (1993): 263–294. As Mitchell shows, transnational capitalism across the Pacific Rim is not a nameless, faceless totality, but is a system driven by local agents with specific interests and strategies for linking up locales like Vancouver to the transnational flow of profit and pleasure.

49 Meaghan Morris, "Metamorphoses at Sydney Tower," *New Formations* 11 (1990): 9. Internet and fax networks, to some extent, have overcome the tyranny of metropolitan distance in the Asia/Pacific region, not to mention such effects as the globalization of cultural studies that renders Morris (or the Indo-Fijian critic, Vijay Mishra) key agents

of the new knowledge formations affiliated paradoxically with both Birmingham and Pacific locales.

50 Meaghan Morris, "Tooth and Claw: Tales of Survival, and *Crocodile Dundee*," *The Pirate's Fiancée: Feminism, Reading, Postmodernism* (London and New York: Verso, 1988), p. 248.

51 Juliet S. Kono, "Yonsei," *The Best of Bamboo Ridge*, p. 52. Kono's claim that her *yonsei* (fourth generation) Japanese American son is "mired into this locality," which I have used as a celebratory signifier of Bamboo Ridge localism, is later concretized into the ethnic signifier of "*zoris . . .* caked with mud," in *Hilo Rains* (Honolulu: Bamboo Ridge Press, 1988), p. 103.

52 Rodney Morales, "The Speed of Darkness," in *The Speed of Darkness* (Honolulu: Bamboo Ridge Press, 1988), p. 127.

53 Joseph P. Balaz, "Da Mainland To Me," *Chaminade Literary Review* 2 (1989): 109.

54 June Watanabe, "Dig Turns up Best Look Yet at Old Hawaii," *Honolulu Star-Bulletin*, Nov. 5, 1992, p. A1. Watanabe quotes from Joseph Kennedy, head of Archaeological Consultants of Hawaii.

55 Samuel M. Kamakau, *The Works of the People of Old* (*Na Hana a ka Po'e Kahiko*), trans. Mary Kawena Pukui (Honolulu: Bishop Museum Press, 1992), p. 7. Kamakau recorded this impression on November 11, 1869; the Great Mahele land redistribution, he lamented, had forever disturbed this Hawaiian sense of space as running from mountain to sea.

56 To counter the transnational reconfiguration of the Pacific in places like Honolulu Chinatown into global/local sites of capitalist retooling, I would like to end on an affirmative place-bound note, with this quotation from Mililani Trask, leader of Ka Lāhui Hawai'i (key Hawaiian sovereignty group). She evokes the *genius loci* of the Hawaiian locale in these terms: "[I]n our constitution we do not use Jesus, Jehovah, Pele or any of that; we just use the generic terms *Akua* (spirit). Personally, I consider that my religious practices are appropriate to all of my bloodlines [Catholic and native Hawaiian, as well as the later path of Tibetan Buddhism]." She continues: "In Ka Lāhui, we believe that the first element of sovereignty is a strong and abiding faith in the Akua, and that is in the constitution. It's very culturally appropriate for us to anchor ourselves in spiritual practice. In the traditional [Hawaiian] way it [spirit/*Akua*] governed everything, including your diet, your social life, all of that." "Trask on the Task," Mililani Trask interviewed by Derek Ferrar, *Honolulu Weekly* 4 (Jan. 12, 1994): 6. Also see *The Wai'anae Book of Hawaiian Health: The Wai'anae Diet Program Manual* (Wai'anae, Oahu, Hawaii: Wai'anae Coast Comprehensive Health Center, 1993) for the development of a pre-Cook taro-based diet and counterregime to the Western junk-food diet that has given Hawaiians the worst health profile (overweight, diabetes, heart attack) of any ethnic group in the United States. Chinatown, too, was once the site of taro ponds and fresh water (see note 55).

THE CASE OF THE EMERGENT CULTURAL CRITICISM COLUMNS IN TAIWAN'S NEWSPAPER LITERARY SUPPLEMENTS: GLOBAL/LOCAL DIALECTICS IN CONTEMPORARY TAIWANESE PUBLIC CULTURE

Ping-hui Liao

As hybrid spaces are being created by exiles, migrations, and nomadisms, regions now override national borders and give rise to new forms of transcultural public sphere in which bilingual or diasporic intellectuals move about and write from one world to another. This new critical space across cultures opens up and enlivens, in the words of Rob Wilson and Wimal Dissanayake in the introduction to this collection, with its "global/local synergy" the very textures of everyday life and reshapes structures of feeling we "all too commonly banalize as 'postmodern' or hypertextually consecrate as 'postcolonial' " (p. 2). In part a response to the new relations between increasingly globalizing institutional structures and public discourse which often addresses issues of local cultural politics, the emergent cultural criticism columns in Taiwan's newspaper literary supplements have, since the late eighties, entered a brave new world of cultural studies, exemplifying the problem of cultural appropriation and nativist resistance, of the global/localizing processes in the literary public sphere.

Before 1987, the year martial law was lifted, there had been intense, prolonged assaults on high and low modes of cultural production, circulation, and consumption by the Government Information Office and Garrison Headquarters of Taiwan. The press and bookstore chains were concentrated in the hands of a few large corporations owned by the Kuomingtang (KMT) party, which could censor controversial or confrontational art and public discourse that might upset social stability. As a result, only works of "pure" literature, such as the historical novel, romance, poetry, fiction, or kung fu serial were published in the newspaper literary supplements and considered to be "fair" or "safe" use of words and images by the public. However, the system of power elites instituted by Chiang Kai-shek in the early fifties was challenged by the market economy and the new ruling class—*chung-hsiao-chi-yeh* (middle-or-small-size corporation owners)—during the late seventies and early eighties, the era of Chiang Ching-kuo who supplemented his father's totalitarian right-wing agenda with a toned-down neoconservatism, a new order of economic and political relationships.[1] The new educated and largely Taiwanese middle class came together to form a developing "bourgeois public sphere" in which the role of property owners and the role of human beings converge to increase the effectiveness of rational-critical discourse in the sociopolitical realm.[2] With the rise of the affluent Taiwanese middle class and the fragmentation of the power bloc or the old ruling class, the problems of national, cultural, gender, or ethnic identity were further complicated by international economic and political trends—recognition of the PRC by the UN or the end of cold war ideology, for example. Attention shifted gradually from local politics to culture and communication as organized from afar by the transnational symbolic capital and its network.

Through the expanding transnational network and new educational system global and "hegemonic" forces, images, codes, styles, and technologies were introduced in the context of "postmodernist" culture and new social movement to the younger generation. As more bilingual intellectuals trained in Europe or the United States returned to Taiwan in the early eighties, motivated by the social and economic changes of the time, critical theory, French poststructuralism, feminism, and models of cultural studies became increasingly popular in the universities. Students began to identify themselves as cultureworkers, feminists, left-wing radicals, and so on. The contents of the newspaper literary supplements changed because the body of reading public changed: college students who had been interested in reading literature turned to the study of culture and theory, while the majority of formerly light literature readers were attracted to new forms of entertainment provided by cable or satellite TV. The everyday subjects produced and experienced at the intersection of the global and the local, of various fields and gaps, thence became a major feature in the newspaper literary supplements, especially the cultural criticism columns. Questions of origins and belonging, of gender and identity, of the relations between social practices and cultural expression, etc. were constantly asked and continue to be raised by contributors to the supplements, in response to the processes and procedures of radical transformation.

In order to write carefully and affectionately about everyday subjects, the columnists often defamiliarize them by drawing on foreign models and then recontextualize them within multiple histories of the local communities. Henri

Lefebvre's point on the role of intellectuals to drive the "organized passivity" and banality out of everyday life is relevant here, in particular his observation of the interpenetration of the global and the local. For Lefebvre, our world has been unevenly modernized, "socio-political contradictions are realized spatially" in the cities, places, and cultures where capital would globalize its everyday operations. While this "postmodern" space is still dominated by contradictions and disjunctures in which "local knowledges and subjects" remain to be suppressed or ignored, culture-workers can seek to articulate and highlight "conflicts between local powers and central powers, wherever they may occur in the world."[3]

II

As a response in part to the mobile global cultural flow in several dimensions,[4] cultural criticism columns in Taiwan's newspaper literary supplements—those of the *China Times, Independence Morning Post, China Times Express,* and *Commons Daily,* in particular—have recently been developed to address problems of meaning, value, and social practice as they affect people's everyday existence. These columns that we have broadly defined as belonging to the field of cultural criticism are mostly written by bilingual intellectuals to promote changes in public policy or to advocate notions of new social movement, cultural nationalism, regional coalition, or various strategies of localization. Among the topics discussed are the unstable mixtures of new ideas, fashions, or music from abroad with local politics in Taiwan or China; the resurgence of indigenous and traditional cultures in relation to modernization; oppositional projects of ethnic identity and cultural location; racial and sexual politics of incorporation and distanciation; emergence of new cityscapes and urban social relations; forms of cultural production and consumption; art of survival measured against neocolonial domination and manipulation; impacts of minor media in the form of calling-in to the station; relations between institutional structures and critical public discourse; and possibilities of alternate cultural studies on and in Taiwan.

A novel feature in Taiwan's 1994 newspaper literary supplements, cultural criticism columns devoted to certain types of problems and written by specific groups of bilingual intellectuals, evolved from the public sphere in the world of letters to replace the earlier newspaper serials. Frequently the contributors have their columns as the designated critical spaces to respond and comment on issues at hand in a very personal and at times idiosyncratic way. These bilingual intellectuals were largely trained in the West or were local writers with easy access to foreign symbolic or cultural capital. Speaking and often writing in more than one language, they try to come up with a perspective which is neither global nor local. As "neither-nor," they seem to have an insider-outsider view of the complex micropolitics of location and memory which is beginning to flourish and interact with the changing realities. Doing cultural criticism from within, they negotiate with and appropriate indigenous traditions— among them, literary supplementary modes of writing, for example—to locate themselves in a present-day Taiwanese context and that in relation to the radical changes in southern China. For they desire to be the articulators of new Taiwanese or Chinese subjectivities as they are formed by new patterns of sociability and cultural signification.

These bilingual intellectuals, coming from varied backgrounds and having multiple layers of experience, draw on their expert and common knowledge to talk about Western concepts such as civil society, cultural politics, consumerism, gender, media, neocolonialism, and national identity, but these concepts only provide a general framework for discussing the contexts of internal struggle and the global marketing of place and culture. Often the scholars warn that in appropriating these terms one may merely be buying a new, soft, more supple form of orientalist knowledge and transnational control rephrased as "postmodern" or "postcolonial" collaboration. A major crisis in present-day Taiwan's public culture, as these intellectuals see it, lies in its chaotic fluidity and instability. In the face of the uneven indigenizing and globalizing processes in the emergence of the new (counter-)public spheres, how to assess in cultural terms the rapid and ambivalent changes in sociopolitical life has become a critical issue, as the changes raise questions of the adequacy of available critical discourses or models. How, for instance, will the prosperity and instability of present-day Taiwan translate in cultural values, in light of developments in the Americas, Germany, Japan, Singapore, Korea, Russia, and especially Hong Kong and southern China?

It is within this context that bilingual intellectuals appropriate the tradition of newspaper literary supplements to propagate their cultural criticism. Several groups of intellectuals have further organized themselves around common themes and created cultural criticism columns for the newspaper literary supplements that appear on particular weekdays. (In the case of *Independence Morning Post*, these columns show up every day and are so arranged that they resemble the earlier serial literature in form, though not in content.) *San-sao-shih-chuang-chi* (columns created by three youngsters with four scholars in their fifties), for example, appear regularly in the *China Times* literary supplements. The team is an interestingly mixed group which in itself manifests the global-local dialectical character in contemporary Taiwanese public culture. For Nan Fang-shuo, one of the local representative writers for the column, is a leading intelligentsia and also an editor for *New Journalism,* an influential monthly news magazine, that exposes governmental corruption and discusses various issues arising in everyday social life. Lung Ying-tai and Liu Ta-p'ei, on the other hand, represent the voices from outside: Lung is an academic in Germany, while Liu is a writer residing in America. The younger generation contributors to the column are cultural critics in their early thirties and reveal strong interdisciplinary research interests in psychoanalysis, communication, anthropology, and so on. Even within a group like *shih-ch'i sho* (47 club, whose members were all born in 1947), which has a special weekly column in *Independence Evening Post* and argues of the need for a local cultural craze, some of its spokesmen—Chen Fang-ming and Chang Liang-che, for instance—stayed in the United States or Japan for many years before they returned to Taiwan in 1987. The literary supplement section of the *Commons Daily* is aptly named *hsiang-tu wen-hua* (local culture), but most of its writers relocate sociopolitical issues on the trajectory of transnational information flows, linking their attentions to local conjunctures to global processes so that they may theorize and develop rational-critical discourses from the inside out.

In Taiwan's 1993 newspaper literary supplements, an expanded weekend version with in-depth reports on contemporary cultural issues was introduced by the *China Times, China Times Express, United Daily,* and *Independence Morning Post.* These supplements stood out by devoting six to eight pages to cover such themes as new humanities, new space for public debate, new public opinion, and book or film reviews. The expanded weekend version continues to grow in Taiwan's major newspapers, although not in the *Independence Morning Post,* in part because of the 1994 takeover of the newspaper by a millionaire KMT member of the legislature. However, the *Post* now has daily cultural criticism columns written by a limited group of critics, and the subjects are always on media, gender, identity politics, etc. What it previously introduced only in the weekends now appears every day though in a smaller scale, and one can sense from reading the essays the internal strife (or local struggle) in the editorial office. As a result, the emergence of several politically significant topics in the public sphere can be seen not only on the streets where demonstrators gather on a weekly basis to speak about their identities, interests, and needs, but also in these cultural criticism columns where rational-critical discourse interacts with the events of everyday life. By appropriating the Chinese-Western traditions of writing intimate essays and turning the tradition into a cultural critique from within,[5] the bilingual intellectuals have written "to the moment" (in the words of Samuel Richardson) so that their readers can participate in the public sphere without losing sight of the international public sphere.

III

In *The Structural Transformation of the Public Sphere,* Jürgen Habermas notes that with the rise of Western modernity the new public sphere was developed to bringing together people who had already carved out a "private" space as economic agents and owners of property, as well as an "intimate" sphere which was the locus of their family life. He traces the change from the presentational publicity of absolute monarchies to the sensibilities and subjectivities of a bourgeois liberal public sphere. The new "metatopical" common spaces, in Charles Taylor's terminology,[6] evolved from the public sphere in the world of letters, that is, the literary public sphere of the late seventeenth and early eighteenth century. It developed in England through a network of coffee houses, newspapers, literary journals, and reading clubs; in France, a dynamic of reading, narration, commentary, debate, and criticism flourished in and through salons; and in Germany, similar activities began with the learned table societies and literary societies (*Tischgesellschaften*). Habermas highlights the vital role of the domestic fiction in constituting modern subjectivity and the public sphere. He links the intimate sphere with the public sphere, suggesting that the public sphere arose in the broader strata of the bourgeoisie as "an expansion and at the same time completion of the intimate sphere of the conjugal family."[7] "Living room and *salon* were under the same roof," he goes on, "just as the privacy of the one was oriented toward the public nature of the other, and as the subjectivity of the privatized individual was related from the very start to publicity, so both were conjoined in literature that had become 'fiction'" (50). In other words, as a group of private people make use of their reason and establish a sphere of criticism of public authority, they have already turned "the experiential complex of audience-oriented privacy . . . into the political realm's public sphere" (51). In a similar way, cultural criticism columns in Taiwan's newspaper literary supplements have functionally converted the public sphere in the world of letters, a sphere held together by the medium of the press with its serial literature and institution of the reading public, into a public domain of professional criticism within which "the subjectivity originating in the interiority of the conjugal family, by communicating with itself, attained clarity about itself" (51).

In a Confucian analogy, the body can be a metonymy for the intimate sphere of the family and an extended synecdoche for the state-governed public sphere. As Wang Hui and Leo Lee have most recently pointed out, it is hard for Chinese discourse to translate precisely concepts—"public sphere" (*Offentlichkeit*), for example—which as yet have no corresponding experience and reality. "The semantic fields of Chinese language encode other kinds of presuppositions dominated largely by Confucian ideology," they indicated, "but with various counterdiscourses and spaces that allow for contestations."[8] In a sense, the end-of-the-month literary supplements of the *China Times Express,* which carry the results of a "physical examination" of the China and Taiwan political bodies along with prescriptions and suggestions on how to correct their malfunctions, may be regarded as a crucial step toward instituting a public sphere in the world of letters. In fact, cultural criticism columns in Taiwan's—as well as in Hong Kong's—newspaper literary supplements,[9] in particular, can be interpreted as an important feature of a "Chinese" public sphere in the world of letters that generates rational-critical debates about public issues.

Cultural criticism columns in Taiwan's newspaper literary supplements have thus developed as a discursive arena in which members of subordinated—hence *fu-kang*—social groups, in the words of Nancy Fraser, "invent and circulate counterdiscourses to formulate oppositional interpretations of their identities, interests, and needs."[10] And as global cultural flows can be appropriated, writers tend to work through indigenous and imported genres or discourses, mingling local knowledge with information from abroad, to establish a sphere of criticism in which a mobile vision of the global and the macropolitical may open up the possibilities for contestation and resistance within a system of power to alter that system. Early this year, a group of feminists, for instance, defended Teng Ru-wen who had killed her husband after a long period of sexual abuse by continuously writing essays critiquing patriarchal codes. They drew on examples from other parts of the world and finally managed to pressurize the judge to sentence Teng not guilty. Another major achievement of calling upon the global-local dialectics has been the resurgence of Taiwan's indigenous and traditional cultures which have, for many years, been suppressed, misrepresented, or almost driven to the verge of extinction. With the help of bilingual intellectuals who are equally anxious to develop local voices, some aboriginal scholars have brought forward a series of in-depth reports and commentaries on the aborigines' life and experience since the Dutch invasion.

Translations of American Indian or Australian nativist writings appear in cultural criticism columns quite frequently, sometimes in juxtaposition with the work of Taiwan's aborigines. As a result of these forums for public discourse and discussion, more and more aboriginal intellectuals now openly denounce their Han identity, and several literary magazines devoted to aboriginal writings have been created. And in terms of other subaltern counterpublic spheres that are being established, gay and lesbian theories are the emergent critical discourses in the columns; they contribute to the process of making visible or even toward the goal of legitimating homosexuality. These are but instances of how the local can put the global into use in the form of "neocolonial" mimicry, in the mode of cultural bricolage or reproduction, that helps constitute multiple lines of invention and transformation.

IV

However, as these columns treat public issues, they also help manufacture publicity and generate the desire to decode public culture in an industrialized and commodified cultural knowledge: a desire for the simple formulation of social circumstances, in order to experience and perceive the everyday as mediated within the learning rhythms of immediate application of cultural studies.[11] Part of the reason for the desire to organize collective experience is that readers tend to see cultural studies people as radicals and experts diagnosing or making visible social problems in a largely "culture-consuming" (and at times "culture-debating") public sphere.[12] This is in part due to the respectability of intellectuals or literati in the Taiwanese society and the attempt on the part of these bilingual intellectuals to keep in touch with the needs of the people. In a small island like Taiwan, it is easier for a piece of writing to travel and to be read by the general public, especially when it is published in a leading newspaper. Bilingual intellectuals then use the cultural criticism columns to fight the alienation and the disintegration of the public sphere in the world of letters on the one hand and to be recognized by the public on the other.

With the rise of modern media, Habermas observed, "the public is split apart into minorities of specialists who put their reason to use nonpublicly and the great mass of consumers whose receptiveness is public but uncritical" (175). The mass media are based on the "commercialization of the participation in the public sphere," an expanded public sphere made accessible to the masses but losing its political character "to the extent that the means of 'psychological facilitation' could become an end in itself for a commercially fostered consumer attitude" (169). This sort of commercialization of the production of knowledge of the everyday has been the dark side of the emergent cultural criticism in Taiwan's newspaper literary supplements, though ironically it is also an incentive that helps keep the literary supplements tradition alive. In between the socially integrated forms of culture consumption and the critical mode of imaginative cultural analysis that textualizes and historicizes everyday life, the emergent cultural criticism brings academic discourse closer to the aims and techniques of older, nonacademic essay writing. Yet, as the bilingual intellectuals loosen and disseminate the academic authority of cultural studies, they nonetheless reproduce the pedagogical function by asking the readers to accept it. This is made more apparent by some cultural critics who constantly appropriate Western critical terms or models of cultural studies that have globalizing effects on the level of the local.

The hybrid nature of academic and nonacademic public discourse of the emergent cultural criticism columns contributes in fact to the popularity of its reception but also helps create the counterpublics—those of gays and lesbians, for example. Most recently, however, the columns have become more and more oriented toward the intimate sphere and organized around banal topics of the everyday—news, sports, fashions, personal fantasy or reverie, and so on—to such an extent that the public sphere becomes "the sphere for the publicizing of private biographies, so that the accidental fate of the so-called man in the street or that of systematically managed stars attain publicity, while publicly relevant developments and decisions are garbed in private dress and through personalization distorted to the point of unrecognizability."[13] Frequently, it is the same group of cultural critics writing for special columns that return every other day or weekly in a kind of repetition compulsion. It is as if the bilingual intellectuals were so fed up by real politics and the commodification of the everyday that they turn to the inner life or problems of private existence in a self-indulgent or narcotic mode. This is most noticeable in the *tati* (good earth) literary supplements of the *Independence Morning Post* and *jenchien* (human world) of the *China Daily*. Since the takeover of the *Independence Morning Post* by a KMT tycoon in early 1994, the content of its literary supplements, as I have mentioned, has dwindled and suffered from self-censorship. The previously six-to-eight-page weekend expanded version covering various subjects has been reduced to two pages of book review. Though the *China Daily* still publishes its weekend expanded version of the literary supplements, it is no longer vigorous.

As a result of the transformation of the newspaper literary supplements from a culture-decoding (or debating) to a culture-consuming public, writers and readers turn their attention to the "public opinion" sections, especially those of the *United Daily* and the *China Daily*. In response to the rejection of the "proletarian context of living," to use Oskar Negt and Alexander Kluge's terminology (17), the subaltern groups have created radio and cable TV stations that still remain to be legitimated by the Government Information Office for people to call in and to comment on. TNT, Voices of the Taiwanese, TVBS, and others draw a great number of cab drivers, opposition party members, housewives, and the working class to form a proletarian public sphere which is far more vital and mobile than the bourgeois literary public. As an immediate way to get the people to express and exchange their general opinions through and across the radio waves, calling-in has been the most popular and carnivalesque form of public discourse set against existing institutional structures. TVBS, a Hong Kong satellite TV created for audiences of southern China with Taiwanese money, has recently played an important role in inviting the Taiwanese people to respond to the December mayoral and gubernatorial elections on their own terms. Such calling-in programs draw on Euro-American models but appropriate them for the development of local politics. In relation to these new forms of local cultural expression, the bilingual intellectuals are beginning to write essays in their columns raising the question of immediacy and transparency of calling-in and of the implication of local politics for global culture. This may constitute a new phase of "global-local times" in which cosmopolitans would have to situate themselves in localities to make sense of the local-global relations.

Notes

1 Thomas B. Gold, "Civil Society and Taiwan's Quest for Identity," in *Cultural Change in Postwar Taiwan*, ed. Steven Harrell and Huang Chun-chieh (Boulder, Colo.: Westview, 1994), pp. 54–58.

2 Cf. Jürgen Habermas, *The Structural Transformation of the Public Sphere: An Inquiry into a Category of Bourgeois Society*, trans. Thomas Burger (Cambridge: MIT Press, 1989), pp. 55–56.

3 Henri Lefebvre, *The Production of Space*, trans. Donald Nicholson-Smith (Oxford: Blackwell, 1991), p. 379.

4 Arjun Appadurai proposes that an elementary framework for exploring the fundamental disjunctures between economy, culture, and politics is to look at the relationship between five dimensions of global cultural flow which can be termed: ethnoscapes, mediascapes, technoscapes, finanscapes, and ideoscapes. See "Disjuncture and Difference in the Global Cultural Economy," in *The Phantom Public Sphere*, ed. Bruce Robbins (Minneapolis: University of Minnesota Press, 1993), p. 275.

5   Classical Chinese essay writing started quite early; however, the *hsiao-pin-wen* (familiar essay) was a most popular mode of literary expression only in Ming. Lu Xun and his generation revived the tradition and turned it to bitter social criticism. See Leo Ou-fan Lee, "Critical Spaces: The Construction of Cultural Criticism in Modern China," a paper delivered at the Comparative Approaches to Civil Society and the Public Sphere Conference at Ballagio, Italy, August 12–16, 1993.

6   Charles Taylor, "Modernity and the Rise of the Public Sphere," in *The Tanner Lectures on Human Values* (New York: Columbia University Press, 1992), p. 229.

7   Habermas, *Structural Transformation*, p. 50.

8   Wang Hui, Leo Ou-fan Lee, and Michael M. J. Fischer, "Is the Public Sphere Unspeakable in Chinese? Can Public Spaces (*gonggong kongjian*) Lead to Public Spheres?" *Public Culture* 6, no. 3 (1994): 604.

9   In "Hong Kong fu-kang chin-hsi," *Yu-shih wen-yi* 488 (August 1994): 5–8, Liu Shaoming talks about the rise of column essays in Hong Kong's newspaper literary supplements in response to William Tay's paper on Hong Kong literary magazines. There Liu also refers to the changes in Taiwan's newspaper literary supplements since the 1980s.

10 Nancy Fraser, "Rethinking the Public Sphere," in *Habermas and the Public Sphere,* ed. Craig Calhoun (Cambridge: MIT Press, 1992), p. 123.

11 Cf. Oskar Negt and Alexander Kluge, *Public Sphere and Experience: Toward an Analysis of the Bourgeois and Proletarian Public Sphere,* trans. Peter Labanyi et al. (Minneapolis: University of Minnesota Press, 1993), pp. 27–28.

12 Cf. Habermas, *Structural Transformation*, pp. 160–175.

13 Habermas, *Structural Transformation*, pp. 171–172.

SOUTH KOREA AS SOCIAL SPACE

Fredric Jameson interviewed by Paik Nak-chung,
Seoul, 28 October 1989

●

Paik: This is your first visit to Korea, but you have been a week in Seoul, and perhaps we may begin with some of your impressions and thoughts on Korea.

Jameson: Well, I don't know that you necessarily want my physical impressions of the city, but this is a very stunning landscape and wonderful time to be here. These gingko trees, which must be very specific to Korea, are just electrifying to see, especially at this time of the year and with the mountains surrounding the city. So all that's very impressive. I feel I've learned a lot on this trip, and I have now a great deal to think about and to sort out. Above all it has become increasingly clear to me, the degree to which Korea has been in effect repressed from the political consciousness—certainly of the United States, and surely of the First World. We know of our guilt in situations like India and Vietnam, obviously; some of us are aware of our guilt in the Middle East and to a certain degree in Ireland—at least our British comrades are, or should be. Those are political wounds that are visible. But we don't remember not merely what happened to Korea in the past, but the continued involvement of the entire life of this country in the cold war-derived presence of the United States. I've been to a number of Third World countries, but this is the only one I think whose productivity is such that, as I understand it, if the two Koreas were unified you'd be more powerful in all kinds of ways than any European nation-state, and in any case you have a much older history. But the surprise is the way in which a country with this enormous industrial prosperity and productivity is still profoundly political. The Third World countries I've visited have been essentially very poor, desperate countries, from Nicaragua to the Philippines and Palestine and so on, whereas we are accustomed to think that prosperous First World countries depoliticize gradually, cease to be political in the classical way. Here it makes a very odd impression to find a bustling, prosperous industrial country in which everyone has both suffered politically and is politically conscious. So what I want to reflect on and what I want to take away as something I've learned is not the idea that Korea would be an aberration or an exception in that respect but perhaps that it is the classical example of how politics functions and that it is the rest of these countries, both First World and Third World, that are in some respects exceptions.

Paik: I would like to come back later to this question of Korea's being apparently exceptional but essentially typical or classical. But now I want to ask your impressions about the conference you've just been participating, the International Conference on Marxism and the New Global Society.

Jameson: Well, there are very few world conferences of Marxist intellectuals and scholars. My presence is something of an oddity because I come out of Marxist philosophy and cultural studies more than sociology or economics, although I sometimes feel that Marxists are often as bad as bourgeois scholars in the way in which they allow themselves to become compartmentalized— Marxist economists don't have a clue as to the importance of culture and Marxist cultural critics don't interest themselves in economics, and so forth. Here I felt an atmosphere of greater exchange, but I did think that the conference tended to be deflected into two ways that weren't necessarily directly related—one, the obligatory review of what's happening in all the Communist regimes or Communist parties today and, second, Marxist theory itself, how it is flourishing today and how it comes to terms with these things. I think there was something of a conflict of directions, as I may say, with some people attempting to demonstrate that Marxism was dead and the rest of us trying to show that Marxist theory was very vigorous indeed. For me the most important thing is what eventually the students will get out of this and what kinds of new approaches or avenues open up for them when the symposium comes out in Korean as well as in English. I had hoped for a more vigorous participation by the Soviet group. It may be that they are still sorting their thoughts out. I agreed with what one of the Soviets said, that we will eventually have very interesting and innovative interpretations of Marx from the Soviets; we don't have them yet, but that's not surprising. But then there must also be a background to this that I am not aware of, the experience of the Soviet group here in Korea. I don't know how often they come, and so I think there is a whole area here which is very important for you and for them that I don't perceive.

Paik: Your presentation was on "Postmodernism and the Market." Whereas most of the participants, being economists and sociologists and so on, seemed to be mainly interested in the introduction of the market *mechanism* into socialist economies, and thus tended perhaps inadvertently to support the thesis that planning is out and we should all adopt the free market system, you concentrated on the market *ideology* and strongly argued that this was incompatible with Marxism or socialism or any idea of people controlling their own destinies. And I think your characterization of the market ideology as "Leviathan in sheep's clothing" was not only a telling polemical point but well worth the name of a "dialectical image." But I am afraid your point didn't seem quite to get across to most of the other participants.

Jameson: I think there were two points of difference between my approach and that of many of the others. The first is, as may be predictable from my background and training, that my emphasis was on ideology and culture and the role of the image of the market in contemporary politics, and I think those of us in cultural studies are aware that certainly today in media society these images and ideologemes are very powerful objective political forces and have to be addressed. But I find that my colleagues in the social sciences are very often more naive, old-fashioned philosophical realists in that they think reality is out there and you either talk about the market or about planning; but that there is also an idea of the market or an idea of planning which has a force different from but as important as the thing itself they don't always grasp. The second point of difference I would say is that with a few exceptions—and there were exceptions, in particular my friend Alain Liepietz who is I think one of the most interesting economists at work today—most of the Marxist scholars had a conception of an objective scholarship which ruled out the matter of socialist politics as a perspective in a conference of this kind. That's something that I can't do, and my contribution was directed very much toward the matter of some future contribution to socialist or left politics in this conjuncture. So certainly, insofar as the other participants didn't share that perspective, they didn't quite know what to do with my suggestions, or were (if they were antisocialists) delighted that the market ideology was triumphing in this particular way that I described.

Paik: This brings us to the problem of postmodernism, a subject which seems to have occupied you a great deal over the past few years. Now would you briefly explain your notion of the postmodern in a way which would be helpful to many Korean readers not familiar with your work and yet would also contribute to the ongoing debate.

Jameson: Yes, I gather it is maybe also my vision of history and my notion of this current stage of capitalism as a postmodern one that may make my position a little bit unclear. Although postmodernism is a cultural word and has generally been taken to describe first of all the style of certain forms of contemporary architecture and after that certain kinds of image—production and other kinds of cultural products—and while I believe that these cultural changes are significant and important symptoms and clues to the underlying thing itself—I really use the word as the name for a whole mutation or transformation in this current stage of capitalism which I distinguish sharply from the two previous stages. To be very general about it, after the political triumph of the middle classes we have first a stage of a national capitalism of a classical type in which exchange and production take place within the borders of individual advanced countries, and then, toward the end of the nineteenth century, the second stage (which has been classically called by Lenin and others the monopoly stage or the stage of imperialism, since those two things seem to come at once)—the amalgamation of businesses into large national monopolies and then the carving up of the world into a set of spheres of influence controlled by classical colonial powers. To each of those corresponded a certain set of cultural forms and forms of consciousness. Very crudely, it seems to me in this first stage of national capitalism it's essentially in literature and culture what one may call the moment of realism, dominated by essentially realistic forms and artistic languages and, of course, certain kinds of philosophical conceptions. The moment of monopoly or of imperialism, however, seems to me the moment in which modernism as such emerges and that's been very interesting to me as a literary critic; but my premise has been that that stage seems to have come to an end, probably after the work of reconstructing after World War II was completed. There seem to have been all kinds of economic symptoms as well as cultural ones that indicate this and foretell the emergence of a whole new moment no longer characterized by colonization of the old imperialist type but by decolonization and neocolonialism, by the emergence of great multinational corporations, the spread of business to parts of what had hitherto been thought to be the Third World (and obviously the Pacific Rim is the most famous example of this internationalization of capitalism) and also the transformation of a whole range of cultural forms, which are therefore no longer modern. Now one other cultural but also economic and industrial, technological feature one must mention is, of course, the media and television. As far as terminology is concerned, one can talk about media society or multinational society—these are all various words of different types for the postmodern. Daniel Bell's famous "postindustrial society" is another—it's of course a conception that claims that class struggle is over and that our new "mode of production" is dominated by knowledge rather than profit—something not terribly plausible for anybody who reads the newspapers; but it does rely on the notion that we are entering a new kind of industrial production which is not classical, second-stage industrial production but now based on computers, information, scientific research: something one could also call a postindustrial production, with automation and cybernetics. So my premise has been that we should explore both culturally and infrastructurally, socially and economically, this whole new third moment of capitalism. If those of us who believe this third stage is at hand are correct, then that means that a certain number of classical forms of politics, of aesthetics, but also of psychology and a whole range of other things are no longer really valid, and that we need new ones which are not the traditional ones. This doesn't mean as some people have said that Marxism is over but that there certainly needs to be a vigorous response from the Marxist tradition to this transformation which is in fact, in my opinion, implicit in Marxist theory. Ernest Mandel in the book I draw on here, *Late Capitalism,* takes the following position: everybody says Marx's *Capital* describes an older form of capitalism, obviously today things are very different and he couldn't have foreseen them, and so on; no, on the contrary, capitalism today is a purer form of capitalism than the very uneven situation about which Marx wrote and there is a way therefore in which the ideal model of *Capital* may correspond better to our situation than it did to that of the nineteenth-century British and continental one.

Paik: One of the points I tried to make as discussant on your panel was that if you were at all correct in your main thesis—and many of the phenomena you cite are obvious even to someone living far away from the most advanced societies of this era—then perhaps it raised a whole set of really *old* questions as part of the needed new response. I mean concepts like nature and human nature may acquire a new relevance which perhaps you haven't quite done justice to. For instance, you speak of the "obliteration of nature" in this postmodern era. First, I'd like to know more precisely what you mean by this, whether it isn't something of an exaggeration, whether nature is a thing that *can* be obliterated. Secondly, insofar as something of this sort has advanced to any serious extent, then I wonder if it doesn't call for a new attitude on our part to the old categories of "nature," "human nature," and so on.

Jameson: First of all, let me try to make a little clearer my position on the disappearance of nature. I think when one talks about the obliteration of nature, in some deep practical way what one means is the end of Third World agriculture—that is, the industrialization of agriculture and the transformation of peasants or farmers into agricultural workers. This is part of the whole Green

Revolution; it involves junking all the traditional modes of extraction plus the forms that went with that village life and so forth and introducing the application of chemical fertilizers to the soil as an industrial unit. I think that would be the most basic sense of all this. Pollution, although it's horrifying and dangerous, is maybe simply a spin-off of this new relationship to nature. We had a number of papers at the conference on ecology and ecological politics and so on, and I think we all have to be very concerned about those things, but our experience in the West—that is to say, my observation of these things in the West—is that ecological politics tends to be bourgeois politics, that lower-class people are interested in other things besides that, that are sometimes incompatible. I think that things can be achieved ecologically, but they have to be part of some larger collective political project, and that has not been forged yet, I think. And it would involve the control of big business; it seems clear to me that a capitalist country, even if it passes some laws about pollution, about the emission of chemicals from the smokestack, is very unwilling to put together the kind of bureaucracy necessary to police all those things. It's either not able to afford to do that, or it isn't really interested in doing that. It also seems to me fairly obvious that, whatever the records of the Soviet Union up to now, it would be much easier to achieve under a socialist system. So those are crucial dimensions of the question of ecology.

Now the other place where nature exists is, I think, the unconscious. That is to say, in the classical German aesthetics from which all this comes—Lukács used to argue (as Terry Eagleton has again done recently) that Marxism itself could be seen as coming out of Schiller's aesthetics in some way—for classical German aesthetics, art or the cultural was the one sphere that was not colonized by either knowledge-production or commodity-production; and I think one could include in that all the things that Freud described in terms of the unconscious. That is, there has been a place in human nature which includes the aesthetic and the realms of desire and the deeper personality and so forth, which has been in a sense outside the range of forces of older forms of capitalism or of the social system itself. Today I think one of the characteristics of the postmodern is very precisely this penetration and colonization of the unconscious. Art is commodified, the unconscious is itself commodified by the forces of the media and advertising and so on, and therefore it is also in that sense that one can claim a certain kind of nature is gone. Now, Sartre, who has had I think a certain importance here in Korea as well, always used to make fun of the more conservative or nostalgic defenses of nature, and Sartreanism is at least one version of the expression of a great optimism about the triumph over nature and the release of human life from its traditional limits, a release that allows human beings to construct their own selves and their destinies. And I think it's proper to insist on that feature of all this, too—that is, there is a certain freedom involved in being no longer constrained by traditional forms of human nature. On the notion of human nature itself, I guess I remain somewhat ambivalent; I suppose I think that it has a great political value when it is oppositional and that notions of human nature should be oppositional notions. When they become dominant notions, then one must be much more suspicious. But then in that case what I would like to suggest is—and this is very consistent with the whole postmodern period where people lament the disappearance of the older, inner-directed personality, the acquisitive individual, the centered subject, and all those things—that instead of replacing those with the rhetoric of psychic frag-mentations, schizophrenia, and so on, one should return again to notions of collective relations, but collectivities of new types, not of traditional kinds. That would, it seems to me, be a way of looking at human nature as a social thing that would be in my opinion the most productive socially and culturally, and politi-cally as well.

Paik: I share your ambivalence toward the concept, and I'd even stress the importance of maintaining that ambivalence, but I think denying the concept altogether like Sartre is something else—something quite different from Marx's attitude as well. I for one find quite convincing Norman Geras's argument in his book, *Marx and Human Nature,* that Marx at least never meant to say that there was no such thing as human nature; he just happened to work at a moment when it was the oppositional attitude to attack the existing concepts of human nature. But now the point that I want to raise is, whether we haven't reached, precisely because of the phenomena you refer to, a point where the opposi-tional attitude *now* is rather to bring forward again the notion of human nature—in a new way of course. I mean, with the commodification and media-tization of almost the entire human universe there is the danger that anything the market or the media say will go for human nature, and you have to stand up somewhere and say that man *isn't* like that, all this is "against human nature," that the desires mobilized by the mediatized market are false desires, faked desires, and so on. And in the ecology session we were talking about the need to reintroduce use values into the critique of political economy. Now if you are going to bring in the concept of use value and still make some kind of a science of the critique of political economy, you'd have to find a way of quantifying the use values, and you obviously couldn't do this unless the beings to whom those values are useful have a certain "nature"—changing, to be sure, but changing in a certain given way.

Jameson: Well, that was the most scandalous position taken at the very beginning of the postmodern by Marcuse. His notion that there were false desires, false forms of gratification and even happiness was taken poorly by a great many populist leftists, since it suggested that the philosopher-king could decide that lots of working-class people watching television only thought they were happy but were not really happy after all. But I think there remains a great deal that's powerful in Marcuse's way of thinking. My position, however, is a little different—I very much take the point of everything you are saying—but I think it goes back to a notion which has been lost (and this ties into my political perspective which I mentioned in the beginning) the loss not only of a vision of socialism but of a vision of the transformation of human beings that was a crucial part of socialism. That was, I think, essentially a modern matter, a modernist matter; the moderns in their various ways and all the great classical socialisms had this picture of the transformation of human beings in a future society—of a certain utopian transformation of the self as well as of the social world—and therefore their conception of human nature was a conception of human possibilities in that future; and I think that's what one finds in the early Marx, even though Marx is of course notoriously reluctant to spell these things out. But that evocation of the potentialities of human beings under radically different circumstances—if one could recapture *that,* then I think one would have the right set of coordinates on a possible human nature in terms of which judgments could be made on what the Frankfurt School calls the degradation of culture, the degradation of human psychology, and so on. So I think nature stands in a dialectical relationship with utopia and with the time of the future, rather than involving a deduction of a static human nature here and now which is somehow being commodified or vulgarized by contemporary society.

Paik: Let's now come to the question of periodization—of realism to modernism to postmodernism, which as you say you base on Mandel's scheme concerning capitalism. The difficulty I have with this periodization is that it lumps together under "realism" two periods which someone like Lukács would consider crucially different. As you well know, Lukács finds most of the great realists *before* 1848—and 1848 for him is *the* great watershed. Of course, he finds exceptions like Tolstoy who comes later because he is a Russian, and so on, but given your periodization, the distinction he is very keen on making between authentic realism and naturalism would be lost sight of.

Jameson: You see, Lukács has meant a great deal to me, and not least in thinking about these matters. I think that Lukács, although he is very hostile to the modern which he sees dialectically as the culmination of naturalism and symbolism, and is profoundly hostile to that, nonetheless made some very interesting descriptions of it. One can take those over and use them in other ways without his particular value judgments. Now, for him 1848 is important ideologically and politically in the sense that it means the emergence of the first glimpse of a possible working-class culture and therefore the first moment in which bourgeois universalism must then recognize its own class limits and class guilt or else must pass over into that other culture as Marx himself did. I think that the crucial account of the difference between Balzac and Flaubert in this respect is very important. All that is very powerful Lukács. But as the Tolstoy example suggests, I think one has to understand this as a matter of the unequal rates of speed in the various national situations, and then also, not merely unequal rates of speed but also superimposed developments, so that a realistic art and certain conditions that correspond to the older capitalism persist in the middle of a later kind of economic organization and culture, just as today (to come back to the stage I add on to Lukács, namely, postmodernism) it's very plausible I think even in the most advanced countries and certainly in the Third World that one gets a postmodern veneer of some sort and certain kinds of postmodern production. One has a classical form of modern productivity, and then one has enclaves of older kinds of production, too, and those things hold economically and culturally, and thus they coexist. So I think that complexifies Lukács's schema and makes it somewhat less peremptory and judgmental. He takes into account Tolstoy; the other very great realist author, for me almost the greatest although in Lukács's sense a little tainted by naturalism, he never mentions at all, and that is Pérez Galdós in Spain, who is writing in the 1880s to the 1920s. But I think if one made this a little less rigid one could accommodate some of these things.

Now I also believe we have to rethink Naturalism. I haven't found any theory of Naturalism that is satisfactory to me. There is a return to some of the Naturalist writers in the United States after a long period of neglect. I consider Dreiser a realist, but we have some very strange Naturalists as well, like Norris. Some people have seen Naturalism as a very interesting social but also psychic formal symptom. There is a beautiful description by Gilles Deleuze, in his new books on film, of filmic naturalists (Buñuel and Stroheim), their combination of deep psychic unconscious fetishism and attention to certain zones of the social, which also seems to me very interesting in connection with Zola. The other thing about Naturalism is very important I think—you will tell me if this is wrong, but my impression is that when one is talking about the export of the Western novel and the arrival of the Western novel in the East or the Third World generally, it is not Lukács's realism we are talking about, but it is Zola and Naturalism. The Naturalist novel was as powerful (I would almost like to say) a French invention and export as the automobile or the cinema. And therefore coming to terms with Naturalism may involve doing more things than Lukács was willing to do. My understanding is that one of the reasons Lukács attacked Naturalism so severely was that it was, for him living in the Moscow of the thirties a code word for a very vulgar socialist realism, so that his attacks may have meant more in the situation of the Soviet Union than they did in the West, because Western literature had largely advanced beyond Naturalism at that point.

Paik: To a student of English literature, which in a very inadequate way I am, the year 1848 is bound to be somewhat less significant than it is to Lukács, and also as an admiring reader of D. H. Lawrence, T. S. Eliot, and other moderns I have strong disagreements with Lukács's specific discriminations—to which I could add some philosophical quarrels as well. But I think what is important is his attempt to distinguish those realist works which adhere to what you would call a totalizing vision—or, to draw on an observation in *The Political Unconscious,* those works that succeed in producing "the privileged narrative forms" in which the modernist "strategy of containment" does not operate—and those other works which fail to do so. Now, I think you are correct in saying that the Naturalist novels have the greatest impact when they are introduced to the Third World countries not previously familiar with the Western novelistic tradition, but I doubt that this invalidates Lukács's basic point. For one thing, I believe the Naturalist novels have that kind of impact because they are perceived by the readers as addressing precisely those total questions, questions concerned with their whole destiny including the political destiny of the nation. And in this connection I recall a remark in the auto-biography of Richard Wright where he relates how deeply he was moved by reading the works of Dreiser, Norris, Sinclair Lewis, and so on, because they seemed to speak directly to his own life situation—which of course may be said to share many Third World characteristics. Another point is that Naturalism as something of a simplification of Lukács's realism would be more accessible in the initial stage of contact with the Western novel.

Jameson: I think you are right to insist on the category of totality. This is Lukács's great contribution to the study of novelistic form, I think, and one can perhaps use it in other ways than he does. Surely anyone looking at some of the classics of the modern, if you think of *Ulysses*—if there was ever an attempt to mold an image of social totality, it was that. So I think one can sometimes use Lukács against himself, and then I would like to do it like this. That is, I would like to say that the artist attempting (just to speak very crudely) to produce a model of totality, not to say a representation of totality, is always working against certain given limits in his society which prevent its subjects from perceiving the social totality. It seems to me that as society grows more complex and as capitalism develops, the access to a picture of social totality is increasingly difficult, and it is according to that dialectic, in my opinion, that one observes the transformations of art. That is, in the realist period I think there is a socially simpler situation in which a vision of totality can be achieved with relatively more accessible narrative strands and constructs; in the modernist period, however—and I think one of the great features of modernism is specifically to raise the issue of representation as the crucial one—there is a crisis in the possibility of representing the totality, whence these extraordinary modernist formal attempts to reinvent that in an imperialist world-system where it is increasingly difficult to show how things fit together. Now in our global system I would say we've reached yet a third realm of difficulty, and here I think if one had any political judgment to make on the current forms of postmodernism, it is that they have given this attempt up altogether—that is, they have now decided that representation is impossible, that totality doesn't exist, and therefore what made for the tensions and the ambitions of realism and modernism alike in their distinct situations is gone. Now I don't think that's necessarily a permanent thing; I think there will be political postmodernisms. There will be postmodernisms that attempt once again to rise to this task of somehow making a model or having a vision of a global system, and at the end of my essay "Postmodernism, the Cultural Logic of Late Capitalism" I propose a notion—the word has had some currency, I don't know if the concept has caught on—of what I call "cognitive mapping," which was meant to do that, that is, to suggest that our task today as artists or critics or whatever is somehow to reach some way in which we recapture or reinvent a new form of representation of this new global totality.

Paik: Lukács's contention was that the modernist writers, those you call the "high modernist" ones, had already given up on this attempt to capture the social totality. Now, you and I agree that he was unfair to many of these people, but his point seems more applicable, as you yourself suggest, to the postmodernist writers rather than to the high modernists. So in a way one might rephrase your point and say—I believe you have actually gone so far as to say "postmodernism is in some sense *more* modern than modernism"—but why couldn't one go a step further and say, postmodernism is a *purer form* of modernism than high modernism, indeed in the same sense in which Mandel says late capitalism is a stage of purer capitalism than the previous ones.

Jameson: Well, I think that's an attractive formula, and it certainly allows us to rewrite Lukács to a certain degree since one can then transfer many of his critiques of modernism that one doesn't absolutely agree with and to see those as prophetic of postmodernism. I think that makes a lot of sense, including Lukács's recommendations—one always had the feeling in Lukács that he was lecturing these modernist writers and that the solution was either joining the party outright or at least having some sympathy like Thomas Mann and then they could be saved. Well, I don't know what would be our current recommendation, but certainly it seems to me implicit in this diagnosis that without some very keen sense of political and economic crisis itself the postmodern artist cannot achieve this image of totality because there is no longer any point or motivation to do so. That is, this form of cognitive mapping is essentially politically, fully as much as aesthetically, motivated.

Paik: I think the main virtue of rephrasing it that way would be to salvage Lukács's main point, which is that the issue of his "realism" vs. "modernism" remains the continuing and central struggle from the beginning of the capitalist age until it is overcome. And this has a special attractiveness for many of us Korean writers, because here we have the experience of the modern and postmodern pouring in at once, or almost at once, and primarily in the form of neocolonial cultural invasion. We realize of course that we can't deal with this situation simply by going back to our traditional forms or by adopting the older forms of Western art and literature such as the nineteenth-century forms of realism, but we are very committed that we should have some kind of realism in the sense of keeping alive this totalizing vision, which should pass through all these new influxes without quite submitting to them. So in that sense we are after something which may be called postmodern realism—but in this case changing the spelling a bit to indicate that we want to go beyond both high modernism *and* postmodernism. Maybe we need a new name altogether, but in this connection I came upon something in your essay on the Lukács-Brecht debate which I found fascinating. Well, let me read it to you from the volume *Aesthetics and Politics:* "In these circumstances, indeed, there is some question whether the ultimate renewal of modernism, the final dialectical subversion of the now automatized conventions of an aesthetics of perceptual revolution, might not simply be . . . realism itself! . . . In an unexpected dénoument, it may be Lukács—wrong as he might have been in the 1930s—who has some provisional last word for us today." Now, I find that very attractive.

Jameson: Of course, I wrote that before postmodernism had surfaced as a reality and a concept, so it would be perhaps a little more complicated now. My sense is this—I wish I could speak in any way about Korean literature, and I hope to remedy that ignorance insofar as we have translations, and I think we need more of those—but my sense is that first of all there are ways in which a multidimensional Third World social reality may be more interesting for an artist than an increasingly one-dimensional First World one. That explains to me why in my observation—and I don't know whether this is so in Korea but it is certainly so in China and in many other parts of the world—the most interesting novelistic form anywhere is that of the Latin Americans, García Márquez in particular. Now, I would add—and I don't do this out of chauvinism or anything, but because I think it's significant—that in my opinion García Márquez also comes out of Faulkner, and that therefore Faulkner for a great many reasons has shown a new mode of narrative possibilities and certain kinds of realism, which has been maybe the most important global influence since the Naturalists. At least this is the idea that I came to talk to Chinese writers about when I was in China a few years ago, who at that time were experimenting with a new kind of novel that they called the "roots" movement. My sense was this— and it's very consistent with Lukács's descriptions of the eighteenth and nineteenth centuries—that their forms of social realism before that had been static ones of the social surface and that one of the things that the Cultural Revolution did in China was to create a profound, deep sense of history and of historical scars and transformations; so that what they found in Faulkner then and in Márquez was a new kind of narrative apparatus that allowed the writer both to register the social surface and also, like a seismograph, to pick up this ongoing influence of this deeper history. Now your history is obviously even more catastrophic and traumatic than that, and I would see that being the fulfillment of Lukács's thesis: Lukács moves from the way in which the English eighteenth century perceives the surface of society to Scott's and Balzac's discovery of deeper history and how one integrates that. That seems to me what we are seeing recapitulated here on a much vaster scale, in the sense that you've got— you do have postmodern realities as well as ancient peasant realities and all the rest of it, so that whatever this is and however apt this description of Lukács, it must now include many more things and thereby be more complicated and more interesting, I would think.

Paik: Absolutely. Ours is surely another instance of Ernst Bloch's *Gleich-zeitigkeit des Ungleichzeitigen,* and while this could of course be simply an ephemeral moment before we are integrated to the one-dimensional global society, nobody who is seriously committed to praxis can accept that kind of defeatism in advance. So I would like to think that we do have a rare historical opportunity which may no longer be available to the First World, for achieving and sustaining a totalizing vision. I find that in your reply to critics in the latest issue of *New Left Review* (176) you refer to the conditions of possibility for the kind of totalizing thought that would produce a concept like "modes of pro-duction"; and in many ways Márquez's Latin America, or even Faulkner who comes from a backward region—

Jameson: A backward region of the United States, yes, a Third World part of the United States.

Paik: Very close in some ways to the conjunctures you mention in that article, like the Scottish Enlightenment or prerevolutionary France.

Jameson: Yes, absolutely, I agree with that.

Paik: Well, then, in this conjuncture of ours the national struggle, the national question, and the concept of a national literature happen to be very important to us. But I believe these are terms which don't have much meaning to most of the intellectuals in the West. Of course, they shouldn't be meaningful in the old ways, but what would be your reaction to this?

Jameson: I've been very struck by this in Korea and this is another matter that I must think more about. I guess my major frame of reference for a positive conception of nationalism—certainly in an embattled situation like that of the Palestinians' nationalism is obvious and inevitable and progressive, I think anyone can see that—but in terms of a postrevolutionary situation I have been most impressed with the role of nationalism in Cuba and the way in which a Cuban nationalism, a sense of Cuban exceptionalism, has gone hand in hand with the construction of socialism, has not been xenophobic, has been able for example to frame multiple personalities for the Cubans so that they feel them-selves to be part of Latin America; they feel themselves to be part of that very different thing the Caribbean; they feel themselves to be a black country linked to Africa; and they feel themselves also very close to us the North Americans since they were in effect our last colony. So it seems to me that a powerful sense of the unity of the national situation does not necessarily involve xenophobia or narrowness but can be a whole opening to both political praxis and very vigorous kinds of cultural expression, something which seems uniquely the case here in Korea. I'm tempted to say if the First World doesn't understand this—and it's clear why, except for the strange case of Japan, the superstate in the United States or this new Europe has really no place for this kind of thing— then too bad for the First World: that is to say, there are realities that it needs to think about some more, and those are the index of its blind spots and its repressions and the things it doesn't want to know about in the outside world.

Paik: Would you care to comment on the relevance of this issue to the Second World also? You've discussed Cuba, of course, but that's as much Third World as Second.

Jameson: Obviously the Soviet Union is a federation which has to think about these things in another way. Then one would have to compare the German example—but of course Germany has a tradition of having non-national states, Prussia was not a national state, so that as to the viability of the socialist Germany of the East, the German Democratic Republic, there are presents in German history for a non-national formation that maybe do not really exist in other parts of the world.

Paik: I think that's one of the major differences between the German case and the Korean, for we did have a unified national life for many, many centuries before the division in 1945. Another important difference would be that the division of Germany had at least some legitimacy or historical rationale in that it was a punishment meted out to a powerful aggressor and in a way a measure to prevent the repetition of the same tragedy, whereas Korea was a victim of Japanese aggression—

Jameson: Well, Jon Halliday has put that even more strongly in saying that the occupation and division that should have been visited on Japan were transferred to you.

Paik: Right. So there is a very strong feeling throughout Korea demanding reunification; I am sure I can speak for most Koreans, North *and* South, that we do have this feeling. But of course to have the feeling is not the same thing as to see the way to the thing or to have a theory for realizing it. Now, one of the difficulties is that the country *has* been divided for nearly a half-century, and much more violently and rigidly, too, than the two Germanies, and as a result we have two very different social formations, perhaps even different kinds of nationalisms in spite of a very strong common national feeling. But in either case I think the nationalism is a progressive one, even though there is involved a certain amount of xenophobia—.

Jameson: Well, some of that can be progressive if it's a matter of political consciousness and not just the refusal of the alien or the other.

Paik: In any case, Korean nationalism *has* to be progressive because, for one thing, it has to take an oppositional stance toward the hegemonic powers that do not want to see the country reunified. Also, it's inherently impossible to get most Koreans to agree that *any kind* of reunification would be desirable. This is a point which so far hasn't received enough open debate in Korea, but it is obvious, for instance, that a good many South Koreans would not want reunification on North Korean terms, at least insofar as these have become known to them, and the North Koreans would certainly oppose any idea of— well, we used to have this slogan of "Marching North and reunifying the country," and they would no doubt oppose that. So we need to work out a solution, a practicable response to the common national feeling which would serve the real interests of the Korean people, that is to say the preponderant majority of the population both North and South. The problem is that while we are in many ways still a single nation with a long history of unified life and an acute sense of that history, we have had two virtual nation-states or rather seminational for over forty years now, with two almost diametrically opposed social systems, and therefore with very different individual and collective experiences. So how does one work out a solution which will satisfy both the common and the inevitably heterogeneous aspirations and yet manage to be practical? This makes the Korean case quite exceptional, but I think here we have rather a confirmation of your original point that Korea in being apparently exceptional may in fact be more typical, because we really face the same kinds of problems when we try to solve the difficulties facing the entire world today.

Jameson: It's as though you had two distinct opportunities for social transformation, as though it were given to Korea to have two lives at the same time so to speak, which could involve a very rich set of possibilities.

Paik: But would you care to elaborate on your original remark about Korea's being not so much an anomaly as a classical example?

Jameson: I always try to make it clear, in my version of development or "stages" theory, that the stages coexist, overlap, and that one must not think of these things as separate. But in most theories of stages one posits distinct kinds of politics that are relative to the stages themselves: wars of national liberation, and relatively nationalist struggles, that would be the stage of decolonization; socialist revolutions would be another type; now perhaps we can foresee struggles against a whole postmodern apparatus of domination that would again be distinct from those. And so what tends to happen as one looks around the world is that in poor Third World countries one sees wars of national liberation with the nationalist dominant; in more advanced countries, labor struggles and issues of social change of that kind are present. But in most places these seem to be separate, whereas in South Korea all these seem to be taking place in the same social space: this is both an advanced and a Third World country in some sense, the way places like Cuba and China are both Second and Third World countries. I think that's very interesting and it seems to me rather exceptional.

Paik: Korea is exceptional above all in being a *divided* country, and I think the division has—

Jameson: So that you are in a way both First, Second *and* Third World—

Paik: Yes, yes, exactly. So the problems of all these worlds are concentrated here. Well, let me give you my sense of Korea's exceptionalism and typicality. You mention in your reply to critics (*New Left Review* 176, p. 44): "Local struggles and issues are not merely indispensable, they are unavoidable; but . . . they are effective only so long as they also remain figures or allegories for some larger systemic transformation." Now, whether you take the level of South Korean society by itself or of the two Koreas, the national struggle for reunification is an unavoidable, perhaps *the* unavoidable, local issue, but this particular national struggle happens to have certain inbuilt guarantees that it cannot succeed in the old-fashioned nationalist way—if only because we have more than one nationalism (perhaps it isn't even a case to *two* nationalisms but something more like one-and-half). And thus the *social content* of the nationalism or nationalisms becomes much more important than in a "less exceptional" national or decolonization struggle. At the same time, connections with larger worldwide issues turn out to be inevitable—for instance, in the fact that the two Koreas belong to different ideological blocs and thus questions arising from the division of the world system into two contending blocs is superimposed on the local issue. And then, too, when you are to think of any concrete situation with any measure of concreteness, you have to look not only at the society within the national border and the world system as a whole, but also at the intermediate regional configuration. In our case it involves Japan and China, and the Soviet Union, and inevitably the United States.

Jameson: Yes, inevitably!

Paik: So even at the regional level you have practically every one of the prime agents in the world scene. And then, coming back to the question of division, in our case there is not only the regional but *peninsular* configuration to take into account—which is more than a configuration, I think it's actually a *system* of two sharply contending but sometimes perhaps also colluding state apparatuses. So one has to be able to think at once of the part (South Korea) and the whole (the contemporary world in its concreteness), and also to think of the Korean peninsula as both one and two—a dialectical feat which I assume everyone in today's world has to learn if he or she is to carry out the local struggle in the successful manner that you call for.

Jameson: Yes. I would like to say something more about this later but I wish you would repeat here what you were telling me the other day about industrialization and Confucianism—that is, whether here and in Taiwan, Singapore, and so on Confucianism as a substitute for the Protestant ethic is sufficient explanation for the tremendous industrial takeoff in these parts of East Asia.

Paik: No, I don't think it's a sufficient explanation, although I do agree that Confucianism had something to do with the kind of economic success that the so-called Asian NICs have had. Only, the curious thing is that people who are touting this Confucian ethic as a key to development are in many cases the same ones who were saying a few decades ago that East Asia—except for Japan which had a feudal system like the European—was not successfully industrializing *because of* the Confucian ideology, the solution presumably being for us to turn into Christians as rapidly as possible. But as I say, I agree Confucianism was an important factor, especially in securing the relatively high level of national integration and education of the population in these societies. But I believe that even more crucial was the strategy of the global capital, and in this connection I recall an interesting remark by William Hinton criticizing Deng Xiaoping's strategy of development, which according to Hinton is an attempt to emulate South Korea, of course without giving up the Communist party control; and he says this won't work because the primary reason for South Korea's success was the fact that China had gone socialist, and (says Hinton) if Brazil were a socialist country, Panama would now be an economic power.

Jameson: Very funny!

Paik: Of course it's an exaggeration, and Hinton probably meant it as such; I don't think Panama has the kind of infrastructure to make it another Taiwan or South Korea. But I do believe there is a valid point to it: I mean, the United States doesn't have the kind of strategic stake in seeing, say, Mexico or Brazil become successful economies as in the case of South Korea; also the United States or the reigning multinational capital would be more afraid of Brazil developing a really successful national economy.

Jameson: Yes, and I think you also insist on the fact that division is very significant in South Korea or Taiwan, that perhaps it prevents the takeoff miracle state from becoming a nation which then has the power in its own right to pose dangers to—

Paik: That's right. On the one hand, the world capital cannot *afford* to have an economic debacle in these lands—not that it can afford a real debacle in Brazil or Mexico, either, but at least it could live with much more obvious failures there—and on the other hand, with the kind of built-in military and political dependency ensuing from division, it can tolerate a good deal of economic success on the part of these countries.

Jameson: Now, what I want to say about all this is, first of all, that my description of postmodernism in general, this whole moment in general, is characterized by a new significance of space as opposed to time or temporality in the modern. One of the most interesting newer forms of Marxism emerging is coming from the radical geographers and is what I would call a spatial Marxism, an analysis of both the urban and of geography, geopolitics, and so forth; there is a new book by Ed Soja called *Postmodern Geographies,* David Harvey who has moved to Oxford is one of the leading Marxist geographers who has written a number of important books including a new one on post-modernism. It seems to me that that kind of spatial analysis is something to be developed and would be squarely in the line of what you are calling for here, because the way you are laying out the Korean situation is essentially in this newer sense a spatial dialectic.

Paik: That's very interesting and I confess spatial Marxism is an area which is new to me. Up to now I've been rather uncomfortable with all this talk about space and spatiality in postmodernism as opposed to a presumed importance of time in high modernism, because at least one of the main tendencies of capitalism is to abolish space and turn everything into time—in the Marxian sense that finally all value is a matter of temporality. So the emphasis on space would be significant only if it is in opposition to this general trend, an attempt to recover the concreteness of space that capitalism makes disappear.

Jameson: Yes, that's precisely what I wanted to say. One of the features of this—I think Jim O'Connor in the paper "Global Interdependency and Ecological Socialism" which I read in his stead at the conference brought this out—is that in the postmodern there is a new kind of dialectic between international-ism and regionalism; and it seems to me that's a new kind of link as well as opposition that is very fruitful and that has a lot of political possibilities, so that where in older historical moments the attachment to the region very often meant a regressive politics, today it may not at all, and it may be very closely linked to a sense of the whole international thing. So I think that would be a key to find the benefits of this new kind of spatial thinking.

Paik: I see it does tie in very well with what we were discussing—not only about economic development but about nationalism as well. So perhaps we may now turn more particularly to the concept of "national literature," a topic of rather intense debate with us. Its proponents at least (including myself) see it as quite compatible with internationalism, indeed *necessary* to any desirable conception of world literature. I know you are not yet very familiar with how the concept actually works out in the Korean context, but I would like nevertheless to have some of your thoughts on it.

Jameson: This is a period in which the counterpart to multinational capitalism and its organization of global relations has to be, on the part of the left and a progressive culture, an internationalization as well. I have pointed out that, in Goethe's original description of "world literature," what seems to have been most prominent in his mind were the new media organs, like the journals that permitted contact between intellectuals in the various European countries, so that he, Goethe, would read *The Edinburgh Review,* the *Revue des deux Mondes,* and be in closer touch with intellectuals in other national situations. "World literature" was then for him that set of relations and not simply the emergence of great classics. If something like that could be imagined, it would be a way of respecting the primacy of the national situation and also making it possible for an international network of intellectuals and cultures very much in the spirit of the dialectic I just mentioned between the regional and the international. It seems to me it may be possible today that the powerful construction of a national culture is an act of internationalism rather than a withdrawal from the international situation. I tried in another place to push a slogan which was "the internationalism of national situations"; that our intellectual and cultural relations to each other should *pass through* the primacy of the national situation understood in the larger sense, through the concrete regional situation, and that we would understand each other through those situations rather than in some timeless way from masterpiece to masterpiece. So if the Korean project is that of producing a "national literature," then the most important thing would be perhaps to think that such a literature has not yet existed, that the creation of a national literature in this new sense is a wholly new process that may not really have significant precedents, and that we are not talking about older forms of national culture at all but the forging of a whole new one in a whole new global situation, in which then that act may have a special paradigmatic value.

Paik: If such a project is to have any measure of success, don't you think we would need a more precise sense as to the extent to which the so-called global capital *is* global, and where it is not yet that global after all—

Jameson: This is the matter of unevenness, the "synchronicity of the non-synchronous," which makes me think of a remark of Sartre's that has to do with publics. (We already are developing in the area of film, which is more immediate, a more sophisticated international public for the reception of a variety of cultures but the literary thing is more difficult because of the translations and so on.) But Sartre remarks in "What Is Literature?" that it's much better for the writer to have to address two or more publics at once: if you have only one public, then you know what they know, certain kinds of efforts need not be made; but to address several publics, a number of things have to be mobilized to transfer a sense of reality to publics to which it is alien. So there may be a sense in which a newly emergent global cultural public is a benefit to writers in a variety of situations. The other thing I think is this: this is just an idea that occurs to me, and I don't know if it really makes any sense, but I can imagine this kind of situation: let's say in a remote village there is a life experience that's still relatively traditional, that today in 1989 people are living in ways that are still analogous to the twenties or to the nineteenth century. Now I can see that writers of an older period, even if their project was only to register village life as such, would have described those realities differently than a writer today who describes the survival of this village life in a world from which most of it has vanished. That is to say, it seems to me that the global perspective would do something even to the representation of older and more traditional realities. In other words, part of the development of new realism may involve not so much a change in techniques and content as the whole perspective in which this content is embedded in our new global system.

Paik: In other words, "cognitive mapping" is quite crucial.

Jameson: Well, that remains my thought.

Paik: Now, let's come to the old question of "what is to be done." Of course you've already mentioned cognitive mapping, and I was interested to see in your *New Left Review* reply that you sort of came out and admitted that this was translatable as "class consciousness"—

Jameson: But class consciousness on a new global scale, in ways that we don't have the categories for yet.

Paik: Yes. But you must be aware that there are critics of your work who find it insufficiently related to concrete political practice. For instance, Neil Larsen in his very interesting introduction to the collected volumes of your essays remarks that, while your notion of ideology is very fruitful, it leaves out or at least tends to neglect the canonical notion of "inversion" and thus limits the practical relevance of your work. Would you care to respond to that?

Jameson: Well, look, I think when one is talking about politics one should always remember there are multiple politics—we are engaged in lots of them—and there is no single-shot definition of what is to be done that really is satisfactory. So on one level for me it's very important, as I tried to say at this conference, to participate in the reinvention of some conception of socialism which is appropriate to the new global situation. On the level of internationalism it's important for us to forge a whole new network of intellectuals in the way that we are doing right now, a worldwide network of intellectuals—I think that's crucial. Larsen's objection surprises me in the sense that I have often said that there still existed ideology in the bad sense, false consciousness of the classic stamp. I've tried to insist a little more within the First World situation of media culture on ways in which the utopian and symbolically political impulses were expressed in the media. Indeed maybe now we've insisted so much on the utopian dimensions of these things that we should insist more again on the more classical ones of demystification and false consciousness and so forth. The original study of the media on the left essentially came from that perspective, because the media was seen as a very fundamental reason for the explanation of the failure of the working class to develop the appropriate revolutionary consciousness and to seize power in the West. That is, culture and consciousness began to be studied by Western Marxism essentially in the effort to explain the failure of a mass political movement and, of course, also the arrival of fascism. I think we can't transfer these analyses completely to the postmodern situation, but I would certainly hate to have us lose that negative and critical dimension that was present in those things. But it's much harder to sustain a kind of uncompromising negative critique of false consciousness in a situation in which—and I'm talking about the United States now—one doesn't really have the makings of a mass political movement in terms of which one could make that critique. So that obviously conditions what intellectuals in the United States can do, but I think there is for us in the First World a whole dimension of critique of culture that must be sustained, and that's another very important task.

Finally, I thought that this was a moment—and I know a little bit for the visual arts and from contacts, friends, writers in science fiction—that this was a moment in which maybe again critics could, if not make suggestions to the artists, at least participate in the coming into being of new art. I think for a long time Stalinism and what resulted from that made us reluctant to offer any suggestions to artists; this may again be a period in which that kind of collaboration may be possible. So those are a few projects of very different kinds of cultural politics. Meanwhile, it does not seem superfluous, particularly in the context of this particular discussion, to observe that a new emphasis on and a new openness to a properly global cultural production, to Nicaraguan poetry, say, fully as much as to U.S. writing, to the modern Korean tradition as much as to that of continental and Western Europe, ought to function politically too, if only to sensitize its readership to the role of the United States in all these places and to form readers who are also militant opponents of North American interventionism. Indeed, Paul Sweezy recently, in a rather bleak mood, suggested that preventing intervention and supporting liberation movements in other countries was just about *all* the U.S. left could hope to accomplish nowadays: I hope there's more, but it should be clear that the study and teaching of so-called Third World literature has a significant part to play in achieving that much. And finally, philosophically, the preservation and development of dialectical way of thinking about things as over against a dominant positivism, or a one-dimensional technological thought, is also a very crucial matter.

Paik: Let me now end with a directly personal question. How do you feel this project of preserving a dialectical mode of thought is faring in your immediate surroundings? Do you feel it is going well, better than it used to, or that even this is being increasingly co-opted by the mediatized universe?

Jameson: I think it's dialectical to hope that one is often spurred on to make stronger statements in a situation in which one is in a minority and under adverse conditions. I've just gone back to the Frankfurt School and finished a long book on Adorno, about whom I think a good deal more positively than I have at some moments in the past, and this is a first attempt of mine to return to a certain dialectic and describe that. I am teaching Marx's *Grundrisse* right now and working with Marx's own text and Hegel again. So I hope that part of my current work will lead me back to the dialectic itself and to newer ways of projecting that, and I think I wouldn't be doing that unless the dialectic seemed an endangered species, so to speak.

Addendum (1993)

Among the many changes in the world since I interviewed Jameson in October 1989, the end of the Berlin Wall later that year and the subsequent collapse of East German and other Communist regimes in the former Soviet bloc would call for a special mention. While neither of us may claim to have displayed notable prescience concerning the imminent events, I feel the geopolitical change has if anything increased the relevance of Jameson's preoccupation with global capitalism and his emphasis on "the dialectic between the regional and the international."

In South Korea the same change has turned Germany first into a model of unification through capitalist takeover, then gradually into a lesson in the dangers both of division and unwise unity. This has also further isolated the North Korean regime and exacerbated its internal problems. Which, in tandem with the continued development of South Korea's capitalist economy and the considerable domestic reforms since the inauguration of the first civilian president in over three decades, implies an entirely new phase in the politics of Korean unity. Yet both the persistence of the status quo years after German unification and the perceived perils of its abrupt termination seem to me to render the notion of a *system* of division—briefly alluded to in the interview and further developed in my article "South Korea: Unification and the Democratic Challenge" (*New Left Review* 197, Jan.–Feb. 1993)—more useful in projecting the right combination of local, national, and global struggles as well as in the analysis of the given situation.

Finally, while Jameson's global perspective and his expressions of solidarity with our political and literary projects have inspired many Korean readers, I must say some of us retain a certain skepticism about his concept of postmodernism. Contemporary capitalism, on this view, would be better described as full or perhaps late modernity rather than postmodernity. And the foregrounding of the modernism/postmodernism axis, with consequent relegation of "realism" to a twice-removed past or at best to special pockets of global postmodernity, not only diverges from our local endeavors toward a renewed conception of realism as a critical guide for assessing *both* modernism and postmodernism of the imperial West, but seems also to limit the perception and mobilization of the West's own accumulated resources in creative representations of reality, which, in the nature of the case, involved even in premodernist days a wrestling with the question of representation as such. I needn't add that it is Jameson's rare distinction among practitioners of the postmodern discourse to always insist on the difficult grappling with representation and to have given generous attention to instances of such in the non-Western world.

AFTERWORD:

''GLOBAL/LOCAL'' MEMORY

AND THOUGHT

Paul A. Bové

●

Rob Wilson and Wimal Dissanayake lay out the problem for us in their "Introduction: Tracking the Global/Local," and it is not just the problem of this
volume, but the problem critical intellectuals and, perhaps, all people must now
face. We see the problem in something like an aside, in their mention of Henri
Lefebvre's classic study of space, a book that, as we all now know, influenced
Jameson and others, in drawing attention to the problems of space over and
against what had seemed modernism's obsessions with time. Oddly, though,
the problem emerges in the temporal or historicist nature of this aside, and we
should look into it for a bit. What Wilson and Dissanayake do there is let us see
how in place the models and movements of historicist thinking remain even in
a time of severe displacement of almost all relations, a displacement it is the
purpose of this volume to excavate, and of possible opportunities for new
formations of transnational local communities to emerge in the spaces of capital's intense but uneven global localizations.

The gesture is interesting, though, for many reasons. First, of course, it
shows us that good scholars know the movements of thought and can follow
lines of resistance, what appear to be turns and fractures within thinking, and
draw them out for us to see: "Lefebvre prefigured the rise of post-Fordist geographers in the 1980s like David Harvey, Mike Davis, [and] Edward Soja . . .
for whom the local . . . is [fully] global in its uneven and contradictory
makeup, . . . [and] transpacific filmmakers like Ridley Scott or Stephen Okazaki
for whom Tokyo and Southern California comprise an interlocked Asian/Pacific
space" (p. 4). Tracing lines across the spaces of intellectual-cultural production is
one accepted task of culture-workers within modernity—no matter the politics
involved. The effect is, as Deleuze might say, to "striate space." Also, though, the

gesture gives us a characteristic of thought: metaphors of priority transform into figures of influence and precedence producing narratives of cultural resources valuable for their ability to clarify and for their instrumentality in thinking farther along a line, a degree of inflected practice. What is curious about this, though, is the temporal structure of the gesture, aside from its figurality, that this volume should have as its beginning such a characteristically modern gesture of recall, a gesture of memory as characteristic, let us say, of Jameson's own totalizing globalisms as it might be of the less rigidly binary construction of "global/local" Wilson and Dissanayake hope to further in this project.

The oddity of this gesture, though, is its fissured-like quality. It opens the text so that we can see the continuing presence of precisely those formations of thought that one might have expected not to see. Oddly, and this is, I think, true increasingly of criticism that intends to respond to the various crises and opportunities induced and afforded by globalization and the so-called end of the Cold War, we come up against familiar forms, theories, and models of thinking that, despite their witty transformations, confront us with long-familiar concepts, consequences, forms, and hopes. I mean to say nothing more than Wilson and Dissanayake have given us one of the nice effects of current opposition: a moment of specular recognition in which we can all find ourselves at home. There is an uncanny familiarity about it all; we might recognize the pattern as typical of avant-gardism or we might think of it has having to do with structures of repetition, but the effect is that we discover and are expected to discover few if any new intellectual resources for thinking about the present age. This is not to say, of course, that the work contained here and throughout the increasing corpus of oppositional speculation around related matters is not "original." "Originality" is no longer an issue for a criticism that politically engages itself with the task of clarification, resistance, and community formation. Nor is it right to say it produces no new knowledge; when, for example, we see clearly how exiled filmmakers discover their own space to be constricted by the effects of globalization, this paradoxical realization adds significantly to our efforts to transmit an understanding of our individual and group experiences. But when we look for surprises, for the discoveries and disclosures that do not follow the movements of already traced thinking, then, given the insistence upon economic and civilizational rupture that oddly defines one base of projects such as these efforts to fill in the configurations, "global/local"—then we might wonder aloud about the relation between thinking and the new formations that evidently, for many, are there and the persistence of our intellectual resources which we constantly attempt to reconfigure in order to make them do the work needed to transform this putatively new world (order?) into something recognizable. It would not, I think, strike any reader as odd that matters of economy and historical periods undergird most of the superstructure of this outstanding collection's efforts to advance thought into the sphere of global/local constructions. On the contrary, one can imagine that certain Jurassic belletrists might be deeply offended by the mere appearance of such a volume precisely for its now near-exemplary completion of the critical turn away from literary toward cultural and political matters, especially, given this volume's focus on circulation, its turn toward the media as a space of reproduction and unique multinationality. But if we set aside the William Pritchards and Denis Donogues as types no longer meriting serious attention—despite their function as "Newt-onian" allies in the culture wars—then the issue remains: why do we find what we expect? Oddly, the question is not posed.

One must open an aside here and reflect upon the event of Masao Miyoshi's extraordinary essay, "A Borderless World?" Miyoshi, long-recognized as the leading U.S.-based scholar of Japanese literature and culture, indeed, the critical figure with whose work all followers must wrestle in writing about the Japanese novel, modern Japan, and Japan's current cultural role—Miyoshi makes a massive departure from some of the characteristics which mark his previous writings and noting those transformations alone makes this an important volume for intellectual historians. Of course, longtime readers of Miyoshi's criticism note that there are always persistent concerns in his work, and these appear in this essay and in other of his recent pieces, especially those in and following *Off Center: Power and Culture Relations between Japan and the United States*. Nonetheless, "A Borderless World?" embodies a turn in Miyoshi's work that must give us all pause.

Simply, "A Borderless World?" is not an act of literary criticism. Nor is it an act of high theory. It is scholarly, archival writing. It draws upon journalism, specialized studies, governmental and quasi-governmental documents, economics, sociology, and the complex discourses of international political economy. It is a movement in Miyoshi's thinking, a change in his focus, a shift in the object of attention, and it explains the reasons for its own shift as both the compelling injustices of globalizing capital in the form of transnational corporations and the irresponsible indifference of (especially U.S.) intellectuals to the predations of these TNCs and the new politics the TNC system obliges us to think. The essay overwhelms that indifference with the clear results of an undistracted and lucid examination of the record of TNC activity. Yet its story sounds with an undertone of sadness and disappointment suggesting that its own lucidity, its desires for struggle give little reason to hope—either for the success of reorganization and resistance or the transformation of intellectual work to the places where resistance is most needed.

But what is this literary critic doing telling us about such matters as Mexico's Televisa? Or trying to make sense of Robert Reich's badly thought-out efforts to understand globalized capital? Miyoshi's opening paragraph mentions Edward W. Said's *Culture and Imperialism* and by way of contrast one remarks that Miyoshi has no intent on following Said into the literary historical and critical project of studying interlinked, hybrid worlds and experiences. By contrast, Said's "vision" is too humanistic, too "literary," rather, we might say, by contrast "anachronistic." It is one symptom, though, of the intellectual times and their call to critics to examine the realities that appear in our experience and knowledge of new horizons, new forms, and brutal facts.

If we take seriously, as I think we must, the basic thesis of this collection and its thematic expression in Miyoshi's programmatic essay, then the decline of the state-form cannot be admitted without very substantial reorganization of critical, intellectual work. This collection of essays is one effort to produce work under these new presumably poststatist conditions. Oddly, though, the basic intellectual formations of statism and its knowledge system are clearly recognizable in this collection. This must be said not to dismiss the essays or the project that gathers and intends them. Nor is our interest to mark the so-called limits that are revealed when older intellectual formations approach newer forms under changed and changing conditions. Of course, symptomatically, the ability to gather critical essays in complex dialogue, as a form of "multicasting" across regions and locales in a cybernetic age, is novel and a response to the demands the shifts in state and nonstate powers place upon knowledge production, reproduction, and distribution. Symptoms, however, normally require something like a referent; we usually speak of symptoms as "of something." We are left wondering just what this "something" is and at a time when, if the basic claims about poststatism are to be believed, the entirety of the referential field to which ideology, symptomology, semiotics and so on belong no longer exists. In other words, we are caught in a conundrum resulting from the fact that whatever is has not yet sprung itself fully upon us probably because, if we speak in Vichian terms, we are not yet done making it. But, we might ask, where would such notions lead us?

We are accustomed to speaking of the speed with which global consumerism and its cybernetic constructs outstrip the efficacy of critical reflection, especially in prose. So we prosers are condemned, we might say, to the eternity of belatedness which is sometimes called irrelevance. But where else might we be? Miyoshi's essay strikes one over and again for its ascetic effect. Oddly, here is an essayist who has stripped away the apparatus of theory, the knowledge of literary history, of aesthetic form to take on something like a hard body: tough, clean, glaring examination of the unjust processes and transformations that occur in global economy, passing almost unnoticed by "literary critics." Miyoshi's asceticism strips away all the organizing organs of the literary intellectual and leaves us—where? We are somewhere between, not in the sense meant by Rushdie or Said when, with others, they speak of hybrid subjectivities resulting from diasporic shifts within and after colonialism. We are "between" because we are neither this nor that: Miyoshi's ascetic move is significant not because he has (here) given up literary criticism for political economy of TNCs. It is significant because it does not complete the move *out of* the intellectual constructions of state formations.

Literary critical state formations are essentially literary historical. They can, of course, be formalist hermeneutic and semiotic structural. In the formation of nation-states, however, the historical canon-forming effect has priority over the others—at least politically. Miyoshi's essay knows that literary historical criticism cannot stand if it is the case that the state formation dissolves in the emerging functions of TNCs. Simply, literary criticism has no place outside a dominant state system.

But what of empirical political economy? Where is that to be found? We are all familiar with the various "after Marx" notions which "place" Marx within the general practices of nineteenth-century problems and which either attempt, theoretically-politically, to identify the (unique) significance of his text's play with these matters or to dismiss them as predictable variations on Hegel, statism, and so on—especially since "the end of the cold war." We don't want to replicate such efforts; they fall within the common modernist paradigm identified by Foucault as filling in the gaps at the origins of "discursive practice." "Deconstructing" those gaps in the heirs is of no interest. But when a leading critic makes a move like Miyoshi's, when that critic's regime requires a "moving aside" from a place of mastery to a place of provocation and necessity (if not despair) then the very "in-between-ness" of the move must be thought about.

Retaining the terms of political economy and honoring the need to get the facts out and down (one thinks of Chomsky as the model here)—all this follows the path of the familiar. One would be tempted to dismiss this move as a repetition, as a following of a trace, working to deepen already striated space. It would be wrong to make the dismissal too easily. Putting aside the likelihood that political economy might lead to both understanding and transformation of global capital, it is still appropriate to notice the simultaneous existence of a (modernist?) desire to deal with the new (TNCS) and to throw over the inherited obfuscations that block even the preliminary act of knowing, of recognizing and limning the enemy. Miyoshi sets up a hard challenge: take the death of the state seriously and describe its effects (and causes) prior to the existence of fully poststatist intellectual formations of critique. Put differently, political economy is a statist form and its thinker is a state philosopher. This kind of Deleuzian notion rests on carefully thinking about the way intellectual as well as geographical space is striated by the state system in alliance with capital; the result is microfascism and possibly, we should add, "after the cold war," the development of "macrofasicm" or, at least, its public legitimation as in Italy.

While Karen Kelsky, among others in this volume and elsewhere, speaks of social and cultural "hybridity" as a fact of global/local relations and struggles, the hybridity of the intellectual's work, the fact of being within modernity and the state while trying to be in but not of postmodernity and globalization produces as yet unfulfilled demands for thinking, a process that can only be satisfied in a movement that does not work within the tread-marks of previous intellectual systems themselves principally attendant upon either modern state formations (and their epiphenomena) or romantic embrasures of local "struggles" against "global" forces—struggles that too often and too easily are shaped by David-Goliath archetypes. (One thinks here of Mary Louise Pratt's MLA prize-winning book, *Imperial Eyes: Travel Writing and Transculturation* [1992].)

Miyoshi rightly emphasized that rather than attempting to develop a critical attitude toward the new knowledges produced by the TNCs and their global partners, academics are rushing to embrace TNC power and culture. There is a chance in this, although it is hard to keep it in mind. The knowledge needed by the TNCs finds its way into the academy or is in part produced there. Importantly, this gives the academy a reason for existence that it no longer does or can derive from its traditional especially humanistic cultural work carried out on statist lines. Foucault used to urge that intellectuals become experts, which, in this context, we might say means acquiring the TNC knowledge produced within and distributed to and by the university. Of course, there is, as Wilson and Dissanayake make very clear, a politically dangerous allure for humanists in globalism; the end of nation-statism leads us to think and see that a new class of globalized humanists whose job it is to produce and circulate the global culture of TNC political economy has emerged from within and spaces near to the university. Also, other academics have embraced and usurped the indigenous and local within the same construction. (On this point, Gayatri Spivak's incomparable essay, "Can the Subaltern Speak?" is essential reading.)

Better for the hybrid academic intellectual to become expert in the knowledges of the TNC than to enlist, intellectually/professionally, on the side of the local struggles. Expertise suggests that the hybrid intellectual can acquire something like a "cosmopolitan" as opposed to a global persona and function; the "cosmopolitan" can take up the perspectives and knowledge needed to acquire a point of view on the global whether imaged as total or seen in struggle with the local. The cosmopolitan has expertise and also, if you will, what Said calls, paradigmatically, "critical consciousness." "Critical consciousness" is not meant to be an idealist, free-floating detachment but rather both a process and its result: it acquires education, knowledge, critical judgment, and, above all, the ability to take notice. This means to see not only what appears within the apparently empirical evidence of the day—which is, after all, merely the results of established systems' efforts to represent experience. It means rather to see those places where, as it were, the new knowledges produce anomalous effects upon the ruling institutions and systems; to identify the misprision between the political adaptations of those new knowledges and the social forces they intend to direct. It also means having fully developed analyses of which intellectual discursive formations, often inherited from modernity or from the postmodern media apparatus (one thinks throughout these remarks of Newt Gingrich's putative grasp on cybernetics and information), cannot accomplish the often liberatory results their intellectual practitioners hope to derive from them. In this context, the futile efforts to reimagine society within globalized economy around the notion of "civil society" comes to mind, especially in its Cultural Studies avatar, as a particularly clear and egregious example of such failure.

Gramsci occasionally worried about cosmopolitanism because cosmopolitans were transformed within Italian history into universal intellectuals. Contemporary critics, often adapting Gramsci, have understood, as Edward Said and others make clear, the spatial nature of Gramsci's thinking, which links the particularities of history to those of certain places. We might say that Gramsci's thinking about the "southern question" is a precedent for reporting and stressing local cultural activities within and against global capital. This volume, then, appears as one of the heirs of Gramsci. But cosmopolitans, we recall, had two functions—as Gramsci recognized. On the one hand, they extended the reach of the universal church and its Holy Roman Imperial allies; in this, cosmopolitans are like Virgil's Jupiter prophesying the universal rule of Rome. On the other hand, the cosmopolitans had the reach to understand as well as make the world. Of course, what we would call "class" has a role to play in thinking this matter; yet, cosmopolitans like Michelangelo, Kepler, Montaigne, Copernicus, Rabelais, and Cervantes, to say nothing of Dante or Donne, knew the new knowledges of their time and, while critical of them when necessary, aspired both to know them in their relations and to adapt them as possible to the formation of the future. The process comes to some sort of conclusion in Spinoza whose life involves attending to what is newly produced, examining, theorizing, extending, and displacing it—one thinks of his geometric recasting of Descartes—not to form a social movement (new or old) but to clarify the intellectual resources needed to bring to clarity the significant items necessary for thought so that it might lead society into forms that better emerge from the given—rather than the worse forms that seem automatistically to be emerging. We might say, simply, Spinoza thinks through the emerging market and state-police formations to a noncontract theory as a way of denying developing statism its, until recently, historically decisive role in capital formation. Or, to put the matter more "positively," Spinoza's thinking produces concepts that are other than those which come to be predominant.

Among all the extraordinary things about Spinoza, his cosmopolitanism stands out. Declared anathema by his church and large elements of his political society, traveling little, engaging in small but important correspondence, study-ing the ancients and the strongest contemporaries, observing the new politics and economics of emerging market forces, and thinking hard not only the relations among these elements but their likely outcome as well as forceful alternatives, Spinoza invented concepts, methods, and, if you will, discursive potentialities left untouched for decades. Spinoza comes to mind as the cos-mopolitan intellectual who is not belated; who shares no orthodoxy (even if he attempted to produce a certain dogmatics); and, most important, does not lose himself in the pursuit of an even then rapidly accelerating contemporaneity.

It would be unfair to demand of the editors and authors of this or any collection that they produce the "Spinozism" we need. Yet, the collection moves us in the direction of thinking just such demands. The hybridity which we notice in intellectuals moving from their disciplinary bases to the new places they must be to carry out their political, ethical, and personal responsibilities involves a hybridity of knowledges, but not only the obvious hybridity that mixes the knowledge of Iranian TV with the discourses of dialectics or the finance of TNCs with the indifference or disinterest of academic globalists. It involves as well a fundamental *temporal* shift in knowledge, a metaphor well worth establishing in this volume with its postcolonial emphases upon space.

Modern intellectuals could and did occupy one time. Despite the persistent traces of premodern formations in modernity—for example, those represented by the "primitivism" of SoHo in Lawrence's *Women in Love*—modernity has a coherence to its knowledge. Whether taken as totality in Hegelian or Marxist terms, or as narrative inclusion à la Proust or Balzac or Joyce, or as the construction of empire and its narratives—as Said shows in *Culture and Imperialism*—modernity preceded the fragmenting effects of representation's failures and so had confidence in its knowledges and their ability to make known. In what we now call globalism—which is not coherent with postmodernism theory, given not only the failures of representation but of participation and identity—intellectuals practice and theorize with no assurance but the absence of coherence. After all, declaring the state formation to be dead means as well the end of history since one cannot easily imagine any historicism without the state form as its ground and end. But if this is so how do we account for the compelling historicizations within the thinking of the global/local relations and the hybridity of knowledges that mark current intellectual production? Belatedness is one answer; we can derive such stories from Gramsci and Raymond Williams or from Nietzsche; we can even adapt the Jamesonian paradigm that historicizes the postmodern as just that which is a- or antihistorical, as that historyless hypercommodification that ends history as part of its own establishment. Another similar answer might have it that intellectuals continue to practice as moderns in form even if the cause of the recast work they attempt is the thematized sense of the end of modernity in the focalizing of the global/local. Importantly, this implies that as intellectuals we are neither here nor there; more precisely, neither now nor then—no matter whether the then is what was or what will be. Or, even better, temporal hybridity means the intellectuals are in this moment both then and now—a very painful way to be and one that demands for its easing precisely the emergence of "Spinoza."

Intellectuals are then in the practices that belong to what was: we write with certain totalizing ambitions; such ambitions can only have superhuman, that is, state or superstates as their audience or readership. Wlad Godzich has made this point about *Don Quixote*. And we are where we are which means certainly no longer then, although we are not yet where we want to be: we do not yet have the knowledge or the discourse to deal with the TNC-world Miyoshi—after Gibson and others—summons as the nightmare fact of the global division of labor. And, as we speak of it this way, we realize there are matters pressing on the present—precisely as part of the TNC-world—which somehow cannot be talked about from within the very rhetoric, "division of labor." (One always thinks of Gayatri Spivak as having worked in these areas before one arrives.) "Division of Labor," for example, has trouble catching the "disappearance of work," a phenomenon that in itself causes crises for the worker-centered modes of critical reflection and organized politics. But this is a simple and manageable example. More complex, I think, is indeed the persistence of "historicization," a persistence found in the very texture of critical figuration that lets Wilson and Dissanayake speak of Lefebvre as "preceding" the postmodern geographers, Soja et al. Even if diasporics are historicized and local semiotics of work habits are historicized, the problem remains for thinking that the invention of historicism, as noble and humanistic as it has been, exists to fix knowledge within modernity as available to the state form. This is an issue which no less a historian than Henry Adams has dealt with in *Mont Saint Michel and Chartres*. The desire to avoid this issue on the part of historical and politically committed intellectuals is very great. Among the intemperate, even raising the issue is a sign of "idealism" and "class collaboration." Of course, we cannot forget the challenge to historicism that took place in the middle of this century when structuralism and language-centered theories provoked strong criticism of and polemical exchanges with historicizing thinkers. Lévi-Strauss and Sartre argue endlessly over the priority of history as change and structure as analysis. That sort of event is evocative, not because one wants to reembrace the structuralism paradigm but because, along with Foucault, one wants to think about how and why it is that "humankind" chooses to represent itself, natural phenomena, experience, and its traditions in figures the complex of which come to be called "historical." This emergence of historicized knowledge and mechanisms for knowledge production is not *natural*. Weak perspectivism historicizes the emergence of history as a form. Spinoza forces geography on Descartes just as, we might say, Vico was (more successfully) forcing history upon him. Despite Jameson's repeated claims about the predominance of ahistoricisms in Western culture and modernity, and putting aside the "ahistoricism" of such things as "analytic philosophy" the problems with which are better put than in terms of not "being historical," history has been the principle within and according to which modern state systems organize knowledge. Those cultural studies admit this when they insist in "contending" or "struggling" over the particular stories or histories that "have" authority in a culture. Oddly, perhaps, there has been a confusing conflation of story and history. Histories can be other than narrations; indeed, they can be modernized jump-cuts. Stories can be other than history as Mahfouz shows us again in his recasting of Scheherazade.

Curiously, when Vico gives us historicism, Spinoza gives us geometry. Modernity had the choice, and although the struggles persist, the state's need for history to establish its role within capital's project of nation-state organization has brought us to the point where, if it is true that the state-form is secondary now to transnational and local formations, the opportunity and need to think the persistence of historicism in our knowledges must be confronted—and more rigorously than the slogan: "Always historicize!" allows. What has come from historicizing? And what can we expect to come from its persistence among a rapidly depleting caste of more or less marginal academic intellectuals who, away from where the action is in the production of knowledge basic to globalization, have only the choice of opposition or complicity—especially since the line between these two is no longer very clear.

If it were true that the state needed historicized knowledge, then what knowledge might the TNC need? Surely, as a form of power it needs and produces and controls and distributes knowledges. Of what kind are these knowledges? Are they familiar from modernity (biology?) or from mass media (information science?) or are they epistemically rooted in and across the formations of knowledge so that their effective novelty is not identifiable in terms of new "fields" or "disciplines" but, rather, as in Spinoza's day, in the tendencies of large epistemic shifts that make themselves potentially knowable everywhere but are not simply localizable anywhere? Nature, for example, has disappeared entirely within postmodernism. This is a basic claim within Jameson's now classical theory: nature is within buildings and always commodified so it cannot be found outside or in opposition to culture. This is, we might say, an intensification of modernity's ecological assault upon nature which makes of earth what Heidegger called "standing reserve." But perhaps a TNC world has done something discontinuous, something unrecognizable to the modern humanist political theories. What might this be? Is it discontinuous to think that TNC society actually *makes* or *produces* what we used to call nature? This might be done in many ways, some intentional—genetics and bioengineering—some unintentional—rapid mass transportation and forest clearing. If we imagine pursuing such thoughts as experiments, then it might appear as if all the historicizing moves which render our "culture" as continuous with what precedes—no matter how we post the "post" of "postmodern"—work in a time long ago, a time when it even made sense to imagine the formation of knowledge and society around the opposition, "nature"/"culture." Lévi-Strauss, for example, debated Sartre in part to displace the evolutionary metaphorics of progress from a nature state. Of course, we know that Lévi-Strauss's thinking stood in relation to the Third World liberation struggles just as immediately if less evidently than Sartre's. But what we now confront, given the dialectics carried out under the sign, "global/local," is a structuration for which such foundational oppositions have no meaning: in the conceptual place once occupied by nature there stands the commodity, but also in that space stands the impossibility of the opposition to and involving nature—whether it be "culture" or the commodity form itself. Reading Marx does not, I think, turn up a notion of commodity as the production of matter itself, of interference in evolution itself, of the making of "artificial life." This means, I think, despite claims to the contrary which generally insist upon continuity and the persistent applicability of older notions like dialectic, base/superstructure, and mediation, that we may well be confronting a rupture in life forms and in knowledge more akin to those that mark the shifts from the medieval to modern than from modern to postmodern. Indeed, "postmodernism theory" seems perfectly to obscure this shift, it blocks the development of the perceptual apparatus needed to theorize the emergent and to take action to modify its development.

"Global/local" metaphors are now privileged, as they should be, by the need to deal with the effects of the so-called third wave or late capital constructions of global capital. Not only do we have a sense, based on life forms and the expressive forms of cultural production, that things have changed significantly, once and for all, but we know that there are, almost everywhere, from the center of Los Angeles to the poetry/sovereignty groups of Hawaii and elsewhere, efforts at what used to be called "resistance." Efforts to save whatever "smooth spaces," to adapt Deleuze, there might yet be from the striating efforts of capital and its effectively "naturalized" global market. These efforts we call "local" and honor them, as these essayists do, as struggles to direct the ways in which capital will, as it certainly always will, striate or mark the spaces which are either still smooth—the Pacific Ocean itself—or are the previously striated, that is, colonized spaces like Hawaii, itself, as they are repositioned by capital in the new flows of capital production and circulation.

These efforts oblige intellectuals, especially cosmopolitan intellectuals, to recognize the misfit between their previously developed cultural capital tools and the new realities trying to emerge. Indeed, I take it that "global/local" names the effort at the emergence of this new thinking and these new discourses. As change once required the development of a "geometrical method" to substitute for the order of knowledge that goes under the sign, "flogistan," so emergence of new orders requires we at least consider giving up our inherited modern discourses even as we think the modernist burden of the past. To think the circulation of blood, to conceive the body as a place of organic motion, required epistemological shifts greater than those we see in the critical efforts to sustain Marxism, for example, in "postmodern theory." Attending to the universities' roles in the production of new knowledges and looking elsewhere where that knowledge is produced alone can give the critical humanist the chance to meet the demands of the time—which demands, we must recall, cannot be merely explicatory or oppositional, but must also be creative, directive, productive, that is, they must forge the devices needed to produce not only understanding and knowledge but also the new institutions and relations whose potentialities, we might say, lie dormant within the emergent forces.

Even the Deleuzian figuration of state and nonstate intellectuals will not carry us far enough in accepting this challenge—although one can and must imagine Deleuze and Guattari's efforts as precisely attempts to move to the new knowledge and discourses. Of course, all of us, as heirs to Nietzsche and other genealogists, accept the deconstructive burden that tells us neither Deleuze nor we can move now to completely new spaces unencumbered by the masterful forms we have often acquired—or, in Heidegger's sense, which have acquired us. But this awareness, which is an element of modernity's limits upon intelligence, does not license the persistence of practice tied dyingly to past formations. And past formations, we surely now know, include such apparently "nouveau" things as Marxist readings of video.

Spinoza's efforts to move thinking into spaces where it had never been before rests upon an understanding that intelligence is itself only at those times when it moves with the shifting of forms, when it commits itself to the task of perfecting itself by thinking as the way to bring to completion the finest rational possibilities of the leading or emergent form that being takes. In Negri's rather too particular terms, we might say that Spinoza thinks the market even as or, if you will, "before" the market appears and does so to produce the perfection of production in which the market inheres. Sadly, we might say, Spinoza's thinking succeeds but the market, with the contract-based state form, better succeeds in establishing itself as what Spinoza would call the "sinful" incompletion of modern production and modern life forms.

It would be silly to demand of a thinking about "global/local" that it produce this new Spinozan effort. And yet, the effort needs to be made and its need appears when thinking the "global/local" is put in the best light, namely, as the effort to think in the lacuna, the interstice, that gloms at us from the transitional space between state and superstate (or no state) and the national and transnational forms of capital. The local/global figure is in some ways a figure of neocolonial struggle, but that is itself the name for the existence of a system that, as global, puts itself outside our reach, outside our vision. For, where must one stand to see this globe? Some would say it cannot be seen; others are convinced that Marx gives us still the devices to see this globe—for those people, where they stand is where they have always thought they stood, namely in the domain of "science." But there are few who would willingly denominate their standpoint by that now tarnished term.

Students who take up this volume should see it as a report from what I want to call "the interregnum," that place and time when there is as yet no rule, when there are ordering forces but they have not yet summoned their institutional rule into full view. Intellectuals have the task of bringing these forces into view and, like Spinoza, of giving thought the task of directing the new moment into social forms that it might not otherwise take. Achieving perfection is harder than following the course that reserves potential in the satisfaction of what can easily be. Of course, historicizing the matter will let us tell a story about who and what desires this easy but sinful course. But since our stories are always of what we always know, we should resist the temptation to obscure knowledge in recognition or to condemn thought to specularity rather than the direction of the emergent.

If Wilson and Dissanayake have accomplished so much as to make clear that we are in an interregnum that demands of us all even greater effort, it is because they exercised a critical judgment that allows them to find strong traces of the need to supersede the resident past. "Global/local" turns out, then, to be not merely a challenge to modern mappings and imperial forces, but to the work of intellectual memory. It reminds us of how and why such as Nietzsche always warned us that to remember is to die. Critics should exercise caution in their efforts at resuscitation. Thinking the "global/local" perhaps uniquely gives us reason to brood for whatever time is necessary over whatever it is that is needful.

INDEX

●

CONTRIBUTORS' NOTES

●

Jonathan L. Beller received his Ph.D. in cinema and social theory from the Program in Literature at Duke University in 1994. He has published in a variety of scholarly journals including *Postmodern Culture* and *Communication Research*. Among his film and video work is "Interventions in a *Field of Dreams* with Ariel Dorfman," which he made for Paper Tiger Television and which has also been published in *Learning History in America* (1994).

Paul A. Bové is Professor of English and Comparative Literature at University of Pittsburgh and editor of the journal *boundary 2*. His most recent publications include *In the Wake of Theory* (1991) and *Mastering Discourse: The Politics of Intellectual Culture* (1992).

Christopher L. Connery teaches Chinese literature and cultural studies in the Program in Literature at the University of California at Santa Cruz. He has published essays and reviews in diverse journals, including *boundary 2, The Journal of Asian Studies,* and *Postmodern Culture,* and has an essay on Pacific Rim discourse in *Asia/Pacific as Space of Cultural Production* (1995).

Arif Dirlik is presently a fellow at the Center for Studies of Ethnicity and Race in America at the University of Colorado at Boulder. He is the author of many books on China, anarchism, globalization, and the Asia-Pacific Region, including *What Is in a Rim?: Critical Perspectives on the Pacific Region Idea* (1993) and *After the Revolution: Waking to Global Capitalism* (1994).

Wimal Dissanayake is Senior Fellow at the East-West Center and editor of *East-West Film Journal.* He is the author of several works concerning Asian literature and film, including *Sholay, A Cultural Reading* (1992), and editor of the collection of essays, *Colonialism and Nationalism in Asian Cinema* (1994).

Mike Featherstone teaches sociology and cultural studies at Teeside Polytechnic University in England, where he edits *Theory, Culture & Society.* He is the editor of several books, including *Global Culture: Nationalism, Globalization and Modernity* (1990) and *Cultural Theory and Cultural Change* (1992), and author of *Consumer Culture & Postmodernism* (1991) and, most recently, *Undoing Culture* (1995).

Fredric Jameson is William A. Lane, Jr. Professor of Comparative Literature and Director of the Graduate Program in Literature and the Duke Center for Critical Theory, Duke University. He is the author of numerous studies, including *Signatures of the Visible* (1990), *Postmodernism, Or, The Cultural Logic of Late Capitalism* (1991), and *The Seeds of Time* (1994).

Karen Kelsky received her doctorate in anthropology at the University of Hawaii at Manoa in 1995. She has published an essay called "Intimate Ideologies: Transnational Theory and Japan's 'Yellow Cabs' " in *Public Culture* and has lectured at universities in Hawaii and Japan.

Ping-hui Liao is Professor of English at National Tsing Hua University in Taiwan, where he has been the director of the Institute of Literature and is presently serving as president of the International Comparative Literature Association in Taiwan. He has published essays in *Public Culture, Musical Quarterly,* and *Cultural Critique* and has a study of orientalism in opera forthcoming with Princeton University Press.

Masao Miyoshi is Hajime Mori Professor of English and Comparative Literature and director of the Program in Japanese Studies at the University of California at San Diego. His recent publications include *Off Center: Power and Cultural Relations between Japan and the United States* (1991) and *Japan in the World* (coedited with Harry Harootunian) (1993).

Katharyne Mitchell is Assistant Professor of Geography at the University of Washington in Seattle. Her studies of cultural and transnational dynamics in Pacific Rim cities have appeared in *Antipodes* and other journals, and in *Asia/Pacific as Space of Cultural Production* (1995).

Hamid Naficy teaches media studies in the Department of Art and Art History at Rice University. His latest books include *The Making of Exile Cultures: Iranian Television in Los Angeles* (1993) and *Otherness and the Media: The Ethnography of the Imagined and the Imaged* (1993).

Paik Nak-chung is Professor of English at Seoul National University in South Korea. He is the author of several books published in Korea and Japan on world literature and Korean national literature, and editor of the important cultural-political journal, *Changjak-kwa-bipyong [Creation and Criticism] Quarterly,* where his interview with Fredric Jameson in this collection first appeared.

Dana Polan is resident director of the Centre Parisien d'Etudes Critiques, a program in Paris for students from around the world to study film, philosophy, literature, and contemporary culture. He is the author of a study of film spectacles called *Power and Paranoia* (1986), and his most recent book *In a Lonely Place* (1994) is in the British Film Institute's Film Classics Series.

Ella Shohat is Associate Professor of Women's Studies and Cultural Studies at the City University of New York—Graduate Center, and the Coordinator of the Cinema Studies Program at CUNY–College of Staten Island. Coeditor of *Social Text,* she is the author of *Israeli Cinema: East/West and the Politics of Representation* (1989) and has published essays in *Screen, Public Culture, Third Text* and other journals. She is coeditor (with Robert Stam) of the collection, *Unthinking Eurocentrism: Multiculturalism and the Media* (1994).

Robert Stam is Professor of Cinema Studies at New York University. He is the author of *Reflexivity in Film and Literature, Subversive Pleasures: Bakhtin, Cultural Criticism, and Film* (1989), and coauthor (with Randal Johnson) of *Brazilian Cinema* (1982) and (with Robert Burgoyne and Sandy Flatterman-Lewis) of *New Vocabularies in Film Semiotics* (1992).

Rob Wilson teaches in the English Department at the University of Hawaii at Mānoa. During 1995, he was a National Science Council Fellow at National Tsing Hua University in Taiwan, studying the dynamics of globalization and localization and the emergence of an Asian/Pacific Cultural Studies in the region. He is coeditor (with Arif Dirlik) of *Asia/Pacific as Space of Cultural Production* (1995) and of a forthcoming study with Duke University Press called *Reimagining the American Pacific: From "South Pacific" to Bamboo Ridge.*

Mitsuhiro Yoshimoto teaches film at the University of Iowa and has had pathbreaking essays on Japanese film and culture published in *Public Culture* and *boundary 2.*

Library of Congress Cataloging-in-Publication Data
Wilson, Rob
Global/local : cultural production and the transnational imaginary /
Rob Wilson and Wimal Dissanayake, editors.
p. cm. (Asia-Pacific)   Includes index.
ISBN 0-8223-1702-8 (alk. paper). — ISBN 0-8223-1712-5 (pbk. : alk. paper)
   1. Asia—Civilization.   2. Pacific Area—Civilization.   3. Intercultural
communication—Asia.   4. Intercultural communication—Pacific Area.
5. Regionalism—Asia.   6. Regionalism—Pacific Area.
I. Dissanayake, Wimal.   II. Title.
DS12.W48 1996   303.48'2'095—dc20   95-33262CIP